HACKERS TOEFL
LISTENING

200% 활용법

토플 쉐도잉&말하기 연습 프로그램

이용방법 고우해커스(goHackers.com) 접속 ▶
상단 메뉴 [TOEFL → 쉐도잉&말하기 연습] 클릭하여 이용하기

토플 스피킹/라이팅 첨삭 게시판

이용방법 고우해커스(goHackers.com) 접속 ▶
상단 메뉴 [TOEFL → 스피킹게시판/라이팅게시판] 클릭하여 이용하기

토플 공부전략 강의

이용방법 고우해커스(goHackers.com) 접속 ▶
상단 메뉴 [TOEFL → 토플공부전략]
클릭하여 이용하기

토플 자료 및 유학 정보

이용방법 고우해커스(goHackers.com)에
접속하여 다양한 토플 자료 및
유학 정보 이용하기

고우해커스 바로 가기 ▶

교재 MP3

이용방법 해커스인강(HackersIngang.com) 접속 ▶
상단 메뉴 [토플 → MP3/자료 → 문제풀이 MP3] 클릭하여 이용하기

문제풀이 MP3 바로 가기 ▶

단어암기 MP3

이용방법 해커스인강(HackersIngang.com) 접속 ▶
상단 메뉴 [토플 → MP3/자료 → 무료 MP3/자료] 클릭하여 이용하기

MP3/자료 바로 가기 ▶

iBT 리딩 실전모의고사

이용방법 해커스인강(HackersIngang.com) 접속 ▶
상단 메뉴 [토플 → MP3/자료 → 무료 MP3/자료] 클릭 ▶ 본 교재의 실전모의고사 프로그램 이용하기

| H | A | C | K | E | R | S |

TOEFL
LISTENING
Intermediate

해커스 어학연구소

무료 토플자료·유학정보 제공
goHackers.com

최신 토플 경향을 반영한
Hackers TOEFL Listening Intermediate (iBT)
을 내면서

해커스 토플은 토플 시험 준비와 함께 여러분의 영어 실력 향상에 도움이 되고자 하는 마음에서 시작되었습니다. 해커스 토플을 처음 출간하던 때와 달리 이제는 많은 토플 책들을 서점에서 볼 수 있지만, 그럼에도 해커스 토플이 여전히 **독보적인 베스트셀러**의 자리를 지킬 수 있는 것은 늘 **처음과 같은 마음**으로 더 좋은 책을 만들기 위해 고민하고, 최신 경향을 반영하기 위해 끊임없이 노력하기 때문입니다.

이러한 노력의 결실로, 새롭게 변경된 토플 시험에서도 학습자들이 영어 실력을 향상하고 토플 고득점을 달성하는 데 도움을 주고자 **최신 토플 경향**을 반영한 『Hackers TOEFL Listening Intermediate (iBT)』을 출간하게 되었습니다.

토플 리스닝 고득점의 발판을 확실히 마련하기 위한 중급 교재!
『Hackers TOEFL Listening Intermediate (iBT)』은 학습자들이 중급 실력을 완성하고 나아가 상급 듣기 실력으로 발돋움하기 위한 중급용 학습서입니다.

유형별 학습을 통한 완벽한 실전 대비!
학습자들이 실제 시험에 출제되는 문제 유형별로 체계적으로 학습함으로써 보다 수준 높은 듣기 실력을 쌓을 수 있도록 구성하였습니다. 또한, 다양한 문제 유형을 가장 확실하게 풀어낼 수 있는 공략법을 제공하고, 문제 유형을 누적식으로 구성하여 학습자들이 모든 문제 유형을 골고루 공부할 수 있도록 하였습니다.

『Hackers TOEFL Listening Intermediate (iBT)』이 여러분의 토플 목표 점수 달성에 확실한 해결책이 되고 영어 실력 향상, 나아가 **여러분의 꿈을 향한 길**에 믿음직한 동반자가 되기를 소망합니다.

David Cho

Hackers TOEFL

Listening

Intermediate

◇

CONTENTS

온라인 실전모의고사 (HackersIngang.com)
* 실제 시험과 동일한 환경에서도 Actual Test 1, 2를 풀어볼 수 있습니다.

TOPIC LIST ▤

다음의 TOPIC LIST는 교재에 수록된 모든 지문을 주제별로 구분하여 목록으로 구성한 것이다.

교재에 수록된 모든 지문은 실제 iBT 토플 Listening 시험의 주제별 출제 경향을 충실히 반영하여 구성되었다. 따라서, 교재를 처음부터 끝까지 학습하면서 출제율이 높은 주제와 자신이 취약한 주제를 파악한 뒤 집중 학습이 필요하다고 생각하는 주제를 골라 다시 한번 풀어보고, 해당 주제의 단어를 외워서 취약점을 보완한다.

Conversation

Instructor's Office Hours	DT [1-5]	Ch 1 HP [4-6]	Ch 1 HT [18-22]
	Ch 2 HT [1-5]	Ch 2 HT [18-22]	Ch 3 HT [1-5]
	Ch 3 HT [18-22]	Ch 4 HT [1-5]	Ch 5 HP [1-3]
	Ch 5 HT [18-22]	Ch 6 HP [4-6]	Ch 6 HT [1-5]
	Ch 6 HT [18-22]	AT 1 [1-5]	AT 2 [12-16]
Service Encounters	Ch 1 HP [1-3]	Ch 1 HT [1-5]	Ch 2 HP [1-3]
	Ch 2 HP [4-6]	Ch 3 HP [1-3]	Ch 3 HP [4-6]
	Ch 4 HP [1-3]	Ch 4 HP [4-6]	Ch 4 HT [18-22]
	Ch 5 HP [4-6]	Ch 5 HT [1-5]	Ch 6 HP [1-3]
	AT 1 [18-22]	AT 2 [1-5]	

Lecture

Humanities	Architecture	Ch 5 HT [12-17] Airtight Buildings
	Arts	DT [12-17] Rembrandt
		Ch 1 HT [12-17] Still Life
		Ch 2 HT [29-34] Fresco
		Ch 3 HT [23-28] Andrew Wyeth
		Ch 6 HP [10-12] Computer Art
		AT 1 [6-11] Victorian Era Art Audience
	Film	Ch 2 HP [10-12] Film Audiences and Theater
	History	Ch 1 HT [23-28] Gutenberg
		Ch 4 HT [23-28] Cultural Diffusion
	Literature	Ch 4 HP [7-9] Detective Novel: The Moonstone
		Ch 5 HP [7-9] Sentimental Comedy
		Ch 5 HT [29-34] Good-Night, Owl!

	Music	Ch 2 HT [12-17] Rossini
		Ch 6 HT [12-17] Electronica
Social Science	Anthropology	AT 2 [17-22] Mayan Civilization
	Archaeology	Ch 3 HP [7-9] Stone Balls
		Ch 4 HP [10-12] LIDAR
	Economics	Ch 3 HT [6-11] Contingency Planning
	Geography	Ch 6 HT [29-34] Lakes of Rub' al-Khali
	Psychology	Ch 3 HT [29-34] Theory of Mind
	Sociology	Ch 4 HT [6-11] Urbanization Models
Natural Science	Astronomy	Ch 1 HP [10-12] Sunspots
		Ch 3 HT [12-17] Moons of Saturn
		Ch 4 HT [29-34] Brown Dwarfs
		Ch 5 HP [10-12] Uranus
		AT 1 [12-17] Star Catalogs
	Biology	DT [6-11] Polar Bears
		Ch 1 HP [7-9] Camouflage
		Ch 1 HT [6-11] Dormancy and Hibernation
		Ch 2 HT [6-11] Western Chimpanzees
		Ch 2 HT [23-28] Beavers
		Ch 3 HP [10-12] Zooplankton
		Ch 6 HT [23-28] Bacteria Communication
		AT 2 [23-28] Cat's Purring
	Chemistry	AT 1 [23-28] Magnesium
	Earth Science	Ch 1 HT [29-34] Snowmelt
	Engineering	Ch 6 HP [7-9] Thrust and Lift
	Environmental Science	Ch 2 HP [7-9] Renewable Energy
		Ch 5 HT [23-28] Synthetic Fuel
		Ch 6 HT [6-11] Introduced Species
	Geology	Ch 4 HT [12-17] Flooding and River Shape
	Physics	AT 2 [6-11] Semiconductors
	Physiology	Ch 5 HT [6-11] Circadian Rhythm

* **DT:** Diagnostic Test　　**HP:** Hackers Practice　　**HT:** Hackers Test　　**AT:** Actual Test

iBT TOEFL Listening 고득점의 발판, 해커스 토플 리스닝 인터미디엇!

01. 전략적인 학습으로 토플 리스닝 정복!

최신 출제 경향 완벽 반영 및 TOPIC LIST

이 책은 iBT 토플 리스닝의 **최신 출제 경향**을 철저히 분석하여 모든 지문과 문제에 반영하였다. 또한, 교재에 수록된 모든 지문의 TOPIC을 목록으로 제공하여, 학습자가 특히 취약한 주제를 골라 공부하는 등 다양하게 활용할 수 있도록 하였다.

Diagnostic Test 및 4주/6주 학습플랜

실제 토플 시험의 구성 및 난이도로 제작된 Diagnostic Test를 통해 학습자가 자신의 실력을 스스로 점검할 수 있도록 하였으며, 이 결과에 따라 자신의 수준에 맞는 **4주/6주 학습플랜**을 활용하여 고득점을 위한 리스닝 실력을 완성할 수 있도록 하였다.

02. 체계적인 학습으로 실력 다지기!

문제 살펴보기 & 문제 공략하기

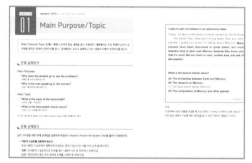

문제 유형에 대하여 간략히 소개하고 실제 시험에서는 어떤 형태로 출제되는지 제시하였다. 또한, 각 문제 유형의 가장 효과적인 공략법과 적용 사례를 통해 논리적인 문제 해결 능력을 키울 수 있다.

Hackers Practice & Hackers Test

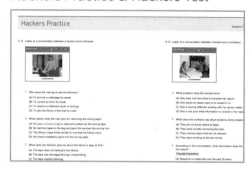

앞서 배운 문제 유형별 공략법을 실제 시험과 유사한 연습 문제에 적용하여 풀어봄으로써 유형별 집중 학습이 가능하며, 실제 시험에 대한 적응력 또한 키울 수 있다.

Vocabulary List

각 챕터의 모든 지문에 등장한 어휘 중 **토플 필수 어휘**를 선별하여 리스트로 제공하였다. 또한, 제공된 어휘에 대한 **퀴즈를 활용**하여 어휘를 효율적으로 암기할 수 있다.

Actual Test

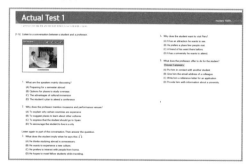

실제 시험과 유사한 구성 및 난이도로 제작된 문제를 풀어보며 iBT 토플 리스닝 학습을 효과적으로 마무리할 수 있다.

03. 정확한 해석과 정답단서로 실력 UP!

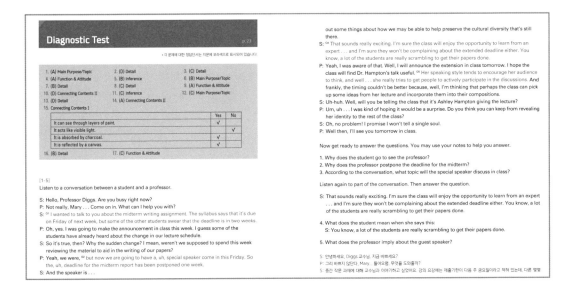

스크립트, 해석 및 어휘

교재에 수록된 **모든 지문의 스크립트를 매끄러운 해석 및 중요 어휘**와 함께 제공하여, 학습자가 보다 정확하게 지문의 흐름을 이해하고 어휘 실력까지 함께 향상할 수 있도록 하였다.

정답단서

교재에 수록된 실전 형태의 문제에 대한 정답단서를 해석과 함께 제공하여, **정답과 오답의 근거를 학습자 스스로 파악**할 수 있도록 하였다. 이를 통해, 학습자는 보다 능동적이고 효과적인 학습을 할 수 있다.

04. 해커스만의 다양한 학습자료 제공!

해커스인강(HackersIngang.com)

해커스인강 사이트에서 해커스 어학연구소에서 자체 제작한 실전모의고사 프로그램을 무료로 제공한다. 이 프로그램을 통해 교재에 수록된 2회분의 Actual Test를 실제 iBT TOEFL Listening 시험과 동일한 환경에서 풀어볼 수 있다. 또한, **교재에 수록된 Vocabulary List의 어휘가 녹음된 무료 단어암기 MP3**를 다운로드 받아 학습 효과를 극대화할 수 있으며, 본 교재에 대한 유료 **동영상강의**를 통해 선생님의 상세한 설명을 들으며 토플 리스닝 문제 유형을 체계적으로 학습할 수 있다.

고우해커스(goHackers.com)

온라인 토론과 정보 공유의 장인 **고우해커스 사이트**에서 다른 학습자들과 함께 교재 내용에 대해 서로 의견을 교류하고 학습 내용을 토론할 수 있으며, **다양한 무료 학습자료와 TOEFL 시험 및 유학에 대한 풍부한 정보**도 얻을 수 있다.

iBT TOEFL 소개

■ iBT TOEFL이란?

iBT(Internet-based test) TOEFL(Test of English as a Foreign Language)은 종합적인 영어 실력을 평가하는 시험으로 읽기, 듣기, 말하기, 쓰기 능력을 평가하는 문제 외에도, 듣기-말하기, 읽기-듣기-말하기, 읽기-듣기-쓰기와 같이 각 능력을 연계한 통합형 문제가 출제된다. iBT TOEFL은 Reading, Listening, Speaking, Writing 영역의 순서로 진행되며, 4개의 시험 영역 모두 노트테이킹을 허용하므로 문제를 풀 때 노트테이킹한 내용을 참고할 수 있다.

■ iBT TOEFL 구성

시험 영역	출제 지문 및 문항 수	시험 시간	점수 범위	특징
Reading	· 2개 지문 출제 지문당 길이: 약 700단어 지문당 10문항 출제	36분	0~30점	· 지문 길이가 길고, 다양한 구조의 지문이 출제됨 · 사지선다 형태, 지문 클릭(지문에 문장 삽입하기) 형태, 또는 정보를 분류하여 요약표나 정보 분류표에 넣는 형태 등이 출제됨
Listening	· 2개 대화 출제 대화당 길이: 약 3분 대화당 5문항 출제 · 3개 강의 출제 강의당 길이: 3~5분 강의당 6문항 출제	41분	0~30점	· 대화 및 강의의 길이가 길고, 실제 상황에 가까움 · 사지선다 형태, 다시 듣고 푸는 형태, 표 안에 정보를 분류하거나 순서대로 배열하는 형태 등이 출제됨
Speaking	· 독립형 1문항 출제 · 통합형 3문항 출제	17분 준비: 15~30초 답변: 45~60초	0~30점	· 독립형 문제(1번) 특정 주제에 대한 의견 말하기 · 통합형 문제(2~4번) 읽고 들은 내용에 기초하여 말하기
Writing	· 통합형 1문항 출제 · 토론형 1문항 출제	35분	0~30점	· 통합형 문제 읽고 들은 내용에 기초하여 글쓰기 · 토론형 문제 토론 주제에 대한 글쓰기
		2시간 내외	총점 120점	

■ iBT TOEFL 접수 및 성적 확인

실시일	ETS Test Center 시험은 1년에 60회 이상 실시되며, 홈에디션 시험은 일주일에 약 4~5일 정도 실시됨
시험 장소	ETS Test Center에서 치러지거나, 집에서 홈에디션 시험으로 응시 가능 (홈에디션 시험 응시 가능한 장비 및 환경 요건은 ETS 토플 웹사이트에서 확인 가능)
접수 방법	ETS 토플 웹사이트 또는 전화상으로 접수
시험 비용	(2024년 현재 기준이며, 가격 변동 있을 수 있음) ・시험 접수 비용 US $220 ・추가 리포팅 비용 US $25 (대학당) ・시험일 변경 비용 US $60 ・취소한 성적 복원 비용 US $20 ・추가 접수 비용 US $40 ・Speaking/Writing 재채점 비용 US $80 (영역당) (응시일로부터 2~7일 전에 등록할 경우)
시험 당일 주의사항	・공인된 신분증 원본 반드시 지참하며, 자세한 신분증 규정은 ETS 토플 웹사이트에서 확인 가능 ・홈에디션 시험에 응시할 경우, 사전에 ProctorU 프로그램 설치하여 정상 작동 여부 확인 ・홈에디션 시험에 응시할 경우, 휴대폰 또는 손거울, 화이트보드 또는 투명 시트와 지워지는 마카 지참(일반 종이와 필기구, 헤드폰 및 이어폰은 사용 불가)
성적 및 리포팅	・시험 응시 후 바로 Reading/Listening 영역 비공식 점수 확인 가능 ・시험 응시일로부터 약 4~8일 후에 온라인으로 성적 확인 가능 ・시험 접수 시, 자동으로 성적 리포팅 받을 기관 선택 가능 ・MyBest Scores 제도 시행 (최근 2년간의 시험 성적 중 영역별 최고 점수 합산하여 유효 성적으로 인정)

iBT TOEFL Listening 소개 및 학습전략

iBT TOEFL Listening 영역은 크게 대화(Conversation)와 강의(Lecture)로 구성되어 있다. 대화는 주로 대학에서 일어날 수 있는 상황에 대해, 강의는 주로 대학 수업에서 다루는 학문 분야에 대해 묻는다. 대화 및 강의를 들으면서 노트테이킹을 할 수 있으므로, 기억력에 의존하기보다는 내용을 듣고 이해하면서 정리하는 능력이 요구된다.

■ iBT TOEFL Listening 구성

시험은 2개의 Part로 구성되며, 각 Part에는 다음과 같이 1개의 대화와 1~2개의 강의가 나온다. 이때, 1개의 강의가 나오는 Part가 먼저 나올 수도 있고, 2개의 강의가 나오는 Part가 먼저 나올 수도 있다.

Part 구성 예시 1 (1개의 강의가 나오는 Part)	Conversation 1	3분 정도 소요	5문항 출제
	Lecture 1	3~5분 정도 소요	6문항 출제
Part 구성 예시 2 (2개의 강의가 나오는 Part)	Conversation 1	3분 정도 소요	5문항 출제
	Lecture 1	3~5분 정도 소요	6문항 출제
	Lecture 2	3~5분 정도 소요	6문항 출제

■ iBT TOEFL Listening 특이사항

· 대화와 강의의 길이가 길며, 화자의 어투가 실제 상황처럼 자연스럽다.
· 정답이 2개 이상인 문제가 출제된다.
· 대화 및 강의의 일부 내용을 다시 들려주는 문제가 출제된다.

■ iBT TOEFL Listening 문제 유형 소개

문제 유형		유형 소개
Basic Comprehension 들은 내용에 대한 기본적인 이해를 요하는 문제	Main Purpose/Topic	대화나 강의의 주제/목적을 가장 잘 나타낸 것을 선택하는 유형
	Detail	대화나 강의의 주요 세부 정보를 파악하는 유형
Pragmatic Understanding 들은 내용의 기저에 놓인 실질적인 의미를 파악하는 문제	Function & Attitude	화자의 의도와 태도를 가장 잘 나타낸 것을 선택하는 유형
Connecting Information 들은 내용을 종합해서 풀어야 하는 문제	Connecting Contents	주어진 정보들 간의 관계 또는 지문의 전개 구조를 묻는 유형
	Inference	지문에서 명백하게 설명되지는 않았지만 제시된 정보로 추론이 가능한 것을 선택하는 유형

■ iBT TOEFL Listening 학습전략

1. 정확한 영어 발음 및 억양을 익힌다.

정확한 영어 듣기를 위해서는 원어민의 발음과 억양, 말하는 속도 등에 익숙해져야 한다. 원어민의 음성을 자주 들으면서 다양한 발음 및 억양을 정확하게 익히도록 한다.

2. 토플에 자주 출제되는 토픽에 관한 배경지식을 쌓는다.

배경지식을 많이 알고 있을수록 들리는 내용도 많으므로, 시험에 자주 출제되는 토픽과 관련된 내용을 많이 알아두는 것이 좋다. 교재에 수록된 지문들과 함께, 평소에 다양한 분야의 학술·시사적인 내용을 많이 읽어두도록 한다.

3. 어휘력을 기른다.

모르는 단어는 잘 들리지 않으므로, 평소에 교재에 수록된 단어를 비롯하여 다양한 빈출 어휘를 외워두도록 한다. 단어를 외울 때에는 철자와 뜻뿐만 아니라 정확한 발음까지 함께 알아두는 것이 중요하다.

4. 문장을 많이 받아써 본다.

영어 문장을 계속해서 받아쓰다 보면 자신이 영어 듣기에서 어느 부분에 취약한지, 어떤 단어가 잘 들리지 않는지를 쉽게 파악할 수 있다.

5. 노트테이킹 연습을 한다.

iBT TOEFL Listening 시험에서는 들으면서 노트테이킹이 허용되므로, 이를 잘 활용할 수 있어야 한다. 음성을 들으면서 핵심 내용을 중심으로 간략하게 노트테이킹하는 것을 연습하도록 한다.

* 효과적인 노트테이킹 방법에 관해서는 교재 p.18에서 자세히 다룬다.

iBT TOEFL Listening 화면 구성

음량 조절 화면

시험이 시작되기 전에 음량을 조절할 것인지를 묻는 화면이다. ● Volume 버튼을 클릭하면 음량을 조절할 수 있는 창이 나타난다. 시험을 보는 동안에도 음량을 조절할 수 있다.

Listening Direction 화면

리스닝 영역의 전반적인 시험 진행 방식에 대한 설명이 나오고, 같은 내용이 음성으로도 제시된다. 리스닝 시험에는 11문제 또는 17문제로 구성된 Part가 2번 나오며, 각 Part는 대화 1개와 강의 1~2개로 이루어져 있다는 설명이 등장한다.

■ 시험 도중에 ● Help 버튼을 누르면 시험 진행 과정과 관련된 정보를 볼 수 있다. 이때 시험 시간은 계속해서 카운트 된다.

지문을 들을 때 제시되는 화면

대화를 들을 때, 두 화자의 사진이 나오며 사진을 통해 화자들의 관계 및 대화가 이루어지는 장소를 짐작할 수 있다. 강의를 들을 때에는 교수 혹은 교수와 학생들의 사진이 나오며, 강의의 주제와 관련된 사진이 나오는 경우도 있다. 사진 아래의 바는 지문의 진행 정도를 보여준다.

■ Hide Time Hide Time 버튼을 누르면 시간 카운트가 창에서 사라지고 Show Time Show Time 버튼이 나타나며, Show Time 버튼을 누르면 시간 카운트가 Hide Time 버튼과 함께 창에 다시 나타난다.

문제가 나오는 화면

문제가 나올 때 보이는 화면이다. 문제를 들려준 후 보기가 화면에 나오면, 보기 앞에 있는 동그라미를 클릭하여 답을 표시한다. 답을 클릭한 후 **Next 버튼**을 누르고 **OK 버튼**을 클릭하면 답이 확정되며, 이전 문제로 돌아갈 수 없다. 답이 2개 이상인 문제는 반드시 모든 답을 표시해야 다음 문제로 넘어갈 수 있다.

다시 듣고 푸는 문제의 Direction 화면

대화 및 강의의 일부를 다시 듣고 푸는 문제에서 주어지는 디렉션 화면이다. 이 화면이 나온 후 지문의 일부를 다시 듣게 된다.

iBT TOEFL Listening 시험과 동일한 환경에서도 교재에 수록된 Actual Test 2회분을 풀어볼 수 있습니다.

* **온라인 실전모의고사 프로그램 이용 경로**
　해커스인강(HackersIngang.com) 접속 → [MP3/자료] 클릭 → [실전모의고사 프로그램] 클릭

Note-taking

iBT TOEFL Listening에서는 대화와 강의를 듣는 동안 노트테이킹이 허용된다. 효과적인 노트테이킹은 전체적인 대화 또는 강의의 흐름을 파악하고 세부 정보를 기억하는 데 도움을 주며, 각 정보의 연관성을 쉽게 파악할 수 있도록 해준다. 한 가지 유의해야 할 점은 반드시 들은 내용을 이해한 후에 노트테이킹해야 한다는 것이다. 또한, 효과적인 노트테이킹을 위해서는 들은 내용을 모두 기록하기보다는 핵심 내용만을 간략하게 정리하는 요령을 길러야 한다.

■ Note-taking 방법

주로 대화와 강의의 첫 부분에서 소개되는 중심 내용과, 대화와 강의의 전반에 걸쳐 등장하는 세부 내용을 문제를 풀 때 쉽게 떠올릴 수 있도록 정리한다. 아래의 예문을 통해 노트테이킹 과정을 차근 차근 따라가며, 효과적인 노트테이킹 방법을 익혀보자.

1. 기호 및 약어를 이용한다.

   노트테이킹을 할 때에는 들리는 말을 모두 받아쓰는 것보다 기호 및 약어 표현을 이용하여 필요한 정보만 간략하게 쓰는 것이 좋다. 그리고 나중에 혼동을 주지 않기 위해서는 통용되는 기호나 통일된 형태의 약어를 사용해야 한다.

   기호 및 약어를 이용한 노트테이킹의 예

   18th century's comedy in England ⇒ 18C comedy @ Eng.
   Native American tribes did not use a writing system ⇒ Native Ame.: X writing sys.

2. 중심 내용을 간략하게 쓴다.

   도입부에서 중심 내용을 듣고 이해한 후, 키워드를 이용하여 간략하게 정리한다. 중심 내용은 첫 문장부터 등장하는 경우도 있고 어느 정도 내용을 들은 후에 등장하는 경우도 있으므로, 주의하여 들으며 기록한다.

   Script

   > Today, we'll be discussing the gymnosperm and the angiosperm, two types of plants that are believed to have evolved from the early vascular plants.
   > It was in Devonian period that gymnosperms first evolved. This was perhaps 360 million years ago. The gymnosperm plants were the most abundant type of plant until the Cretaceous period about 66 to 144 million years ago.
   > Now let's talk about the angiosperms, which, as I said earlier, include all flowering plants that produce seeds and in some angiosperms, fruit . . .

   Note

   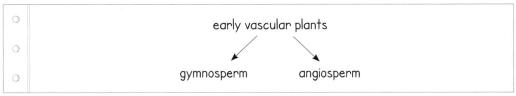

3. 세부 화제에 따라 내용을 구분하여 노트테이킹한다.

내용이 본격적으로 전개되기 시작하면 각 세부 화제별로 내용을 파악하고 정리하는 것이 좋다. 세부 화제가 전환될 때 자주 쓰이는 표시어(Another, First of all, Later, Well, Then 등)를 잘 파악하면, 세부 화제의 변화를 자연스럽게 알 수 있다. 강의의 경우에는 용어 정의, 예시, 나열, 비교 및 대조 등 각 설명 방식에 맞게 노트테이킹을 하는 것이 좋다. 그러나 중요하지 않은 세부 사항을 단순히 덧붙이는 설명 방식이 사용되는 경우도 있다.

Script

> Today, we'll be discussing the gymnosperm and the angiosperm, two types of plants that are believed to have evolved from the early vascular plants.
> It was in Devonian period that gymnosperms first evolved. This was perhaps 360 million years ago. The gymnosperm plants were the most abundant type of plant until the Cretaceous period about 66 to 144 million years ago.
> Now let's talk about the angiosperms, which, as I said earlier, include all flowering plants that produce seeds and in some angiosperms, fruit. These flowering plants evolved from the gymnosperms about 140 million years ago.

Note

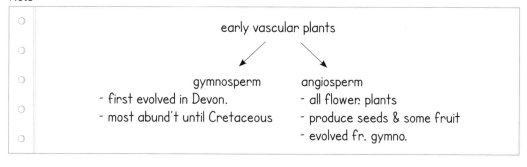

```
                    early vascular plants


              gymnosperm          angiosperm
          - first evolved in Devon.   - all flower. plants
          - most abund't until Cretaceous   - produce seeds & some fruit
                                       - evolved fr. gymno.
```

해커스 학습플랜

Diagnostic Test(p.23)의 결과에 따라 본인의 점수대에 맞는 학습플랜을 참고하여 스스로 계획을 세워 학습하시면 효과적입니다.

4주 학습플랜 (맞은 개수: 12~17개)

	Day 1	Day 2	Day 3	Day 4	Day 5
Week 1	DT	Ch 1 HP	Ch 1 HT	Ch 1 HT	Ch 2 HP
Week 2	Ch 2 HT	Ch 2 HT	Ch 3 HP	Ch 3 HT	Ch 3 HT
Week 3	Ch 4 HP	Ch 4 HT	Ch 4 HT	Ch 5 HP	Ch 5 HT
Week 4	Ch 5 HT	Ch 6 HP	Ch 6 HT	Ch 6 HT	AT 1, 2

* 8주 학습플랜을 진행하고 싶은 학습자는 4주 학습플랜의 하루 학습 분량을 이틀에 걸쳐 공부합니다.

6주 학습플랜 (맞은 개수: 11개 이하)

	Day 1	Day 2	Day 3	Day 4	Day 5
Week 1	DT	DT	Ch 1 HP	Ch 1 HP	Ch 1 HT
Week 2	Ch 1 HT	Ch 2 HP	Ch 2 HP	Ch 2 HT	Ch 2 HT
Week 3	Ch 3 HP	Ch 3 HP	Ch 3 HT	Ch 3 HT	Ch 4 HP
Week 4	Ch 4 HP	Ch 4 HT	Ch 4 HT	Ch 5 HP	Ch 5 HP
Week 5	Ch 5 HT	Ch 5 HT	Ch 6 HP	Ch 6 HP	Ch 6 HT
Week 6	Ch 6 HT	AT 1	AT 1	AT 2	AT 2

* **DT:** Diagnostic Test   **HP:** Hackers Practice   **HT:** Hackers Test   **AT:** Actual Test

학습플랜 활용법

1. 매일매일 정해진 학습 분량을 공부합니다. 문제 공략하기를 먼저 꼼꼼히 학습한 후, 이를 Hackers Pratice와 Hackers Test에 적용하면서 익힙니다.

2. 실전에 임하는 자세로 문제를 풀고, 문제를 다 푼 후에는 스크립트와 해석을 참고하여 음성을 다시 들어 보고 정답단서를 참고하여 모든 문제의 정답과 오답을 분석합니다.

3. 각 챕터의 모든 Hackers Practice와 Hackers Test를 학습한 후에 Vocabulary List를 통해 마무리합 니다. 해커스인강(HackersIngang.com)에서 Vocabulary List의 어휘가 녹음된 단어암기 MP3를 무 료로 다운로드할 수 있습니다.

4. 교재에서 이해가 되지 않는 부분은 고우해커스(goHackers.com)의 [해커스 Books > 토플 리스닝 Q&A]를 통해 확인합니다.

5. 당일의 정해진 학습 분량을 마치지 못했을 경우에는, 계속 진도를 나가되 일주일이 지나기 전에 해당 주 의 학습 분량을 모두 끝냅니다.

무료 토플자료·유학정보 제공

goHackers.com

Hackers TOEFL

Listening

Intermediate

Diagnostic Test

Diagnostic Test

[1-5] Listen to a conversation between a student and a professor.

1. Why does the student go to see the professor?

   (A) To clarify an important deadline
   (B) To complain about a test grade
   (C) To inquire about a special lecture
   (D) To request an extension for her paper

2. Why does the professor postpone the deadline for the midterm?

   (A) To schedule an extra review day
   (B) To allow revisions of the test to be made
   (C) To give students more time to study
   (D) To make time for a guest speaker

3. According to the conversation, what topic will the special speaker discuss in class?

   (A) Latin American literature
   (B) Cultural developments in South America
   (C) Brazil's native traditions
   (D) Languages spoken in Brazil

Listen again to part of the conversation. Then answer the question.

4. What does the student mean when she says this: 🎧

(A) She thinks the students have been worried about meeting the deadline.

(B) She believes the students are doing their papers carelessly.

(C) She does not think the new deadline will give the students enough time.

(D) She thinks the special lecture may distract the students from doing their papers.

5. What does the professor imply about the guest speaker?

(A) She can train other teachers.

(B) She is skilled at drawing out ideas.

(C) She will talk about the students' reports.

(D) She requires students to speak.

[6-11] Listen to part of a lecture in a zoology class.

6. What aspect of polar bears does the lecturer mainly discuss?

   (A) The threats faced by this species in the Arctic

   (B) Their adaptation to the extreme physical environment

   (C) The impact of climate change on polar bear populations

   (D) Variations in their hunting patterns at different times of the year

7. What does the professor say about the polar bear's fur?

   (A) It changes from brown to white when the bear is young.

   (B) It looks white but is actually completely clear.

   (C) It stays pure white throughout the bear's lifespan.

   (D) It turns green for part of the year.

8. According to the professor, what is the reason some people think the camouflage theory is wrong?

   (A) The eyesight of the polar bear's prey is not very good.

   (B) The skin of the polar bear is actually black.

   (C) Polar bears hunt primarily in the dark.

   (D) Not all polar bears have white fur.

Listen again to part of the lecture. Then answer the question.

9. What does the professor mean when she says this:

   (A) She does not fully agree with one of the theories.

   (B) She thinks it is difficult to support only one argument.

   (C) She thinks both theories are correct.

   (D) She has her own ideas regarding the fur's function.

10. Why does the professor mention infrared photographs?

   (A) To prove that the polar bear's fur reflects sunlight

   (B) To show that the polar bear is sensitive to light

   (C) To explain the polar bear's low body temperature

   (D) To demonstrate the polar bear's ability to retain heat

Listen again to part of the lecture. Then answer the question.

11. What does the professor imply when she says this:

   (A) People should conduct more research on the behavior of polar bears.

   (B) People can learn from the walking habits of polar bears.

   (C) People want to utilize their stored fat in the same way.

   (D) People have a more efficient physiology than polar bears.

[12-17] Listen to part of a lecture in an art history class.

12. What is the main topic of the lecture?

(A) Why fake versions of Rembrandt's works are so common

(B) The characteristics of Rembrandt's self-portraits

(C) How an imitation of Rembrandt's work was detected

(D) A controversy about Rembrandt's painting style

13. Why have a lot of paintings been mistakenly classified as the works of Rembrandt?

(A) He left many of his pieces unfinished.

(B) He used a wide variety of painting methods.

(C) He allowed other artists to alter his paintings.

(D) He let pupils copy his works.

14. Why does the professor mention the Dutch royal family?

(A) To explain why a painting's origin was not questioned

(B) To show that Rembrandt's paintings were highly valued

(C) To state that a portrait's subject remains unidentified

(D) To identify the owner of many of Rembrandt's works

15. In the lecture, the professor describes the qualities of infrared light. Indicate whether each of the following is a quality.

Click in the correct box for each sentence.

	Yes	No
It can see through layers of paint.		
It acts like visible light.		
It is absorbed by charcoal.		
It is reflected by a canvas.		

16. What does the professor say about the sketches made by Rembrandt?

(A) They are based on other works of art.

(B) They do not include a lot of details.

(C) They were used to train other artists.

(D) They did not absorb infrared light.

Listen again to part of the lecture. Then answer the question.

17. Why does the professor say this:

(A) To express concern that a word may be unfamiliar

(B) To imply that paintings are not easy to recreate

(C) To indicate that a term may be misunderstood

(D) To suggest that an idea was mentioned previously

정답·스크립트·해석·정답단서 p.188

＊채점 후 p.20을 보고 본인의 맞은 개수에 해당하는 학습플랜을 참고하세요.

CHAPTER 01

Main Purpose/Topic

Main Purpose/Topic

Main Purpose/Topic 문제는 대화나 강의의 중심 내용을 묻는 유형이다. 대화에서는 주로 학생이 교수나 교직원을 찾아간 목적이 무엇인지를 묻고, 강의에서는 교수가 설명하고 있는 내용의 주제가 무엇인지를 묻는다.

▶ 문제 살펴보기

Main Purpose

- Why does the student go to see the professor?
  학생은 왜 교수를 찾아가는가?

- Why is the man speaking to the woman?
  남자는 왜 여자와 이야기하는가?

Main Topic

- What is the topic of the lecture/talk?
  강의의 주제는 무엇인가?

- What is the lecture/talk mainly about?
  강의는 주로 무엇에 관한 것인가?

※ 간혹 2개 이상의 정답을 고르는 Main Purpose/Topic 문제가 출제되기도 한다.

▶ 문제 공략하기

실전 고득점을 위한 문제 공략법을 꼼꼼하게 학습하고 Hackers Practice와 Hackers Test를 풀면서 적용해 본다.

- **지문의 도입부를 집중하여 듣는다.**
  중심 내용은 도입부에서 명확하게 언급되는 경우가 많으므로 이를 주의 깊게 들어야 한다.
  대화: 인사말이나 일상적으로 안부를 묻는 내용이 나온 후 목적이나 주제 언급
  강의: 첫마디부터 혹은 이전 강의의 주제를 소개한 후 주제 언급

- **중심 내용을 언급할 때 자주 쓰는 표현에 유의하여 듣는다.**
  대화나 강의의 주제를 언급할 때 화자가 자주 쓰는 표현들을 알아두면 주제를 정확하고 쉽게 파악할 수 있다.
  중심 내용을 언급할 때 쓰이는 표현들은 다음과 같다.

대화	강의
I'm interested in ~	Let's talk about ~
I wanted to talk to you about ~	I want to take a look at ~
I came here to speak to you about ~	Today, I'd like to talk about ~
I was wondering if ~	Let us continue our study on ~

※ 간혹 지문에서 주제가 확실하게 언급되지 않는 경우에는 지문 전체를 듣고 전반적인 내용을 파악해야 한다.

Listen to part of a lecture in an astronomy class.

Today, I'd like to talk about a planet named by the Romans ... the planet they observed moving faster than any other planets. I guess you know I'm talking about Mercury. Many planets have been discussed in great detail, but most teachers tend to skim over Mercury because they know only that it's much like our moon in color, surface area, and lack of atmosphere.

What is the lecture mainly about?

(A) The similarities between Earth and Mercury
(B) The research on Mercury
(C) The facts about planet Mercury
(D) The composition of Mercury and other planets

지문 해석 p.195

강의에서 주제를 언급할 때 교수가 자주 쓰는 표현인 "Today, I'd like to talk about ~" 이하의 내용을 주의 깊게 들어야 한다.

CHAPTER 1

CH 2

CH 3

CH 4

CH 5

CH 6

Hackers TOEFL Listening Intermediate

해설

도입부에서 중심 내용을 언급할 때 쓰는 표현인 "Today, I'd like to talk about ~" 이하에 오는 수성에 대한 소개를 통해 강의의 중심 내용이 수성에 대한 정보임을 알 수 있다. 따라서, 정답은 (C)이다.

Hackers Practice

[1-3] Listen to a conversation between a student and a librarian.

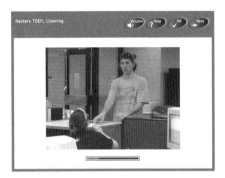

1. Why does the man go to see the librarian?

   (A) To borrow a videotape he needs

   (B) To correct an error he made

   (C) To reserve a reference book on biology

   (D) To pay the library a fine that he owes

2. What reason does the man give for returning the wrong tape?

   (A) He was in a hurry to go to class and picked up the wrong tape.

   (B) He had two tapes in his bag and gave the woman the wrong one.

   (C) The library's tape looks similar to one that his friend owns.

   (D) His friend mistakenly gave him the wrong tape.

3. What does the librarian assume about the library's tape at first?

   (A) The tape does not belong to the library.

   (B) The tape was damaged through mishandling.

   (C) The tape needed cleaning.

   (D) The tape is mechanically faulty.

---

lead to ~으로 이어지다 diversity[divə́rsəti] 다양성 waiting list 대기자 명단 turn into ~으로 변하다 immediately[imí:diətli] 바로
physically[fízikəli] 물리적으로 malfunction[mælfʌ́ŋkʃən] 오작동 circulation[sə̀ːrkjuléiʃən] 유통 late fee 연체료
get in touch with ~에게 연락하다

[4-6] Listen to a conversation between a student and a professor.

4. What problem does the woman have?

(A) She does not have time to complete her report.

(B) She wants an easier topic to do research on.

(C) She is having difficulty working with her group mates.

(D) She is not sure what information to include in her report.

5. What does the professor say about students doing research projects?

(A) They do not know where to begin.

(B) They have trouble narrowing the topic.

(C) They choose topics that are not relevant.

(D) They start working at the last minute.

6. According to the conversation, what information does the student decide to include in her report?

Choose 2 answers.

(A) Research on asteroids over the past 30 years

(B) Significant scientific discoveries on greatest impacts

(C) The largest asteroid collisions with Earth

(D) Data supporting asteroid impact predictions

---

upcoming[ʌ́pkʌ̀miŋ] 다가오는 asteroid[ǽstərɔ̀id] 소행성 impact[ímpækt] 충돌 allot[əlát] 할당하다 stuff[stʌf] 자료
collision[kəlíʒən] 충돌 omit[oumít] 생략하다 pointer[pɔ́intər] 조언 crater[kréitər] 분화구 frequency[fríːkwənsi] 빈도
destroy[distrɔ́i] 멸종시키다 set aside 제쳐놓다

[7-9] Listen to part of a lecture in a biology class.

7. What is the main topic of the lecture?

    (A) Methods animals use to change color

    (B) Why animals can look similar to each other

    (C) A way some animals can disguise themselves

    (D) How animals adjust to their habitats

8. What does the professor say about the Pacific octopus?

    (A) It matches the color of its prey.

    (B) It imitates the behavior of other species.

    (C) It can change color when required.

    (D) It is less effective at hiding in daylight.

9. What makes the leaf insect's camouflage so impressive?
Choose 2 answers.

    (A) It is effective enough to fool caterpillars.

    (B) It copies irregular patterns in leaves.

    (C) It changes its colors to match the seasons.

    (D) It includes more than one color.

---

predator[prédətər] 포식자 tactic[tǽktik] 전략 camouflage[kǽməflà:ʒ] 위장 background matching 배경에 맞추기
blend[blend] 섞이다 pacific octopus 참문어 coral[kɔ́:rəl] 산호 prey[prei] 먹이 surrounding[səráundiŋ] (주위의) 환경
stand out 도드라지다 resemble[rizémbl] 닮다 mimic[mímik] 모방하다 vein[vein] (식물의) 잎맥 marking[má:rkiŋ] 무늬
caterpillar[kǽtərpìlər] 애벌레 imitate[ímətèit] 모방하다 edge[edʒ] 가장자리

[10-12] Listen to part of a lecture in an astronomy class.

10. What is the main topic of the lecture?

(A) The differences between solar flares and sunspots

(B) The origins of the Sun's magnetic field

(C) The Sun's basic chemical structure

(D) The features of a solar phenomenon

11. According to the professor, what causes sunspots?

(A) Excess heat coming off the Sun's surface

(B) Disturbances in the Sun's magnetic field

(C) Temperature changes in the Sun's atmosphere

(D) Magnetic objects hitting the Sun's exterior

12. What does the professor say about solar flares?

Choose 2 answers.

(A) They absorb energy from the Sun.

(B) They emit particles into space.

(C) They look like dark shadows on the Sun.

(D) They are triggered by sunspots.

정답·스크립트·해석·정답단서 p. 195

composition[kàmpəzíʃən] 구성 요소　sunspot[sʌ́nspàt] 태양 흑점　patch[pætʃ] 반점　expand on ~에 대해 더 상세하게 말하다
magnetic storm 자기 폭풍　across[əkrɔ́ːs] 직경으로　rotation[routéiʃən] 자전　equator[ikwéitər] 적도
pole[poul] (천체·지구의) 극　distort[distɔ́ːrt] 일그러뜨리다　magnetic field 자기장　break through ~을 뚫고 나가다
solar flare 태양면 폭발　magnetic force 자력　go off 터지다　electrically charged particle 대전입자

CHAPTER 1

CH 2

CH 3

CH 4

CH 5

CH 6

Hackers TOEFL Listening Intermediate

Hackers Test

[1-5] Listen to a conversation in a listening lab.

1. Why does the student visit the listening lab?

    (A) To rent a video to take home

    (B) To view required course material

    (C) To prepare a recording for class

    (D) To check out the TV/VCR system

2. What does the woman say about the TV/VCR?

    (A) It is being used.

    (B) It was set up incorrectly.

    (C) It is malfunctioning.

    (D) It needs to be replaced.

3. According to the conversation, what is a reason the listening lab staff had the TV/VCR brought to the technical services department?

    (A) They do not have the time to repair machines.

    (B) They do not have the skills to fix the equipment in the lab.

    (C) They are not responsible for maintaining the TV/VCR.

    (D) They damaged the TV/VCR further when they were trying to fix it.

4. Why does the woman hesitate to give the man a time slot for the day after?

(A) She is worried the tape the man needs may still be out.

(B) She remembers that other students have reserved time slots ahead of the man.

(C) She realizes the TV/VCR will still be at the repair shop.

(D) She is concerned that the TV/VCR may be damaged from overuse.

5. According to the conversation, what are some ways the man can resolve his problem if the TV/VCR is not returned the next day?

Choose 3 answers.

(A) Check the video shops for a copy of the tape

(B) Ask another student to switch time slots

(C) Wait in case the TV/VCR becomes free

(D) Try looking for a video file on the Internet

(E) Ask the professor to postpone the essay exam

[6-11] Listen to part of a lecture on biology.

6. What does the professor mainly discuss in the lecture?

   (A) The hibernation habits of the ground squirrel

   (B) The characteristics of mammalian dormancy

   (C) The manner in which hibernation and dormancy differ

   (D) The reasons animals hibernate and become dormant

7. According to the professor, what is true of bears in the winter?

   (A) They remain asleep for the entire season.

   (B) They refrain from going to the bathroom.

   (C) They struggle to keep their cubs warm.

   (D) They feed occasionally throughout the period.

8. According to the professor, how do dormant bears conserve energy?

   (A) They cease all physical activity.

   (B) They sleep close to other bears.

   (C) Their body temperatures are lowered.

   (D) Their hearts beat less often.

9. What does the professor say about snakes and turtles?

(A) They store food in their shelters during their rest period.

(B) They wake from a deep sleep several times during the winter.

(C) Their bodies can become overheated by exposure to sunlight.

(D) Their body temperatures are determined by external conditions.

10. According to the professor, why do hibernating animals eat more before winter?

(A) They want to protect themselves against freezing temperatures.

(B) They need to amass fat for energy consumption.

(C) They must take advantage of dwindling food supplies.

(D) They use increased food consumption as a trigger for hibernation.

11. What are two differences between dormancy and hibernation?

Choose 2 answers.

(A) The extent to which body temperature declines

(B) The ability to give birth to offspring in winter

(C) The need to occasionally consume food

(D) The possibility of becoming conscious quickly

CHAPTER 1

CH 2

CH 3

CH 4

CH 5

CH 6

Hackers TOEFL Listening Intermediate

[12-17] Listen to part of a lecture from an art history class.

12. What is the main topic of the lecture?

   (A) The influence of the Dutch on still life painters

   (B) The development of a new style of painting

   (C) The background elements of 15th-century paintings

   (D) The use of decorative objects by early painters

13. What inspired many artists to focus on depicting objects?

   (A) Books published in Asia and the Americas

   (B) Artworks brought back from foreign lands

   (C) Drawings made during trips to distant lands

   (D) Illustrations discovered in ancient documents

14. What does the professor say about *Butcher's Stall with the Flight into Egypt*?

   (A) It does not make effective use of the background.

   (B) It is unusual because it shows a butcher's shop.

   (C) It is the first painting to focus on everyday objects.

   (D) It does not have human subjects in the foreground.

15. Why were Dutch people interested in paintings of tulips?

(A) Tulips were available in a broad assortment of colors.

(B) Tulips were associated with high social status.

(C) Tulips were a symbol of the Dutch Republic.

(D) Tulips were used to beautify table settings.

16. What is a characteristic of the tabletop scenes painted by 17th-century Dutch artists?

(A) The objects were all very costly.

(B) The table was larger than usual.

(C) The food was very traditional.

(D) The dishes were made only of glass.

17. What qualities of still life paintings appealed to hunters?

Choose 2 answers.

(A) The inclusion of realistic details

(B) The accurate representation of a setting

(C) The depiction of exotic animals

(D) The life-sized portrayal of subjects

CHAPTER 1

CH 2

CH 3

CH 4

CH 5

CH 6

Hackers TOEFL Listening Intermediate

[18-22] Listen to a conversation between a student and an academic advisor.

18. What are the speakers mainly discussing?

    Choose 2 answers.

    (A) Why the student is having difficulties in a class

    (B) Which class the student should register for next semester

    (C) How the student can improve his grade in a class

    (D) Whether the student should withdraw from a class

19. What does the advisor say about the comparative literature course?

    (A) It is far too advanced for the student to be taking.

    (B) Other students are having difficulties in the class.

    (C) The professor of that course is not suitable.

    (D) The class is only for advanced graduate students.

20. Why did the student initially decide to take the course?

    (A) He was considering changing his major to literature.

    (B) He realized he had no other options.

    (C) He remembered that he needed it to graduate.

    (D) He was interested in gaining a wider academic view.

21. According to the conversation, what is the main reason the student is thinking of dropping the class?

(A) He is already carrying a full credit load.

(B) He prefers subjects related to math and the sciences.

(C) He does not understand the Greek language.

(D) He is unable to comprehend the discussions in class.

22. According to the conversation, what are some reasons for not dropping the course?
Choose 3 answers.

(A) It was recommended by a friend of the student.

(B) It will be included in the student's academic records.

(C) It would likely result in the loss of financial assistance.

(D) It is too late in the semester to enroll in another class.

(E) It will affect the student's overall grade.

CHAPTER 1

CH 2

CH 3

CH 4

CH 5

CH 6

Hackers TOEFL Listening Intermediate

[23-28] Listen to part of a lecture in a history class.

23. What is the main topic of the lecture?

(A) The benefits of the printing press

(B) The importance of printing in China

(C) Theories on the origins of movable type

(D) The early history of printing

24. According to the lecture, in what way were eyeglasses helpful in spurring the invention of the printing press?

(A) They gave Gutenberg the idea for movable type.

(B) They made it easier for people to read printed texts.

(C) They utilized a technology that was applied to the printing press.

(D) They helped typesetters see smaller movable characters.

25. What does the professor say about Gutenberg's metal movable type?
Choose 2 answers.

(A) It was more resilient than the woodblocks used in Europe.

(B) It could only be used with a sticky type of ink.

(C) It was not the first metal movable type invented.

(D) It could produce a limited range of characters

26. According to the professor, why was woodblock printing superior to movable type for Chinese texts?

    (A) It was easier to find wood than metal in China.

    (B) It took less effort to carve letters into woodblocks.

    (C) It did not require access to a special type of ink.

    (D) It was a more efficient method to produce text with many characters.

27. According to the professor, what are two characteristics of Bi Sheng's invention?
    Choose 2 answers.

    (A) It consisted of a solid block of type that simplified the printing process.

    (B) It was too delicate for printing jobs that were considerable in scope.

    (C) It made use of heat to make the ink more permanent.

    (D) It had to be aligned before it could be used.

28. According to the professor, what is the significance of Gutenberg's molds?

    (A) They enabled the manufacture of movable type in large quantities.

    (B) They allowed the individual carving of each metal type.

    (C) They initiated the move from ceramic to metal type.

    (D) They permitted the production of large metal plates.

CHAPTER 1

CH 2

CH 3

CH 4

CH 5

CH 6

Hackers TOEFL Listening Intermediate

[29-34] Listen to part of a lecture on earth science.

29. What does the professor mainly discuss?

(A) Measuring snowmelt for the water needs of an area

(B) Types of surface water hydrology

(C) Causes of flooding in agricultural areas

(D) New technologies in measuring snowmelt

30. According to the professor, what difference is there between snow and other types of precipitation?

(A) The runoff from snowmelt is less polluted.

(B) Snowmelt is not immediately usable as a water source.

(C) More water is obtainable from snowmelt.

(D) Snowmelt is easier to measure than rain water.

31. Why is snowmelt of concern to residents where it occurs?

(A) Because it affects the level of water in rivers

(B) Because it represents a critical supply of water

(C) Because it is 90 percent unusable

(D) Because it is critical to business revenues

32. According to the lecture, what are some factors that affect the amount of snowmelt?
Choose 3 answers.

(A) The amount of moisture in the snow

(B) The type of crop grown by the farmer

(C) The type of soil common to the area

(D) The amount of snowmelt in previous years

(E) How quickly the snow melts

33. According to the professor, what is the significance of a long winter?

(A) It will be difficult to obtain an accurate measurement of snowmelt.

(B) Various measurements will be necessary as snow continues to fall.

(C) There will be an insufficient amount of runoff in early spring.

(D) The snow cover on the mountains will have a harder crust.

34. According to the lecture, what are two factors that can cause flooding in areas with snowmelt?
Choose 2 answers.

(A) The ground consists of clay.

(B) There is a large amount of snowmelt.

(C) The soil is icy and solid.

(D) The runoff is not used by residents.

정답·스크립트·해석·정답단서 p. 200

VOCABULARY LIST

Chapter 1에서 선별한 다음의 토플 필수 어휘를 단어암기 음성을 들으며 암기한 후 퀴즈로 확인해 보세요.

* 해커스 동영상강의의 포털 해커스인강(HackersIngang.com)에서 단어암기 음성파일을 무료로 다운로드할 수 있습니다.

diversity[divə́ːrsəti] 다양성

malfunction[mælfʌ́ŋkʃən] 오작동

circulation[sə̀ːrkjuléiʃən] 유통

asteroid[ǽstərɔ̀id] 소행성

allot[əlát] 할당하다

collision[kəlíʒən] 충돌

omit[oumít] 생략하다

pointer[pɔ́intər] 조언

crater[kréitər] 분화구

frequency[fríːkwənsi] 빈도

set aside 제쳐놓다

predator[prédətər] 포식자

tactic[tǽktik] 전략

camouflage[kǽməflàːʒ] 위장

resemble[rizémbl] 닮다

mimic[mímik] 모방하다

vein[vein] (식물의) 잎맥

composition[kàmpəzíʃən] 구성 요소

across[əkrɔ́ːs] 직경으로

rotation[routéiʃən] 자전

equator[ikwéitər] 적도

go off 터지다

ritual[rítʃuəl] (종교적인) 의식

priority[praiɔ́ːrəti] 우선권

time slot 시간대

ecosystem[ékousìstəm] 생태계

perspire[pərspáiər] 땀을 흘리다

hibernation[hàibərnéiʃən] 동면

dormancy[dɔ́ːrmənsi] 휴면

prototypical[pròutətípikəl] 대표적인

give birth to ~을 낳다

fluctuate[flʌ́ktʃuèit] 변동하다

reserve[rizə́ːrv] 저장물

awareness[əwɛ́ərnis] 의식

foreground[fɔ́ːrgràund] (그림·사진 등의) 전경

decorative[dékərətiv] 장식용의

still life 정물화

voyage[vɔ́iidʒ] 항해

appreciate[əpríːʃièit] 진가를 인정하다

butcher[bútʃər] 푸줏간

obsess[əbsés] 사로잡다

diminish[dimíniʃ] 줄어들다

afford[əfɔ́ːrd] ~을 살 여유가 있다

nobleman[nóublmən] 귀족

illusion[ilúːʒən] 환상

broaden[brɔ́ːdn] 넓히다

perspective[pərspéktiv] 시야

dabble in 한 번 해 보다

theoretical[θìːərétikəl] 이론적인

keep up with ~을 따라가다

in the dark 모르는

stick to 계속하다

Quiz

각 단어의 알맞은 뜻을 찾아 연결하시오.

01 obsess	ⓐ 시야	06 omit	ⓐ 땀을 흘리다
02 reserve	ⓑ 사로잡다	07 give birth to	ⓑ 변동하다
03 malfunction	ⓒ 분화구	08 perspire	ⓒ 생략하다
04 perspective	ⓓ 저장물	09 dormancy	ⓓ 넓히다
05 camouflage	ⓔ 위장	10 fluctuate	ⓔ ~을 낳다
	ⓕ 오작동		ⓕ 휴면

01 ⓑ 02 ⓓ 03 ⓕ 04 ⓐ 05 ⓔ 06 ⓒ 07 ⓔ 08 ⓐ 09 ⓕ 10 ⓑ

demonstrate[démənstrèit] (증명해) 보이다

financial aid 학비 지원

tutorial[tju:tɔ́:riəl] 개별 지도의

advanced[ædvǽnst] 고급 단계의

undergraduate[ʌndərgrǽdʒuət] 학부생

screen[skri:n] 선발하다

appropriately[əpróuprièitli] 제대로

give it a try 한 번 시도해 보다

contribute[kəntríbju:t] 공헌하다

printing press 인쇄기

sticky[stíki] 끈적거리는

stepping stone 발판

precede[prisí:d] 앞서다

movable type 가동 활자

detachable[ditǽtʃəbl] 분리할 수 있는

punctuation mark 문장 부호

unquestionably[ʌnkwéstʃənəbli] 의심할 나위 없이

durable[djúərəbl] 내구성 있는

scribe[skraib] 필경사

time-consuming[táimkənsù:miŋ] 시간 소모적인

tedious[tí:diəs] 지루한

fragile[frǽdʒəl] 부서지기 쉬운

mold[mould] 주형

carve[kɑːrv] 조각하다

hydrology[haidrálədʒi] 수문학

application[æ̀pləkéiʃən] 응용

snowmelt[snóumèlt] 해빙

precipitation[prisìpətéiʃən] 강수

significant[signífikənt] 상당한

runoff[rʌ́nɔ̀:f] 유거수

constitute[kánstətjù:t] 차지하다

replenish[ripléniʃ] 다시 채우다

surface water 지표수

cache[kæʃ] 저장소

measurement[méʒərmənt] 측정

resident[rézədənt] 거주자

disaster[dizǽstər] 재해

project[prádʒekt] 예측하다

shortfall[ʃɔ́:rtfɔ̀:l] 부족

adjustment[ədʒʌ́stmənt] 조정

shortage[ʃɔ́:rtidʒ] 부족

modify[mádəfài] 조절하다

cultivate[kʌ́ltəvèit] 경작하다

conservation[kànsərvéiʃən] 비축

measure[méʒər] 대책

variable[véəriəbl] 변수

elevation[èləvéiʃən] 고도

moisture[mɔ́istʃər] 습기

content[kántent] 함유량

partially[pá:rʃəli] 부분적으로

crust[krʌst] 표면

seep into ~으로 스며들다

Quiz

각 단어의 알맞은 뜻을 찾아 연결하시오.

01 resident   ⓐ 분리할 수 있는

02 elevation   ⓑ 지루한

03 application   ⓒ 거주자

04 fragile   ⓓ 고도

05 tedious   ⓔ 부서지기 쉬운

     ⓕ 응용

06 variable   ⓐ 공헌하다

07 durable   ⓑ 변수

08 stepping stone   ⓒ 조절하다

09 contribute   ⓓ 차지하다

10 constitute   ⓔ 내구성 있는

     ⓕ 발판

ⓓ 01 ⓔ 60 ⓕ 80 ⓔ ⁄0 ⓑ 90 ⓑ ⑤0 ⓔ ⁊0 ⓕ ⑥0 ⓓ Z0 ⓒ l0

CHAPTER 02

Detail

CHAPTER 02 Detail

Detail 문제는 대화나 강의에서 등장하는 세부 사항에 대한 정보를 이해한 후, 1개 또는 2개 이상의 답을 골라 완성하는 유형이다. 화자가 언급한 내용 중 중심 내용과 연관된 주요 세부 사항을 묻는다.

문제 살펴보기

- According to the conversation, what is ~?
  대화에 따르면, ~은 무엇인가?
- What is an example the man gives of ~?
  남자가 ~에 대해 드는 한 가지 예는 무엇인가?

정답이 2개 이상인 경우
- According to the professor, what are some reasons for ~? Choose 2 answers.
  교수에 따르면, ~의 몇 가지 이유는 무엇인가? 2개의 답을 고르시오.
- According to the employee, what are examples of ~? Choose 3 answers.
  직원에 따르면, ~의 예는 무엇인가? 3개의 답을 고르시오.

문제 공략하기

실전 고득점을 위한 문제 공략법을 꼼꼼하게 학습하고 Hackers Practice와 Hackers Test를 풀면서 적용해 본다.

- **지문의 주요 세부 사항을 파악하며 듣는다.**
  화자는 여러 가지 세부 사항들을 언급하는데, 지문에서 언급되는 주요 세부 사항은 다음과 같다.

  대화: 제안 또는 충고, 질문 또는 대답, 이유 및 결과 설명
  강의: 특징 또는 방법, 질문 또는 대답, 이유 및 결과 설명

- **주요 세부 사항을 언급할 때 쓰는 표현에 유의하여 듣는다.**
  중심 내용과 관련된 내용을 언급할 때 종종 쓰이는 표현들을 통해 세부 사항을 정확하고 쉽게 파악할 수 있다. 지문에서 주요 세부 사항을 나타내는 표현들은 다음과 같다.

강조	I'd like to point out ~ / It is important ~
부연 설명	What's more interesting is ~ / It's surprising ~
인과	That's because ~ / The reason why ~ / As a result, ~
비교/대조	Similarly / In the same way / On the other hand / In contrast / While ~
역접	Ironically / But / However / Nevertheless

Listen to part of a lecture in an astronomy class.

Mariner 10 covered about 45 percent of the surface of Mercury. That may not seem like much . . . but the pictures show that Mercury is pockmarked with craters and very large multi-ring basins, like our moon. That's because the Moon and Mercury both have thin atmospheres, and this makes them easy targets for meteorites and other debris. Both also have temperature extremes . . . Mercury's goes down to minus 170 degrees Celsius at night and 350 degrees Celsius during the day, and the Moon's temperature ranges from minus 100 to 340. The only big difference between them is density.

강의에서 주요 세부 사항을 언급할 때 교수가 자주 쓰는 표현인 "That's because ~" 이하의 내용을 주의 깊게 들어야 한다.

What does the professor say about the craters of Mercury and the Moon?

(A) They were formed by lava flows from now extinct volcanoes.
(B) They are quite dissimilar in appearance.
(C) They result from having little protective gases.
(D) They cover only about half of the surface of both celestial bodies.

지문 해석 p. 213

해설
주요 세부 사항을 언급할 때 쓰는 표현인 "That's because ~" 이하에 오는 내용에서, 강의의 주요 세부 사항이 달과 수성은 둘 다 얇은 대기층을 가지고 있어서 운석들과 다른 파편들의 표적이 된다는 내용임을 알 수 있다. 따라서, 정답은 (C)이다.

CH 1

CHAPTER 2

CH 3

CH 4

CH 5

CH 6

Hackers TOEFL Listening Intermediate

Hackers Practice

[1-3] Listen to a conversation between a student and a career advisor.

1. What are the speakers mainly discussing?

   (A) Enrolment in summer school

   (B) Work for the summer

   (C) Advantages of being a tutor

   (D) Places to eat on campus

2. According to the conversation, what is the objective of the math club?

   (A) To allow students to socialize

   (B) To give better students a chance to compete

   (C) To help out less capable students

   (D) To give students a group with whom to identify

3. What does the woman say about the library assistant position?

   (A) It is too far from her home.

   (B) It requires working until late.

   (C) It would not pay her enough.

   (D) It comes with a heavy workload.

---

flexible[fléksəbl] 융통성 있는 suit[su:t] 잘 맞다 minor[máinər] 부전공 posting[póustiŋ] 공고 via[vaiə] ~을 통해
geometry[dʒiámətri] 기하학 calculus[kælkjuləs] 미적분학 keep in mind 기억해두다 just in case 만약을 위해서
rowdy[ráudi] 난폭한 spread[spred] 분배하다 load[loud] 업무량

[4-6] Listen to a conversation between a student and a university bookstore employee.

4. Why does the student visit the bookstore?

   (A) To trade in used books

   (B) To buy course textbooks

   (C) To use the store's printer

   (D) To return a textbook

5. What problems did selling used books cause?

   Choose 2 answers.

   (A) Used books took up too much storage space.

   (B) The store was charged extra fees.

   (C) The store earned no profit from used books.

   (D) The store had too many unsold new books.

6. What does the employee say about new editions of books?

   (A) They are more popular with students.

   (B) They can be ordered online.

   (C) Professors prefer that their students buy them.

   (D) Students can trade old editions for them.

---

introduction[ìntrədʌ́kʃən] 입문 carry[kǽri] 취급하다 secondhand[sékəndhæ̀nd] 중고의 hurt[həːrt] 손해를 입히다
financially[finǽnʃəli] 재정적으로 assume[əsúːm] 생각하다 dead stock 팔다 남은 상품 take up 차지하다 charge[tʃɑːrdʒ] 청구하다
fee[fiː] 수수료 outweigh[àutwéi] ~보다 더 크다 be willing to 기꺼이 ~하다 sustain[səstéin] (피해 등을) 입다
practice[prǽktis] 관행 end up 결국 ~하게 되다

[7-9] Listen to part of a lecture in an environmental science class.

7. What is the discussion mainly about?

(A) Methods of collecting solar power

(B) Disadvantages of wind turbines

(C) Types of renewable energy

(D) Devices used to harness natural energy

8. What is one reason that renewable energy sources are not widely used?

(A) Their costs are difficult to estimate.

(B) They are less efficient than nuclear power.

(C) They are not abundant in quantity.

(D) They rely upon certain weather conditions.

9. According to the discussion, what are two advantages of wind turbines?

Choose 2 answers.

(A) Use readily available wind

(B) Take up minimal space

(C) Create adequate power

(D) Are extremely cost efficient

---

renewable energy 재생 에너지   existing[igzístiŋ] 현존하는   replenish[ripléniʃ] 다시 채우다   geothermal heat 지열
biomass[báioumæs] 바이오매스(에너지원으로 이용되는 생물 자원)   reliable[riláiəbl] 신뢰할 만한   availability[əvèiləbíləti] 이용 가능성
solar panel 태양 전지판   secondary[sékəndèri] 2차적인   windmill[wíndmil] 풍차   mechanism[mékənìzm] 기계
drawback[drɔ́ːbæ̀k] 단점   visual[víʒuəl] 시각적인

[10-12] Listen to part of a lecture in a film class.

10. What is the main purpose of the lecture?

(A) To describe the first motion picture devices

(B) To explain why the film industry was a success

(C) To show how early film audiences and venues changed

(D) To discuss the technological innovations in theaters

11. According to the professor, why were nickelodeons popular with members of the working class?

Choose 2 answers.

(A) They did not have a formal atmosphere.

(B) They could be enjoyed in relative privacy.

(C) They charged fees that were affordable.

(D) They had very comfortable furnishings.

12. What does the professor say about movie palaces?

Choose 3 answers.

(A) They were decorated more elaborately.

(B) They allowed people to choose from a collection of films.

(C) They sometimes involved live musicians.

(D) They employed workers to maintain the atmosphere.

(E) They were places where people of different backgrounds mixed.

정답·스크립트·해석·정답단서 p.213

fair[fɛər] 박람회   permanent[pə́ːrmənənt] 상설의   slot[slɑt] (자동판매기 등의) 구멍   in private 다른 사람이 없는 데서
appreciate[əpríːʃièit] 환영하다   venue[vénjuː] 장소   sit through 끝까지 앉아서 보다   playhouse[pléihàus] 극장
accommodate[əkámədèit] 수용하다   admission[ædmíʃən] 입장   establishment[istǽbliʃmənt] 시설   cut across 가로지르다

Hackers Test

[1-5] Listen to a conversation between a student and a professor.

1. Why does the student go to see the professor?

   (A) To talk about job possibilities for art history majors

   (B) To get advice on his academic future

   (C) To discuss paintings they viewed in class

   (D) To ask about the merits of studying business

2. What does the professor say about majoring in art history?

   (A) It is more difficult than majoring in business.

   (B) It is a choice that she is partial to.

   (C) It offers more rewards than majoring in business.

   (D) It gave her problems when she was in college.

3. What does the student say about the CEO he met?

   (A) He double majored in college like the professor did.

   (B) He said the job market was promising for business majors.

   (C) He felt that art history was actually more interesting than business.

   (D) He influenced the student's current choice of major.

4. Why does the student want to major in art history?

   (A) He is very stimulated by his art history classes this semester.
   (B) He admires his art history professors and wants to emulate them.
   (C) He was inspired by an artist he spoke with.
   (D) He is excited about the job prospects of art history majors.

5. According to the professor, what are two benefits she received from having a double major?

   Choose 2 answers.

   (A) Having a job that is rewarding and well-paid
   (B) Being able to examine her more inventive side
   (C) Improving her strategic and analytical abilities
   (D) Learning about hard work and dedication

CH 1

CHAPTER 2

CH 3

CH 4

CH 5

CH 6

Hackers TOEFL Listening Intermediate

[6-11] Listen to part of a lecture in a biology class.

6. What is the main topic of the lecture?

   (A) The three different chimpanzee groups in Africa

   (B) The behaviors shared by all types of chimpanzees

   (C) The link between chimpanzee behavior and habitat

   (D) The various ecosystems that chimpanzees inhabit

7. What does the professor say about the diet of chimpanzees?

   (A) They are able to consume plants and animals.

   (B) They prefer to eat meat whenever it is available.

   (C) They can digest a limited variety of vegetation.

   (D) They are unable to eat large amounts of insects.

8. Why is finding food more challenging for western chimpanzees?

   (A) The methods they use to hunt are less effective.

   (B) The rain forest that they inhabit is smaller.

   (C) The region in which they live is drier.

   (D) The plants they gather are less nutritious.

9. According to the professor, what are two examples of tool use specific to western chimpanzees?

   Choose 2 answers.

   (A) Knocking down fruits with wood

   (B) Stabbing animals with sharp sticks

   (C) Breaking open nuts with stones

   (D) Opening ant nests with rocks

10. How do chimpanzees in the savanna avoid the sun?

    (A) They find shade in forested areas.

    (B) They rest in natural shelters.

    (C) They wake up later in the day.

    (D) They only search for food at night.

11. Why is it noteworthy that western chimpanzees go into pools of water?

    (A) They swim in a manner similar to humans.

    (B) Other chimpanzees are reluctant to enter water.

    (C) They share the water with other animals.

    (D) Some chimpanzees swim as a form of bonding.

CH 1

CHAPTER 2

CH 3

CH 4

CH 5

CH 6

Hackers TOEFL Listening Intermediate

[12-17] Listen to part of a lecture in a music class.

12. What is the lecture mainly about?

(A) The traditions followed by opera composers

(B) The relationship between opera and theater

(C) The career of a talented composer of operas

(D) The development of opera in 16th-century Italy

13. According to the professor, what was Rossini's first significant accomplishment as a composer?

(A) He revised sonatas that were written by his music teacher.

(B) He composed music that was performed by his father's group.

(C) He worked with an experienced composer to create an opera.

(D) He produced several pieces of music in a short period of time.

14. What does the professor say about *Demetrio e Polibio*?

(A) The music was composed in stages.

(B) The style was very unconventional.

(C) The story's ending was criticized.

(D) The music was made after the lyrics.

15. How did studying with Cavedagni influence Rossini?

(A) It inspired him to compose music with simple melodies.

(B) It pushed him to write opera music for the first time.

(C) It encouraged him to imitate the writers of folk music.

(D) It motivated him to break the rules of composition.

16. According to the professor, what are the key aspects of Rossini's style?

Choose 3 answers.

(A) An emphasis on the music rather than the singers

(B) The use of musical elements from another genre

(C) A reliance on complex rhythms to produce tension

(D) The repetition of melodies for dramatic effect

(E) A focus on showcasing different types of vocalists

17. Why was there early public interest in *The Barber of Seville*?

(A) It was written with another composer's help.

(B) It included characters from Italian history.

(C) It was based on an existing theatrical work.

(D) It featured a singer who was popular in Europe.

CH 1

CHAPTER 2

CH 3

CH 4

CH 5

CH 6

Hackers TOEFL Listening Intermediate

[18-22] Listen to a conversation between a student and a professor.

18. Why does the student visit the professor?

(A) To register as a volunteer for a concert

(B) To discuss his favorite opera performer

(C) To provide feedback on a class activity

(D) To ask about attending a performance

19. According to the professor, why is it impossible for the student to participate in the field trip?
Choose 3 answers.

(A) The professor does not have an additional ticket.

(B) The student is not registered in the class.

(C) The student has not paid all of his tuition fees.

(D) The professor cannot contact the administration office.

(E) The student missed a registration deadline.

20. Why does the student have very little money right now?

(A) He is unemployed right now.

(B) He paid his tuition fees for next semester.

(C) He is volunteering instead of earning money.

(D) He had to buy a new computer for class.

21. According to the professor, what kinds of tasks do volunteers do at the arts center?
    Choose 2 answers.

    (A) Give out free passes to promote attendance

    (B) Help concert attendees find their seats

    (C) Make monthly schedules for the shows

    (D) Assist with writing performance pamphlets

22. According to the conversation, why is the student uncertain about volunteering?

    (A) He has a lot of assignments this semester.

    (B) He wants to find a paying job instead.

    (C) He is going to be traveling a lot and unavailable.

    (D) He is nervous about working with the public.

CH 1

CHAPTER 2

CH 3

CH 4

CH 5

CH 6

Hackers TOEFL Listening Intermediate

[23-28] Listen to a talk on beavers' decision making.

23. What does the professor mainly discuss?

(A) The results of an experiment studying beavers' selection of trees

(B) The similarities between the human and animal decision making processes

(C) The design methods used by beavers in building their dams

(D) The manner of decision making demonstrated by beavers

24. According to the lecture, what purpose does a dam serve?

(A) It makes traversing a stream easier.

(B) It traps fish for beavers to consume.

(C) It floods a particular area with water.

(D) It provides a home for beaver groups.

25. According to the lecture, what is true of beavers when finding dam-building materials?

(A) They often cut down trees they do not eventually use.

(B) They can carry cut-down trees with their strong jaws.

(C) They are prone to selecting certain kinds of trees.

(D) They prefer trees and branches already in the water.

26. What does the professor say about the beaver's predators?

(A) They often destroy the beaver's dams.

(B) They are unable to hunt the beaver in water.

(C) They cannot outrun the beaver on land.

(D) They live in the trees that the beaver cuts down.

27. What are two disadvantages of beavers choosing the far tree in the experiment?
Choose 2 answers.

(A) A longer trip puts them at greater risk of predation.

(B) More wood can be acquired by chopping down the nearby trees.

(C) Getting to the far tree involves navigating upstream.

(D) It takes more energy to move a large tree over a longer distance.

28. What do beavers and their predators have in common?

(A) They use wood to build their lodges.

(B) They spend most of their time in rivers.

(C) They exhibit complex decision making.

(D) They are awake during the same hours.

CH 1

CHAPTER 2

CH 3

CH 4

CH 5

CH 6

Hackers TOEFL Listening Intermediate

[29-34] Listen to part of a lecture from an art history class. The professor is discussing Renaissance art.

29. What is the main topic of the lecture?

(A) The techniques used by Renaissance artists

(B) The differences between oil paintings and frescoes

(C) The development of the visual arts in Europe

(D) The characteristics of a type of Renaissance painting

30. What are the disadvantages of the fresco method?
    Choose 2 answers.

(A) The plaster cannot be removed from the wall.

(B) The colors change after the paint is applied.

(C) The artist cannot easily correct mistakes.

(D) The paint can be damaged by moisture.

31. What distinguishes *The School of Athens* from other Renaissance frescoes?

(A) Its subject matter

(B) Its large size

(C) Its color scheme

(D) Its complex style

32. Why were only certain colors used when painting a fresco?

   (A) Many paints were too costly for Renaissance artists.

   (B) Some paint ingredients were destroyed by plaster.

   (C) Artists only had access to a few pigments during this period.

   (D) Most colors appeared too bright against white plaster.

33. What does the professor say about the color transitions in *The School of Athens*?

   (A) They involve careful blending.

   (B) They are difficult to detect.

   (C) They occur very abruptly.

   (D) They were not well planned.

34. How did artists make certain elements of a fresco more noticeable?

   (A) They used lighter colors to create an outline.

   (B) They applied additional layers of plaster.

   (C) They switched to a different type of paint.

   (D) They pushed in certain area of wet plaster.

정답·스크립트·해석·정답단서 p. 218

CH 1
CHAPTER 2
CH 3
CH 4
CH 5
CH 6

Hackers TOEFL Listening Intermediate

VOCABULARY LIST

Chapter 2에서 선별한 다음의 토플 필수 어휘를 단어암기 음성을 들으며 암기한 후 퀴즈로 확인해 보세요.

* 해커스 동영상강의 포털 해커스인강(HackersIngang.com)에서 단어암기 음성파일을 무료로 다운로드할 수 있습니다.

flexible[fléksəbl] 융통성 있는

minor[máinər] 부전공

posting[póustiŋ] 공고

via[vaiə] ~을 통해

geometry[dʒiámətri] 기하학

calculus[kǽlkjuləs] 미적분학

rowdy[ráudi] 난폭한

spread[spred] 분배하다

introduction[ìntrədʌ́kʃən] 입문

secondhand[sékəndhæ̀nd] 중고의

dead stock 팔다 남은 상품

outweigh[àutwéi] ~보다 더 크다

sustain[səstéin] (피해 등을) 입다

practice[prǽktis] 관행

end up 결국 ~하게 되다

existing[igzístiŋ] 현존하는

geothermal heat 지열

reliable[riláiəbl] 신뢰할 만한

secondary[sékəndèri] 2차적인

mechanism[mékənìzm] 기계

drawback[drɔ́:bæ̀k] 단점

fair[fɛər] 박람회

permanent[pə́:rmənənt] 상설의

appreciate[əprí:ʃièit] 환영하다

venue[vénju:] 장소

accommodate[əkámədèit] 수용하다

admission[ædmíʃən] 입장

establishment[istǽbliʃmənt] 시설

perspective[pərspéktiv] 관점

biased[báiəst] 편향된

inspire[inspáiər] 영감을 주다

critique[krití:k] 평론

wind up 결국 ~하게 되다

devotion[divóuʃən] 전념

hone[houn] 기르다

appealing[əpí:liŋ] 매력적인

pros and cons 장단점

grassy[grǽsi] 풀로 덮인

primate[práimeit] 영장류

seasonal[sí:zənl] 주기적인

edible[édəbl] 식용의

locate[lóukeit] 찾아내다

proficient[prəfíʃənt] 능숙한

engage in ~에 관여하다

come up with ~을 찾아내다

submerge[səbmə́:rdʒ] 잠수하다

tradition[trədíʃən] (예술 등의) 양식

costume[kástʃu:m] 분장

inevitable[inévətəbl] 필연적인

prominent[prámənənt] 유명한

thrive[θraiv] 잘 성장하다

text[tekst] 원고

Quiz

각 단어의 알맞은 뜻을 찾아 연결하시오.

01 permanent	ⓐ 편향된
02 inevitable	ⓑ 기하학
03 hone	ⓒ 상설의
04 geometry	ⓓ 필연적인
05 biased	ⓔ 기르다
	ⓕ 미적분학

06 primate	ⓐ 영장류
07 proficient	ⓑ 중고의
08 secondhand	ⓒ 장소
09 devotion	ⓓ 2차적인
10 venue	ⓔ 능숙한
	ⓕ 전념

10 ⓒ   09 ⓕ   08 ⓑ   07 ⓔ   06 ⓐ   05 ⓐ   04 ⓑ   03 ⓔ   02 ⓓ   01 ⓒ

profound[prəfáund] 지대한

rigid[rídʒid] 융통성이 없는

sit well with ~와 어울리다

rebel[rébəl] 반항적인 사람

incorporate[inkɔ́ːrpərèit] 결합하다

showcase[ʃóukèis] 소개하다

contemporary[kəntémpərèri] 당대의

all time 전례 없는

household[háushòuld] 누구나 아는

composition[kàmpəzíʃən] 작곡

make it a point to 반드시 ~하다

extra[ékstrə] 여분의

restricted[ristríktid] 한정된

field trip 현장 학습

enroll[inróul] 등록하다

liability[làiəbíləti] 책임

exception[iksépʃən] 예외

permission[pərmíʃən] 허가

limited[límitid] 많지 않은

brochure[brouʃúər] (안내·광고용) 책자

newsletter[njúːzlètər] 회보

free pass 무료 입장권

dwelling[dwéliŋ] 주거지

shelter[ʃéltər] 은신처

lodge[ladʒ] 오두막

gnaw away at ~을 갉아대다

aspen[ǽspən] 미루나무

willow[wílou] 버드나무

pine[pain] 소나무

genetically[dʒənétikəli] 유전적으로

programmed[próugræmd] 정해진

preference[préfərəns] 선호

expenditure[ikspénditʃər] 소비

chop down 베다

wolverine[wùlvəríːn] 오소리

nocturnal[naktɔ́ːrnl] 야행성의

outline[àutláin] 개요를 서술하다

plaster[plǽstər] 석고 반죽

lime[laim] 석회

apply[əplái] 바르다

water-based[wɔ́ːtərbèist] 수성의

wipe off 닦다

stunning[stʌ́niŋ] 훌륭한

strike[straik] 주의를 끌다

contrasting[kəntrǽstiŋ] 대비를 이루는

robe[roub] 예복

corrosive[kəróusiv] 부식을 일으키는

pigment[pígmənt] 색소

transition[trænzíʃən] 변화

intense[inténs] 짙은

take advantage of ~을 이용하다

stand out 눈에 띄다

Quiz

각 단어의 알맞은 뜻을 찾아 연결하시오.

01 liability	ⓐ 책임	06 dwelling	ⓐ 색소
02 restricted	ⓑ 훌륭한	07 pigment	ⓑ 주거지
03 stunning	ⓒ 선호	08 corrosive	ⓒ 대비를 이루는
04 rigid	ⓓ 한정된	09 household	ⓓ 야행성의
05 preference	ⓔ 융통성이 없는	10 nocturnal	ⓔ 누구나 아는
	ⓕ 허가		ⓕ 부식을 일으키는

01 ⓐ 02 ⓓ 03 ⓑ 04 ⓔ 05 ⓒ 06 ⓑ 07 ⓐ 08 ⓕ 09 ⓔ 10 ⓓ

Hackers TOEFL Listening Intermediate

CH 1

CHAPTER 2

CH 3

CH 4

CH 5

CH 6

CHAPTER **03**

Function & Attitude

Function & Attitude

Function & Attitude 문제는 대화나 강의에서 화자가 한 말의 기저에 놓여있는 의도나 태도를 묻는 유형이다. Function은 화자가 특정한 말을 한 의도가 무엇인지를 묻고, Attitude는 화자의 의견이나 태도를 묻는다.

▶ 문제 살펴보기

Function

- **Why does the professor say this:**
  교수는 왜 이렇게 말하는가:

- **What does the professor mean when he/she says this:**
  교수는 이렇게 말함으로써 무엇을 의미하는가:

Attitude

- **What is the professor's attitude toward ~?**
  ~에 대한 교수의 태도는 무엇인가?

- **What is the professor's opinion of ~?**
  ~에 대한 교수의 의견은 무엇인가?

▶ 문제 공략하기

실전 고득점을 위한 문제 공략법을 꼼꼼하게 학습하고 Hackers Practice와 Hackers Test를 풀면서 적용해 본다.

Function

- **지문의 맥락을 파악하며 듣는다.**
  다시 들려주는 부분의 앞뒤 맥락을 통해 화자가 한 말의 의도를 파악할 수 있다.

- **문제가 나올 수 있는 부분을 예측하며 듣는다.**
  지문에서 화자가 돌려 말하거나 어조를 다르게 하여 표면적인 내용과는 다른 의도를 표출하는 부분을 주의 깊게 들어야 한다.

Attitude

- **화자가 주관적인 생각을 말하는 부분에 주의하여 듣는다.**
  화자가 자신의 의견, 제안, 느낌 등을 말하는 부분을 주의 깊게 들어야 화자의 태도를 파악할 수 있다.

- **어조를 통해 화자의 전반적인 태도를 파악하며 듣는다.**
  지문에 나타난 화자의 어조가 positive(긍정적인), negative(부정적인), uncertain(불확실한), encouraging(격려하는), critical(비판적인)한지 판단함으로써 화자의 의도나 태도를 파악할 수 있다.

CH 1

CH 2

CHAPTER 3

CH 4

CH 5

CH 6

Listen to part of a conversation between a student and a librarian.

W: Hello, uh . . . One of my assignments is, um, to write a report about a unique old book. So do you think you have a good one for me to use?

M: A unique old book . . . let me see . . . Oh, I have one. This is a cookbook.

W: You're kidding! You mean . . . recipes? But, um . . . What can I do with this book? I mean, it's just recipes.

M: You know what, this isn't just an old cookbook. The recipes in this book and how the author presents them reveal a lot about the culture of the olden days.

W: Oh, the author says something about the recipes . . . Well, that should provide enough material, then. Maybe I should borrow that book for a couple of days.

M: Sorry, that's not how it works. The policy in this library—or, for that matter, other libraries—is to allow patrons to look at these old, rare books only in the library.

화자가 학생의 질문에 표면적인 내용과는 다른 의도를 가지고 "Sorry, that's not how it works."라고 답하는 것을 주의 깊게 들으며 의도를 파악해야 한다.

Listen again to part of the conversation. Then answer the question.

W: Maybe I should borrow that book for a couple of days.

M: Sorry, that's not how it works. The policy in this library—or, for that matter, other libraries—is to allow patrons to look at these old, rare books only in the library.

Q. Why does the man say this:
   M: Sorry, that's not how it works.

(A) To warn the woman that her topic probably will not work

(B) To point out that the woman cannot check out the book

(C) To express concern about the woman's carelessness with the old book

(D) To make clear that the woman has to wait to borrow the book

지문 해석 p. 231

해설
화자가 "Sorry, that's not how it works."라고 말하며 표면적인 내용과는 다른 의도를 표출하는 부분을 주의 깊게 들음으로써 대출이 불가능하다는 의미를 파악할 수 있다. 따라서, 정답은 (B)이다.

[1-3] Listen to a conversation between a student and an employee at the university fitness center.

Listen again to part of the conversation. Then answer the question.

1. What does the student mean when he says this: 🎧

(A) He is confused by the woman's question.

(B) He is unsure whether he brought his ID.

(C) He is aware of the requirement to show ID.

(D) He is surprised by the woman's request.

Listen again to part of the conversation. Then answer the question.

2. What does the employee mean when she says this: 🎧

(A) She is interested in the student's sports activities.

(B) She knows why the gym is popular with students.

(C) She is sympathetic to the student's situation.

(D) She realizes that the student wants to exercise.

Listen again to part of the conversation. Then answer the question.

3. Why does the student say this: 🎧

(A) To show that he is reluctant to take the suggestion

(B) To emphasize that he has a flexible workout schedule

(C) To indicate that he has little time to use the gym

(D) To suggest that he does not understand a plan

---

out-of-state[àutəvstéit] 다른 주의 pass[pæs] 출입증 hassle[hæsl] 번거로운 상황 strict[strikt] 엄격한 security[sikjúərəti] 보안
fair[fɛər] 타당한 policy[páləsi] 규정 frustrating[frʌstreitiŋ] 불만스러운 facility[fəsíləti] 시설 copy[kápi] 사본
issue[íʃuː] 발급하다 recommend[rèkəménd] 추천하다 morning person 아침형 인간

[4-6] Listen to a conversation in a registrar's office.

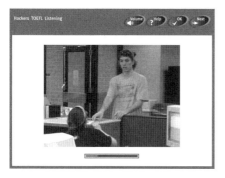

4. Why does the student visit the registrar's office?

   (A) To inquire about loan repayment options

   (B) To check on the balance of his account

   (C) To collect money from a scholarship

   (D) To settle the rest of his tuition fees

Listen again to part of the conversation. Then answer the question.

5. Why does the woman say this: 🎧

   (A) To express uncertainty about her own explanation of the process

   (B) To check the man's understanding of the registration procedure

   (C) To verify if the student is already familiar with the rules

   (D) To indicate disagreement with the process of re-registration

Listen again to part of the conversation. Then answer the question.

6. Why does the man say this: 🎧

   (A) To express his agreement with her statement

   (B) To show surprise at her comment

   (C) To clarify whether or not she was joking

   (D) To check if he heard her correctly

---

tuition[tʃuːíʃən] 수업료 check[tʃek] 수표 balance[bǽləns] 잔액 account[əkáunt] 계정 student ID 학생증
payment[péimənt] 납부금, 납부 due[djuː] ~까지인; 수업료 in a bind 곤란한 상황인 negotiate[nigóuʃièit] 조정하다
convince[kənvíns] 설득하다 mediator[míːdièitər] 중재인 in any case 어쨌든

[7-9] Listen to part of a lecture from an archaeology class.

7. What is the lecture mainly about?

(A) The various patterns of ancient tools

(B) The discovery of an ancient Scottish weapon

(C) The possible uses of a type of artifact

(D) The origins of a stone-carving technique

Listen again to part of the lecture. Then answer the question.

8. Why does the professor say this:

(A) To test the students' understanding of a point

(B) To offer evidence that disproves a theory

(C) To suggest that some measurements were wrong

(D) To provide a reason for an opinion

9. Why is it likely that the stone balls were part of a weapon?
Choose 2 answers.

(A) They could be attached to ropes easily.

(B) They were heavy enough to cause serious harm.

(C) They could be produced very quickly.

(D) They were decorated with complex designs.

---

artifact[ɑ́ːrtəfæ̀kt] 공예품 elaborate[ilǽbərət] 정교한 spiral[spáiərəl] 나선 primitive[prímətiv] 원시의 weight[weit] 추
diameter[daiǽmətər] 지름 bola[bóulə] 볼라(끝에 쇳덩어리가 달린 수렵 기구) fasten[fæsn] 단단히 고정시키다 wrap[ræp] 휘감다
sphere[sfiər] 구 intricate[íntrikət] 복잡한 in favor of ~을 지지하는 prized[praizd] 소중한 gravesite[gréivsàit] 묘지

[10-12] Listen to part of a lecture in a biology class.

10. What is the lecture mainly about?

(A) The ways zooplankton avoid predators

(B) The daily migration of an organism

(C) The elements of the ocean's food chain

(D) The physical traits of migratory zooplankton

Listen again to part of the lecture. Then answer the question.

11. What does the student mean when she says this:

(A) She wishes to provide a supporting fact.

(B) She wants to check a term's definition.

(C) She thinks that a statement needs to be modified.

(D) She needs the professor to clarify the topic.

12. According to the professor, how do zooplankton move through water?

Choose 2 answers.

(A) By pushing against it with their legs

(B) By allowing themselves to be carried by currents

(C) By squeezing water out from their bodies

(D) By using a body part to drag themselves forward

정답·스크립트·해석·정답단서 p.231

---

organism[ɔ́ːrɡənìzm] 생물 zooplankton[zòuəplǽŋktən] 동물성 플랑크톤 convert[kənvə́ːrt] 바꾸다 habitat[hǽbitæt] 서식지
migration[maiɡréiʃən] 이동 microorganism[màikrouɔ́ːrɡənìzm] 미생물 feed on ~을 먹고 살다 depth[depθ] 밑바닥
interrupt[intərʌ́pt] 방해하다 in relation to ~에 비해 resistance[rizístəns] 저항력 flap[flæp] 펄럭거리다
ocean current 해류 make progress 전진하다 sink[siŋk] 가라앉다 dense[dens] 밀도가 높은

Hackers Test

[1-5]   Listen to a conversation between a student and a professor.

1. What is the conversation mainly about?

    (A) References for a research paper

    (B) Films being shown at a festival

    (C) A student's topic for a presentation

    (D) The differences between film and literature

Listen again to part of the conversation. Then answer the question.

2. Why does the student say this:

    (A) To indicate agreement with her professor

    (B) To inquire about an important question

    (C) To show excitement about her project

    (D) To express uncertainty about her topic

3. What does the professor suggest the student do?

    (A) Work on her public speaking skills

    (B) Choose a different topic

    (C) Attend an upcoming film festival

    (D) Narrow the scope of a theme

4. What paper does the student want to present at the film festival?

(A) A history of film and literature

(B) Films based on literary masterpieces

(C) Film and literature in the 20th century

(D) Story-telling techniques in film and literature

Listen again to part of the conversation. Then answer the question.

5. What does the professor mean when he says this: 🎧

(A) He thinks the student's idea may be promising.

(B) He thinks the student needs help.

(C) He wants to discourage the student.

(D) He is not confident about the student's proposal.

[6-11] Listen to part of a lecture in an economics class.

6. What is the lecture mainly about?

    (A) Methods that management can use to increase profits

    (B) Techniques to prevent a crisis from occurring

    (C) A common problem many different companies face

    (D) An aspect of the crisis management procedure

7. According to the professor, what are the benefits of contingency planning?
  Choose 3 answers.

    (A) The correct action is taken.

    (B) Less money is lost.

    (C) The crisis is avoided.

    (D) Little time is wasted.

    (E) Fewer employees are needed.

Listen again to part of the lecture. Then answer the question.

8. What does the student mean when he says this:

    (A) He has heard a term before.

    (B) He would like to clarify the question.

    (C) He is unfamiliar with a concept.

    (D) He believes the risks are exaggerated.

9. What is the professor's attitude toward a crisis response team?

   (A) It requires too many company resources.

   (B) It should be established in advance of a crisis.

   (C) It complicates the development of a plan.

   (D) It should be a temporary arrangement.

10. What is the final stage of the contingency planning process?

    (A) The team members are selected.

    (B) The measures are regularly updated.

    (C) The company is significantly expanded.

    (D) The potential threat is eliminated.

Listen again to part of the lecture. Then answer the question.

11. Why does the professor say this:

    (A) To stress the impressiveness of an accomplishment

    (B) To check whether the class understands a point

    (C) To introduce an idea that contradicts the previous one

    (D) To suggest that successful mining rescues are infrequent

[12-17] Listen to part of a lecture on astronomy.

12. What is the professor mainly discussing?

(A) The properties of Saturn's regular satellites

(B) The similarities between Titan and Dione

(C) The discovery of new moons around Saturn

(D) The atmospheric conditions on Saturn's moons

Listen again to part of the lecture. Then answer the question.

13. Why does the professor say this:

(A) To discount the possibility of life outside of Earth

(B) To contrast a common opinion with that of experts

(C) To show disagreement with speculative science

(D) To emphasize that life on Titan might be plausible

14. According to the professor, what are three ways in which Titan is similar to the Earth? Choose 3 answers.

(A) Its atmosphere is abundant in nitrogen.

(B) Its size is comparable to the size of Earth.

(C) It is not protected from harmful radiation from the Sun.

(D) Its elements create rivers, valleys, and dunes.

(E) Its atmospheric conditions produce a greenhouse effect.

15. What does the professor say about Dione's terrain?

    (A) It was formed by the process of erosion.

    (B) It contains see-through sections made of ice.

    (C) It is not a result of the moon's tectonic movements.

    (D) It is unusually smooth and contains few variations.

16. What do some researchers suppose about Dione?

    (A) It is bombarded by meteors more often than Saturn's other moons.

    (B) It is the most geologically active moon in the solar system.

    (C) Ice and heavy winds are making it erode at a rapid pace.

    (D) A large object collided with it and caused it to turn.

17. What is the professor's opinion about research on Saturn's moons?

    (A) She thinks not enough research is being conducted.

    (B) She does not think that current research is accurate.

    (C) She feels that research findings have not been fully supported.

    (D) She is confident that continued research will lead to new findings.

CH 1

CH 2

CHAPTER 3

CH 4

CH 5

CH 6

Hackers TOEFL Listening Intermediate

[18-22] Listen to a conversation between an academic advisor and a student.

18. Why does the student talk to the professor?

(A) To ask him what journalism classes he is offering for the semester

(B) To check the requirements for a switch to mass communications

(C) To determine who the easiest professors in journalism are

(D) To get his recommendation on an elective she wants to take

Listen again to part of the conversation. Then answer the questions.

19. Why does the professor say this: 🎧

(A) To indicate that the electives the student wants are not available

(B) To encourage the student to try harder to fulfill her electives

(C) To express disagreement with what the student said

(D) To assure the student that he doubts her request will be rejected

20. According to the conversation, what are two reasons the student gives for choosing an elective in journalism?

Choose 2 answers.

(A) To satisfy her elective requirements for the semester

(B) To study something different from her field

(C) To prepare for a career in writing

(D) To take courses related to her major

21. What does the professor say about studying under Professor Meyer?

    (A) He provides students with a topic when they do research papers.
    (B) He has rigorous standards that stimulate his students to do their best.
    (C) He is an appealing and entertaining professor in the classroom.
    (D) He makes research easier by giving students a list of source materials.

Listen again to part of the conversation. Then answer the question.

22. What does the student mean when she says this: 🎧

    (A) She thinks writing for the university paper was difficult.
    (B) She does not think writing for the paper was worth the effort.
    (C) She believes she should have studied journalism first.
    (D) She thinks she should have worked on more interesting articles.

[23-28] Listen to part of a talk on art history.

23. What is the talk mainly about?

(A) The mixed reactions to the realist paintings of Andrew Wyeth

(B) The gradual evolution of Wyeth's realist style

(C) The subject matter of popular realist masterpieces

(D) The prevalence of abstract expressionism in the mid-20th century

Listen again to part of the lecture. Then answer the question.

24. What does the professor mean when he says this: 🎧

(A) He does not think that Andrew Wyeth had talent.

(B) He wants to correct some information he gave about Andrew Wyeth.

(C) He does not understand why N.C. Wyeth taught his son painting techniques.

(D) He thinks N.C. Wyeth had a reason to give his son assistance.

25. What does the professor say about *Christina's World*?

(A) It became famous only after Wyeth's death.

(B) It was inspired by a woman who Wyeth knew.

(C) It contrasted sharply with the fashionable art at the time.

(D) It differed significantly from works Wyeth had done earlier in life.

26. According to the professor, why were many artists and critics unwilling to give Wyeth's art any acclaim?

(A) They claimed that it put too much emphasis on natural beauty.

(B) They felt that his technical ability as an artist was overrated.

(C) They thought that he was too strongly influenced by an earlier artist.

(D) They contended that it was insignificant from the viewpoint of contemporary art.

Listen again to part of the lecture. Then answer the question.

27. Why does the student say this:

(A) To show that she understands the professor's point

(B) To indicate her familiarity with exhibits at art museums

(C) To explain that she has a different idea from the professor

(D) To express that she is in agreement with the curator's perspective

28. What is the professor's opinion of the controversy surrounding Wyeth's work?

(A) It is irrelevant considering the art's market value.

(B) It reflected the critics' resentment of Wyeth's fame.

(C) It contributed to the high prices of some of his paintings.

(D) It is the primary reason the American public became aware of Wyeth's works.

[29-34] Listen to part of a lecture on psychology.

29. What is the main topic of the lecture?

(A) The applicability of the Sally-Anne test to animals

(B) How vervet monkeys behave toward new monkeys

(C) Views on whether vervet monkeys have a theory of mind

(D) The reasons vervet monkeys sound false alarm calls

Listen again to part of the lecture. Then answer the question.

30. Why does the professor say this:

(A) To suggest that the students will obtain similar results

(B) To express uncertainty about the results of the test

(C) To encourage the students to research a topic

(D) To indicate the reason she described the experiment

Listen again to part of the lecture. Then answer the question.

31. Why does the professor say this:

(A) To provide the meaning of a word she just mentioned

(B) To find out if the students understood what she said

(C) To explain a criterion used in the experiment

(D) To emphasize the significance of a term she used

32. What does the professor say about vervet monkey alarm calls?

(A) They are only made when monkeys from outside the group approach.

(B) Monkeys make them only if their immediate family is endangered.

(C) They sound different depending on the type of threat.

(D) High-ranking monkeys in the group typically make them.

33. According to the professor, what is a reason some scientists believe that vervet monkeys have a theory of mind?

(A) A monkey may understand how a false alarm can affect another monkey.

(B) Monkeys deliberately ignore false alarms.

(C) Monkeys are concerned with their own social status.

(D) Some monkeys know where to look for the marble.

34. What is the professor's attitude concerning a theory of mind in animals?

(A) Experiments have proved it to be credible.

(B) It likely does not exist in all animals.

(C) Its viability has not been proven or disproven.

(D) It does not exist except in humans.

정답·스크립트·해석·정답단서 p. 238

VOCABULARY LIST

Chapter 3에서 선별한 다음의 토플 필수 어휘를 단어암기 음성을 들으며 암기한 후 퀴즈로 확인해 보세요.

*해커스 동영상강의 포털 해커스인강(HackersIngang.com)에서 단어암기 음성파일을 무료로 다운로드할 수 있습니다.

hassle[hǽsl] 번거로운 상황

frustrating[frʌ́streitiŋ] 불만스러운

balance[bǽləns] 잔액

in a bind 곤란한 상황인

negotiate[nigóuʃièit] 조정하다

convince[kənvíns] 설득하다

mediator[mí:dièitər] 중재인

artifact[ɑ́:rtəfæ̀kt] 공예품

spiral[spáiərəl] 나선

primitive[prímətiv] 원시의

diameter[daiǽmətər] 지름

fasten[fǽsn] 단단히 고정시키다

intricate[íntrikət] 복잡한

prized[praizd] 소중한

habitat[hǽbitæt] 서식지

depth[depθ] 밑바닥

dense[dens] 밀도가 높은

barge in on 갑자기 찾아오다

far-fetched[fɑ̀:rfétʃt] 억지스러운

in terms of ~의 관점에서

make use of ~을 사용하다

fine-tune[fàintʃúːn] 다듬다

evolution[èvəlúːʃən] 발달

cinematography[sìnəmətágrəfi] 영화 촬영법

thorough[θə́ːrou] 면밀한

overview[óuvərvjù:] 개관

terminology[tə̀:rmənálədʒi] 용어

manage[mǽnidʒ] 잘 해나가다

get stuck 난관에 봉착하다

run out of ~이 바닥나다

management[mǽnidʒmənt] 경영진

scramble[skrǽmbl] 급히 서두르다

strike[straik] 발생하다

maintenance[méintənəns] 유지

personnel[pə̀:rsənél] 직원의

viability[vàiəbíləti] 실행 가능성

up-to-date[ʌ̀ptədéit] 최신 정보에 근거한

in place ~을 위한 준비가 되어 있는

drag on 계속되다

classification[klæ̀səfikéiʃən] 분류법

albeit[ɔːlbíːit] 비록 ~이지만

prograde[próugrèid] 순행의

inclination[ìnklənéiʃən] 경사

equatorial plane 적도면

retrograde[rétrəgrèid] 역행의

account for ~을 차지하다

mass[mæs] 질량

fuel[fjuːəl] 부추기다

building block 구성 요소

sustain[səstéin] 존재하게 하다

radiation[rèidiéiʃən] 복사광

terrain[təréin] 지형

Quiz

각 단어의 알맞은 뜻을 찾아 연결하시오.

01 mass	ⓐ 경사
02 inclination	ⓑ 질량
03 terminology	ⓒ 용어
04 convince	ⓓ 분류법
05 sustain	ⓔ 존재하게 하다
	ⓕ 설득하다

06 terrain	ⓐ 지형
07 diameter	ⓑ 순행의
08 overview	ⓒ 개관
09 intricate	ⓓ 역행의
10 retrograde	ⓔ 지름
	ⓕ 복잡한

01 ⓑ 02 ⓐ 03 ⓒ 04 ⓕ 05 ⓔ 06 ⓐ 07 ⓔ 08 ⓒ 09 ⓕ 10 ⓓ

depression[dipréʃən] 함몰

fracture[fræktʃər] 균열

tectonic[tektánik] 지각의

wispy[wíspi] 희미한

transparent[trænspɛ́ərənt] 투명한

face away 반대쪽을 향하다

meteor[mí:tiər] 유성

probe[proub] 탐색하다

elective[iléktiv] 선택 과목

requirement[rikwáiərmənt] 필수 과목, 필수 요건

stringent[stríndʒənt] 엄격한

reporting[ripɔ́:rtiŋ] 보도

feature[fí:tʃər] 기사, 특집

genuinely[dʒénjuinli] 진심으로

synonymous[sinánəməs] 같은 뜻을 의미하는

accomplished[əkámpliʃt] 뛰어난

go without saying 두말할 나위가 없다

tip[tip] 예측

pay off 성공하다

renowned[rináund] 유명한

abstract[æbstrǽkt] 추상적인

polarize[póuləràiz] (사람들을) 대립시키다

contradictory[kàntrədíktəri] 모순되는

rebel[rébəl] 저항

incessant[insésnt] 끊임없는

instill[instíl] 불어넣다

sentiment[séntəmənt] 정서

in hindsight 돌이켜 보았을 때

controversy[kántrəvə̀:rsi] 논란

relevance[réləvəns] 타당성

rage[reidʒ] 맹렬하게 계속되다

put on ~을 꾸미다

skit[skit] 토막극

marble[má:rbl] 구슬

desire[dizáiər] 욕구

intent[intént] 의도

urge[ə:rdʒ] 권하다

suitable[sú:təbl] 적당한

cite[sait] 인용하다

alarm call 경고음

low-ranking[lòurǽŋkiŋ] 하위 계급의

speculate[spékjulèit] 추측하다

subordinate[səbɔ́:rdənət] 부하

put oneself in the shoes of ~의 입장에 서다

perception[pərsépʃən] 인식

anecdotal[æ̀nikdóutl] 일화적인

refute[rifjú:t] 반박하다

have no bearing on ~과 관련이 없다

impairment[impɛ́ərmənt] 장애

mental deficiency 지능 장애

induction[indʌ́kʃən] 귀납

overwhelming[òuvərʰwélmiŋ] 강력한

Quiz

각 단어의 알맞은 뜻을 찾아 연결하시오.

01 tectonic	ⓐ 투명한	06 fracture	ⓐ 귀납
02 intent	ⓑ 같은 뜻을 의미하는	07 speculate	ⓑ 유성
03 cite	ⓒ 지각의	08 incessant	ⓒ 추측하다
04 elective	ⓓ 선택 과목	09 induction	ⓓ 일화적인
05 synonymous	ⓔ 의도	10 anecdotal	ⓔ 균열
	ⓕ 인용하다		ⓕ 끊임없는

CHAPTER 04

Connecting Contents I

Connecting Contents I

Connecting Contents I(List, Matching, Ordering) 문제는 대화나 강의에 등장하는 여러 가지 정보의 상호 관계를 이해한 후, 표를 완성하는 유형이다. List는 제시된 각 정보의 사실 여부를, Matching은 각 정보가 속하는 범주를, Ordering은 사건이나 대상의 진행 과정, 혹은 발생 순서를 파악하고 있는지를 묻는다.

문제 살펴보기

List

- Indicate whether each of the following is ~.
  다음의 항목이 ~인지를 표시하시오.

	Yes	No
Statement A		
Statement B		
Statement C		

Matching

- Indicate for each example what type of ~.
  각 예시가 ~의 어떤 유형인지를 표시하시오.

	Type A	Type B	Type C
Ex 1			
Ex 2			
Ex 3			

Ordering

- The professor explains the steps ~. Put the steps listed below in the correct order.
  교수는 ~의 단계를 설명한다. 아래의 단계들을 올바른 순서대로 나열하시오.

Step 1	
Step 2	
Step 3	

문제 공략하기

실전 고득점을 위한 문제 공략법을 꼼꼼하게 학습하고 Hackers Practice와 Hackers Test를 풀면서 적용해 본다.

List

- **하나의 범주에 대한 여러 가지 정보가 나열될 때에는 List 문제를 예상하며 들어야 한다.**

  특징, 제안, 이유 등과 관련된 정보가 자주 출제된다.

  Example

  대화: 도서관 이용 규칙 변경 사항, 보고서에 추가해야 할 사항

  강의: 석회암 동굴의 특징, 뉴욕이 세계적인 대도시가 될 수 있었던 이유

Matching

- **두 개 이상의 범주와 각 범주에 관한 정보들이 나열될 때에는 Matching 문제를 예상하며 들어야 한다.**

  장점/단점, 유사점/차이점, 비교/대조 등과 관련된 정보가 자주 출제된다.

  Example

  대화: 학생이 쓴 리포트의 장점/단점, 두 전공 수업의 유사점/차이점

  강의: 천연진주와 양식진주의 유사점/차이점, 두 예술가의 비교/대조

Ordering

- **여러 가지 정보들이 순서대로 나열될 때에는 Ordering 문제를 예상하며 들어야 한다.**

  절차, 과정 등과 관련된 정보가 자주 출제된다.

  Example

  대화: 수강 신청 절차, 교환학생 선발 과정

  강의: 화학 실험 과정, 산업혁명의 진행 과정

CH 1
CH 2
CH 3
CHAPTER 4
CH 5
CH 6

Hackers TOEFL Listening Intermediate

Listen to part of a lecture in an astronomy class.

Now, a space probe, the Mariner 10, visited Mercury three times and took around 2,700 pictures. In 1965, scientists calculated that Mercury rotated every 59 days, give or take 5 days. The Mariner 10, however, was able to determine that the rotation is actually 58.646, plus or minus 0.0005 days.

OK . . . another thing the Mariner 10 learned is that Mercury has a magnetic field about 100 times weaker than the Earth's. The interesting thing is . . . for a planet to have a magnetic field, it has to have a core that's partially molten, that is, liquid metal or liquid rock. A solid core cannot produce a magnetic field. Scientists believed that Mercury's core was once liquid iron, but assumed that it had become cold and solid all these billions of years. However, the Mariner 10 did detect a magnetic field, albeit a weak one.

One other point I'd like to make is . . . both the Moon and Mercury have temperature extremes . . . Mercury's goes down to minus 170 degrees Celsius at night and 350 degrees Celsius during the day, and the Moon's temperature ranges from minus 100 to 340. The only big difference between them is density. The Moon's lower density suggests that it's made of mostly igneous rock from lava flows, but Mercury's higher density means that it has an iron core.

지문 해석 p. 252

교수가 수성과 관련된 여러 개의 특징을 나열하기 시작할 때, List 문제를 예상하며 주의 깊게 들어야 한다.
특징 1 – 수성의 자전이 생각보다 더 빈번하게 일어난다.

특징 2 – 수성에는 지구보다 약한 자기장이 있다.

특징 3 – 수성의 기온 차는 크다.

In the lecture, the professor describes the characteristics of Mercury. Indicate whether each of the following is a feature of Mercury.

Click in the correct box for each sentence.

	Yes	No
Rotation occurs over a period of 5 days.	√	
Magnetic field exists but is faint.	√	
Temperature ranges are extreme.	√	
Density is similar to the Earth's moon.		√

해설

화자가 나열하는 수성에 관한 여러 가지 특징을 주의 깊게 들음으로써, 제시된 정보들 중 사실인 것을 골라 표를 완성할 수 있다. 따라서, 정답은 수성의 자전이 본래 생각되던 것보다 자주 일어나고 그곳에는 약한 자기장이 존재하며, 기온 차가 심하다는 것이다.

CH 1

CH 2

CH 3

CHAPTER 4

CH 5

CH 6

Hackers TOEFL Listening Intermediate

Hackers Practice

[1-3] Listen to a conversation between a student and a librarian.

1. What is the student's problem?

(A) She does not know the author of a book she wants to borrow.

(B) She damaged a book that she checked out from the library.

(C) She needs information about the status of a library book.

(D) She is uncertain about the library policy on book returns.

2. What improvements are included in the updated computer system? Indicate whether each of the following is included.

Click in the correct box for each phrase.

	Included	Not Included
Easier access to online publications		
Improved organization of the website		
Additional options for book reservations		
An enhanced search function		

3. What does the librarian offer to do for the student?

(A) Contact her professor about an assignment

(B) Put a book that is being fixed on hold

(C) Email another library about a copy of a book

(D) Suggest other sources to use for a research paper

---

catalogue[kǽtəlɔ̀ːg] 목록 status[stéitəs] 상태 spine[spain] (책의) 등 rough[rʌf] 거친 comment[kάment] 언급하다
navigate[nǽvəgèit] (웹사이트를) 여기저기 찾다 setup[sétʌp] 구성 orderly[ɔ́ːrdərli] 정돈된 insistent[insístənt] 주장하는
insight[ínsàit] 통찰력 circulation[sə̀ːrkjuléiʃən] 유통 notification[nòutəfikéiʃən] 알림 extension[iksténʃən] 연장

[4-6] Listen to a conversation between a student and an employee in the Student Activity Center.

4. Why does the student visit the Student Activity Center?

(A) To inquire about San Francisco attractions

(B) To discuss an upcoming club activity

(C) To ask about funding for a club trip

(D) To sign up for an architecture club event

5. The employee explains the steps in the process for getting a change in travel plans approved. Put the steps listed below in the correct order.

Drag each answer choice to the space where it belongs.
One of the answer choices will not be used.

Step 1	
Step 2	
Step 3	

- Pick up some forms from another office
- Provide schedule and route information
- Arrange an inspection of the bicycles
- Recalculate the travel costs

6. Why did the university recently introduce a new regulation regarding cycling trips?

(A) There was a complaint made by a club official.

(B) There was an injury to a pedestrian on campus.

(C) There was a problem at the university bike shop.

(D) There was an accident involving other students.

---

in charge of ~을 담당하는 last-minute [lをstmínit] 막바지의 adjustment [ədʒʌ́stmənt] 수정 notify [nóutəfài] 알리다
paperwork [péipərəðːrk] 서류 작업 straightforward [strèitfɔ́ːrwərd] 간단한 itinerary [aitínərèri] 일정
treasurer [tréʒərər] 회계 담당자 certify [sə́ːrtəfài] 증명하다 mechanical [məkǽnikəl] 기계적인

[7-9] Listen to part of a lecture on literature. The professor is discussing a detective novel.

7. What does the professor mainly discuss?

(A) The most popular novels written during the Victorian period

(B) The characteristics of modern English detective novels

(C) The features that make *The Moonstone* the first full-length detective novel

(D) The unique characters that are portrayed in *The Moonstone*

8. What does the professor say about Sergeant Cuff?

(A) He was the first example of a detective hero.

(B) He was an ineffective professional investigator.

(C) He was overly absorbed in details.

(D) He was the most important character.

9. In the lecture, the professor describes typical characteristics of modern detective fiction novels. Indicate whether each of the following is a characteristic.

Click in the correct box for each sentence.

	Yes	No
A number of misleading hints are given.		
Two detectives compete to solve a crime.		
A perceptive and eccentric detective solves the crime.		
The story revolves around a crime and a criminal.		
Several people are directly responsible for the crime.		

---

full-length[fùlléŋθ] 장편의 detective[ditéktiv] 탐정 undisclosed[ʌ̀ndisklóuzd] 밝혀지지 않은 plot[plɑt] 줄거리
prototype[próutətàip] 시초 inept[inépt] 서투른 incompetent[inkámpətənt] 무능한 perceptive[pərséptiv] 통찰력 있는
civilized[sívəlàizd] 교양 있는 eccentric[ikséntrik] 괴짜인 deduction[didʌ́kʃən] 추리 reason[ríːzn] 추리하다

[10-12] Listen to part of a lecture in an archaeology class.

10. What is the lecture mainly about?

(A) A comparison of tools used in archaeology

(B) A technique for locating archaeological sites

(C) A method used to preserve ancient ruins

(D) An analysis of how archaeology benefits from technology

11. In the lecture, the professor explains the sequence of steps used to create a three-dimensional map of an area. Put the steps listed below in the correct order.

Drag each answer choice to the space where it belongs.
One of the answer choices will not be used.

Step 1	
Step 2	
Step 3	
Step 4	

- The distance to an object is calculated.
- Data is collected over a large area.
- Information is compared to historical data.
- Light is transmitted onto objects on the ground.
- Several types of measurements are compared.

Listen again to part of the lecture. Then answer the question.

12. Why does the professor say this: 🎧

(A) To point out that archaeologists must be patient

(B) To suggest that a project took longer than expected

(C) To stress the significance of an accomplishment

(D) To express doubts about a device's advantages

정답·스크립트·해석·정답단서 p.252

muon[mʃuːɑn] 뮤온 ruin[ruːin] 유적 buried[bérid] 파묻힌 radio wave 전파 light wave 광파 unit[júːnit] 장치
low-flying[lóuflàiiŋ] 저공 비행의 aircraft[ɛ́ərkræft] 항공기 enter into ~에 입력하다 shift[ʃift] 이동하다
man-made[mǽnméid] 인공의 hazard[hǽzərd] 위험 요소

Hackers Test

[1-5] Listen to a conversation between a student and a professor.

1. Why does the student go to see the professor?

    (A) To inquire about changing a presentation topic

    (B) To ask for a definition of an economic principle

    (C) To request assistance with a class assignment

    (D) To ask a question about the significance of the factors of production

2. What does the professor say about the factors of production?

    (A) They apply only to an industrial setting.

    (B) They are limited to raw materials.

    (C) They vary depending on the situation.

    (D) They are often difficult to identify.

3. According to the professor, what is an important aspect of the law of diminishing returns?

    (A) The overall level of production declines.

    (B) Increases in output get progressively smaller.

    (C) The cost of additional input becomes higher.

    (D) Output becomes significantly greater over time.

Listen again to part of the conversation. Then answer the question.

4. What does the student mean when she says this:

(A) She regrets choosing a difficult topic.

(B) She wishes she had more time to prepare.

(C) She does not fully understand a concept.

(D) She needs to start her presentation soon.

5. The professor suggests several ways for the student to learn more about a law of economics. Indicate whether each of the following is included.

Click in the correct box for each phrase.

	Suggested	Not Suggested
Consult with another professor		
Search for relevant websites		
Review a unit in the textbook		
Get texts from the library		

CH 1

CH 2

CH 3

CHAPTER 4

CH 5

CH 6

Hackers TOEFL Listening Intermediate

[6-11] Listen to part of a lecture in a sociology class.

6. What is the lecture mainly about?

    (A) Theories regarding the causes of urbanization

    (B) Models that explain how cities are organized

    (C) The history of urban development in North America

    (D) A comparison of residential and industrial areas

7. What does the professor say about the ring model?

    (A) It was criticized for being inaccurate.

    (B) It describes many patterns of urban development.

    (C) It replaced an earlier theory about sectors.

    (D) It is unable to account for the presence of the CBD.

8. In the lecture, the professor explains the steps in the urbanization process according to Hoyt. Put the steps listed below in the correct order.

    Drag each answer choice to the space where it belongs.
    One of the answer choices will not be used.

Step 1	
Step 2	
Step 3	

    - Factories are built along roads and railway lines.
    - Residential areas form in relation to industrial areas.
    - Transportation routes project from the CBD.
    - Wealthy neighborhoods attract more businesses.

Listen again to part of the lecture. Then answer the question.

9. What does the student mean when he says this: 🎧

(A) He heard something that contradicts the professor's statement.

(B) He wants to make sure that he understands a concept correctly.

(C) He learned about an alternate theory that he would like to share.

(D) He has a different idea based on his personal experience.

10. What are key elements of the multiple nuclei model?

Choose 3 answers.

(A) The CBD does not determine a city's organization.

(B) There are many centers throughout a city.

(C) The city center has a wide range of functions.

(D) Each center is based around a key institution.

(E) Residential areas are included in the CBD.

11. According to the professor, what is an advantage of the multiple nuclei model?

(A) It is compatible with previous theories.

(B) It predicts property values more accurately.

(C) It shows how to slow the urbanization process.

(D) It is more adaptable than other models.

CH 1
CH 2
CH 3
CHAPTER 4
CH 5
CH 6

Hackers TOEFL Listening Intermediate

[12-17] Listen to part of a lecture in a geology class.

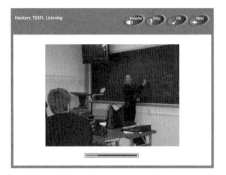

12. What is the main topic of the lecture?

(A) A feature shared by various types of rivers

(B) The importance of rivers in some regions

(C) A process that affects the shape of a river

(D) The relationship between rivers and rain

13. What are the factors that determine the frequency of floods in a river system?
Choose 2 answers.

(A) The composition of the surrounding land

(B) Significant loss of soil and rocks

(C) The overall size of a river system

(D) Seasonal increases in precipitation

14. What happens during flooding to cause a river channel to become deeper?

(A) Material piles up on the river's edges.

(B) Rocks are removed from the river's bottom.

(C) Water destroys the banks of the river.

(D) Soil is transported from low areas of land.

Listen again to part of the lecture. Then answer the question.

15. What does the professor mean when she says this: 🎧

(A) Floodwaters occasionally create new levees.

(B) Rivers do not usually have levees on their banks.

(C) Levees are sometimes difficult to detect.

(D) Floods are not always prevented by levees.

16. What is the professor's opinion of the Jamuna River?

(A) She considers it an interesting subject of study.

(B) She wishes that it was easier to observe.

(C) She thinks the students should research it.

(D) She finds it visually appealing in photographs.

17. In the lecture, the professor describes several characteristics of the Jamuna River. Indicate whether each of the following is a characteristic.

Click in the correct box for each sentence.

	Yes	No
It is divided into multiple channels.		
It has extremely high banks.		
It includes unstable islands.		
It contains little sediment.		
It experiences regular floods.		

[18-22] Listen to a conversation between a bookstore attendant and a student.

18. Why does the man visit the bookstore?

    (A) To pick up a political science book that has just come in

    (B) To purchase a replacement political science textbook

    (C) To order a book on his science class reading list

    (D) To order a book that was sold out at another bookstore

Listen again to part of the conversation. Then answer the question.

19. What does the woman mean when she says this: 🎧

    (A) She does not understand why the man has not bought the book yet.

    (B) She realizes she does not have a copy for the student.

    (C) She thinks the publisher is taking too long to deliver the order.

    (D) She does not think they will have copies any time soon.

20. Why does the man need to order the book?

    (A) He wants to reference it for an essay.

    (B) He has to study for an exam.

    (C) He lost his friend's copy.

    (D) He is required to bring it to class.

21. What does the woman say about the textbook?

    (A) It is no longer used for Political Science 101.
    (B) It is not included in the warehouse inventory.
    (C) It will be available before the end of the summer.
    (D) It is sold only at selected bookstores.

22. The bookstore clerk suggests what the man should do. Indicate whether each of the following is a suggestion.

    Click in the correct box for each phrase.

	Suggested	Not Suggested
Search for an item online		
Visit a different bookstore		
Borrow the book from the library		
Visit the university's storage unit		
Ask the professor if he will order more books		

[23-28] Listen to part of a lecture in a history class.

23. What is the lecture mainly about?

(A) The importance of cultural exchanges

(B) A comparison of different writing systems

(C) An example of an historical process

(D) The characteristics of the Latin alphabet

Listen again to part of the lecture. Then answer the question.

24. Why does the professor say this:

(A) To show that languages share alphabets

(B) To stress that pronunciation is important

(C) To indicate that pronunciation rules vary

(D) To introduce the Latin writing system

25. What was unusual about the symbols of the Phoenician writing system?

(A) They represented complex concepts.

(B) They were all similar in appearance.

(C) They stood for specific sounds.

(D) They were based on Egyptian ones.

26. In the lecture, the professor explains the changes made by the Greeks to the Phoenician alphabet. Indicate whether each of the following is a change.

Click in the correct box for each sentence.

	Yes	No
They altered the forms of many letters.		
They eliminated most of the vowels.		
They combined a few of the consonants.		
They created some additional symbols.		

27. How did the Greek writing system spread to Italy?

(A) Greek merchants settled in the region.

(B) Roman colonies were set up in the Middle East.

(C) Greek rulers tried to conquer the peninsula.

(D) Roman scholars traveled to Greek cities.

28. Why was the Latin alphabet still used after the end of the Roman Empire?

Choose 2 answers.

(A) Religious leaders communicated with each other in Latin.

(B) Merchants recorded their financial transactions in Latin.

(C) Government officials could produce clearer documents with it.

(D) Scholars could easily express their own languages with it.

[29-34] Listen to part of a lecture from an astronomy course.

29. What is the lecture mainly about?

   (A) The process by which stars gain mass

   (B) The source of the Sun's energy

   (C) The characteristics of a kind of star

   (D) The differences between planets and stars

30. What does the professor say about the size of a brown dwarf?

   (A) It is greater than that of other type of stars.

   (B) It results in the star having a very low density.

   (C) It causes the matter in the star to expand.

   (D) It is comparable to that of a large planet.

Listen again to part of the lecture. Then answer the question.

31. Why does the student say this:

   (A) To show that brown dwarfs are similar to large planets

   (B) To indicate that he is uncertain about how to respond

   (C) To suggest that the answer to the question is obvious

   (D) To demonstrate that he is familiar with brown dwarfs

32. In the lecture, the professor explains the steps in the formation process of a brown dwarf. Put the steps listed below in the correct order.

Drag each answer choice to the space where it belongs.
One of the answer choices will not be used.

Step 1	
Step 2	
Step 3	

- The accumulation of matter stops.
- Dust and gas combine in outer space.
- A nuclear reaction produces a lot of energy.
- An object increases significantly in mass.

33. According to the professor, why are brown dwarfs difficult to detect with telescopes?

(A) They are located in distant galaxies.

(B) They radiate little energy.

(C) They are not very common.

(D) They produce infrared radiation.

34. What is the professor's attitude toward the recent estimate about the number of brown dwarfs?

(A) It should be viewed with doubt.

(B) It is likely to be confirmed soon.

(C) It has been disproven by new research.

(D) It is more accurate than an earlier one.

정답·스크립트·해석·정답단서 p. 259

VOCABULARY LIST

Chapter 4에서 선별한 다음의 토플 필수 어휘를 단어암기 음성을 들으며 암기한 후 퀴즈로 확인해 보세요.

*해커스 동영상강의의 포털 해커스인강(HackersIngang.com)에서 단어암기 음성파일을 무료로 다운로드할 수 있습니다.

catalogue[kǽtəlɔ̀ːg] 목록

status[stéitəs] 상태

spine[spain] (책의) 등

rough[rʌf] 거친

comment[kámen t] 언급하다

setup[sétʌp] 구성

orderly[ɔ́ːrdərli] 정돈된

insistent[insístənt] 주장하는

insight[ínsàit] 통찰력

extension[iksténʃən] 연장

in charge of ~을 담당하는

last-minute[lǽstmínit] 막바지의

adjustment[ədʒʌ́stmənt] 수정

straightforward[strèitfɔ́ːrwərd] 간단한

itinerary[aitínərèri] 일정

treasurer[tréʒərər] 회계 담당자

certify[sə́ːrtəfài] 증명하다

full-length[fùlléŋθ] 장편의

detective[ditéktiv] 탐정

undisclosed[ʌ̀ndisklóuzd] 밝혀지지 않은

prototype[próutətàip] 시초

inept[inépt] 서투른

incompetent[inkámpətənt] 무능한

perceptive[pərséptiv] 통찰력 있는

civilized[sívəlàizd] 교양 있는

eccentric[ikséntrik] 괴짜인

deduction[didʌ́kʃən] 추리

reason[ríːzn] 추리하다

ruin[rúːin] 유적

buried[bérid] 파묻힌

radio wave 전파

unit[júːnit] 장치

shift[ʃift] 이동하다

man-made[mǽnméid] 인공의

hazard[hǽzərd] 위험 요소

struggle with ~으로 고심하다

supplemental[sʌ̀pləméntl] 추가적인

lost[lɔːst] 이해할 수 없는

go over 검토하다

production[prədʌ́kʃən] 생산, 생산량

fertilizer[fə́ːrtəlàizər] 비료

constant[kánstənt] 변함없는

element[éləmənt] 원리

output[áutpùt] 생산량

practical[prǽktikəl] 현실적인

term[təːrm] 조건

boost[buːst] 증가

urbanization[ə̀ːrbənizéiʃən] 도시화

district[dístrikt] 구역

sector[séktər] 부문

commercial[kəmə́ːrʃəl] 상업의

residential[rèzədénʃəl] 주거의

Quiz

각 단어의 알맞은 뜻을 찾아 연결하시오.

01 inept	ⓐ 서투른	06 deduction	ⓐ 탐정
02 supplemental	ⓑ 통찰력 있는	07 straightforward	ⓑ 괴짜인
03 adjustment	ⓒ 구성	08 detective	ⓒ 추리
04 perceptive	ⓓ 추가적인	09 element	ⓓ 현실적인
05 prototype	ⓔ 시초	10 eccentric	ⓔ 원리
	ⓕ 수정		ⓕ 간단한

01 ⓐ 02 ⓓ 03 ⓕ 04 ⓑ 05 ⓔ 06 ⓒ 07 ⓕ 08 ⓐ 09 ⓔ 10 ⓑ

neighborhood [néibərhùd] 주민, 지역
uniform [jú:nəfɔ̀:rm] 일정한
nuclei [njú:kliài] 핵(nucleus의 복수형)
institution [ìnstətjú:ʃən] 기관
flexibility [flèksəbíləti] 유연성
vegetation [vèdʒətéiʃən] 식물
in place 제자리에
alter [ɔ́:ltər] 바꾸다
overflow [òuvərflóu] 범람하다
spill out 넘쳐 흐르다
rainfall [réinfɔ̀:l] 강우량
river channel 수로
dig out ~을 파내다
sediment [sédəmənt] 침전물
deposit [dipázit] 퇴적시키다
levee [lévi] 제방
barrier [bǽriər] 장벽
stream [stri:m] 개울
downstream [dàunstrí:m] 하류
political science 정치학
go out of print (서적이) 절판되다
storage facility 보관 시설
warehouse [wɛ́ərhàus] 창고
used copy 중고책
promising [prámisiŋ] 가능성이 있는
diffusion [difjú:ʒən] 확산

spread [spred] 전파
Latin alphabet 로마자
phonetic [fənétik] 음성의
stand for ~을 나타내다
versatile [və́:rsətl] 만능의
originate [ərídʒənèit] 유래하다
trace back to 기원이 ~까지 거슬러 올라가다
adopt [ədápt] 차용하다
colony [káləni] 식민지
peninsula [pənínsjulə] 반도
rise to power 권세를 얻다
conquer [káŋkər] 정복하다
collapse [kəlǽps] 무너지다
official [əfíʃəl] 당국자
star [stɑ:r] 항성
brown dwarf 갈색 왜성
Jupiter [dʒú:pətər] 목성
planet [plǽnit] 행성
compress [kəmprés] 압축하다
infrared radiation 적외선
protostar [próutoustɑ̀:r] 원시성
nuclear fusion 핵융합
spot [spɑt] 발견하다
astronomer [əstránəmər] 천문학자
estimate [éstəmət] 견해
skeptical [sképtikəl] 회의적인

Quiz

각 단어의 알맞은 뜻을 찾아 연결하시오.

01 uniform	ⓐ 확산
02 versatile	ⓑ 반도
03 levee	ⓒ 일정한
04 peninsula	ⓓ 항성
05 diffusion	ⓔ 만능의
	ⓕ 제방

06 adopt	ⓐ 천문학자
07 skeptical	ⓑ 차용하다
08 astronomer	ⓒ 바꾸다
09 warehouse	ⓓ 견해
10 estimate	ⓔ 회의적인
	ⓕ 창고

01 ⓒ 02 ⓔ 03 ⓕ 04 ⓑ 05 ⓐ 06 ⓑ 07 ⓔ 08 ⓐ 09 ⓕ 10 ⓓ

CHAPTER **05**

Connecting Contents II

Connecting Contents II

Connecting Contents II(Purpose, Organization) 문제는 대화나 강의의 전개 구조를 묻는 유형이다. Purpose는 화자가 언급한 특정 내용이 지문 속에서 흐름상 또는 구조상 어떤 역할을 하는지를 묻고, Organization은 화자가 정보를 전달하는 방식에 대해 묻는다.

문제 살펴보기

Purpose

- Why does the professor mention ~?
  교수는 왜 ~을 언급하는가?

- Why does the professor talk about ~?
  교수는 왜 ~에 관해 이야기하는가?

Organization

- How does the professor introduce/clarify/explain ~?
  교수는 ~을 어떻게 소개/명시/설명하는가?

- How does the professor organize ~?
  교수는 ~을 어떻게 구성하는가?

※ Organization 유형은 주로 강의에서 출제된다.

문제 공략하기

실전 고득점을 위한 문제 공략법을 꼼꼼하게 학습하고 Hackers Practice와 Hackers Test를 풀면서 적용해 본다.

Purpose

- **중심 내용과 관련이 적어 보이는 발언의 목적을 파악한다.**
  화자가 주제와 관련이 적어 보이는 발언을 할 때, 그것을 언급한 진짜 목적이 무엇인지를 파악해야 한다. 화자는 주로 예증, 강조, 배경지식 제공 등을 위해 이러한 발언을 한다.

Organization

- **화자가 정보를 전달하는 방식을 파악한다.**
  화자가 정보를 전달하는 방식에 유의하면서 각 정보의 상관관계를 파악해야 한다. 화자의 정보 전개 방식에는 비교 및 대조, 시간의 흐름에 따른 설명, 구체적인 예 제시, 서로 다른 범주로의 분류 등이 있다. 지문에서 화자의 정보 전개 방식을 알려주는 표현은 다음과 같다.

비교/대조	in comparison to ~ / similar to ~ / on the other hand / however
순차적인 설명	the first step is / next / and then
예시	for example / like / such as
분류	there are two types of ~ / have three groups of ~

Listen to part of a lecture in an astronomy class.

P: Today I'd like to talk about a planet named by the Romans . . . the planet, Mercury. Well, maybe you can tell me what you know about Mercury.

S: It's the closest to the Sun.

P: Yes. Anything else?

S: I think it's the same size as our moon . . . or is that Pluto?

P: You were right the first time—our moon. Uh, any other comments? Nothing more? OK, well, my point exactly. Many planets are discussed in great detail, but most teachers tend to skim over Mercury because they know only that it's much like our Moon in color, surface area, and lack of atmosphere. Now, one reason we don't have a whole lot of information about Mercury is that . . .

How does the professor introduce his discussion of Mercury?

(A) By describing the distance of Mercury from Earth
(B) By drawing attention to the lack of knowledge about Mercury
(C) By comparing Mercury and the Earth's Moon
(D) By stating information about other planets

지문 해석 p. 273

교수는 학생들에게 질문하는 방식을 통하여 수성에 관한 정보가 적다는 것에 주목하도록 한다. 이처럼 논의 대상에 대한 화자의 정보 전달 방식을 주의 깊게 들어야 한다.

해설

화자는 수성에 대한 질문을 통해 학생들이 후에 나오는 중심 내용, 즉 수성에 관한 정보가 적다는 사실에 주목하도록 하며 논의를 시작한다. 따라서, 정답은 (B)이다.

CH 1

CH 2

CH 3

CH 4

CHAPTER 5

CH 6

Hackers TOEFL Listening Intermediate

Hackers Practice

[1-3] Listen to a conversation between a professor and a student.

1. Why does the student visit the professor?

   (A) To discuss changing his major to theater
   (B) To get advice about acting opportunities
   (C) To request a bigger role in a class play
   (D) To inquire about a new club policy

2. What does the student say about the drama club?

   (A) It puts on several performances each semester.
   (B) It gets no financial support from the university.
   (C) It is only open to students with specific majors.
   (D) It does not attract large audiences to its shows.

3. Why does the professor mention a scene on a train?

   (A) To recommend a play that the student should watch
   (B) To indicate that the student can have a speaking role
   (C) To explain why a theater production needs extras
   (D) To demonstrate the importance of set design

---

perform[pərfɔ́ːrm] 공연하다 give it a try 한 번 해 보다 support[səpɔ́ːrt] 후원 put on 상연하다
membership[mémbərʃip] 회원 자격 a series of 일련의 act out 연출하다 a bunch of 많은 elaborate[ilǽbərət] 정교한
stage production 연극 작품 audience[ɔ́ːdiəns] 관중

[4-6] Listen to a conversation between a student and an employee at the Campus Security Office.

4. Why does the student visit the campus security office?

   (A) To get advice on locating a missing device
   (B) To report a theft from her dormitory
   (C) To check if an item has been dropped off
   (D) To turn in a laptop she found on campus

5. What does the student say about the Facilities Management Office?

   (A) It provides computers for students to use.
   (B) It is not well-known among the students.
   (C) It has the only lost and found on campus.
   (D) It is not open during the summer vacation.

6. Why does the employee discuss the university's online community?

   (A) To suggest a solution to the student's problem
   (B) To confirm that the student knows the website
   (C) To explain why the student's plan is unwise
   (D) To urge the student to buy a new computer

---

common room 휴게실 supervisor[súːpərvàizər] 관리인 turn in 반납하다 stop by ~에 들르다 suffer[sʌ́fər] 나빠지다
Facilities Management Office 시설 관리 사무소 administration[ædmìnəstréiʃən] 행정 lost and found 분실물 보관소
take advantage of ~을 이용하다 bother[báðər] 신경 쓰다 guarantee[gæ̀rəntíː] 보장

[7-9] Listen to part of a lecture on history.

7. What is the lecture mainly about?

(A) The various types of Restoration comedies

(B) The influence of religion over English plays

(C) The characteristics of 18th century comedy in England

(D) The distinguishing features of English playwrights

8. Why does the professor mention the Puritans?

(A) To show that England preferred coarse comedies

(B) To make a point about the common people's need for entertainment

(C) To explain why theater was prohibited

(D) To contrast theater during the reign of Charles I and Charles II

9. Why does the professor discuss Cibber's play *Love's Last Shift*?

(A) To describe a prototypical sentimental comedy from the 17th century

(B) To identify the inappropriate themes often found in Restoration comedies

(C) To emphasize the sustained popularity of the sentimental comedy genre

(D) To provide an example of a work with themes from two styles of comedies

---

flourish[flə́:riʃ] 번성하다 Puritan[pjúərətn] 청교도 Protestant[prátəstənt] 신교도 monarchy[mánərki] 군주
reinstate[rì:instéit] 복위하다 vulgar[vʌ́lgər] 저속한 sentimental[sèntəméntl] 감상적인 conservative[kənsə́:rvətiv] 보수적인
righteousness[ráitʃəsnis] 올바름 demographic[dì:məgrǽfik] 인구통계학적인 enthrone[inθróun] 왕위에 오르다
immorality[ìmərǽləti] 부도덕성 profanity[proufǽnəti] 모독 tribulation[trìbjuléiʃən] 동요 innate[inéit] 천성적인
stint[stint] 기간 exploit[éksplɔit] 행적 climactic[klaimǽktik] 절정의 elicit[ilísit] 이끌어내다

[10-12] Listen to part of a lecture in an astronomy class.

10. What is the main topic of the lecture?

(A) The development of Uranus' rings

(B) The characteristics shared by all gas giants

(C) The ways planetary movements are measured

(D) The discovery of a planet in the solar system

11. Why does the professor mention ships on the horizon?

(A) To explain how astronomers tracked Uranus' orbit

(B) To provide an example of a comet's movements

(C) To describe the orbital path taken by 34 Tauri

(D) To demonstrate an effect created by distance

12. According to the professor, why did Herschel name the new planet George's Star?

(A) He was asked to do so by Great Britain's ruling king.

(B) He wanted to acknowledge an astronomer's contribution.

(C) He was making a political statement against America.

(D) He felt it would be helpful for dating the discovery.

정답·스크립트·해석·정답단서 p. 273

---

outer planet 외행성 **gas giant** 가스상 거대 혹성 **Saturn**[sǽtərn] 토성 **Uranus**[júərənəs] 천왕성 **solar system** 태양계
mistake for ~으로 오인하다 **star catalog** 성표 **horizon**[həráizn] 지평선 **illusion**[ilú:ʒən] 착각 **comet**[kámit] 혜성
trail[treil] 자국 **orbit**[ɔ́:rbit] 궤도를 돌다 **honor**[ánər] 영예 **object**[əbdʒékt] 반대하다

Hackers Test

[1-5]   Listen to a conversation between a student and a student center employee.

1. Why does the student visit the student center?

    (A) To change her volunteering hours
    (B) To ask about volunteer positions
    (C) To check the schedule of a piano class
    (D) To get extra lessons related to her major

Listen again to part of the conversation. Then answer the question.

2. What does the student mean when she says this:

    (A) She believes the employee misspoke.
    (B) She prefers Tuesdays over Thursdays.
    (C) She has a scheduling problem.
    (D) She is unsure when she is free.

3. Why is the student unwilling to volunteer at Clearview Community Center next
    semester?

    (A) She wants to teach then.
    (B) She will have graduated.
    (C) She will be too busy.
    (D) She will have another volunteer job then.

4. What does the employee say about the hospital's music performances?

   Choose 2 answers.

   (A) They are for the sick patients.

   (B) Their purpose is to procure funding.

   (C) They require a lot of volunteers.

   (D) They are still in the planning stage.

5. Why does the student mention her study group?

   (A) To identify people who might want to volunteer

   (B) To prove she is studying music seriously

   (C) To explain why she cannot submit an application today

   (D) To indicate where she got the idea to earn extra credit

CH 1
CH 2
CH 3
CH 4
CHAPTER 5
CH 6

Hackers TOEFL Listening Intermediate

[6-11] Listen to part of a talk on the circadian rhythm.

6. What does the professor mainly discuss?

   (A) How the circadian rhythm developed in humans
   (B) The causes and effects of circadian rhythm disorders
   (C) Treatments for circadian rhythm disorders
   (D) The functions of the circadian rhythm

Listen again to part of the lecture. Then answer the question.

7. What does the professor mean when he says this:

   (A) He thinks he may be speaking too quickly.
   (B) He is talking about a topic not related to the lecture.
   (C) He realizes he was discussing something out of turn.
   (D) He does not want to consider something the students cannot understand.

8. According to the professor, what major role does the circadian rhythm play?

   (A) It adjusts the body to differences in time zones.
   (B) It alters the sleeping patterns of human beings.
   (C) It resets the biological clock when a person lacks sleep.
   (D) It coordinates the timing of specific functions of the body.

9. Why does the professor discuss a blind person?

   (A) To explain how a blind person copes when his SCN is impaired
   (B) To demonstrate new ways of treating circadian rhythm disorders in the blind
   (C) To explain why the circadian rhythm also functions by using external cues
   (D) To show how the SCN adjusts when a person has a visual impairment

10. According to the professor, what are two ways the circadian rhythm can be disrupted?
    Choose 2 answers.

    (A) Strenuous physical activity
    (B) Getting up at dawn
    (C) Changing time zones
    (D) Working after midnight

11. What point does the professor make when he refers to round-the-clock workers?

    (A) Doctors are only beginning to understand what the circadian rhythm is.
    (B) Working hours for employees in various industries need changing.
    (C) Ailments related to an out-of-sync rhythm are common.
    (D) There are far too many people working after midnight.

CH 1
CH 2
CH 3
CH 4
CHAPTER 5
CH 6

Hackers TOEFL Listening Intermediate

[12-17] Listen to part of a lecture in an architecture class.

12. What is the talk mainly about?

(A) New methods in airtight building construction

(B) The minimization of air leakage through airtight buildings

(C) Techniques used to improve building ventilation

(D) The effects of airtight buildings on physical health

13. What are two aspects of the sealed polyethylene approach?
Choose 2 answers.

(A) Buildings are made mostly of plaster and cement.

(B) Special materials are used to prevent air from leaking out.

(C) Buildings are enclosed in specially designed covering.

(D) Double walls are used to keep air inside the building.

14. According to the professor, why did doctors take years to discover the reason for the sharp increase in health ailments in the 1970s?

(A) Because the symptoms vanished after people left the buildings

(B) Because the health problems people experienced were not physical

(C) Because people had already quit their jobs and obtained other work

(D) Because the doctors could not determine where their patients worked

15. How does the professor clarify her point about contaminants found in any building?

    (A) By explaining the connection between air flow and illness

    (B) By stating that mold can grow in any damp environment

    (C) By outlining the steps taken by doctors to identify symptoms

    (D) By providing examples of common sources of toxic materials

16. What does the professor say about solids and liquids in a room?

    (A) They begin to discharge poisonous fumes at a certain temperature.

    (B) They are fairly safe if the room temperature remains constant.

    (C) They do not emit fumes as long as they are handled properly.

    (D) They can become volatile over an extended period of time.

17. What is the professor's opinion of the government's solution to save on energy costs?

    (A) It was well thought out.

    (B) It was not effective.

    (C) It was too expensive.

    (D) It was too complex.

CH 1
CH 2
CH 3
CH 4
CHAPTER 5
CH 6

[18-22] Listen to a conversation between a student and a professor.

18. Why does the student go to see the professor?

   (A) To report a problem with registration
   (B) To gain his permission to sit in on a class
   (C) To ask him to expand his course's enrollment
   (D) To discuss some difficult course concepts

19. What does the professor say about the course on Freud?

   (A) It is for a general audience.
   (B) It will also run the following term.
   (C) It can be audited by anyone.
   (D) It usually has free spaces.

20. Why does the student mention an undergraduate thesis?

   (A) To explain her interest in taking course on Freud
   (B) To show the professor that she has studied Freud
   (C) To emphasize that she needs academic advice
   (D) To show that she has the prerequisites for a class

21. What condition does the professor put on the student's attendance in his class?

    (A) She has to sign up for another class.

    (B) She must write about Freud's dream theories.

    (C) She has to make an outline for a paper.

    (D) She must participate in discussions on reading materials.

22. Why does the professor mention the psychology department's summer research program?

    (A) To suggest a program for the student to join

    (B) To provide an alternative to writing a thesis

    (C) To describe his expectations for the students

    (D) To demonstrate that he will have a busy schedule

CH 1
CH 2
CH 3
CH 4
CHAPTER 5
CH 6

Hackers TOEFL Listening Intermediate

[23-28] Listen to part of a lecture in an environmental science class.

23. What is the main topic of the lecture?

(A) A process to convert gasoline into diesel

(B) The environmental benefits of synthetic fuel

(C) A method used to produce an alternative fuel

(D) The causes of the decline in oil availability

24. Why does the professor mention the German government?

(A) To identify the first use of a chemical process

(B) To explain why a discovery was not publicized

(C) To show the efficiency of production method

(D) To emphasize the importance of a type of fuel

25. According to the professor, what is synthetic fuel commonly made from?

(A) Crop fertilizer

(B) Oil byproducts

(C) Industrial waste

(D) Plant matter

26. In the lecture, the professor explains the sequence of steps involved in the production of synthetic fuels. Put the steps listed below in the correct order.

Drag each answer choice to the space where it belongs.
One of the answer choices will not be used.

Step 1	
Step 2	
Step 3	
Step 4	

- A gas is filtered to get rid of contaminants.
- An element is added to a gas to cause a reaction.
- A gas is allowed to cool and become a liquid.
- A catalyst is placed in a liquid to remove pollutants.
- A material is heated and pressurized.

27. What are the advantages of synthetic fuel?
Choose 3 answers.

(A) It is produced from renewable substances.
(B) It is more efficient than diesel or gas.
(C) It causes little environmental damage.
(D) It can be used to power car engines.
(E) It can be made in a variety of locations.

Listen again to part of the lecture. Then answer the question.

28. Why does the professor say this: 🎧

(A) To demonstrate the public's dislike of synthetic fuel
(B) To show that synthetic fuel is difficult to purchase
(C) To introduce an obstacle to the use of synthetic fuel
(D) To state that synthetic fuel is dangerous to distribute

[29-34] Listen to part of a talk on literature.

29. What is the lecture mainly about?

 (A) How to establish the theme of a literary work

 (B) Two approaches to reading literature

 (C) Different ways in which children's books may be read

 (D) How to recognize the artistic value of literature

30. What does the professor say about extensive reading?

 (A) Its purpose is to comprehend the main idea of a literary work.

 (B) It is the least popular means of understanding literature.

 (C) It requires a grasp of the author's reason for writing a literary piece.

 (D) It is a critical skill that all readers should learn.

31. Why does the professor mention "curling up in an armchair to read a book"?

 (A) To explain why the American public was once a reading public

 (B) To illustrate the enjoyment associated with the aesthetic aspect

 (C) To demonstrate how readers should approach reading a book

 (D) To show that people need to be relaxed when they read

32. According to the professor, what are two characteristics of the aesthetic aspect of reading?

Choose 2 answers.

(A) The reader has a personal response to the literary work.

(B) The reader is concerned with accuracy of information in the work.

(C) The reader has enjoyment of the literature as a purpose for reading.

(D) The reader wants to have the same experience as the author of the work.

33. Why does the professor talk about Pat Hutchins' *Good-Night, Owl!*?

(A) To provide background for a discussion on children's books

(B) To give an example of a literary work that can only be appreciated aesthetically

(C) To emphasize the importance of reading to children out loud

(D) To explain how literature may be read using the two reading aspects

Listen again to part of the lecture. Then answer the question.

34. Why does the professor say this:

(A) To find out whether the students are familiar with the writing technique the author used

(B) To indicate that the students will not understand her point unless they read the book

(C) To encourage the students to read children's books more often

(D) To remind the students that the book was given as a reading assignment

정답·스크립트·해석·정답단서 p.279

VOCABULARY LIST

Chapter 5에서 선별한 다음의 토플 필수 어휘를 단어암기 음성을 들으며 암기한 후 퀴즈로 확인해 보세요.

*해커스 동영상강의 포털 해커스인강(HackersIngang.com)에서 단어암기 음성파일을 무료로 다운로드할 수 있습니다.

put on 상연하다

act out 연출하다

administration[ædmìnəstréiʃən] 행정

bother[báðər] 신경 쓰다

flourish[flə́:riʃ] 번성하다

monarchy[mánərki] 군주

reinstate[rì:instéit] 복위하다

vulgar[vʌ́lgər] 저속한

sentimental[sèntəméntl] 감상적인

conservative[kənsə́:rvətiv] 보수적인

demographic[dì:məgrǽfik] 인구통계학적인

enthrone[inθróun] 왕위에 오르다

profanity[prouǽnəti] 모독

tribulation[trìbjuléiʃən] 동요

innate[inéit] 천성적인

stint[stint] 기간

exploit[éksplɔit] 행적

climactic[klaimǽktik] 절정의

elicit[ilísit] 이끌어내다

Saturn[sǽtərn] 토성

Uranus[júərənəs] 천왕성

mistake for ~으로 오인하다

comet[kámit] 혜성

trail[treil] 자국

object[əbdʒékt] 반대하다

commit to ~에 할당하다

tricky[tríki] 곤란한

put off 미루다

manageable[mǽnidʒəbl] 감당할 만한

demanding[dimǽndiŋ] 부담이 큰

qualified[kwáləfàid] 자격을 갖춘

work around ~을 피해서 일하다

graveyard shift 야간 근무

circadian rhythm 생체리듬

depressed[diprést] 우울한

anxious[ǽŋkʃəs] 불안한

stabilize[stéibəlàiz] 안정시키다

digestive[didʒéstiv] 소화액

secretion[sikrí:ʃən] 분비

out of sync 조화가 깨진

pacemaker[péismèikər] 조절 기관

cue[kju:] 자극; 신호를 보내다

go against 어긋나다

abnormality[æbnɔ:rmǽləti] 이상

round-the-clock[ràundðəklák] 밤낮으로 일하는

conserve[kənsə́:rv] 보존하다

airtight[ɛ́ərtàit] 밀폐형의

ailment[éilmənt] 질환

sealed[si:ld] 밀봉된

building paper 방습지

laminate[lǽmənèit] 얇은 판을 씌우다

necessitate[nəsésətèit] 동반하다

Quiz

각 단어의 알맞은 뜻을 찾아 연결하시오.

01 profanity	ⓐ 모독	
02 secretion	ⓑ 질환	
03 necessitate	ⓒ 천성적인	
04 ailment	ⓓ 분비	
05 conservative	ⓔ 보수적인	
	ⓕ 동반하다	

06 elicit	ⓐ 군주	
07 bother	ⓑ 이상	
08 monarchy	ⓒ 신경 쓰다	
09 vulgar	ⓓ 곤란한	
10 tricky	ⓔ 이끌어내다	
	ⓕ 저속한	

ⓓ 01 ⓕ 60 ⓔ 80 ⓒ ㄴ0 ⓔ 90 ⓔ S0 ⓑ ㄴ0 ⓕ E0 ⓓ ㄷ0 ⓐ 10

gypsum [dʒípsəm] 석고

respiratory [réspərətɔ̀:ri] 호흡의, 호흡기와 관련된

dizziness [dízinis] 현기증

irritation [ìrətéiʃən] 염증

nausea [nɔ́:ziə] 구역질

ascertain [æ̀sərtéin] 확인하다

contaminant [kəntǽmənənt] 오염 물질

varnish [vá:rniʃ] 니스

damp [dæmp] 눅눅한

mold [mould] 곰팡이

fungi [fʌ́ndʒai] 균류(fungus의 복수형)

volatile [válətl] 휘발성의

chronic [kránik] 만성적인

asthma [ǽzmə] 천식

full-blown [fùlblóun] 악화된

fit [fit] 발작

sick leave 병가

absenteeism [æ̀bsəntí:izm] 결근

amount [əmáunt] ~에 달하다

audit [ɔ́:dit] (수업을) 청강하다

get overwhelmed 난처해지다

condition [kəndíʃən] 조건

commitment [kəmítmənt] 책무

armed forces 군대

conversion [kənvə́:rʒən] 전환

remains [riméinz] 유해

waste product 폐기물

break down into ~으로 분해하다

carbon monoxide 일산화탄소

impurity [impjúərəti] 불순물

catalyst [kǽtəlist] 촉매제

molecule [máləkjù:l] 분자

renewable [rinjú:əbl] 재생 가능한

compatible [kəmpǽtəbl] 호환되는

any time soon 곧장

extensive [iksténsiv] 광범위한

extract [ikstrǽkt] 발췌하다

aesthetic [esθétik] 심미적인

curl up 웅크리고 앉다

armchair [á:rmtʃɛ̀ər] 안락의자

evoke [ivóuk] 불러일으키다

association [əsòusiéiʃən] 연관

affirm [əfə́:rm] 확신하다

protagonist [proutǽgənist] 주인공

racket [rǽkit] 큰 소음

annoyed [ənɔ́id] 화가 난

screech [skri:tʃ] 비명을 지르다

onomatopoeia [ànəmǽtəpí:ə] 의성법

pick up 이해하다

crunch [krʌntʃ] 오도독 소리

chipmunk [tʃípmʌŋk] 줄다람쥐

acorn [éikɔ:rn] 도토리

Quiz

각 단어의 알맞은 뜻을 찾아 연결하시오.

01 catalyst		ⓐ 악화된
02 asthma		ⓑ 주인공
03 volatile		ⓒ 휘발성의
04 commitment		ⓓ 천식
05 protagonist		ⓔ 책무
		ⓕ 촉매제

06 evoke		ⓐ 호환되는
07 absenteeism		ⓑ 불순물
08 impurity		ⓒ 비명을 지르다
09 aesthetic		ⓓ 불러일으키다
10 compatible		ⓔ 결근
		ⓕ 심미적인

01 ⓕ 02 ⓓ 03 ⓒ 04 ⓔ 05 ⓑ 06 ⓓ 07 ⓔ 08 ⓑ 09 ⓕ 10 ⓐ

CHAPTER **06**

Inference

Inference

Inference 문제는 대화나 강의에서 제시된 정보에 근거하여 직접적으로 언급되지 않은 사실을 유추하는 유형이다. 이 유형은 지문의 일부 혹은 전체 맥락과 주어진 정보의 종합적인 이해를 통해 논리적으로 추론할 수 있는 사실을 묻는다.

문제 살펴보기

- **What can be inferred about ~?**
  ~에 관해 추론할 수 있는 것은 무엇인가?

- **What does the professor imply about ~?**
  교수는 ~에 관해 무엇을 암시하는가?

- **What will the woman do next?**
  그 여자는 다음에 무엇을 할 것인가?

※ 강의의 일부를 다시 듣고 푸는 Inference 문제도 있다.

문제 공략하기

실전 고득점을 위한 문제 공략법을 꼼꼼하게 학습하고 Hackers Practice와 Hackers Test를 풀면서 적용해 본다.

- **화자가 전달하고자 하는 바가 무엇인지 파악하며 듣는다.**
  화자가 언급한 정보를 통해 간접적으로 알 수 있는 사실을 추론하며 들어야 한다.

- **화자가 반복적으로 언급하는 내용의 결론을 생각하며 듣는다.**
  화자가 자신의 생각을 강조하기 위해 그와 관련된 내용을 여러 번 말하는 경우가 있는데, 이를 바탕으로 화자가 말하고자 하는 결론이 무엇인지를 추론하며 들어야 한다.

- **화자의 다음 할 일이 언급되는 부분에 주의하며 듣는다.**
  화자가 다음으로 할 일은 주로 지문이 마무리되는 부분에서 언급되므로, 끝까지 놓치지 않고 들어야 한다.

Listen to part of a lecture in an astronomy class.

Another thing the Mariner 10 learned is that Mercury has a ■
magnetic field about 100 times weaker than the Earth's. The
interesting thing is . . . for a planet to have a magnetic field, it
has to have a core that's partially molten—that is, liquid metal
or liquid rock. A solid core cannot produce a magnetic field.
Scientists believed that Mercury's core was once liquid iron,
but assumed that it had become cold and solid all these
billions of years. However, the Mariner 10 did detect a
magnetic field, albeit a weak one.

교수는 수성이 자기장을 가지고 있다
는 사실에 대해 설명한 뒤 자기장을
가진 행성의 특징을 언급하는데, 이
를 통해 간접적으로 알 수 있는 사실
을 추론하며 들어야 한다.

What can be inferred about Mercury?

(A) It looks exactly like Earth's Moon.
(B) Its magnetic field attracts debris.
(C) Its craters were formed by geological activity.
(D) It may have a core that is partly liquid.

지문 해석 p. 292

해설

수성에 약한 자기장이 존재한다는 것이 밝혀졌으며 용해된 핵을 가진 행성만이 자기장을 가질 수 있다는 화자의 설명을 통해,
수성의 핵이 부분적으로 액체라는 것을 추론할 수 있다. 따라서, 정답은 (D)이다.

CH 1

CH 2

CH 3

CH 4

CH 5

CHAPTER 6

Hackers TOEFL Listening Intermediate

Hackers Practice

[1-3] Listen to a conversation between a teaching assistant and a student.

1. Why does the man go to the professor's office?

    (A) To discuss a grade he received in a business course

    (B) To request a transfer to another university

    (C) To ask for advice regarding a marketing course

    (D) To see whether he can drop a course

Listen again to part of the conversation. Then answer the question.

2. What does the student imply when he says this:

    (A) It is good that the university accepts cross enrollment.

    (B) It is a pity that some courses do not meet curriculum requirements.

    (C) It would be unfortunate if he could not speak to Professor Platt.

    (D) It is not too difficult to complete the requirements.

3. What does the woman suggest the man do to get credit for the marketing course?

    (A) Have Northwestern send his school records

    (B) Get a passing mark in the course

    (C) Complete his assignment at Raiders, Inc.

    (D) Ask the professor to contact Northwestern University

---

tie-up[taiʌp] 협력 제도 Inc.[iŋk] 주식회사(=incorporated) breakthrough[bréikθrùː] 기발한 lucrative[lúːkrətiv] 돈을 많이 버는
hands-on[hǽndzán] 실무의 setting[sétiŋ] 환경 course description 수업 소개서 curriculum[kəríkjuləm] 이수과정
academic affair 교무처 registrar[rédʒistrɑ̀ːr] 학적 담당 사무원 transcript[trǽnskript] 성적 증명서 window[wíndou] 빈 시간

[4-6] Listen to a conversation between a professor and a student.

4. Why does the student go to see the professor?

Choose 2 answers.

(A) To request a chance to raise his exam score

(B) To get advice about an assignment topic

(C) To discuss how to improve his biology paper

(D) To clarify a concept discussed in class

Listen again to part of the conversation. Then answer the question.

5. What can be inferred about the professor when she says this: 🎧

(A) She doubts if the student understands a concept.

(B) She believes that the student should consider many options.

(C) She thinks that the student has a better idea for a topic.

(D) She feels that the proposal made by the student is not the best.

6. What does the professor imply about desert animals?

(A) They are more likely to be nocturnal than those of other ecosystems.

(B) They store water underground because it is too hot on the surface.

(C) They avoid nocturnal hunters by hiding in underground shelters.

(D) They have much greater access to water at night than during the day.

---

makeup test 재시험   sleep-wake cycles 수면 각성 주기   nocturnal[nɑktɔ́ːrnl] 야행성인   night vision 야간 시력
predator[prédətər] 포식 동물   rodent[roudnt] 설치류   hawk[hɔːk] 매   at dusk 해 질 무렵에   in the open 공공연하게
prey[prei] 피식자   overheat[òuvərhíːt] 과열되다   conservation[kànsərvéiʃən] 보존   retain[ritéin] 유지하다

[7-9] Listen to part of a lecture in an engineering class.

7. What is the main topic of the lecture?

(A) The design of the first airplane

(B) The basic principles of flight

(C) The main parts of an airplane

(D) The history of human flight

Listen again to part of the lecture. Then answer the question.

8. What does the professor imply when he says this:

(A) Airplanes produce less thrust than the student thinks.

(B) Planes need big engines to deal with wind resistance.

(C) Engine power is not as important as the student believes.

(D) Engineers have different opinions on the role of thrust.

9. Why does the professor mention birds?

(A) To illustrate the importance of lift when flying

(B) To suggest that airplane designs can be improved

(C) To show the link between air pressure and flight

(D) To identify the origins of the airplane wing

---

thrust[θrʌst] 추진력 lift[lift] 양력 propeller[prəpélər] 추진기 engine power 엔진 출력 friction[fríkʃən] 마찰
aerodynamic[ɛ̀əroudainǽmik] 공기 역학적인 sleek[sliːk] 매끈한 swiftly[swíftli] 재빠르게 low-powered[lóupàuərd] 저출력인
the other way around 반대로 cross section 단면도 prominent[prámənənt] 돌출된 airfoil[ɛ́ərfɔ̀il] (항공기·프로펠러 등의) 익형

[10-12] Listen to part of a lecture on computer art.

10. What is the main purpose of the talk?

(A) To discuss the effect art implements have on artistic creativity

(B) To compare computer art and painting

(C) To explain how artists produce a work of art

(D) To describe the processes involved in producing art

11. The professor describes the features of computer art and painting. Indicate for each type the feature that characterizes them.

Click in the correct box for each phrase.

	Computer Art	Painting
Encourages risk taking		
Uses numerous strokes with a handheld implement		
Provides instant results when settings are altered		
Is guided by reflections and emotions		

12. What does the professor imply about an image on a computer screen?

(A) It contains more strokes than a painting.

(B) It is possible to see only bits of the image.

(C) It has a more emotional quality than a canvas image.

(D) It can be changed without much difficulty.

정답·스크립트·해석·정답단서 p.292

league[liːg] 범주 implement[ímpləmənt] 도구 easel[íːzəl] 이젤 pigment[pígmənt] 물감 media[míːdiə] 도구(medium의 복수형)
versus[váːrsəs] ~에 대비하여 stroke[strouk] 획 simulate[símjulèit] 모방하다 step-by-step 단계적인
inspiration[ìnspəréiʃən] 영감 agony[ǽgəni] 고통

Hackers Test

[1-5] Listen to a conversation between a professor and a student.

1. What is the main topic of the conversation?

   (A) Developments in racial studies

   (B) The history of the southern region of Spain

   (C) The student's involvement in clubs

   (D) Opportunities afforded by the writing club

Listen again to part of the conversation. Then answer the question.

2. What does the professor imply when she says this:

   (A) The professor's comments regarding the student's paper are not important.

   (B) The student does not have to feel anxious about his paper.

   (C) The paper the student wrote contains as many errors as the student believes.

   (D) The topic of the student's paper was appropriate and well chosen.

3. How does the student feel about becoming a member of the writing club?

   (A) He thinks it is a waste of time.

   (B) He is concerned that he may not be qualified.

   (C) He feels he will not get along with the other writers.

   (D) He is annoyed by the requirements of the club.

4. According to the conversation, what are two activities the members of the writing club do?
   Choose 2 answers.

   (A) Attend talks on writing

   (B) Have writing contests

   (C) Invite other writers

   (D) Hold discussions on written works

Listen again to part of the conversation. Then answer the question.

5. What can be inferred about the student?

   (A) He is not planning to join the writing club now.

   (B) He is not sure if he will be allowed to become a writing club member.

   (C) He is concerned that the writing club will take him away from more important activities.

   (D) He expects to join the writing club when his writing skills improve.

CH 1
CH 2
CH 3
CH 4
CH 5
CHAPTER 6
Hackers TOEFL Listening Intermediate

[6-11] Listen to part of a lecture on environmental science. The professor is discussing introduced species.

6. What is the main topic of this lecture?

   (A) The benefits of native plants to an ecosystem

   (B) The decorative value of exotic species

   (C) The effects that introduced plants have on a region

   (D) The traits that make invasive species successful

7. Why does the professor mention the wind?

   (A) To demonstrate the ease with which exotic plants are transferred

   (B) To provide an example of how introduced species can be distributed

   (C) To differentiate between introduced species and exotic species

   (D) To illustrate the difficulties of eliminating of non-native plants

8. What can be inferred about introduced plants?

   (A) They are usually the preferred source of food for birds.

   (B) They are a problem only if released into the wild.

   (C) They are less of a nuisance in the northern regions.

   (D) They are most commonly found in the United States.

9. According to the professor, what is one negative effect of the dense shade produced by the Russian olive?

   (A) It increases the consumption of resources.

   (B) It lowers the temperature of the surrounding area.

   (C) It limits the amount of available groundwater.

   (D) It prevents the growth of other young trees.

10. According to the professor, what is a reason the Russian olive grows well in the southwestern United States?

    (A) The tree is dependent on birds to reproduce.

    (B) The tree requires a significant amount of sunlight.

    (C) The tree is only considered decorative in certain areas.

    (D) The tree needs a special type of soil to survive.

Listen again to part of the lecture. Then answer the question.

11. What can be inferred about the professor? 🎧

    (A) He is unsure whether the groups' ideas will be effective.

    (B) He doubts the motives of certain types of environmental groups.

    (C) He is optimistic about the future of a category of plant.

    (D) He feels that a problem is likely to be resolved very soon.

CH 1

CH 2

CH 3

CH 4

CH 5

CHAPTER 6

Hackers TOEFL Listening Intermediate

[12-17] Listen to part of a lecture in a music class.

12. What is the main topic of the lecture?

(A) The impact of technology on music

(B) Different styles of electronica

(C) Electronic music trends in the 1990s

(D) An overview of a type of electronic music

13. Why does the professor mention ambient music?

(A) To illustrate the great popularity of electronica

(B) To show that electronica is more than dance music

(C) To provide an example of music with catchy rhythms

(D) To demonstrate that electronic music has merit

14. Why did some critics claim that electronica was not real music?
Choose 3 answers.

(A) It uses samples of existing works.

(B) It could not be performed live.

(C) It features unidentifiable instruments.

(D) It lacks the basic song elements.

(E) It is not made by conventional musicians.

15. What does the professor imply about early fans of electronica?

(A) They often attended concerts at major venues.

(B) They appreciated the uniqueness of this music.

(C) They preferred songs with emotional lyrics.

(D) They first heard this music on the radio.

16. Why was the synthesizer important to the development of electronic music?

(A) It generates a variety of sounds.

(B) It is played in the same way as a piano.

(C) It is used to edit digital audio files.

(D) It records sounds in a variety of formats.

Listen again to part of the lecture. Then answer the question.

17. What does the professor mean when he says this:

(A) He thinks that advertisers tend to overuse electronica.

(B) He is uncertain about the benefits of music in advertising.

(C) He believes that electronic music is ideal for marketing.

(D) He is confused about why advertisers like electronica.

CH 1

CH 2

CH 3

CH 4

CH 5

CHAPTER 6

Hackers TOEFL Listening Intermediate

[18-22] Listen to a conversation between a professor and a student.

18. Why does the professor want to see the student?

(A) To talk about differences between lecture and seminar classes

(B) To inform the student of her record of attendance for a literature seminar

(C) To encourage the student to participate more in class discussions

(D) To compliment the student on her exceptional responses during class

19. What does the professor imply about the student's performance in his literature class?

(A) It is so poor that she may get a failing mark.

(B) It has not been as good as in another class she is enrolled in.

(C) It has been below average compared to the other students.

(D) It has been satisfactory up to a certain point.

20. What does the student imply about literature?

(A) Most students who take mathematics are reluctant to study literature.

(B) Literature is a subject that does not require a lot of background information.

(C) Questions concerning literature do not always have clear answers.

(D) She is not as interested in literature as she is in mathematics.

21. According to the professor, what is the objective of the seminar?

    (A) Allow students the chance to question their professors

    (B) Give students more training in seminar preparation

    (C) Let students share ideas and learn from each other

    (D) Provide students the opportunity to obtain debate skills

22. Why does the professor discuss Realism and Naturalism?

    (A) To alert the student to pay more attention to the class topics

    (B) To show the student that she is capable of expressing her opinion

    (C) To evaluate the student's understanding of literature

    (D) To help the student prepare a presentation for the next seminar

CH 1

CH 2

CH 3

CH 4

CH 5

CHAPTER 6

Hackers TOEFL Listening Intermediate

[23-28] Listen to part of a lecture on biology.

23. What does the professor mainly discuss?

(A) The effect of toxins on quorum-sensing bacteria

(B) A method by which bacteria share information

(C) The role of bacteria in causing serious illnesses

(D) A type of ocean-dwelling bacteria that lights up

24. What does the professor say about Ken Nealson?

(A) He discovered quorum sensing while researching bacteria.

(B) He was not pleased with the research on quorum sensing.

(C) He wanted to find a treatment for bacterial infections.

(D) He researched *Vibrio fischeri* with a fellow student.

Listen again to part of the lecture. Then answer the question.

25. Why does the professor say this: 🎧

(A) To remind the students of an idea he had previously covered

(B) To distinguish between two different meanings of the same word

(C) To describe a part of the university's decision-making process

(D) To explain the origin of a strange-sounding concept

Listen again to part of the lecture. Then answer the question.

26. What does the professor imply when he says this:

    (A) The process is very energy efficient.

    (B) The *Vibrio fischeri* expend too much energy.

    (C) There is a more energy efficient way to detect the presence of bacteria.

    (D) The bacteria save energy only when enough of them are present.

Listen again to part of the lecture. Then answer the question.

27. What does the professor mean when he says this:

    (A) He thinks the students are not following the discussion.

    (B) He wants the students to provide their own examples.

    (C) He thinks the example was very clear to the students.

    (D) He wants to test the students' understanding of the material.

28. Why does the professor mention computer hacking?

    (A) To provide an analogy for how quorum sensing can be disrupted

    (B) To clarify how bacterial behavior mimics that of computer viruses

    (C) To compare the negative effects of bacteria with those of hackers

    (D) To describe how scientists genetically engineered new bacteria

CH 1
CH 2
CH 3
CH 4
CH 5
CHAPTER 6

Hackers TOEFL Listening Intermediate

[29-34] Listen to part of a lecture on geography. The professor is discussing lakes of the Rub' al-Khali.

29. What is the professor mainly discussing?

(A) The reasons geologists study dried-up lakes

(B) Differences between ancient lakes and present-day lakes

(C) Ancient sand dunes in the empty quarter

(D) The evidence that points to the presence of lakes in a desert

Listen again to part of the lecture. Then answer the question.

30. What can be inferred about the monsoon rains?

(A) They are known to change course frequently.

(B) It is common for them to affect deserts.

(C) It is not a confirmed fact that their path changed.

(D) The intervals between monsoon rains were longer in the past.

31. According to the professor, why was clay or silt necessary to form the lakes?

(A) They prevent water from seeping into the ground.

(B) They are very effective at absorbing water.

(C) They provide ideal conditions for snails and clams to breed.

(D) They make dunes that help collect the rain.

32. According to the professor, what are two characteristics of the older lakes?

Choose 2 answers.

(A) They persisted longer than the newer lakes.

(B) They were incapable of supporting large animals.

(C) They formed in an elongated shape.

(D) They were shallower than the newer lakes.

33. What is the professor's opinion on animal migration to the lakes?

(A) It has not been confirmed by archaeological evidence.

(B) It was necessary for the animals' continued survival.

(C) It provided the conditions for life to thrive there today.

(D) It ended up being a tremendous error.

34. According to the professor, what is the evidence that the lakes were very salty?

Choose 2 answers.

(A) The presence of mineral deposits

(B) The uniformity of the salt crust on the soil

(C) The drying up of the only freshwater source

(D) The lack of fossilized fish

정답·스크립트·해석·정답단서 p.298

VOCABULARY LIST

Chapter 6에서 선별한 다음의 토플 필수 어휘를 단어암기 음성을 들으며 암기한 후 퀴즈로 확인해 보세요.

*해커스 동영상강의 포털 해커스인강(HackersIngang.com)에서 단어암기 음성파일을 무료로 다운로드할 수 있습니다.

tie-up[taiʌp] 협력 제도

Inc.[iŋk] 주식회사(=incorporated)

breakthrough[bréikθrùː] 기발한

lucrative[lúːkrətiv] 돈을 많이 버는

hands-on[hændzán] 실무의

course description 수업 소개서

curriculum[kəríkjuləm] 이수과정

academic affair 교무처

registrar[rédʒistràːr] 학적 담당 사무원

transcript[trǽnskript] 사본

window[wíndou] 빈 시간

makeup test 재시험

rodent[roudnt] 설치류

at dusk 해 질 무렵에

in the open 공공연하게

retain[ritéin] 유지하다

thrust[θrʌst] 추진력

lift[lift] 양력

friction[fríkʃən] 마찰

aerodynamic[ɛ̀əroudainǽmik] 공기 역학적인

sleek[sliːk] 매끈한

swiftly[swíftli] 재빠르게

the other way around 반대로

cross section 단면도

prominent[prámənənt] 돌출된

league[liːg] 범주

implement[ímpləmənt] 도구

pigment[pígmənt] 물감

media[míːdiə] 도구(medium의 복수형)

versus[vɔ́ːrsəs] ~에 대비하여

stroke[strouk] 획

simulate[símjulèit] 모방하다

inspiration[ìnspəréiʃən] 영감

agony[ǽgəni] 고통

racial[réiʃəl] 인종의

exceptional[iksépʃənl] 뛰어난

prejudice[prédʒudis] 편견

forum[fɔ́ːrəm] 공개 토론회

student council 학생회

take up 차지하다

naturalize[nǽtʃərəlàiz] 귀화시키다

pest[pest] 해충

invasive[invéisiv] 침입하는

prosper[práspər] 잘 자라다

ornamental[ɔ̀ːrnəméntl] 장식용 식물

perennial[pəréniəl] 다년생의

shrub[ʃrʌb] 관목

foliage[fóuliidʒ] 잎

dense[dens] 울창한, 빽빽한

hedge[hedʒ] 울타리

habitation[hæ̀bitéiʃən] 주거지

deposit[dipázit] 놓다

Quiz

각 단어의 알맞은 뜻을 찾아 연결하시오.

01 simulate   ⓐ 모방하다

02 breakthrough   ⓑ 사본

03 implement   ⓒ 도구

04 transcript   ⓓ 기발한

05 naturalize   ⓔ 귀화시키다

   ⓕ 매끈한

06 rodent   ⓐ 설치류

07 exceptional   ⓑ 돈을 많이 버는

08 prominent   ⓒ 돌출된

09 thrust   ⓓ 장식용 식물

10 lucrative   ⓔ 뛰어난

   ⓕ 추진력

01 ⓐ   02 ⓓ   03 ⓒ   04 ⓑ   05 ⓔ   06 ⓐ   07 ⓔ   08 ⓒ   09 ⓕ   10 ⓑ

outcompete[àutkəmpíːt] 능가하다

sapling[sǽpliŋ] 묘목

mature[mətʃúər] 성장하다

respective[rispéktiv] 각각의

subgenre[sʌ́bʒàːnrə] 하위 장르

ambient music 환경 음악

catchy[kǽtʃi] 기억하기 쉬운

underground[ʌ́ndərgràund] 비전통적인

conventional[kənvénʃənl] 전통적인

convincingly[kənvínsiŋli] 그럴듯하게

manipulate[mənípjulèit] 조작하다

mainstream[méinstrìːm] 주류

incorporate[inkɔ́ːrpərèit] 포함하다

commercial[kəmɔ́ːrʃəl] 광고

controversial[kàntrəvɔ́ːrʃəl] 논란의 여지가 있는

contribute[kəntríbjuːt] 의견을 말하다

subjective[səbdʒéktiv] 주관적인

valid[vǽlid] 타당한

appreciate[əpríːʃièit] 감상하다

objectively[əbdʒéktivli] 객관적으로

idealize[aidíːəlàiz] 이상화하다

sympathetic[sìmpəθétik] 동정적인

freeze up 얼어붙다

microbiologist[màikroubaiálədʒist] 미생물학자

luminescence[lùːmənésns] 발광

quorum[kwɔ́ːrəm] 정족수

autoinducer[ɔ̀ːtouindjúːsər] 자가 유도 물질

trigger[trígər] 일으키다

toxin[táksin] 독소

immune system 면역 체계

infection[infékʃən] 감염

credibility[krèdəbíləti] 신빙성

microscopic[màikrəskápik] 미세한

medical condition 질병

devote[divóut] 투입하다

apt[æpt] 적절한

barren[bǽrən] 불모지인

geological[dʒìːəládʒikəl] 지질학적인

teem with ~으로 넘치다

monsoon rain 우기

silt[silt] 토사

distinct[distíŋkt] 별개의

sand dune 사구

choppy[tʃápi] 거친

abrupt[əbrʌ́pt] 가파른

crested[kréstid] 볏이 있는

fossil[fásəl] 화석

livable[lívəbl] 살기에 좋은

hippopotamus[hìpəpátəməs] 하마

indication[ìndikéiʃən] 증거

in abundance 풍부하게

uninhabitable[ʌ̀ninhǽbitəbl] 살 수 없는

Quiz

각 단어의 알맞은 뜻을 찾아 연결하시오.

01 convincingly	ⓐ 객관적으로	06 microscopic	ⓐ 의견을 말하다
02 distinct	ⓑ 포함하다	07 apt	ⓑ 미세한
03 trigger	ⓒ 별개의	08 crested	ⓒ 비전통적인
04 abrupt	ⓓ 그럴듯하게	09 underground	ⓓ 조작하다
05 objectively	ⓔ 가파른	10 contribute	ⓔ 적절한
	ⓕ 일으키다		ⓕ 볏이 있는

ⓐ 01 ⓒ 02 ⓕ 03 ⓔ 04 ⓐ 05 ⓑ 06 ⓔ 07 ⓕ 08 ⓒ 09 ⓐ 10

Hackers TOEFL

Listening

Intermediate

Actual Test

Actual Test 1

* 실전모의고사 프로그램을 통해, 실제 시험과 동일한 환경에서도 Actual Test를 풀어볼 수 있습니다.

[1-5] Listen to a conversation between a student and a professor.

1. What are the speakers mainly discussing?

   (A) Preparing for a semester abroad
   (B) Options for places to study overseas
   (C) The advantages of cultural immersion
   (D) The student's plan to attend a conference

2. Why does the professor mention museums and performance venues?

   (A) To explain why certain countries are expensive
   (B) To suggest places to learn about other cultures
   (C) To express that the student should go to Spain
   (D) To encourage the student to live in a city

Listen again to part of the conversation. Then answer the question.

3. What does the student imply when he says this:

   (A) He thinks studying abroad is unnecessary.
   (B) He wants to experience a new culture.
   (C) He prefers to interact with people from home.
   (D) He hopes to meet fellow students while traveling.

4. Why does the student want to visit Peru?

   (A) It has an attraction he wants to see.
   (B) He prefers a place few people visit.
   (C) A friend of his went there before.
   (D) It has a university he wants to attend.

5. What does the professor offer to do for the student?
   Choose 2 answers.

   (A) Put him in contact with another student
   (B) Give him the email address of a colleague
   (C) Write him a reference letter for an application
   (D) Provide him with information about a university

[6-11] Listen to part of a talk on art history.

6. What does the professor mainly discuss?

   (A) How technological and social changes affected Victorian art

   (B) The influence of Queen Victoria on British artists

   (C) Why Victorian art was popular with upper-class collectors

   (D) The important role of steel-plate printing during the Victorian era

7. What was a benefit of the steel-plate printing process?

   (A) It ensured greater profits for many struggling artists.

   (B) It encouraged artists to publish their own art journals.

   (C) It enabled artists to create original artwork very quickly.

   (D) It allowed the average person to purchase art.

8. Why does the professor mention the 1851 World Expo?

   (A) To provide an example of the increase in the popularity of art at that time

   (B) To indicate why so many artists were based in London

   (C) To suggest that it was the birthplace of Victorian art

   (D) To illustrate how many art collectors there were in London

9. Why does the professor discuss businesspeople?

    (A) To explain why financial growth occurred

    (B) To introduce a new type of art collector

    (C) To suggest that aristocrats rarely purchased art

    (D) To demonstrate the economic value of art

10. What does the professor say about John Sheepshanks?
    Choose 2 answers.

    (A) He collected works from artists of the past.

    (B) He made a donation to a British institution.

    (C) He founded an art museum in London.

    (D) He was an important British businessperson.

11. According to the professor, what was the influence the new class of wealthy individuals had on the art world?

    (A) It led to a significant drop in artistic standards.

    (B) It made art accessible to more of the public.

    (C) It resulted in the rise of specialized art critics.

    (D) It limited the subject matter of artistic works.

[12-17] Listen to part of a lecture in an astronomy class. The professor is discussing star catalogs.

12. What is the main purpose of the lecture?

(A) To provide a brief history of astronomy

(B) To discuss the discovery of a unique space object

(C) To outline the process used to measure stars

(D) To describe the lists used to identify stars

13. How do astronomers determine a star's coordinates?

(A) By taking several measurements hours apart

(B) By comparing the star to other stars in a region

(C) By finding where a pair of angles meet

(D) By observing the star's size in relation to Earth

Listen again to part of the lecture. Then answer the question.

14. What does the student mean when she says this:

(A) She read an interesting theory about star catalogs.

(B) She was particularly impressed with the museum's catalog.

(C) She is curious about why star catalogs were invented.

(D) She cannot recall the exact time she saw a star catalog.

15. Why does the professor mention the Babylonians?

(A) To show that many different cultures observed the stars

(B) To provide an example of a religious use of star catalogs

(C) To identify the origins of the Greek star catalogs

(D) To point out the challenges faced by early astronomers

16. What may have prompted Hipparchus to produce a star catalog?

(A) He was inspired by a story about astronomy.

(B) He discovered a mistake in an earlier catalog.

(C) He wanted to test a technique he developed.

(D) He needed to confirm findings from an experiment.

17. According to the professor, what are some practical uses of star catalogs?
Choose 3 answers.

(A) They guide scientists in their search for habitable planets.

(B) They could be used to determine the time of year.

(C) They can help researchers learn the age of the universe.

(D) They can indicate when a star was first discovered.

(E) They provide a way of determining one's position.

[18-22] Listen to a conversation between a student and a university employee.

18. What is the woman's problem?

(A) Her schedule makes it hard for her to eat meals at the cafeteria.

(B) Her restaurant job takes up much of her time.

(C) She does not like the food at the cafeteria.

(D) She has an unused food account at the university cafeteria.

19. According to the conversation, what are two reasons the student does not eat at the cafeteria often?

Choose 2 answers.

(A) She frequently forgets her meal plan card.

(B) She is fed at her workplace.

(C) Her schedule does not allow it.

(D) Her home is too far away.

Listen again to part of the conversation. Then answer the question.

20. Why does the woman say this: 🎧

(A) To show how tired she is

(B) To express how busy she is

(C) To explain that she has a health problem

(D) To complain about her job

21. What does the service center worker suggest the student do?

(A) Cancel her student food account

(B) Get a refund from Student Services

(C) Always pay for her meals in cash

(D) Adjust her current meal plan

22. What does the service center worker imply about the school's meal plan?

(A) It is cheaper than cooking at home.

(B) Most students choose to enroll in it.

(C) Most students opt for the part-time plan.

(D) It is very popular with students living off-campus.

[23-28] Listen to part of a lecture in a chemistry class.

23. What is the lecture mainly about?

(A) Advantages and disadvantages of thermal reduction

(B) Resource requirements for purifying magnesium

(C) Methods of obtaining metals from mineral ore

(D) Current production processes for magnesium metal

24. In the lecture, the professor describes the process for producing magnesium from seawater. Put the steps listed below in the correct order.

Drag each answer choice to the space where it belongs.

Step 1	
Step 2	
Step 3	
Step 4	

- Use electricity to separate the elements
- Refine the metal and process it for use
- Combine seawater with chemicals
- Purify the solution and allow it to dry

25. According to the professor, why does the thermal reduction process allow almost any country to produce magnesium?

(A) It is only dependent on the availability of coal.

(B) It uses mineral ore abundant in the earth's crust.

(C) It requires little technical knowledge to implement.

(D) It uses less expensive equipment.

Listen again to part of the lecture. Then answer the question.

26. What does the professor mean when she says this: 🎧

(A) She wants the students to refer to the textbook during the lecture.

(B) She thinks an understanding of chemistry is important for this talk.

(C) She wants to present the general sequence in magnesium production.

(D) She does not think the students can understand the technical details.

27. What can be inferred about a coastal country that does not produce magnesium?

(A) The electricity it generates is insufficient for magnesium production.

(B) Its access to mineral-rich seawater is restricted.

(C) It does not have an abundance of mineral ore.

(D) Much of its electricity is directed to residential buildings.

Listen again to part of the lecture. Then answer the question.

28. Why does the professor say this: 🎧

(A) To ask the students for relevant examples

(B) To emphasize the amount of energy used

(C) To check the students' understanding of the process

(D) To illustrate the difficulty of producing electricity

정답·스크립트·해석·정답단서 p.312

ACTUAL
TEST 1

AT 2

Hackers TOEFL Listening Intermediate

Actual Test 2

* 실전모의고사 프로그램을 통해, 실제 시험과 동일한 환경에서도 Actual Test를 풀어볼 수 있습니다.

[1-5] Listen to a conversation between a student and a university employee.

1. Why does the woman visit the financial aid office?

   (A) To solve a problem she has with an aid package

   (B) To apply for a government-subsidized student loan

   (C) To register for federal financial aid

   (D) To inquire into the possibility of work study

Listen again to part of the conversation. Then answer the question.

2. Why does the woman say this: 🎧

   (A) She expected to receive a lower amount.

   (B) She believes an error has been made.

   (C) She wants to confirm what the man said.

   (D) She thought she did not qualify for a grant.

3. What does the man imply about the amount the woman received?

   (A) It was specifically designed for her needs.

   (B) It was provided by an independent agency.

   (C) The woman should be satisfied with it.

   (D) She may supplement it by taking out a loan.

4. What does the man suggest the woman do?

   (A) Appeal to the dean's office
   (B) Take advantage of a work program
   (C) Call her old university to explain the matter
   (D) Borrow money from a finance association

Listen again to part of the conversation. Then answer the question.

5. What does the woman mean when she says this: 🎧

   (A) She believes she received someone else's financial aid report.
   (B) She wants to get perfect marks in college.
   (C) She wants to have her high school grades checked.
   (D) She wants a scholarship that reflects her academic achievements.

[6-11]   Listen to part of a lecture in a physics class.

6. What is the main purpose of the lecture?

    (A) To discuss setting up semiconductor switches in a network

    (B) To explain how semiconductors can solve electrical distribution problems

    (C) To explain why power transmission problems are common

    (D) To illustrate how loop flow can cause electrical disturbances and outages

7. According to the lecture, why does electricity not always take the shortest route as it flows?

    (A) The cables and wires in a grid may not be laid out properly in some sections.

    (B) The flow of electricity may not be strong enough to follow a particular route.

    (C) Insufficient power lines in an area may force electricity to take a different path.

    (D) Impedance in the electrical circuit blocks the flow of the current.

Listen again to part of the lecture. Then answer the question.

8. Why does the professor say this: 🎧

    (A) To encourage the students to analyze how electricity flows

    (B) To indicate that he will explain his illustration

    (C) To check the students' understanding of the path of least resistance

    (D) To express uncertainty about the problem in his illustration

9. The following are steps in the process of loop flow. Put the steps listed below in the correct order.

Drag each answer choice to the space where it belongs.

Step 1	
Step 2	
Step 3	
Step 4	

- Electricity consumption increases.
- Power flows through an indirect route.
- Overloading causes a power outage.
- Backup power flows from an alternative generator.

10. According to the professor, what is the main function of semiconductor switches in the power supply industry?

(A) They reduce the overhead for electricity production.

(B) They facilitate long-term storage of electricity.

(C) They regulate power flow to prevent overloading.

(D) They amplify electrical currents as needed.

11. What does the professor imply about the status of the nation's power networks?

(A) They must provide more power to highly populated areas.

(B) They have to be redesigned to prevent loop flow.

(C) They are expensive to repair when blackouts occur.

(D) They are capable of rerouting electric current in emergencies.

[12-16] Listen to a conversation between a student and a professor.

12. Why does the student go to see the professor?

Choose 2 answers.

(A) To ask about the Comstock Lode

(B) To get help with her paper's focus

(C) To find out her grade on an exam

(D) To request a due date extension

13. Why does the professor mention the bluish clay found in the mines?

(A) To describe what typical silver mines look like

(B) To explain a common obstacle to mining silver

(C) To show that mined silver needs to be purified

(D) To indicate how a silver deposit was discovered

14. Why were new mining technologies developed for the Comstock Lode?

(A) The silver ore contained a toxic material.

(B) The miners did not have access to machinery.

(C) The wooden support blocks were weak.

(D) The tunnels in the mines were unstable.

15. What does the professor say about the mines of the Comstock Lode?
Choose 2 answers.

(A) They cost millions of dollars to operate.

(B) They became less productive after 1880.

(C) They took over 20 years to construct.

(D) They produced a large amount of silver.

Listen again to part of the conversation. Then answer the question.

16. What does the student imply when she says this:

(A) She is bad at choosing essay topics.

(B) She prefers to have a clear deadline.

(C) She is not happy with her recent grades.

(D) She rushed to finish a previous paper on time.

[17-22] Listen to part of a lecture in an anthropology class.

17. What is the main topic of the lecture?

    (A) The reasons for the Mayans' prosperity

    (B) How the Mayans settled Central America

    (C) How the Mayans dominated other cultures

    (D) The decline of the Mayan civilization

18. What can be inferred about the Mayan food supply?

    (A) It was dependent on imports from other regions.

    (B) It was usually sufficient for the population.

    (C) It was unreliable at certain times of the year.

    (D) It was often a concern for average Mayans.

19. What does the professor say about the minerals discovered by the Mayans?

    (A) They were extremely rare and valuable.

    (B) They were traded for fish and corn.

    (C) They had functional and decorative uses.

    (D) They formed the sole basis of the Mayan economy.

20. Why does the professor mention Zapotec civilization?

(A) To show the extent of Mayan influence

(B) To provide an example of cultural exchange

(C) To illustrate the superiority of Mayan society

(D) To identify an important trade route

21. According to the professor, what were the benefits of Mayan wealth?
Choose 3 answers.

(A) The invention of new technologies

(B) The discovery of new crops for farming

(C) The development of a middle class

(D) The ability to support a large population

(E) The resources to conquer neighboring territories

Listen again to part of the lecture. Then answer the question.

22. What does the professor mean when she says this: 🎧

(A) She feels the students have not been paying attention.

(B) She believes the students require additional explanation.

(C) She thinks the students are aware of a similar example.

(D) She wants the students to get excited about economics.

[23-28] Listen to part of a lecture in a biology class.

23. What is the main topic of the lecture?

   (A) The functions of an animal sound
   (B) Purring as a defense mechanism in cats
   (C) Various animal vocalization methods
   (D) Ways cats communicate with each other

24. According to the professor, how do cats produce purring sounds?

   (A) They squeeze and relax their jaw muscles.
   (B) They produce whines from their nose and throat.
   (C) They constrict their vocal passages as they breathe.
   (D) They hold their breath and then release it slowly.

25. Why does the professor mention bread dough?

   (A) To explain how cats show discomfort
   (B) To describe a particular cat behavior
   (C) To stress that cats react strongly to food
   (D) To state why cats need physical contact

26. How do cats motivate people to feed them?

    (A) They purr more and more loudly.

    (B) They try a few different vocalizations.

    (C) They purr and rub their paws together.

    (D) They make a crying sound.

27. How can purring reduce pain?

    Choose 2 answers.

    (A) It distracts the cat from its physical condition.

    (B) It informs the cat owner that the cat needs care.

    (C) It releases natural pain-relief chemicals.

    (D) It produces vibrations that have healing effects.

Listen again to part of the lecture. Then answer the question.

28. What does the professor mean when she says this: 🎧

    (A) She has not considered the problem before.

    (B) Cat vocalizations follow complicated patterns.

    (C) The student has asked an unclear question.

    (D) Different types of purrs sound similar.

정답·스크립트·해석·정답단서 p.324

이로써 교재 학습이 모두 끝났습니다.
Actual Test 1, 2는 실전모의고사 프로그램으로도 제공되니, 실전 환경에서 최종 마무리 연습을 해보시기 바랍니다.

＊ 해커스인강(HackersIngang.com)에서 이용할 수 있습니다.

중급 학습자를 위한 토플 리스닝 학습서

H|A|C|K|E|R|S TOEFL
LISTENING Intermediate

개정 3판 10쇄 발행 2025년 1월 6일
개정 3판 1쇄 발행 2019년 8월 1일

지은이	David Cho │ 언어학 박사, 前 UCLA 교수
펴낸곳	(주)해커스 어학연구소
펴낸이	해커스 어학연구소 출판팀

주소	서울특별시 서초구 강남대로61길 23 (주)해커스 어학연구소
고객센터	02-537-5000
교재 관련 문의	publishing@hackers.com
동영상강의	HackersIngang.com

ISBN	978-89-6542-302-7 (13740)
Serial Number	03-10-01

전세계 유학정보의 중심
고우해커스

goHackers.com

HACKERS

TOEFL
LISTENING
Intermediate

David Cho

정답 · 스크립트 · 해석 · 정답단서

해커스 어학연구소

HACKERS

TOEFL
LISTENING
Intermediate

정답 · 스크립트 · 해석 · 정답단서

해커스 어학연구소

* 각 문제에 대한 정답단서는 지문에 보라색으로 표시되어 있습니다.

1. **(A)** Main Purpose/Topic	2. **(D)** Detail	3. **(C)** Detail
4. **(A)** Function & Attitude	5. **(B)** Inference	6. **(B)** Main Purpose/Topic
7. **(B)** Detail	8. **(C)** Detail	9. **(A)** Function & Attitude
10. **(D)** Connecting Contents II	11. **(C)** Inference	12. **(C)** Main Purpose/Topic
13. **(D)** Detail	14. **(A)** Connecting Contents II	

15. Connecting Contents I

	Yes	No
It can see through layers of paint.	√	
It acts like visible light.		√
It is absorbed by charcoal.	√	
It is reflected by a canvas.	√	

16. **(B)** Detail   17. **(C)** Function & Attitude

[1-5]

Listen to a conversation between a student and a professor.

S: Hello, Professor Diggs. Are you busy right now?

P: Not really, Mary . . . Come on in. What can I help you with?

S: ^{Q1} I wanted to talk to you about the midterm writing assignment. The syllabus says that it's due on Friday of next week, but some of the other students swear that the deadline is in two weeks.

P: Oh, yes. I was going to make the announcement in class this week. I guess some of the students have already heard about the change in our lecture schedule.

S: So it's true, then? Why the sudden change? I mean, weren't we supposed to spend this week reviewing the material to aid in the writing of our papers?

P: Yeah, we were, ^{Q2} but now we are going to have a, uh, special speaker come in this Friday. So the, uh, deadline for the midterm report has been postponed one week.

S: And the speaker is . . .

P: Well, actually Ashley Hampton, the internationally renowned sociologist. She happens to be coming to our campus this week. Her main purpose is to update the faculty of the Latin American Studies Department on her fieldwork.

S: Wow, Dr. Ashley Hampton herself! How did you convince her to speak to our class?

P: She owed me a favor from before, so I've asked her to give a lecture to our class this Friday on her most recent research. ^{Q3} You know, she is doing work on the, um, the indigenous cultures of Brazil, which relates to our survey of South American cultural traditions. If you recall, a few weeks ago we were discussing how European colonization . . . and, uh, more recently, agricultural development . . . put increasing pressure on indigenous tribes—so much so that some entire cultures, along with their languages, have disappeared.

S: Oh, yeah . . . and some people are working to try to save those traditions that remain.

P: Right. Well . . . anyway, Dr. Hampton is here to give an updated report of just how extensive the situation really is. It's a great opportunity to learn from firsthand testimony . . . and also to find out some things about how we may be able to help preserve the cultural diversity that's still there.

S: ᴼ⁴ That sounds really exciting. I'm sure the class will enjoy the opportunity to learn from an expert . . . and I'm sure they won't be complaining about the extended deadline either. You know, a lot of the students are really scrambling to get their papers done.

P: Yeah, I was aware of that. Well, I will announce the extension in class tomorrow. I hope the class will find Dr. Hampton's talk useful. ᴼ⁵ Her speaking style tends to encourage her audience to think, and well . . . she really tries to get people to actively participate in the discussions. And frankly, the timing couldn't be better because, well, I'm thinking that perhaps the class can pick up some ideas from her lecture and incorporate them into their compositions.

S: Uh-huh. Well, will you be telling the class that it's Ashley Hampton giving the lecture?

P: Um, uh . . . I was kind of hoping it would be a surprise. Do you think you can keep from revealing her identity to the rest of the class?

S: Oh, no problem! I promise I won't tell a single soul.

P: Well then, I'll see you tomorrow in class.

Now get ready to answer the questions. You may use your notes to help you answer.

1. Why does the student go to see the professor?
2. Why does the professor postpone the deadline for the midterm?
3. According to the conversation, what topic will the special speaker discuss in class?

Listen again to part of the conversation. Then answer the question.

S: That sounds really exciting. I'm sure the class will enjoy the opportunity to learn from an expert . . . and I'm sure they won't be complaining about the extended deadline either. You know, a lot of the students are really scrambling to get their papers done.

4. What does the student mean when she says this:
   S: You know, a lot of the students are really scrambling to get their papers done.

5. What does the professor imply about the guest speaker?

S: 안녕하세요, Diggs 교수님. 지금 바쁘세요?

P: 그리 바쁘지 않단다, Mary... 들어오렴. 무엇을 도와줄까?

S: 중간 작문 과제에 대해 교수님과 이야기하고 싶었어요. 강의 요강에는 제출기한이 다음 주 금요일이라고 적혀 있는데, 다른 몇몇 학생들은 최종기한이 2주 후라고 단언하거든요.

P: 오, 그래. 이번 주 수업 시간에 공지하려고 했단다. 몇몇 학생들은 이미 강의 계획 변경에 대해 들은 것 같구나.

S: 그럼 그게 사실인가요? 왜 갑자기 변경된 거죠? 제 말은, 이번 주에는 저희가 보고서 쓰는 것을 도울 자료를 복습하기로 되어있지 않았나요?

P: 그래, 그러기로 했지만, 지금은, 어, 이번 주 금요일에 특별 연사가 오기로 되어 있단다. 그래서 그, 어, 중간 보고서의 최종기한이 한 주 미뤄졌어.

S: 그럼 그 연사는...

P: 음, 사실 국제적으로 유명한 사회학자인, Ashley Hampton이야. 그분이 이번 주에 우연히 우리 학교에 오시게 됐거든. 주요 목적은 중남미 학과의 교수진에게 그녀의 현장 연구를 알리기 위해서란다.

S: 와, Ashley Hampton 박사님이 직접 오신다니! 어떻게 그분이 저희 수업에서 강의를 하도록 설득하셨나요?

P: 전에 내가 그녀의 부탁을 들어준 적이 있어서, 이번 금요일에 우리 수업에서 그녀의 최신 연구에 대해 강의해달라고 부탁했지. 그러니까, 그녀는, 음, 브라질의 토착 문화에 대해 연구하고 있는데, 이는 남미 문화 전통에 대한 우리의 조사와도 관련이 있거든. 네가 기억한다면, 몇 주 전에 우리는 어떻게 유럽 식민지가... 그리고, 어, 더욱 최근에, 농업 발전이, 토착 부족들에게 점점 더 압력을

가해서, 몇몇 문화 전체가, 그들의 언어와 함께, 사라졌는지를 논의했었지.

S: 오, 네... 그리고 몇몇 사람들은 남아있는 그 전통을 구하기 위해 힘쓰고 있다는 것도요.

P: 맞아. 음... 어쨌든, Hampton 박사는 그 상황이 실제로 얼마나 광범위한지에 대한 최신 보고를 해주려고 여기 오는 거야. 그건 직접적인 증언으로부터 배우고... 또한 우리가 어떻게 여전히 그곳에 존재하는 문화적 다양성을 보존하는 데 도울 수 있는지 알아보는 굉장한 기회란다.

S: 정말 흥미로울 것 같아요. 학생들도 분명 전문가로부터 배울 수 있는 기회를 즐거워할 거예요... 그리고 그들이 연장된 최종기한에 대해서도 불평하지 않을 거라 확신해요. 그러니까, 많은 학생들이 보고서를 마무리하기 위해서 정말 급하게 서두르고 있거든요.

P: 그래, 그것에 대해 알고 있단다. 음, 내일 수업 시간에 기한 연장을 공지하마. 학생들이 Hampton 박사의 강의를 유익하게 느끼면 좋겠구나. 그녀의 강의 방식은 청중들이 생각하도록 고무하는 경향이 있고, 음... 사람들이 활발하게 토론에 참여하도록 정말 노력하거든. 그리고 솔직히, 타이밍이 이보다 좋을 순 없어, 음, 왜냐하면 아마도 학생들이 그녀의 강의에서 아이디어를 좀 얻고 그것들을 보고서와 결합할 수 있을 거라는 생각이 들거든.

S: 네. 음, 강의를 하는 분이 Ashley Hampton이라는 것을 학생들에게 알려주실 건가요?

P: 음, 어... 난 그게 좀 놀라운 소식이길 바라고 있었단다. 그녀의 정체를 나머지 학생들에게 밝히지 않을 수 있겠니?

S: 오, 물론이죠! 단 한 명에게도 말하지 않을게요.

P: 그러면, 내일 수업 시간에 보자.

어휘

syllabus[síləbəs] 강의 요강   swear[swɛər] 단언하다   deadline[dédlàin] 최종기한   renowned[rináund] 유명한
sociologist[sòusiálədʒist] 사회학자   indigenous[indídʒənəs] 토착의   colonization[kὰlənizéiʃən] 식민지
agricultural[ὰgrikʌ́ltʃərəl] 농업의   tribe[traib] 부족   extensive[iksténsiv] 광범위한   firsthand[fə̀ːrsthǽnd] 직접적인
testimony[téstəmòuni] 증언   preserve[prizə́ːrv] 보존하다   diversity[divə́ːrsəti] 다양성   extended[iksténdid] 연장된
scramble[skrǽmbl] 급하게 서두르다   extension[iksténʃən] 기한 연장   incorporate[inkɔ́ːrpərèit] 결합하다

[6-11]
Listen to part of a lecture in a zoology class.

In our previous lecture, we discussed some of the ways that animals adapt to the conditions of the habitats where they live. Q6 Today I plan to look at a unique animal, the polar bear. What's so unique about this animal? Well, in an environment that is so inhospitable . . . the Arctic . . . the polar bear has adapted in ways that are really pretty ingenious.

So . . . how did the polar bear wind up in the Arctic in the first place? Scientists believe that the polar bear or *Ursus maritimus*, its scientific name, evolved from the predatory brown bear around 200,000 years ago. It seems the Ice Age forced the bears to live in an environment where temperatures plummeted to minus 45 degrees Celsius! Well . . . those bears had to adapt to the cold. And scientists say they did. They evolved an insulating layer of fat or blubber, and they packed on this layer by devouring up to 100 pounds of seal fat at one sitting. This layer helps prevent heat loss. Actually, polar bears have more problems with overheating than they do with the cold. They quickly overheat when they run. And speaking of running, the polar bears' extra-wide feet help them distribute their weight efficiently on the fragile sea ice, and swim in the Arctic ice waters.

OK, now I'm thinking . . . how come the color of their fur changed? Well, what exactly is the color of a polar bear's fur? Q7 Most people would say it's white, but it's actually pigment-free, colorless. It only looks white because the clear strands scatter the sun's rays. Except, at the San Diego Zoo a few years back, their polar bears' fur turned green for a while because of the algae that got trapped in the hollow shafts of their fur.

But, anyway, there's some debate over why the polar bears' fur is the color it is. In one camp, people say that the fur serves as camouflage for hunting. Q8 But other people argue that polar

bears hunt mainly in the Arctic winter, which, of course, is dark much of the time, so there's no need for camouflage. They say that the fur evolved to help keep them warm in the winter.
Q9 Well, both arguments carry some weight. Although the Arctic winter days are mostly dark, there are several months when polar bears can hunt in some hours of daylight. I kind of fall into the second camp, though. You see, the clear strands allow the sunlight to penetrate through to the black skin. This heat gets trapped and stored by the fat and fur. Q10 Actually, you might find this hard to believe but the polar bear's insulation system is so efficient at trapping heat that in infrared photographs, the only visible heat escaping from their bodies is the puff of air caused by their breath! They experience almost no heat loss.
Now . . . polar bears are active the entire year, unlike brown bears that curl up in caves during the winter season. But it might surprise you to know that they do, in fact, hibernate, but not during the winter. And it's a special kind of hibernation called "walking hibernation". You see, in wintertime, there is no shortage of food, but summer is a real problem because the ice melts and this reduces the habitat polar bears have in which to search for food! Q11 To cope with this, polar bears have developed the ability to slow their metabolism down by walking slowly for extended periods. During these periods, they draw energy from their stores of fat . . . I guess this is a feature that most people would envy.

Now get ready to answer the questions. You may use your notes to help you answer.

6. What aspect of polar bears does the lecturer mainly discuss?
7. What does the professor say about the polar bear's fur?
8. According to the professor, what is the reason some people think the camouflage theory is wrong?

Listen again to part of the lecture. Then answer the question.

P: Well, both arguments carry some weight. Although the Arctic winter days are mostly dark, there are several months when polar bears can hunt in some hours of daylight. I kind of fall into the second camp, though. You see, the clear strands allow the sunlight to penetrate through to the black skin.

9. What does the professor mean when she says this:
   P: I kind of fall into the second camp, though.

10. Why does the professor mention infrared photographs?

Listen again to part of the lecture. Then answer the question.

P: To cope with this, polar bears have developed the ability to slow their metabolism down by walking slowly for extended periods. During these periods, they draw energy from their stores of fat . . . I guess this is a feature that most people would envy.

11. What does the professor imply when she says this:
    P: I guess this is a feature that most people would envy.

지난 강의에서, 우리는 동물들이 그들이 살고 있는 서식지의 환경에 적응하는 몇 가지 방법을 논의해 보았습니다. 오늘은 독특한 동물인, 북극곰에 대해 살펴보려고 합니다. 이 동물의 무엇이 그렇게 독특할까요? 음, 아주 혹독한 환경인... 북극에서... 북극곰은 정말로 대단히 독창적인 방법으로 적응해 왔습니다.
자... 북극곰은 애초에 어떻게 북극에서 살게 되었을까요? 과학자들은 북극곰, 또는 그것의 학명인 'Ursus maritimus'가 약

200,000년 전에 육식성 불곰으로부터 진화했다고 생각합니다. 빙하기가 곰들을 온도가 영하 45도까지 급격히 떨어지는 환경에서 살도록 만든 것 같아요! 음... 곰들은 추위에 적응해야만 했죠. 그리고 과학자들은 그들이 그렇게 했다고 말합니다. 그들은 지방 또는 여분의 지방 단열층을 진화시켰고, 한 번 앉은 자리에서 바다표범의 지방을 100파운드까지 먹어 치우면서 이 층을 쌓았습니다. 이 층은 열 손실을 막아주죠. 사실, 북극곰은 추위보다는 과열 때문에 더 많은 어려움을 겪습니다. 그들이 달리면 빠르게 과열돼요. 그리고 달리기에 대해 말하자면, 북극곰의 대단히 넓은 발은 깨지기 쉬운 해빙 위에서 그들의 체중을 효과적으로 분산시키고, 북극 빙수에서 수영할 수 있도록 도와줍니다.

자, 지금 드는 생각은... 북극곰의 털 색은 왜 변했을까요? 음, 북극곰의 털 색은 정확히 뭔가요? 대부분의 사람들이 흰색이라고 말하겠지만, 사실은 색이 없는, 무색이죠. 투명한 가닥들이 햇빛을 분산시키기 때문에 희게 보이는 것뿐이에요. 몇 년 전 샌디에이고 동물원에서, 털의 빈 줄기 안에 낀 조류 때문에 북극곰들의 털이 잠시 녹색으로 변했던 것은 제외하고 말이죠.

하지만, 어쨌든, 북극곰의 털 색이 왜 그런지에 대한 몇 가지 논쟁이 있어요. 한 쪽에서는, 털이 사냥을 위한 위장의 역할을 한다고 말해요. 하지만 다른 사람들은 북극곰이 주로 북극의 겨울에 사냥을 하고, 이때는, 당연히, 대부분의 시간이 어두워서, 위장할 필요가 없다고 주장하죠. 그들은 털이 겨울에 그들을 따뜻하게 유지해주기 위해 진화한 것이라고 말합니다.

음, 두 견해 모두 어느 정도 일리가 있습니다. 비록 북극의 겨울날들이 대부분 어두운데도 불구하고, 북극곰이 낮에 몇 시간 동안 사냥을 할 수 있는 몇 달이 있겠지만요. 하지만, 저는 두 번째 쪽으로 좀 기우는군요. 그러니까, 투명한 털 가닥들은 햇빛이 검은 피부까지 통과할 수 있도록 해주거든요. 이 열은 지방과 털에 의해 가둬지고 저장됩니다. 사실, 믿기 힘들겠지만 북극곰의 단열 조직은 열기를 보존하는 데 매우 효율적이기 때문에 적외선 사진에서, 그들의 몸에서 빠져나오는 육안으로 볼 수 있는 열기는 숨 때문에 발생되는 입김뿐입니다! 그들은 열 손실을 거의 겪지 않죠.

자... 겨울철에 동굴에서 웅크리고 있는 불곰과 달리, 북극곰은 일년 내내 활동적이에요. 하지만, 그들이 사실, 동면을 하지만, 겨울철에는 하지 않는다는 게 놀라울 수도 있겠네요. 그리고 그것은 '걷는 동면'이라고 불리는 특별한 종류의 동면이에요. 그러니까, 겨울에는, 먹이가 부족하지 않지만, 여름에는 얼음이 녹고 이것이 북극곰이 먹이를 찾을 수 있는 서식지를 줄이므로 정말 문제죠! 이것에 대처하기 위해, 북극곰은 오랜 기간 동안 천천히 걸음으로써 그들의 신진대사를 늦추는 능력을 발전시켜 왔어요. 이 기간 동안, 그들은 저장되어 있는 지방에서 에너지를 끌어내죠... 이 특징은 대부분의 사람들이 탐낼 만한 것이라고 생각되네요.

어휘

adapt[ədǽpt] 적응하다 habitat[hǽbitæt] 서식지 environment[inváiərənmənt] 환경 inhospitable[inháspitəbl] 혹독한
Arctic[áːrktik] 북극; 북극의 ingenious[indʒíːnjəs] 독창적인 predatory[prédətòːri] 육식성의 plummet[plʌ́mit] 급격히 떨어지다
insulating[ínsəlèitiŋ] 단열의 layer[léiər] 층 blubber[blʌ́bər] (여분의) 지방 devour[diváuər] 먹어 치우다 seal[síːl] 바다표범
at one sitting 한 번 앉은 자리에서 overheating[òuvərhíːtiŋ] 과열 fragile[frǽdʒəl] 깨지기 쉬운 pigment[pígmənt] 색
strand[strǽnd] (털, 머리카락 등의) 가닥 scatter[skǽtər] 분산시키다 algae[ǽldʒiː] 조류 hollow[hálou] (속이) 빈
shaft[ʃǽft] 줄기 camp[kǽmp] 쪽 camouflage[kǽməflàːʒ] 위장 penetrate[pénətrèit] 통과하다 trap[trǽp] 가두다
infrared[ìnfrəréd] 적외선 curl[kəːrl] 웅크리다 hibernate[háibərnèit] 동면하다 cope with ~에 대처하다
metabolism[mətǽbəlìzm] 신진대사 feature[fíːtʃər] 특징

[12-17]
Listen to part of a lecture in an art history class.

P: Let's go back to checking the authenticity of old paintings. Art historians have a hard time with this . . . particularly with the works of the 17th-century Dutch master, Rembrandt. There is significant controversy about many of the paintings supposedly done by him. Q12 But in the case of a painting titled *Portrait of Rembrandt with Gorget* . . . well, an innovative technique was used to determine that it is not actually a Rembrandt original.
Before I get into this, though, I should probably explain why Rembrandt is such a problem for art historians. Q13 The main issue is that Rembrandt encouraged his students to imitate his work . . . He would even add finishing touches to their paintings. And many of these imitations were, uh, mistakenly classified as paintings by Rembrandt. To give you an idea of the scale of the problem, there was a time when over 1,000 paintings were thought to be by him. With the development of more accurate verification methods, this number has fallen to about 300. Which brings me to *Portrait of Rembrandt with Gorget* . . . Q14 Until recently, all experts agreed

that this was the work of Rembrandt. It had been in the art collection of the Dutch royal family a very long time, so its history of ownership was well established. I mean, there was no reason to doubt its authenticity. But this all changed when the painting was tested using a technology called infrared reflectography. Um, scanning a painting with infrared light can reveal what lies under the paint . . . such as the initial sketches made by an artist.

S1: Uh, how exactly does this process work? It's hard to believe you can actually see drawings under layers of paint . . .

P: Well, it has to do with the qualities of infrared light. It behaves differently than visible light when it encounters a painting . . . [Q15] It passes through most colors of paint, so the paint layers appear transparent. Um, think of visible light going through a window. On the other hand, infrared light sort of bounces off the underlying canvas. This is because the canvas is white, a color that reflects infrared light. Now, any markings drawn on the canvas in black will absorb infrared light. And artists often used black charcoal to sketch on the canvas. The end result is that these markings are easy to see.

Here, let me show you a picture of the charcoal drawing under *Portrait of Rembrandt with Gorget* . . . As you can see, it is incredibly detailed. And this is actually what led experts to conclude that the painting was done by one of Rembrandt's students. Um, Rembrandt didn't work this way. [Q16] His sketches were very simple . . . just rough outlines to position the important elements of the painting.

S2: So then why do art historians think that this painting was created by one of Rembrandt's students? Couldn't anyone have made it?

P: That's a good question . . . It goes back to what I said earlier about Rembrandt encouraging his students to imitate his work. [Q17] One of the best ways to create a copy of a painting is to use a cartoon. I know what you're thinking . . . Um, let me just make clear that I'm not talking about humorous drawings. In the art world, a cartoon is a detailed drawing of an existing painting that can be used to make a new one. And the drawing discovered using infrared reflectography matches very closely with another painting that was definitely done by Rembrandt. So the most likely explanation is that *Portrait of Rembrandt with Gorget* is a copy of one of Rembrandt's self-portraits. It was probably done by a student who was trying to practice his technique.

Now get ready to answer the questions. You may use your notes to help you answer.

12. What is the main topic of the lecture?
13. Why have a lot of paintings been mistakenly classified as the works of Rembrandt?
14. Why does the professor mention the Dutch royal family?
15. In the lecture, the professor describes the qualities of infrared light. Indicate whether each of the following is a quality.
16. What does the professor say about the sketches made by Rembrandt?

Listen again to part of the lecture. Then answer the question.

P: One of the best ways to create a copy of a painting is to use a cartoon. I know what you're thinking . . . Um, let me just make clear that I'm not talking about humorous drawings. In the art world, a cartoon is a detailed drawing of an existing painting that can be used to make a new one.

17. Why does the professor say this:

P: I know what you're thinking . . .

P: 오래된 그림들의 진위를 확인하는 것으로 돌아가 봅시다. 미술사학자들은 이것 때문에 힘든 시간을 보내죠... 특히 17세기 네덜란드의 거장인 렘브란트의 작품들 때문이에요. 그에 의해 그려진 것으로 추정되는 다수의 그림에 대해 큰 논란이 있습니다. 하지만 'Portrait of Rembrandt with Gorget'이라는 제목을 가진 그림의 경우에는... 음, 그것이 사실 렘브란트의 원본이 아니라는 것을 밝혀내기 위해 혁신적인 기술이 사용되었죠.

하지만, 이를 시작하기 전에, 아마 렘브란트가 미술사학자들에게 왜 그렇게 골칫거리인지 설명해야 할 것 같네요. 주요 쟁점은 렘브란트가 그의 제자들로 하여금 그의 작품을 모방하도록 장려했다는 것입니다... 심지어 그는 그들의 그림에 마무리 손질을 더하기도 했어요. 그리고 이러한 모조품의 다수가, 어, 렘브란트에 의한 그림으로 잘못 분류되었습니다. 그 문제의 규모를 알려주자면, 1,000점 이상의 그림이 그의 것이라고 여겨졌던 때가 있었어요. 더 정확한 검증 방식의 발달로, 이 숫자는 300개 정도로 줄어들었죠. 그것은 저를 'Portrait of Rembrandt with Gorget'으로 이끄는데... 최근까지, 모든 전문가가 이것이 렘브란트의 작품이라고 동의했습니다. 그것은 매우 오랫동안 네덜란드 왕실의 미술 소장품으로 있었기 때문에, 소유권 역사가 매우 확고했죠. 제 말은, 그것의 진위를 의심할 이유가 없었다는 거예요. 하지만 그 그림이 적외선 반사 복사법이라고 불리는 기술을 사용하여 검사되었을 때 이 모든 것이 바뀌었습니다. 음, 적외선으로 그림을 살피는 것은 물감 아래에 무엇이 있는지 밝혀낼 수 있었거든요... 화가가 그린 첫 밑그림 같은 거 말이에요.

S1: 어, 이 과정이 정확히 어떻게 진행되는 거죠? 겹겹의 물감 아래에 있는 밑그림을 실제로 볼 수 있다는 것이 믿기 어려워서요...

P: 음, 그것은 적외선의 특성과 관련이 있어요. 그것이 그림에 부딪히면 가시광선과는 다르게 반응합니다... 적외선은 물감의 색 대부분을 통과해서, 물감의 층이 투명해 보이는 거예요. 음, 창문을 통과하는 가시광선을 생각해 보세요. 한편으로는, 적외선은 뭐랄까 밑에 있는 도화지에 부딪혀 튕겨 나옵니다. 이것은 도화지가 흰색, 즉 적외선을 반사하는 색이기 때문이에요. 자, 도화지에 검은색으로 그려진 모든 표시들은 적외선을 흡수할 겁니다. 그리고 화가들은 대개 검은 목탄으로 도화지에 밑그림을 그렸죠. 최종 결과는 이러한 표시들이 보기 쉽다는 것이고요.

여기, 'Portrait of Rembrandt with Gorget'의 아래에 있는 목탄 밑그림 사진을 보여줄게요... 여러분도 보다시피, 그것은 엄청나게 상세합니다. 그리고 그 그림이 렘브란트의 제자 중 한 명에 의해 그려졌다고 전문가들이 결론짓게 했던 것은 사실 이것이죠. 음, 렘브란트는 이런 식으로 그리지 않았거든요. 그의 밑그림은 매우 간단했어요... 그림의 중요한 요소들을 배치하는 대략적인 윤곽 뿐이었죠.

S2: 그러면 왜 미술사학자들은 이 그림이 렘브란트의 제자에 의해 그려졌다고 생각하나요? 누구든지 그릴 수 있었던 것 아닌가요?

P: 좋은 질문이에요... 그것은 렘브란트가 제자들로 하여금 그의 작품을 모방하도록 장려했다고 앞서 말했던 것으로 거슬러 올라가요. 그림의 복제본을 만드는 가장 좋은 방법 중 하나는 카툰을 이용하는 것이에요. 여러분이 무슨 생각을 하는지 알고 있어요... 음, 제가 익살스러운 그림을 말하는 게 아니라는 것을 분명히 해두죠. 예술계에서, 카툰은 새로운 그림을 만드는 데 사용될 수 있는 기존 그림의 상세한 밑그림이에요. 그리고 적외선 반사 복사법을 이용해 발견된 이 밑그림은 틀림없이 렘브란트에 의해 그려졌던 다른 그림과 매우 정확하게 일치합니다. 그러므로 가장 그럴듯한 설명은 'Portrait of Rembrandt with Gorget'이 렘브란트의 자화상 중 하나의 복제본이라는 것이죠. 그것은 아마 그의 기법을 연습하려 했던 한 제자에 의해 그려졌을 거예요.

어휘
authenticity[ɔ̀ːθentísəti] 진위 Dutch[dʌtʃ] 네덜란드의 master[mǽstər] 거장 controversy[kántrəvə̀ːrsi] 논란
determine[ditə́ːrmin] 밝혀내다 imitate[ímətèit] 모방하다 imitation[ìmətéiʃən] 모조품 classify[klǽsəfài] 분류하다
verification[vèrəfikéiʃən] 검증 ownership[óunərʃìp] 소유권 infrared reflectography 적외선 반사 복사법 layer[leiər] 겹, 층
visible light 가시광선 transparent[trænspéərənt] 투명한 bounce off (~에 부딪혀) 튕겨 나오다 charcoal[tʃáːrkòul] 목탄
self-portrait[sèlfpɔ́ːrtrit] 자화상

CHAPTER 01 Main Purpose/Topic

*각 문제에 대한 정답단서는 지문에 보라색으로 표시되어 있습니다.

문제 공략하기 p.33

오늘은, 로마인들에 의해 이름 지어진 한 행성에 대해 이야기하고 싶습니다... 그들은 이 행성이 다른 어떤 행성들보다 더 빨리 움직이는 것을 관측했습니다. 여러분은 내가 수성에 대해 이야기하고 있다는 것을 알 거예요. 많은 행성들이 굉장히 자세히 논의되어 왔지만, 대부분의 교사들은 수성이 지구의 달과 색깔, 표면적, 그리고 대기가 부족한 점에서 상당히 비슷하다는 것만을 알고 있기 때문에 수성에 대해서 대충 지나가는 경향이 있죠.

HACKERS PRACTICE p.34

1. (B) Main Purpose/Topic	2. (C) Detail	3. (D) Detail
4. (D) Main Purpose/Topic	5. (B) Detail	6. (B), (C) Detail
7. (C) Main Purpose/Topic	8. (C) Detail	9. (B), (D) Detail
10. (D) Main Purpose/Topic	11. (B) Detail	12. (B), (D) Detail

[1-3]

Listen to a conversation between a student and a librarian.

W: Hi . . . Is there something I can help you with?

M: Yes, I hope so. I returned a videotape that I borrowed last week. The title of the video is *How Biological Factors Lead to Insect Diversity*.

W: Oh, yes, I know that video. I believe the waiting list for that particular title is two weeks. So . . . do you want to reserve it again?

M: No, no . . . Q1 Actually, the reason I'm here is that I gave you the wrong videotape by mistake.

W: Pardon me?

M: I gave you the wrong tape. The one I gave to you belongs to my friend. Q2 The tapes look almost the same . . . I mean, they have the same beige label and nearly the same title, but the one that belongs to my friend is the one that I returned to you. When you play it, it seems to be a video on insects at first, but after about a minute, it turns into a videotape of my friend's birthday party.

W: Is that right? Hold on, let me check . . . hmm . . . When did you return it?

M: That was Tuesday last week.

W: I guess you're right. Someone borrowed it after you returned it . . . but returned it almost immediately. He said there was something wrong with the tape. Q3 I thought he meant there was something physically wrong, you know, a malfunction, so I played the tape for a few seconds, and it seemed OK to me, so I put it back in circulation.

M: Is it still here or does someone else have it now?

W: Someone just took it out this morning and won't have to return it till Wednesday.

M: Well, he might return it sooner when he sees that it's not the tape he wants.

W: But . . . where's the library's tape, then?

M: I've got it right here with me.

W: Can I see it?

M: Yes, here it is.

W: Yep, this is clearly the library's tape . . . Anyway, thank you for returning it.

M: No problem, but, uh, do I have to pay a late fee?

W: I think this is a special case, so I'll just let it go this time. But please try to be more careful in the future.

M: Thanks very much. Now then, how do I get my friend's tape back?

W: Well . . . just leave your e-mail address and I'll get in touch with you as soon as the tape is returned . . . or you could just drop by on Wednesday and see if it's been returned.

M: Oh, good. Thanks.

Now get ready to answer the questions. You may use your notes to help you answer.

1. Why does the man go to see the librarian?
2. What reason does the man give for returning the wrong tape?
3. What does the librarian assume about the library's tape at first?

W: 안녕하세요... 제가 도와드릴 수 있는 일이 있나요?

M: 네, 도와주실 수 있었으면 좋겠네요. 제가 빌린 비디오 테이프를 지난주에 반납했어요. 비디오의 제목은 '생물학적 요소가 곤충의 다양성으로 이어지는 방식'이었고요.

W: 오, 네, 그 비디오를 알아요. 그 특정 제목에 대기자 명단이 2주인 것으로 알고 있거든요. 그래서... 다시 예약하고 싶은 건가요?

M: 아니요, 아니에요... 사실, 여기 온 이유는 실수로 잘못된 비디오 테이프를 반납했기 때문이에요.

W: 무슨 말씀이시죠?

M: 잘못된 비디오 테이프를 반납했어요. 제가 드린 건 제 친구 거예요. 그 테이프들은 거의 똑같이 생겼거든요... 제 말은, 같은 베이지색 라벨과 거의 같은 제목을 가지고 있지만, 제가 반납한 건 친구 거예요. 그걸 재생하면, 처음에는 곤충에 관한 비디오인 것 같지만, 잠시 후에, 친구의 생일파티 비디오로 변하죠.

W: 정말요? 잠시만요, 확인해 보죠... 음... 그걸 언제 반납했죠?

M: 지난주 화요일이었어요.

W: 학생 말이 맞는 것 같군요. 학생이 반납한 후에 누군가가 빌려갔는데... 거의 바로 반납했어요. 그는 테이프에 뭔가 문제가 있다고 하더라고요. 저는 물리적으로 잘못된 뭔가가 있다는 건 줄 알고, 그러니까, 오작동 같은 거요, 테이프를 몇 초간 재생시켰는데, 그게 괜찮아 보여서, 다시 유통시켰거든요.

M: 그 테이프가 아직 여기 있나요, 아니면 현재 누군가가 가지고 있나요?

W: 오늘 아침에 어떤 학생이 빌려갔고 수요일까지는 반납하지 않아도 될 거예요.

M: 음, 그가 원했던 테이프가 아닌 것을 알게 되면 더 빨리 반납할 수도 있겠군요.

W: 그런데... 그럼, 도서관 테이프는 어디에 있죠?

M: 바로 여기 가져 왔습니다.

W: 볼 수 있나요?

M: 네, 여기요.

W: 네, 이게 확실히 도서관 테이프군요... 아무튼, 반납해주셔서 감사합니다.

M: 아닙니다, 그런데, 어, 연체료를 지불해야 하나요?

W: 이건 특별한 경우인 것 같으니까, 이번에는 그냥 넘어가도록 할게요. 하지만 다음에는 더 주의해주세요.

M: 정말 감사합니다. 그럼 이제, 친구의 테이프는 어떻게 돌려받을 수 있을까요?

W: 음... 그냥 이메일 주소를 남겨주시면 테이프가 반납되는 대로 학생에게 연락할게요... 아니면 그냥 수요일에 들러서 테이프가 반납되었는지 확인해도 되고요.

M: 오, 좋아요. 감사합니다.

[4-6]

Listen to a conversation between a student and a professor.

S: Professor Watson? Could you spare me a few minutes?

P: Meredith, come on in. I have a class, but I may be able to give you 10 minutes. What can I do for you?

S: [Q4] It's about the research project you assigned us for our upcoming presentations. Um, the topic I chose was asteroid impacts on Earth.

P: Yes, I remember. How's the research coming along?

S: See, I've got so much data that . . . actually, the project has sort of become a bit too big for me to handle.

P: OK, I see your problem . . . and believe me, it's a fairly common one. Well, what you want to do is limit the points to just two . . . otherwise, you'll find yourself trying to cover too much material in the fifteen minutes allotted to you.

S: Right. Well, actually I've got some stuff about the biggest recorded impact in the 20th century . . . I also have data on nearly every major collision that's occurred on Earth as well as material on major research conducted by scientists in the past 30 years . . . [Q4] but I'm not really sure which to include and which to omit. Everything seems so interesting and important . . . that's why I'm hoping for a few pointers from you.

P: [Q5] You know, a lot of students who do a research project tend to believe that every piece of information is important. But . . . you might want to ask yourself what the class would want to know if they wanted to hear a report on the effects of asteroid impacts on Earth.

S: Um . . . [Q6] I guess they'd be interested in learning about the biggest impacts and maybe the most important findings that scientists have made about these impacts.

P: There you are. So do you have a pretty good idea of what impacts you'd like to discuss?

S: Um, the Siberia one and the big crater in Arizona.

P: OK, good . . . and what do you consider the really important research scientists have done regarding asteroid impacts in recent years?

S: [Q6] I'd have to say the frequency of impacts on Earth and the effects of a really big collision, like the asteroid that destroyed the dinosaurs 65 million years ago.

P: There you have it, your two subtopics. Everything else you'll need to simply set aside.

S: OK, I think I've got it. Thanks, Professor.

Now get ready to answer the questions. You may use your notes to help you answer.

4. What problem does the woman have?

5. What does the professor say about students doing research projects?

6. According to the conversation, what information does the student decide to include in her report?

S: Watson 교수님? 시간 좀 내주실 수 있으세요?

P: Meredith, 들어오너라. 수업이 있지만, 10분 정도는 낼 수 있을 것 같구나. 무엇을 도와줄까?

S: 다가오는 발표를 위해 내주신 연구 과제에 관한 건데요. 음, 제가 고른 주제는 지구에 대한 소행성의 충돌이에요.

P: 그래, 기억하고 있단다. 연구는 어떻게 진행되고 있니?

S: 그게, 자료가 너무 많아서... 사실, 제가 감당하기에 뭐랄까 과제가 좀 너무 커진 것 같아요.

P: 그래, 네 문제가 뭔지 알겠어... 그리고 확신하건데, 그건 꽤 흔한 일이야. 음, 네가 해야 할 것은 요점을 단 두 개로 줄이는 것이란다... 그렇지 않으면, 너에게 할당된 15분 안에 너무 많은 자료를 다루려고 애쓰게 될 거야.

S: 맞아요. 음, 사실 저는 20세기에 기록된 가장 큰 충돌에 대한 자료를 좀 가지고 있어요... 또 지난 30년간 과학자들이 해온 주요 연구에 대한 자료뿐만 아니라 지구에서 일어났던 거의 모든 주요 충돌에 대한 자료도 가지고 있고요. 하지만 어떤 것을 포함하고 어

떤 것을 생략해야 할지 정말 모르겠어요. 모든 것이 흥미롭고 중요해 보여서요... 그게 교수님의 조언을 받고 싶은 이유예요.

P: 그러니까, 연구 과제를 하는 많은 학생들은 모든 정보가 중요하다고 생각하는 경향이 있어. 하지만... 소행성 충돌이 지구에 미치는 영향에 대한 보고를 학생들이 듣는다면 무엇을 알고 싶어 할지 너 자신에게 질문해 보렴.

S: 음... 가장 거대한 충돌들과 아마도 이러한 충돌에 대한 과학자들의 가장 중요한 발견에 관심 있을 것 같아요.

P: 바로 그거야. 그래서 어떤 충돌에 대해 논의해야 할지 꽤 좋은 생각이 떠올랐니?

S: 음, 시베리아에서의 충돌과 애리조나의 큰 분화구요.

P: 그래, 좋아... 그리고 최근 몇 년간 소행성과의 충돌에 대해 과학자들이 하고 있는 연구 중 정말 중요하다고 생각하는 게 뭐니?

S: 지구와의 충돌 빈도와 정말 큰 충돌의 영향이라고 생각해요, 6500만 년 전에 공룡을 멸종시켰던 소행성처럼요.

P: 바로 그거다, 너의 두 세부 주제 말이지. 다른 모든 것은 그냥 제쳐놓아야 할 거야.

S: 네, 알 것 같아요. 감사합니다, 교수님.

[7-9]
Listen to part of a lecture in a biology class.

P: Let's begin . . . Most animals use techniques to avoid predators. One of the most interesting tactics involves camouflage. And, uh, just to explain quickly, Q7 camouflage means the various physical traits that allow animals to avoid being seen. There are several types of camouflage, and let me start my lecture by describing one in detail . . .
Background matching is a type of camouflage that enables animals to blend in with their surroundings. One simple form involves color matching. In color matching, an animal's skin, fur, or feathers match the color of its natural habitat. Some animals are born this way, while others can change color when they need to. Um, can anyone provide an example of this?

S1: Um . . . well, I've heard that some species of octopus are able to change their appearance . . .

P: Excellent . . . Yes, Q8 the Pacific octopus, for instance, is quite good at this. It can change its color when necessary. Its natural color is brown like, um, sand. However, it can become the colors of the things around it . . . objects like rocks and coral, and even other animals. This allows it to avoid predators and to capture prey more easily.

S1: Uh, professor? Does color matching work for all animals? I mean, being the same color as the surroundings won't work if an animal stands out in other ways . . . like in size or in how it moves.

P: That brings me to my next point, actually. Now, other animals use a different form of background matching. They are born with physical features that resemble nearby environmental objects. The leaf insect is a good example . . . Its body, as you might expect, is shaped like a leaf . . .
Q9 It not only mimics the general color and shape of a leaf but also the veins and other markings typically found on leaves. This includes bite marks from caterpillars . . .

S2: Do you mean caterpillars actually mistake the leaf insect for a real leaf . . . and eat, I mean, bite into it?

P: No, not at all. Q9 It's just that the leaf insect imitates the patterns of these bite marks. You see, the degree of detail is so great that it matches both the irregular shapes of bite marks and the way leaves turn brown around their edges. This shows how complex background matching can be.

Now get ready to answer the questions. You may use your notes to help you answer.

7. What is the main topic of the lecture?
8. What does the professor say about the Pacific octopus?
9. What makes the leaf insect's camouflage so impressive?

P: 시작해 봅시다... 동물 대부분은 포식자를 피하기 위한 기법들을 사용합니다. 가장 흥미로운 전략 중 하나는 위장을 수반하죠. 그리고, 어, 빠르게 설명하자면, 위장은 동물들이 목격되는 것을 방지해주는 다양한 신체적 특성을 의미합니다. 몇몇 종류의 위장이 있는데, 하나를 자세하게 설명하면서 강의를 시작하도록 하죠...

배경에 맞추기는 동물들이 그들의 주위 환경과 섞이도록 해주는 위장의 한 종류입니다. 한 가지 간단한 형태는 색 맞추기를 포함하죠. 색 맞추기에서는, 동물의 피부, 털, 또는 깃털이 자연 서식지의 색과 일치합니다. 일부 동물들은 이렇게 태어나지만, 다른 동물들은 필요할 때 색을 바꿀 수 있습니다. 누가 이것의 예를 들어 볼 수 있나요?

S1: 음... 저, 모습을 바꿀 수 있는 몇몇 문어 종을 들어본 적이 있어요.

P: 훌륭해요... 네, 예를 들면, 참문어는, 이것에 꽤 능숙하지요. 그것은 필요할 때 색을 바꿀 수 있습니다. 그것의 타고난 색은 갈색이에요, 음, 모래처럼요. 그러나, 그것은 주변 것들의 색이 될 수 있습니다... 바위나, 산호, 그리고 심지어 다른 동물의 색 같은 것으로요. 이는 포식자를 피하고 먹이를 더 쉽게 잡도록 해주죠.

S1: 어, 교수님? 색 맞추기가 모든 동물에게 효과가 있나요? 제 말은, 만약 동물이 다른 식으로 도드라진다면 주위의 환경과 같은 색이 되는 것은 효과가 없잖아요... 크기나 움직이는 방법 같은 걸로 말이에요.

P: 사실, 그것은 다음 요점으로 넘어가게 하네요. 자, 다른 동물들은 배경 맞추기의 다른 형태를 사용합니다. 그들은 근처 환경의 대상을 닮은 신체적 특성을 가지고 태어나요. 나뭇잎 벌레가 좋은 사례죠... 그것의 몸통은, 여러분이 예상한 바와 같이, 잎과 같은 형태로 만들어져 있습니다... 그것은 잎의 일반적인 색과 모양뿐 아니라 잎맥과 나뭇잎에서 전형적으로 발견되는 다른 무늬들도 모방해요. 이는 애벌레에게 물린 자국도 포함하죠...

S2: 애벌레들이 정말로 나뭇잎 벌레를 진짜 잎으로 착각하고... 그리고 먹는다는, 제 말은, 그것을 문다는 말씀인가요?

P: 아니요, 전혀 그렇지 않아요. 그것은 단지 나뭇잎 벌레들이 이러한 물린 자국들의 모양을 모방한다는 거예요. 그러니까, 세밀함의 정도가 너무 대단해서 물린 자국의 불규칙한 모양과 잎의 가장자리 주변이 갈색으로 변하는 방식까지 일치하죠. 이것은 배경 맞추기가 얼마나 복잡할 수 있는지를 보여줍니다.

[10-12]

Listen to part of a lecture in an astronomy class.

P: We're talking about the physical structure and chemical composition of the Sun. At the end of last class, Q10 I mentioned sunspots . . . um, the dark patches that appear on the Sun's surface. This afternoon, we will expand on this . . .

So, what exactly are sunspots? Well, essentially they're magnetic storms that occur on the Sun's surface . . . On average, each one is about 10,000 square kilometers across . . . roughly the same size as our planet. They're quite large and can be observed with a telescope that has a special lens to protect your eyes. They're easy to distinguish because they're darker than the rest of the Sun. Now, these sunspots, they disappear and reappear over time . . . um, they last anywhere from 1 to 100 days.

S1: Does that . . . is that because of the Sun's gravity? Or the movement of planets around the Sun? Why do they do that, exactly?

P: It has to do with the Sun's rotation. Q11 You see, the Sun's interior and exterior move independently. And its exterior spins faster at the equator than at the poles. This complex pattern of movements distorts the Sun's magnetic field. Um, it sort of creates, uh, forces that get twisted and pulled in different directions. And when one of these breaks through the Sun's surface, sunspots are formed . . . Sunspots, therefore, are a result of distortions in the Sun's magnetic field. And they lead to some dramatic effects . . . Can anybody name an example?

S2: Um, well, I'm not sure if they're related, but solar flares are a pretty amazing phenomenon . . .

P: Good. Q12 Yes, solar flares are one effect of sunspots . . . They happen because sunspots produce a lot of magnetic forces . . . and these forces become so powerful that they enter the Sun's atmosphere . . . Now, the atmosphere already stores a lot of magnetic energy. It can't contain all of the additional energy coming from the Sun and must release some of it. This sudden release of energy produces solar flares . . . If you look at this photograph, you'll see that solar flares appear as bright flashes of light. Each of these flashes is a powerful explosion . . . similar to millions of bombs going off at once. ^Q12 They release clouds of electrically charged particles into space. Some of these particles have been known to reach Earth. They interfere with the planet's magnetic field and cause other negative effects.

Now get ready to answer the questions. You may use your notes to help you answer.

10. What is the main topic of the lecture?
11. According to the professor, what causes sunspots?
12. What does the professor say about solar flares?

P: 우리는 태양의 물리적 구조와 화학적 구성 요소에 관해 이야기하고 있습니다. 지난 수업 시간 끝에, 태양 흑점을 언급했는데요... 음, 태양 표면에 나타나는 어두운 반점 말이에요. 오늘 오후에는, 이것에 대해 더 상세하게 말해 볼 거예요... 자, 태양 흑점이란 정확히 무엇일까요? 음, 기본적으로 태양 표면에서 발생하는 자기 폭풍이에요... 평균적으로, 각각은 직경으로 약 10,000km²입니다... 지구와 거의 같은 크기죠. 그것들은 상당히 크고 눈을 보호하기 위한 특수 렌즈를 가진 망원경을 통해 관측될 수 있어요. 그것들은 태양의 나머지 부분보다 더 어두워서 구별하기 쉽습니다. 자, 이 태양 흑점들은, 시간이 지나면서 사라졌다가 다시 나타나요... 음, 1~100일 사이의 얼마 동안 존속하죠.

S1: 그게... 태양의 중력 때문인가요? 아니면 태양 주변 행성들의 움직임 때문인가요? 정확히, 왜 그러는 거죠?

P: 그건 태양의 자전과 관계가 있어요. 보세요, 태양의 내부와 외부는 독립적으로 움직여요. 그리고 그것의 외부는 극에서보다 적도에서 더 빨리 회전하죠. 이 움직임의 복잡한 패턴은 태양의 자기장을 일그러뜨립니다. 음, 그것은 뭐랄까, 어, 서로 다른 방향으로 비틀어지고 당겨지는 힘을 만들어내요. 그리고 이들 중 하나가 태양의 표면을 뚫고 나가면, 태양 흑점이 형성됩니다... 태양 흑점은, 그러므로, 태양 자기장에서의 일그러짐의 결과입니다... 그리고 그것들은 몇 가지 극적인 결과로 이어지죠... 누가 예를 말해볼 수 있나요?

S2: 음, 저, 연관이 있는지는 잘 모르겠지만, 태양면 폭발은 매우 놀라운 현상이에요...

P: 좋아요. 네, 태양면 폭발은 흑점의 한 결과입니다... 그것들은 흑점이 많은 자력을 만들어내기 때문에 발생하죠... 그리고 이 자력은 매우 강력해져서 태양의 대기로 들어갑니다... 자, 대기는 이미 많은 자기 에너지를 축적하고 있어요. 대기는 태양으로부터 오는 모든 추가적인 에너지를 담고 있을 수 없어서 일부를 방출해야 하죠. 이 갑작스러운 에너지의 방출이 태양면 폭발을 만들어냅니다... 이 사진을 보면, 태양면 폭발이 빛의 밝은 섬광처럼 나타난다는 것을 볼 수 있을 거예요. 각각의 섬광은 강한 폭발입니다... 수백만 개의 폭탄이 한 번에 터지는 것과 비슷하죠. 그것들은 대전입자의 구름을 우주로 방출합니다. 입자의 일부는 지구에까지 이른다고 알려져 있어요. 그것들은 지구의 자기장을 방해하고 다른 부정적인 영향들을 초래합니다.

HACKERS TEST

p.38

1. (B) Main Purpose/Topic	2. (C) Detail	3. (B) Detail
4. (B) Detail	5. (A), (C), (D) Detail	6. (C) Main Purpose/Topic
7. (D) Detail	8. (D) Detail	9. (D) Detail
10. (B) Detail	11. (A), (D) Detail	12. (B) Main Purpose/Topic
13. (C) Detail	14. (D) Detail	15. (B) Detail
16. (A) Detail	17. (A), (D) Detail	18. (A), (D) Main Purpose/Topic
19. (B) Detail	20. (D) Detail	21. (D) Detail
22. (B), (C), (D) Detail	23. (D) Main Purpose/Topic	24. (B) Detail
25. (A), (C) Detail	26. (D) Detail	27. (B), (D) Detail
28. (A) Detail	29. (A) Main Purpose/Topic	30. (B) Detail
31. (B) Detail	32. (A), (C), (E) Detail	33. (C) Detail
34. (A), (C) Detail		

[1-5]
Listen to a conversation in a listening lab.

W: Hi. May I help you with something?

M: Yeah, um, this is the listening lab, right?

W: Yep! What do you need?

M: Well, you see, ᴼ¹ I'm in Spanish 105 and my teacher gave us an assignment three or four weeks ago to watch some movie . . . I can't remember the title . . . *Los* something, I think . . . I know it's about, um, well, it's based on Mexican rituals.

W: It sounds like what you're looking for is *Los Ojos de Dios*. Am I right?

M: Wow, impressive! How did you know that?

W: We've had quite a lot of students coming in this week to view it. Apparently there is some, uh, some test or something next week, right?

M: Actually, the test is at the end of this week. That means I have only three days to watch the movie. We have to write an essay on the plot of the film . . . and the essay counts for, like, one-third of the grade. I'm really pushing the limits this time!

W: Well, I'm afraid I have some unfortunate news. ᴼ² There was a problem with the TV/VCR, so you won't be able to view any tapes today. It seems to have been eating all of the videos.

M: What? That can't be . . . When will it be available again?

W: We sent it in to the technical services department earlier this afternoon, which means it should be back sometime tomorrow around, oh, midday or so. ᴼ³ We tried to fix it ourselves, but, well . . . we're just part-time workers, you know. So we don't really have the technical know-how to deal with that kind of thing.

M: So then I can come in tomorrow afternoon or early evening and view the tape?

W: Uh-huh. ᴼ⁴ Wait! I'm sorry . . . I should mention that there are four other students on the waiting list. They will get first priority, so if they show up tomorrow, there may not be any time slots open. But you never know if the students will come or not. Either way, it may be worth checking back . . . Who knows, you might just get lucky.

M: OK, I'll try that. But just in case, are there any other possibilities? My test is in three days and I absolutely must see this film to pass. What do you recommend that I do?

W: Well, you have a couple of options. ᴼ⁵ The first is to try your luck waiting around until the TV/VCR is available. If it isn't back on time, well, that could present a problem . . . ᴼ⁵ Another option is to see if it is at any of the local video stores. I mean, one of the rental shops has to have it. The only problem might be that other students got the same idea . . . and in that case, it might already be rented out. ᴼ⁵ You could also look online to see if it's available for download.

M: Oh, right. Actually, one of my friends works at the rental shop down on Washington Street, so he might be able to help me out. If that doesn't work, I'll check online. I really appreciate your help and advice.

W: No problem . . . I'm just doing my job.

Now get ready to answer the questions. You may use your notes to help you answer.

1. Why does the student visit the listening lab?
2. What does the woman say about the TV/VCR?
3. According to the conversation, what is a reason the listening lab staff had the TV/VCR brought to the technical services department?

CHAPTER 1

Hackers **TOEFL** Listening Intermediate

4. Why does the woman hesitate to give the man a time slot for the day after?

5. According to the conversation, what are some ways the man can resolve his problem if the TV/VCR is not returned the next day?

W: 안녕하세요. 무엇을 도와드릴까요?

M: 네, 음, 여기가 청취 실습실이죠, 맞죠?

W: 네! 무엇이 필요하세요?

M: 음, 그러니까, 저는 스페인어 105 수업을 듣는데 교수님께서 3, 4주 전에 어떤 영화를 보는 과제를 내주셨어요... 제목이 기억나지 않네요... 제 생각에, 'Los' 뭔가인 것 같은데... 그건, 음, 저, 멕시코의 종교적인 의식에 근거한 것이라는 건 알고 있어요.

W: 학생은 'Los Ojos de Dios'를 찾고 있는 것 같은데요? 맞나요?

M: 와, 대단해요! 그걸 어떻게 아셨어요?

W: 이번 주에 그것을 보러 온 학생들이 꽤 많았거든요. 보아하니 어떤, 어, 시험이나 무언가가 다음 주에 있는 것 같던데, 맞죠?

M: 사실, 이번 주 말에 시험이 있어요. 제가 영화를 볼 시간이 단 3일 밖에 없다는 뜻이죠. 저희는 영화의 줄거리에 대한 보고서를 써야 해요... 그리고 그 보고서는, 그러니까, 성적의 약 3분의 1 정도를 차지하고요. 전 이번에 정말 한계를 달리고 있어요!

W: 음, 좋지 않은 소식을 알려줘야 해서 유감이네요. TV/VCR에 문제가 있어서, 오늘은 어떠한 테이프도 볼 수가 없어요. 그게 모든 비디오를 망가뜨리고 있는 것 같거든요.

M: 뭐라고요? 그럴 리 없어요... 언제 다시 사용할 수 있나요?

W: 오늘 이른 오후에 그것을 기술 서비스 부서로 보냈으니, 내일 중, 오, 정오쯤이나 돌아올 겁니다. 우리가 직접 고치려고 노력해 봤어요, 하지만, 음... 그러니까, 우리는 그저 시간제 근로자라서 말이죠. 그래서 사실 그런 종류의 문제를 다룰 수 있는 기술적인 요령이 없어요.

M: 그렇다면 제가 내일 오후나 초저녁에 와서 테이프를 볼 수 있나요?

W: 네. 잠깐만요! 미안한데... 대기자 명단에 4명의 다른 학생들이 있다는 것을 말해줘야겠네요. 그 학생들에게 우선권이 있기 때문에, 그들이 내일 온다면, 빈 시간대가 없을지도 몰라요. 하지만 그 학생들이 올지 안 올지는 알 수 없죠. 어찌 됐건, 다시 확인하는 것이 좋을 거예요... 누가 알아요, 학생에게 운이 따를 수도 있죠.

M: 네, 그렇게 할게요. 하지만 만약을 대비해서, 다른 어떤 방법이 있을까요? 시험이 3일 후인데 통과하려면 반드시 이 영화를 봐야만 하거든요. 제가 어떻게 하는 게 좋을까요?

W: 음, 두 가지 방법이 있어요. 첫째는 TV/VCR이 사용 가능할 때까지 기다리면서 학생의 운을 시험해 보는 거예요. 그게 제시간에 돌아오지 않는다면, 음, 문제가 될 수도 있겠죠... 다른 방법은 아무 동네 비디오 대여점에 가서 테이프가 있는지 찾아보는 겁니다. 제 말은, 대여점 중 한 곳은 꼭 가지고 있을 거예요. 유일한 문제는 다른 학생들도 같은 생각을 했을 수 있다는 거죠... 그리고 그런 경우에는, 그게 이미 대여되었겠네요. 또 학생은 온라인에서 그 영화를 내려받는 것이 가능한지 찾아볼 수도 있고요.

M: 오, 맞아요. 사실, 제 친구 중 한 명이 Washington 가에 있는 대여점에서 일해요, 그러니까 그 친구가 저를 도와줄 수도 있겠네요. 그게 안 되면, 온라인을 확인해 봐야겠어요. 도와주고 조언해 주셔서 정말 감사합니다.

W: 아닙니다... 이게 제 일인 걸요.

어휘

ritual[rítʃuəl] (종교적인) 의식 impressive[imprésiv] 대단한 apparently[əpǽrəntli] 보아하니 midday[míddèi] 정오 know-how[nóuhàu] 요령 priority[praió:rəti] 우선권 time slot 시간대 rental shop 대여점

[6-11]

Listen to part of a lecture on biology.

In the last lecture, I talked about the various traits that allow animals such as camels to survive in desert ecosystems. For example, we discussed how they almost never perspire . . . even in high temperatures. This, uh, ensures that they don't waste bodily fluids and increases the length of time they can go without water. Q6 Today's topic isn't too different—it's another reaction to environmental conditions, a certain type of response that's unique to only a few animals. In short, hibernation.

Now, it's important that you don't confuse hibernation with dormancy . . . They are actually quite different. I'll give a few examples to help clarify what I mean. So, when you think about hibernation, what's the prototypical animal you think of? Bears, right? [Q7] So what do bears do during winter? Are they passed out in a cave for four or five months straight? Not exactly. Bears will get up occasionally—every few days or so—and they'll have a bite to eat, you know . . . and they'll go to the bathroom and, oh, yeah, the females will even give birth to their cubs! [Q11] Also, a bear's temperature will only drop from around 38 degrees to about 34. This is too minor a change to be considered hibernation, so it's incorrect when people say that bears hibernate . . . they actually enter a state of dormancy, which is like very deep sleep. [Q8] During this dormant period, bears are able to conserve energy because their heart rates are lowered and their metabolisms are suppressed.

Also, reptiles like turtles and snakes . . . even though it seems like they hibernate, they don't. However, the reason that they cannot be considered hibernators is different from the one I gave for bears. You see, to hibernate, an animal needs to be able to control its body temperature . . . it's got to be warm-blooded. [Q9] Snakes and turtles are cold-blooded, so their body temperature is determined by the environment around them—it fluctuates.

Let's go back and compare the bear to an animal that really hibernates, like a squirrel. [Q11] When the squirrel hibernates . . . even though it is a warm-blooded creature, its body temperature falls very low. In extremely cold climates, this means a squirrel's temperature might reach one or two degrees below freezing! Strangely enough, squirrels warm up during their hibernation every 15 or 20 days, usually staying awake for less than a day. And just like the bears, they'll go to the bathroom and maybe eat something. [Q10] During hibernation, though, animals typically live off of their fat reserves. They'll eat and eat and eat as winter approaches, fatten up, and then burn the fat over the winter for energy to keep alive.

[Q11] Another big difference between "deep sleepers" like the bear and hibernators like the squirrel is their awareness when hibernating. If there's some sort of emergency, the bear can wake up immediately and respond. This is why bears are dangerous, even when they're dormant—we know not to call it hibernation now, right? So don't mess around with them, because they can awaken very easily . . . and you don't want that. In contrast, the squirrel is dead to the world when it hibernates . . . It takes several hours for it to awaken when it goes through its occasional warming-up phases.

Now get ready to answer the questions. You may use your notes to help you answer.

6. What does the professor mainly discuss in the lecture?
7. According to the professor, what is true of bears in the winter?
8. According to the professor, how do dormant bears conserve energy?
9. What does the professor say about snakes and turtles?
10. According to the professor, why do hibernating animals eat more before winter?
11. What are two differences between dormancy and hibernation?

지난번 강의에서, 낙타와 같은 동물들이 사막 생태계에서 살아남을 수 있게 해주는 다양한 특징에 대해 이야기했습니다. 예를 들어, 우리는 낙타가 거의 땀을 흘리지 않는다는 점을 논의했죠... 높은 온도에서도요. 이것은, 음, 그들이 체액을 낭비하지 않도록 해주고 물 없이 버틸 수 있는 시간을 늘려줍니다. 오늘의 주제도 크게 다르지 않아요, 환경 조건의 변화에 대한 또 다른 반응인데, 몇몇 동물에게 만 유일하게 보이는 특정 유형의 것이죠. 짧게 말해, 동면입니다.

자, 여러분이 동면을 휴면과 혼동하지 않는 것이 중요합니다... 그것들은 실제로 매우 다르거든요. 제 말이 무슨 뜻인지 명확하게 해줄 만한 몇 가지 예를 들어 볼게요. 자, 동면에 대해 생각할 때, 떠오르는 대표적인 동물이 무엇인가요? 곰이에요, 그렇죠? 그럼 곰은 겨울 동안 무엇을 할까요? 4, 5개월 내내 동굴에 쓰러져 있을까요? 사실 그렇지는 않아요. 곰은 때때로, 그러니까, 며칠에 한 번씩 일어나서 조금씩 먹을 거예요... 그리고 화장실에도 가고, 오, 네, 암컷들은 새끼를 낳기도 해요! 또한, 곰의 체온은 38도에서 약 34도 정도로만 떨어질 겁니다. 이는 동면이라고 하기에는 너무 작은 변화예요, 그래서 곰이 동면한다고 하는 건 틀린 말이죠... 실제로는 휴면 상태, 즉 아주 깊은 잠에 빠지는 거니까요. 이 휴면 기간 동안, 곰은 심박수가 줄고 신진대사가 억제되기 때문에 에너지를 보존할 수 있는 거예요.

또한, 거북이나 뱀과 같은 파충류들은... 비록 그들이 동면하는 것처럼 보이지만, 그게 아닙니다. 하지만, 그들이 동면하는 동물로 여겨질 수 없는 이유는 제가 곰에 대해서 제시한 것과는 달라요. 그러니까, 동면을 하기 위해서는, 동물이 체온을 조절할 수 있어야 해요... 정온 동물이어야 하죠. 뱀과 거북은 변온 동물이라서, 그들의 체온은 주위 환경에 의해 결정돼요, 변동하는 거죠.

다시 돌아가서 다람쥐와 같이, 정말로 동면을 하는 동물과 곰을 비교해 봅시다. 다람쥐가 동면할 때... 정온 동물임에도 불구하고, 체온은 아주 낮게 떨어져요. 극도로 추운 기후에서, 이는 다람쥐의 체온이 영하 1, 2도까지 내려갈 수 있다는 것을 의미해요! 참으로 이상하게도, 다람쥐는 15일 또는 20일마다 동면에서 깨어나, 보통 하루가 채 안 되게 깨어 있습니다. 그리고 마치 곰처럼, 화장실에 가고 아마 뭔가를 먹기도 해요. 하지만, 동면 중에, 동물들은 보통 지방 저장물로 살아갑니다. 그들은 겨울이 다가올수록 먹고 또 먹고 또 먹어서, 살을 찌우고, 겨울 동안 살아남기 위해 지방을 태워 에너지를 만들죠.

곰과 같은 "깊은 잠꾼"과 다람쥐와 같이 동면하는 동물들의 또 다른 커다란 차이점은 동면 중의 의식이에요. 만약 어떤 긴급 상황이 생긴다면, 곰은 즉시 일어나서 반응할 수 있어요. 이것이 바로 곰이 휴면하고 있더라도, 위험한 이유예요, 이제 이걸 동면이라고 부르면 안 된다는 것을 알겠죠, 그렇죠? 그러니까 그들 주위에서 장난치지 마세요, 아주 쉽게 깨어날 수 있으니까요... 그리고 여러분은 그걸 원하지 않겠죠. 반면, 다람쥐는 동면할 때 세상 모르고 죽은 듯이 잡니다... 다람쥐는 때때로 몸을 따뜻하게 만드는 단계를 거쳐 깨어나는데 이것은 몇 시간이 걸려요.

어휘

ecosystem[ékousìstəm] 생태계 perspire[pərspáiər] 땀을 흘리다 bodily fluid 체액 hibernation[hàibərnéiʃən] 동면 dormancy[dɔ́ːrmənsi] 휴면 prototypical[pròutətípikəl] 대표적인 pass out 쓰러지다 give birth to ~을 낳다 cub[kʌb] 새끼 warm-blooded[wɔ̀ːrmblʌ́did] 정온의 cold-blooded[kòuldblʌ́did] 변온의 fluctuate[flʌ́ktʃuèit] 변동하다 live off 살아가다 reserve[rizə́ːrv] 저장물 awareness[əwɛ́ərnis] 의식 mess around 장난치다

[12-17]

Listen to part of a lecture from an art history class.

P: OK . . . until the end of the 15th century, all painters followed the same basic rules. They placed the main subject of the painting in the foreground . . . usually, a person. Q12 The background included less important elements . . . decorative items like a vase of flowers, for example. But in the 16th century, Dutch artists began making these objects the focus of their paintings. This new form of art was called still life . . .

The rise of this style of painting occurred during a period of exploration in European history. Q13 Um, Europeans took many voyages to Asia, Africa, and the Americas in the 16th century. After they returned, they published books that included detailed visual depictions of items from these regions. As a result, many artists came to appreciate the beauty of objects. They began paying attention to how they rendered these objects in paintings . . . often moving them to the foreground in place of human subjects. Q14 *Butcher's Stall with the Flight into Egypt* is a good example of this trend. This painting was completed in 1551 by the Dutch artist Peter Aertsen. Here . . . take a look at the picture on the screen. What do you notice about it?

S1: Um, it's mostly just dishes, pieces of meat, and, uh, tools . . . What you would expect to see in any butcher's shop, I guess.

P: Exactly. The foreground is filled with specific and detailed objects . . . and the people are in the background. Soon artists began leaving people out of their paintings altogether . . . This is where we get the term still life, actually . . . it comes from the fact that a painting's subjects are not alive.

Now, in the early 17th century, the Dutch Republic experienced something called tulip mania . . . Uh, the Dutch became obsessed with these flowers. This led many artists to create still life paintings of different colored tulips. Q15 The paintings were popular with wealthy patrons because, um, tulips were incredibly expensive. So they were considered symbols of high status. Um, and even though the popularity of tulips diminished over time, the demand for still life paintings stayed high . . . especially among the members of the upper classes. Dutch artists responded by producing works that appealed to these people . . . Q16 A common scene is a tabletop decorated with items that only the wealthy could afford . . . gold and silver dishes, glass items, gourmet foods . . . things like that. A new trend also developed around this time. Um, by today's standards, it's a little strange . . . I'm talking about paintings of dead animals.

S2: Dead animals? Why would anyone want a painting of that?

P: Well, hunting was a favorite hobby among the wealthy. And to remind them of successful hunts, they often hung the heads of dead animals on their walls . . . These paintings had the same function. Noblemen decorated their houses with them. Q17 And I should say, the artists worked very hard to make these paintings appeal to hunters. Um, first of all . . . they added extra details to, well . . . to make the paintings more realistic. For example, the animals are posed specifically to look like they've just been killed. In addition, the paintings often depict the bodies of animals in their actual size. Um, this is particularly common for paintings of small animals such as ducks . . . The result is a painting that creates the illusion of freshly killed animals hanging on the wall.

Now get ready to answer the questions. You may use your notes to help you answer.

12. What is the main topic of the lecture?
13. What inspired many artists to focus on depicting objects?
14. What does the professor say about *Butcher's Stall with the Flight into Egypt*?
15. Why were Dutch people interested in paintings of tulips?
16. What is a characteristic of the tabletop scenes painted by 17th-century Dutch artists?
17. What qualities of still life paintings appealed to hunters?

P: 자... 15세기 말까지, 모든 화가들은 동일한 기본 규칙을 따랐어요. 그들은 그림의 주요 대상을 전경에 배치했습니다... 일반적으로, 인물이었죠. 배경은 덜 중요한 요소들을 포함했어요... 예를 들면, 꽃병과 같은 장식용 물건 말이에요. 그러나 16세기에, 네덜란드 화가들은 이러한 물건들을 그들 그림의 중심으로 만들기 시작했습니다. 이 새로운 형태의 미술은 정물화라고 불렸죠...
이 화풍의 발생은 유럽 역사에서 탐험의 시기 동안 일어났습니다. 음, 16세기에 유럽인들은 아시아, 아프리카, 그리고 아메리카로 많은 항해를 떠났어요. 돌아온 후, 그들은 이 지역에서 가져온 물건들의 상세한 시각적 묘사를 포함한 책을 출판했습니다. 결과적으로, 많은 화가들은 물체의 아름다움에 대한 진가를 인정하게 되었죠. 그들은 이러한 물체를 어떻게 그림에 표현할지에 주목하기 시작했습니다... 주로 그것들을 인물 대상 대신 전경으로 옮기면서 말이죠. 'Butcher's Stall with the Flight into Egypt'는 이 추세의 좋은 예입니다. 이 그림은 1551년에 네덜란드 화가인 피테르 아르트센에 의해 완성되었어요. 여기... 화면에 그림을 한번 보세요. 여러분들은 무엇을 알아챘나요?

S1: 음, 주로 접시, 고기 조각, 그리고, 어, 도구들뿐이네요... 제 생각에는, 어느 푸줏간에서든 볼 거라고 예상하는 것들이요.

P: 정확해요. 전경은 구체적이고 상세한 물체들로 가득 차 있고... 사람들은 배경에 있죠. 화가들은 곧 그들의 그림에서 인물을 완전히 빼기 시작했습니다... 사실, 바로 여기서 정물화라는 용어가 나왔어요... 그림의 대상이 살아있는 것이 아니라는 사실로부터 온 거죠.
자, 17세기 초에, 네덜란드 공화국은 튤립 파동이라고 불리는 것을 겪었습니다... 어, 네덜란드는 이 꽃에 사로잡혔어요. 이는 많은 화가가 다양한 색상의 튤립 정물화를 그리도록 했습니다. 그 그림들은 부유한 고객들에게 인기 있었고요. 음, 튤립이 엄청나게 비쌌기 때문이죠. 그래서 그것들은 높은 지위의 상징으로 여겨졌거든요. 음, 그리고 시간이 지나면서 튤립의 인기가 줄어들었음에도 불구하고, 정물화에 대한 수요는 계속해서 높았어요... 특히 상류층 구성원들 사이에서요. 네덜란드 화가들은 이러한 사람들의 마음을 끄는 작품을 그림으로써 부응했죠... 흔한 장면은 부자들만이 살 여유가 있었던 물건들로 장식된 탁자 윗면이었어요...

금과 은으로 된 접시, 유리 물품, 고급 식료품... 그런 것들이요. 이 시기 즈음에 새로운 추세 또한 발달했습니다. 음, 오늘날의 기준으로, 약간은 이상해요... 죽은 동물들의 그림에 대해 이야기할 겁니다.

S2: 죽은 동물들이요? 왜 누군가가 그런 그림을 원한 거죠?

P: 음, 부자들 사이에서 사냥은 인기 있는 취미였거든요. 그리고 성공적인 사냥을 되새기기 위해, 그들은 종종 벽에 죽은 동물들의 머리를 걸어 놓았죠... 이 그림들은 같은 기능을 했고요. 귀족들은 이것들로 집을 장식했어요. 그리고, 화가들은 이 그림이 사냥꾼의 마음을 끌도록 매우 열심히 그렸다는 것을 이야기해야겠군요. 음, 우선... 그들은 추가적인 세부사항을 더했어요, 음... 그림을 더 사실적으로 만들기 위해서요. 예를 들어, 동물들은 구체적으로 막 죽임을 당한 것처럼 보이도록 자세가 취해졌죠. 게다가, 흔히 동물들의 실제 몸 크기를 묘사했습니다. 음, 이건 오리와 같은 작은 동물 그림에서 특히 흔했어요... 결과는 갓 죽임을 당해 벽에 걸려있는 동물의 환상을 만들어내는 그림이었죠.

어휘

foreground[fɔ́ːrgràund] (그림·사진 등의) 전경 decorative[dékərətiv] 장식용의 still life 정물화 voyage[vɔ́iidʒ] 항해
appreciate[əpríːʃièit] 진가를 인정하다 butcher[bútʃər] 푸줏간 leave out ~을 빼다 tulip mania 튤립 파동
obsess[əbsés] 사로잡다 diminish[dimíniʃ] 줄어들다 appeal to 마음을 끌다 afford[əfɔ́ːrd] ~을 살 여유가 있다
gourmet food 고급 식료품 remind[rimáind] 되새기다 nobleman[nóublmən] 귀족 illusion[ilúːʒən] 환상

[18-22]

Listen to a conversation between a student and an academic advisor.

P: Hello, Matt. I wasn't expecting to see you today.

S: Hi, Mrs. Nelson. Yeah, I, uh, have a problem I need to talk with you about.

P: Hmm . . . well, have a seat and tell me what's on your mind.

S: You see, [Q18] I'm having a lot of trouble in the comparative literature course I signed up for this semester . . . Literature 401, uh, French Deconstructionist Theory, you know, with Professor Fielding. It is terribly hard for me to understand what is going on in that class.

P: Well, literary theory is not an easy subject . . . and if you throw in French deconstruction, well, you're talking about something that is certainly no picnic. [Q19] Matt, trust me, I'm sure you aren't the only one struggling.

S: I know, but I don't get anything that the professor talks about, much less the readings. [Q20] I took this class to broaden my perspective and to dabble in theoretical study. Actually, one of my friends is a comparative literature major and she recommended the course. She said it would be really interesting, but now I'm not so sure . . .

P: All right, Matt, I understand what you are saying basically, but can you be more specific? What exactly is the problem in the course?

S: OK, well, [Q21] my biggest problem is that I can't keep up with the other students in the discussion sessions. It seems that everyone else gets it, but I'm totally in the dark. They might as well be speaking Greek! I think I'm better off sticking to math and the sciences. [Q18] I never should have registered for the course . . . I'm wondering if I should just drop it.

P: [Q22] Um, since you've already completed half of the semester, if you drop out, you won't be able to replace it with another class . . . and, of course, your transcript will show that you withdrew from the course. I can assure you that's not something you necessarily want on your academic record.

S: On the other hand, if I stay in, it's very unlikely that I'll get a good grade on the final exam. It's an essay test that is designed to demonstrate our ability to write, plus our comprehension of deconstructionist theory. Not only am I poor at writing—actually, I have no idea what deconstruction even means. That kind of stuff is way over my head.

P: Basically you have two choices at this point. [Q22] You can drop the class now, but that will bring your semester credit load down, which means, of course, that you won't have the status of full-time student. The, um, downside to that is you'll probably lose some or even all the financial aid you're getting for this term.

S: That doesn't sound like a great option . . . What's the other one?

P: Very simply, you can stay in the class and do your best. I highly recommend that you seek extra help at the GUTS Tutorial Service Center, where students can get free tutoring in any subject offered on campus. Have you heard about it?

S: Um, yeah, I think so. It is over at Memorial Hall, right?

P: Right. It's on the second floor, across from the International Studies Office. Anyway, I'd also say that you'll be better off requesting a graduate student assistant, since the course you are taking is of such an advanced nature. Also, the undergraduate tutors aren't exactly screened appropriately.

S: I—I'm thinking it is better to, uh, to give it a try. Thank you so much for your help, professor.

Now get ready to answer the questions. You may use your notes to help you answer.

18. What are the speakers mainly discussing?

19. What does the advisor say about the comparative literature course?

20. Why did the student initially decide to take the course?

21. According to the conversation, what is the main reason the student is thinking of dropping the class?

22. According to the conversation, what are some reasons for not dropping the course?

P: 안녕, Matt. 나는 오늘 너를 볼 거라고 예상하지 않았는데.

S: 안녕하세요, Nelson 교수님. 네, 저는, 어, 교수님과 얘기해야 할 문제가 있어서요.

P: 흠... 자, 앉아서 마음속에 있는 것을 말해 보렴.

S: 그러니까, 이번 학기에 수강하는 비교 문학 수업에서 어려움을 많이 겪고 있어요... 문학 401, 어, 그러니까, Fielding 교수님의, 프랑스 해체주의 이론 수업이요. 수업에서 진행되는 것을 이해하는 게 저에게는 너무 어려워요.

P: 음, 문학 이론은 쉬운 과목이 아니란다... 게다가 프랑스 해체주의를 공부한다면, 음, 네가 말하는 건 분명 쉬운 게 아니지. Matt, 정말이지, 힘들어하는 학생이 너 혼자는 아닐 거야.

S: 알아요, 하지만 저는 교수님이 말씀하시는 것을 하나도 이해할 수가 없어요, 읽을 거리는 더 그렇고요. 제 시야를 넓히고 이론적인 공부를 한 번 해 보려고 이 수업을 신청했어요. 사실, 제 친구 중 한 명이 비교 문학 전공인데 그녀가 이 과목을 추천해줬거든요. 그녀는 이게 굉장히 흥미로울 거라고 말했지만, 이젠 잘 모르겠네요...

P: 그래, Matt, 기본적으로 무슨 말인지는 알겠는데, 좀 더 구체적으로 말해줄래? 그 수업에서 문제가 정확히 뭐니?

S: 네, 음, 가장 큰 문제는 토론 시간에 다른 학생들을 따라갈 수가 없다는 거예요. 다른 사람들은 모두 이해하는 것 같은데, 저만 아무 것도 모르고 있어요. 그들이 그리스어를 말한다고 해도 별 차이는 없을 거예요! 수학과 과학을 계속하는 편이 나을 것 같아요. 절대 이 수업을 신청하지 말았어야 했어요... 이 수업을 그냥 수강 취소할까 고민 중이에요.

P: 음, 너는 이미 학기의 반을 끝냈기 때문에, 만약 수강을 취소한다면, 다른 수업으로 대체할 수 없을 거야... 그리고, 물론, 네 성적표는 네가 그 수업을 취소했다는 것을 보여줄 거란다. 장담하건데 그런 건 학적 기록에 반드시 남기고 싶은 것이 아니겠지.

S: 반면에, 제가 계속 남아 있는다면, 기말고사에서 좋은 성적을 받을 가능성이 희박해요. 해체주의 이론을 이해했는지에 덧붙여, 글 쓰는 능력을 보이도록 만들어진 논술 시험이거든요. 저는 글쓰기를 잘 못할 뿐만 아니라, 사실, 해체가 무엇을 뜻하는지도 모르거든요. 이런 종류의 것은 제 수준 밖이에요.

P: 이 시점에서 기본적으로 두 가지 방법이 있단다. 지금 수강을 취소할 수도 있지만, 그렇게 되면 네 학점 이수량이 줄어들 거고, 그럼, 당연히, 넌 정규 학생의 상태가 아니게 되는 거야. 그것의, 음, 단점은 아마 네가 이번 학기에 받는 학비 지원의 일부 또는 전체를 잃게 될 거라는 것이지.

S: 그건 좋은 대안이 아닌 것 같아요... 다른 하나는 뭐죠?

P: 아주 간단히, 수업을 계속 들으면서 최선을 다하는 거야. GUTS 개별 지도 서비스 센터에서 별도의 도움을 얻는 것을 강력하게 추천할게, 그곳에서는 학생들이 교내에 개설된 모든 수업에 대한 무료 개별 지도를 받을 수 있거든. 들어 본 적 있니?

S: 음, 네, 그런 것 같아요. Memorial 홀에 있는 거죠, 그렇죠?

P: 맞아. 국제 연구소 맞은편, 2층에 있단다. 어쨌든, 대학원생 조교를 요청하는 게 더 좋을 거라는 것도 말해주고 싶구나, 네가 듣는 수업이 너무 고급 단계니까 말이야. 게다가, 학부생 개별 교사들은 사실 제대로 선발되지 않거든.

S: 저, 저는, 어, 한 번 시도해 보는 게 좋을 것 같아요. 도와주셔서 정말 감사합니다, 교수님.

어휘

comparative literature 비교 문학   deconstructionist theory 해체주의 이론   broaden[brɔːdn] 넓히다
perspective[pərspéktiv] 시야   dabble in 한 번 해 보다   theoretical[θìːərétikəl] 이론적인   keep up with ~을 따라가다
in the dark 모르는   might as well do ~해도 별 차이 없다   stick to 계속하다   demonstrate[démənstrèit] (증명해) 보이다
at this point 이 시점에서   full-time student 정규 학생   financial aid 학비 지원   tutorial[tjuːtɔ́ːriəl] 개별 지도의
advanced[ædvǽnst] 고급 단계의   undergraduate[ʌ̀ndərgrǽdʒuət] 학부생   tutor[tjúːtər] 개별 교사   screen[skriːn] 선발하다
appropriately[əpróuprièitli] 제대로   give it a try 한 번 시도해 보다

[23-28]

Listen to part of a lecture in a history class.

P: You all probably know that Johannes Gutenberg contributed much to the technology of printing . . . including the invention of the mechanical printing press. And he developed an oil-based ink just for his printing press. Water-based ink has the advantage of drying quickly, but oil ink is stickier, so it attaches to the metal blocks more effectively. Q23 What I want to focus on today, though, are the inventions that came before Gutenberg's printing press, that were stepping stones to it. So . . . can anyone think of an invention that helped make the printing press possible?

S: Well, this may sound silly, but the letters in printed books are small, and my grandma couldn't read until we got her a pair of reading glasses. Perhaps the invention of eyeglasses was a stepping stone?

P: Q24 Yes, it's true that books became more popular after eyeglasses were invented and made it possible for many people to see small print. But there's a major invention that preceded the printing press, and Gutenberg is widely considered to be its inventor . . . metal movable type . . . It's a system of printing that uses detachable pieces, each of which represents a letter, punctuation mark, or character. It was unquestionably an improvement on the woodblock method already in use in Europe. That method of printing used a block of wood. The wood was cut away and what was left behind formed the characters or image to be printed. It was first developed in Asia, but Europeans used the woodblock method to print images on cloth. Anyhow . . . Q25 so movable type is certainly more durable than woodblock. But . . . did Gutenberg really invent movable type?

S: Hmm . . . I'm going to say yes. I mean, before him, they had scribes who copied documents by hand, right?

P: You know what? The Chinese would be surprised to hear your response. Q25 They were using a system of movable characters about 400 years before Gutenberg developed his own version in AD 1450. Let me point out that, although the Chinese invented movable type, Q26 woodblock printing was certainly better suited for Chinese writing system, which consists of more than 40,000 characters. A woodblock could be used again and again to reproduce a page of text or an entire scroll. But if you used movable type, just think of how time-consuming it'd be to rearrange tens of thousands of mobile metal characters in order to print something . . . What a tedious task that would have been!

The Chinese inventor Bi Sheng created the first movable-type system in AD 1040. His type was made of baked clay. He took an iron plate and set his clay types close together, and when the frame was full, he had one solid block of type. He heated up the plate to make it warm. The warmed-up plate softened the clay. Then Bi Sheng took a smooth board and pressed it onto the clay types so that they would all be of the same height. He then inked his clay types and pressed them on paper. When he wasn't using them, he wrapped them in paper and stored them carefully. Q27 If they needed to be used again, they had to be reset on the iron plate and reheated. Now, Bi Sheng's clay types were fragile, so it wasn't practical to apply them to large-scale printing jobs.

Q25 Actually, metal movable type was first created in Korea in the 13th century . . . Q28 but in fairness to Gutenberg, he invented the molds that allowed for mass production of individual pieces of metal type, with each character on a separate block. Before this, each piece of metal type had to be individually carved by hand.

Now get ready to answer the questions. You may use your notes to help you answer.

23. What is the main topic of the lecture?
24. According to the lecture, in what way were eyeglasses helpful in spurring the invention of the printing press?
25. What does the professor say about Gutenberg's metal movable type?
26. According to the professor, why was woodblock printing superior to movable type for Chinese texts?
27. According to the professor, what are two characteristics of Bi Sheng's invention?
28. According to the professor, what is the significance of Gutenberg's molds?

P: 아마 여러분 모두 요하네스 구텐베르크가 인쇄 기술에 대단히 공헌했다는 걸 알고 있을 거예요... 인쇄기의 발명을 포함해서 말이죠. 그리고 그는 자신의 인쇄기에만을 위한 유성 잉크를 개발했어요. 수성 잉크는 빨리 마른다는 장점이 있지만, 유성 잉크는 더 끈적거려서, 금속판에 더 효과적으로 붙죠. 하지만, 오늘 제가 초점을 맞추고 싶은 건, 구텐베르크의 인쇄기 이전에 나온 발명품들이에요, 그것에 발판이 된 것들 말이죠. 그래서... 인쇄기를 만드는 것이 가능하도록 도운 발명품을 생각해 볼 사람 있나요?

S: 음, 우습게 들릴 수도 있지만, 인쇄된 책의 글자는 작잖아요, 그래서 저희 할머니는 저희가 돋보기를 사드리기 전까지 책을 읽으실 수가 없었거든요. 어쩌면 안경의 발명이 발판이 될 수도 있었겠는데요?

P: 맞아요, 안경이 발명되어 많은 사람이 작은 활자를 보는 것이 가능하게 된 이후로 책은 더 인기를 얻었죠. 하지만 인쇄기보다 앞선 대단한 발명품이 있었고, 구텐베르크가 이것의 발명가로 널리 인정되고 있어요... 금속 가동 활자... 이것은 분리할 수 있는 조각들을 사용하는 인쇄 방식으로, 각각의 조각은 글자, 문장 부호, 또는 문자를 나타내요. 의심할 나위 없이 이미 유럽에서 사용되고 있던 목판법이 발전된 것이죠. 목판 인쇄술은 나무판을 사용했어요. 나무를 잘라내고 거기에 인쇄될 문자나 그림을 남기는 거였어요. 이것은 아시아에서 처음 개발되었지만, 유럽 사람들은 옷감에 그림을 찍어내기 위해 목판법을 사용했어요. 어쨌든... 그래서 가동 활자는 목판보다 분명 더 내구성이 있어요. 하지만... 구텐베르크가 정말 가동 활자를 발명했을까요?

S: 흠... 저는 그렇다고 생각해요. 제 말은, 그가 있기 전에는, 손으로 문서를 베끼는 필경사들이 있었잖아요, 그렇죠?

P: 그거 알고 있나요? 중국인들이 학생의 대답을 들으면 놀랄 거예요. 그들은 구텐베르크가 서기 1450년에 자신만의 방식을 개발하기 400년쯤 전부터 이미 가동 활자 방식을 사용하고 있었거든요. 이 점을 이야기해야겠군요, 중국인들이 가동 활자를 발명하긴 했지만, 중국 문자 체계에는 분명 목판법이 더 적합했어요, 40,000개가 넘는 문자로 이루어져 있기 때문이죠. 목판은 한 페이지의 글 혹은 두루마리 전체를 복제하기 위해 계속해서 다시 사용될 수 있었어요. 하지만 가동 활자를 사용한다면, 무언가를 인쇄하기 위해 수만 개의 금속 가동 활자를 재배열하는 게 얼마나 시간 소모적일지 생각해 보세요... 얼마나 지루한 일이었을까요! 중국인 발명가 비셩은 서기 1040년에 첫 가동 활자 방식을 만들어냈어요. 그의 활자는 구운 찰흙으로 만들어졌죠. 그가 금속판을 꺼내 찰흙 활자들을 서로 가깝게 배치하고, 틀이 가득 차면, 한 개의 단단한 활자판이 완성되는 것이었어요. 그는 그 판을 데워서 따뜻하게 만들었어요. 그 데워진 판은 찰흙을 부드럽게 만들었죠. 그러고 나서 비셩은 평평한 판을 가져와 모든 활자들이 같은 높이가 되도록 찰흙 활자를 눌렀어요. 그런 다음 활자에 잉크를 입혀 종이에 눌러 찍었습니다. 활자를 사용하지 않을 때에는, 종이에 싸서 조심스럽게 보관했어요. 만약 다시 사용해야 할 일이 생기면, 활자들을 금속판에 재배치하고 다시 데워야 했죠. 자, 비셩의 찰흙 활자는 부서지기 쉬워서, 대규모의 인쇄 작업에 사용하기에는 실용적이지 않았습니다.

사실, 금속 가동 활자는 13세기에 한국에서 처음 만들어졌어요... 하지만 구텐베르크에게 공평하게 말하자면, 분리된 조각에 각각의 문자가 새겨져 있는, 개별 금속 활자의 대량 생산을 가능하게 만든 주형은 그가 발명한 거예요. 이전에는, 각각의 금속 활자 조각이 손으로 조각되어야만 했거든요.

어휘

contribute[kəntríbjuːt] 공헌하다 printing press 인쇄기 sticky[stíki] 끈적거리는 stepping stone 발판
precede[prisíːd] 앞서다 movable type 가동 활자 detachable[ditǽtʃəbl] 분리할 수 있는 punctuation mark 문장 부호
unquestionably[ʌ̀nkwéstʃənəbli] 의심할 나위 없이 woodblock[wúdblɑk] 목판 durable[djúərəbl] 내구성 있는
scribe[skraib] 필경사 scroll[skroul] 두루마리 time-consuming[táimkənsùːmiŋ] 시간 소모적인 tedious[tíːdiəs] 지루한
fragile[frǽdʒəl] 부서지기 쉬운 mold[mould] 주형 carve[kɑːrv] 조각하다

[29-34]
Listen to part of a lecture on earth science.

Let's continue our discussion on water hydrology. Just to bring to mind what we discussed the last time, hydrology studies the properties, distribution, and effects of water on the surface of the earth, beneath the surface, and in the atmosphere. Q29 But this time, I'll focus on a specific application of hydrology called snowmelt. Now, some of you might not be aware of there being measurable water coming from snow . . . so let me just briefly explain what snowmelt is. It's the water that's created when the temperature is high enough to melt the snow. Pretty straightforward, huh? Snow melts, and when it does, it turns into water . . .

But snowmelt is special in a sense. Q30 The science of hydrology makes a distinction between snow and other forms of precipitation, such as rain, because it takes significant time for snow to fall and then change into water, which can then become runoff. Why should people be so concerned about snowmelt? Q31 Well, it's an important source of water in many parts of the world. In some areas, it constitutes up to 90 percent of the annual water supply. You see, runoff from snowmelt recharges groundwater supplies and replenishes surface water caches, such as rivers and lakes. So having an accurate measurement makes good water management possible and gives us some idea, whether the needs of nature, residents, farmers, and businesses will be met. So I guess I don't have to tell you how important hydrology is . . . Let's look at the ordinary farmer. You know, changes in the amount of snowmelt from year to year can cause a lot of difficulty . . . in some cases, even disaster. Too much runoff can lead to flooding, right? But too little could lead to drought. What if there was a projected shortfall in snowmelt runoff? Here is where such projections are useful . . . because farmers can make adjustments to make up for water shortage.

They can modify the amount of land to cultivate . . . or choose a different type of crop to plant. They could also apply conservation measures so that the existing water supplies can last through the growing season. And this is where it all makes sense. If the forecast turns out to be true, then the planning will have helped the farmer avoid horrendously large financial losses due to crop failure!

Q29 Now we know why we have to measure runoff and make these projections. Well, just how are these projections made? The extent of snow cover is one factor. At first, it seemed to scientists that this would be easy to measure, but they realized that not all places are the same. Q32 But by adding variables like elevation, wind speed, air temperature, the moisture content of the snow, and the rate at which the snow melts, they were able to get a more accurate measure.

Hold on . . . you might've seen different kinds of snow. There's some that's powdery, some that's icy. Powdery snow contains less moisture and usually produces 60 percent less snowmelt than heavy, wet snow. And the temperature of the air is important because if the snow cover partially melts and then refreezes, you'll have this hard crust, and this'll affect how quickly the snow will melt at a later period. Q33 It's even worse if the weather stays cold. It means there'll be very little early spring snowmelt.

OK . . . going back to those factors . . . Q32 the characteristics of the soil can also affect, I mean, affect just how quickly snowmelt can reach a stream or river. Q34 If the soil is frozen or is mostly clay, it'll absorb less water. In this case, the snowmelt would be unable to seep into the ground and make its way to groundwater storage. What will happen? Well, it'll simply become runoff, and this may increase the possibility of flooding.

Now get ready to answer the questions. You may use your notes to help you answer.

29. What does the professor mainly discuss?
30. According to the professor, what difference is there between snow and other types of precipitation?
31. Why is snowmelt of concern to residents where it occurs?
32. According to the lecture, what are some factors that affect the amount of snowmelt?
33. According to the professor, what is the significance of a long winter?
34. According to the lecture, what are two factors that can cause flooding in areas with snowmelt?

수문학에 대한 논의를 계속해 봅시다. 지난 시간에 논의한 것을 떠올려 보면, 수문학은 지구의 표면, 표면 아래, 그리고 대기에 있는 물의 특성, 분포, 그리고 영향에 대해 연구해요. 그런데 이번 시간에는, 해빙이라고 불리는 수문학의 구체적인 응용에 초점을 맞추어 보겠습니다. 자, 여러분 중 몇몇은 눈에서 상당량의 물이 생겨난다는 것을 모르고 있을 겁니다... 그러니까 해빙이 무엇인지 간단히 설명하도록 할게요. 그것은 눈을 녹일 정도로 충분히 기온이 높을 때 생성되는 물입니다. 꽤 간단해요, 그렇죠? 눈은 녹고, 녹으면, 물이 되는 거죠...

하지만 해빙은 어떻게 보면 특별해요. 수문학이라는 과학은 눈을 비와 같은 강수의 다른 형태와 구별하는데, 그 이유는 눈이 내리고 나서 유거수가 될 수 있는 물로 바뀌는 데는 상당한 시간이 걸리기 때문입니다. 왜 사람들이 해빙에 대해 그렇게 관심을 가져야 할까요? 음, 그것이 세계의 많은 지역에서 물의 중요 원천이 되기 때문입니다. 어떤 지역에서는, 연간 물 공급의 90퍼센트까지 차지하죠. 그러니까, 해빙에서 나온 유거수는 지하수 공급을 재충전하며 강이나 호수 같은, 지표수 저장소를 다시 채웁니다. 그래서, 정확한 측정을 하는 것은 수자원을 잘 관리하도록 하며 자연, 거주자, 농부, 그리고 기업의 필요가 충족될 수 있는지에 대한, 방안을 주는 거죠. 그러니까 수문학이 얼마나 중요한지는 말할 필요가 없을 것 같네요... 평범한 농부를 살펴봅시다. 그러니까, 해마다 해빙의 양이 변하는 것은 많은 어려움을 유발합니다... 어떤 경우에는, 심지어 재해가 되죠. 너무 많은 양의 유거수는 홍수를 초래해요, 그렇죠? 하지만 너무 적으면 가뭄으로 이어질 수도 있습니다. 예측된 해빙 유거수의 부족이 있었다면 어떨까요? 바로 여기서 이러한 예측이 도움이 되는 거예요... 농부들이 물 부족을 보완하기 위한 조정을 할 수 있기 때문이죠.

그들은 경작할 땅의 규모를 조절하거나... 또는 다른 종류의 경작할 작물을 선택할 수도 있습니다. 또한 그들은 현재의 물 공급이 작물이 성장하는 계절 내내 지속될 수 있도록 비축 대책을 마련할 수도 있고요. 그리고 이 모든 것들이 일리 있는 부분이 바로 여기입니다. 그 예측이 사실이라고 판명되면, 그럼 그 계획은 농부들이 흉년으로 인한 끔찍하게 거대한 재정적 손실을 피할 수 있도록 도와줄 거니까요!

이제 우리는 왜 유거수를 측정하고 이러한 예측을 해야 하는지 알고 있습니다. 자, 그럼 어떻게 이러한 예측을 할 수 있을까요? 적설의 범위는 한 가지 요소입니다. 처음에, 과학자들은 눈의 양을 쉽게 측정할 수 있다고 생각했지만, 모든 지역이 똑같지는 않다는 것을 나중에 알게 되었어요. 하지만 고도, 풍속, 기온, 눈의 습기 함유량, 그리고 눈이 녹는 속도와 같은 변수들을 추가함으로써, 그들은 더 정확한 측정을 할 수 있게 되었죠.

잠시만요... 모두들 다양한 종류의 눈을 보았을 거예요. 가루 같은 것도 있고, 얼음 같은 것도 있죠. 가루 같은 눈은 습기를 더 적게 함유하고 있으며 무겁고, 축축한 눈보다 해빙의 양이 보통 60퍼센트 더 적습니다. 그리고 기온도 중요한데 만약 적설이 부분적으로 녹고 다시 얼면, 딱딱한 표면이 형성되며, 이는 나중에 눈이 얼마나 빨리 녹는지에 영향을 주기 때문입니다. 날씨가 계속해서 추우면 더 심각해지죠. 초봄에 해빙이 매우 적을 것을 의미하니까요.

좋아요... 이러한 요인들로 돌아가서... 토양의 특성 또한 영향을 줍니다, 제 말은 해빙이 개울이나 강에 얼마나 빨리 도달하는지에 영향을 준다는 거죠. 토양이 얼었거나 대부분이 진흙이라면, 물을 적게 흡수할 거예요. 이런 경우, 해빙은 땅속으로 스며들지 못하고 지하수 저장소에 도달할 수 없겠죠. 무슨 일이 일어날까요? 음, 그것은 그저 유거수가 되어, 홍수의 가능성을 증가시킬 거예요.

어휘

hydrology[haidrálədʒi] 수문학 application[æ̀pləkéiʃən] 응용 snowmelt[snóumèlt] 해빙
straightforward[strèitfɔ́ːrwərd] 간단한 precipitation[prisìpətéiʃən] 강수 significant[signífikənt] 상당한
runoff[rʌ́nɔ̀ːf] 유거수 constitute[kɑ́nstətjùːt] 차지하다 replenish[ripléniʃ] 다시 채우다 surface water 지표수
cache[kæʃ] 저장소 measurement[méʒərmənt] 측정 resident[rézədənt] 거주자 disaster[dizǽstər] 재해
project[prɑ́dʒekt] 예측하다 shortfall[ʃɔ́ːrtfɔ̀ːl] 부족 adjustment[ədʒʌ́stmənt] 조정 shortage[ʃɔ́ːrtidʒ] 부족
modify[mɑ́dəfài] 조절하다 cultivate[kʌ́ltəvèit] 경작하다 conservation[kɑ̀nsərvéiʃən] 비축 measure[méʒər] 대책
variable[vέəriəbl] 변수 elevation[èləvéiʃən] 고도 moisture[mɔ́istʃər] 습기 content[kɑ́ntent] 함유량
partially[pɑ́ːrʃəli] 부분적으로 crust[krʌst] 표면 seep into ~으로 스며들다

CHAPTER 02 Detail

• 각 문제에 대한 정답단서는 지문에 보라색으로 표시되어 있습니다.

문제 공략하기
p.55

마리너 10호는 수성 표면의 45퍼센트 정도를 다루었습니다. 많아 보이지 않을 수도 있지만... 그 사진들은 수성이 지구의 달처럼, 분화구들과 아주 커다란 여러 겹의 분지로 덮혀 있다는 것을 보여줘요. 이것은 달과 수성 모두 얇은 대기를 가지고 있기 때문이고, 이는 그것들이 운석과 다른 파편들의 쉬운 표적물이 되도록 하죠. 또한 둘 다 극한의 온도를 가지는데... 수성의 온도는 밤에 섭씨 영하 170도까지 내려가고 낮에는 섭씨 350도로 올라가는데, 달의 온도는 영하 100도에서 340도까지 이릅니다. 그것들 사이의 유일하게 큰 차이점은 밀도입니다.

HACKERS PRACTICE
p.56

1. **(B)** Main Purpose/Topic	2. **(C)** Detail	3. **(C)** Detail
4. **(B)** Main Purpose/Topic	5. **(B), (D)** Detail	6. **(C)** Detail
7. **(C)** Main Purpose/Topic	8. **(D)** Detail	9. **(A), (C)** Detail
10. **(C)** Main Purpose/Topic	11. **(A), (C)** Detail	12. **(A), (C), (D)** Detail

[1-3]
Listen to a conversation between a student and a career advisor.

W: ᵠ¹ Hello, can you help me go through some summer job options?

M: Sure. Do you know what kind of job you're looking for?

W: I don't want to work full-time, since I'll be in summer school, so I need to find something that's a little flexible.

M: I see. I'm sure we can find something that will suit your needs. By the way, what's your major?

W: Computer science . . . with a minor in mathematics.

M: Then you might be in luck! I just got a job posting via e-mail today. It's for a math tutor at Mayfield High. They're looking for someone to tutor three students in math a couple times a week.

W: Hmm . . . I wonder if they would mind that I'm only minoring in math . . . although my major is pretty math-heavy. Actually, I was also a member of the math club during my last two years of high school. Do you think it would help?

M: Hmm . . . What did you do in it?

W: ᵠ² Well, it's a club where students who are weaker at math can sit with the better students and learn from them. I helped freshmen who were having problems with geometry and calculus.

M: That sounds like good experience for this job . . . I guess you could ask Mayfield High School when you go in for an interview.

W: OK, I will definitely keep it in mind! I should explore other options, though, just in case. What else is available?

M: Let's see here . . . I have some other openings that are part-time—here's one for a server at a bar called the Watering Hole, down on Tucker Street. The hours aren't bad . . . and I'm guessing that the tips could be pretty good on busy nights.

W: I think I'll pass on that one. I've been there, and people tend to get rowdy towards the end of the night, if you know what I mean.

M: I understand. Hmm . . . well, here's another listing you might be interested in. It's for a library assistant . . . shelving books, helping customers, and so on . . . The only problem is that the library decided to spread the work among four assistants, so the load is pretty light.

W: 03 Well, that doesn't sound like it would pay enough to finance my summer school tuition . . . I guess I'll just check out the tutoring position for now.

Now get ready to answer the questions. You may use your notes to help you answer.

1. What are the speakers mainly discussing?
2. According to the conversation, what is the objective of the math club?
3. What does the woman say about the library assistant position?

W: 안녕하세요, 여름 일자리를 몇 개 찾는 것을 도와주실 수 있나요?

M: 물론이죠. 어떤 종류의 일자리를 찾고 있나요?

W: 저는 여름 학기를 들을 예정이기 때문에, 풀타임으로 일하고 싶지는 않아서, 좀 융통성 있는 무언가를 찾아야 해요.

M: 그렇군요. 학생의 필요에 잘 맞는 무언가를 찾을 수 있을 거예요. 그런데, 학생의 전공이 뭐죠?

W: 컴퓨터 공학이요... 수학 부전공을 함께 하고 있어요.

M: 그렇다면 학생은 운이 좋은 것 같네요! 오늘 막 이메일을 통해 일자리 공고를 받았거든요. Mayfield 고등학교의 수학 개별 교사 자리예요. 그들은 일주일에 두 번 정도 세 명의 학생에게 수학 개별 지도를 해줄 누군가를 찾고 있죠.

W: 흠, 제가 수학을 부전공하고 있다는 점을 괜찮아할지 모르겠네요... 제 전공에서 수학의 비중이 꽤 크긴 하지만. 사실, 저는 고등학교 마지막 2년 동안 수학 동아리의 일원이기도 했어요. 그게 도움이 될까요?

M: 흠... 거기서 무엇을 했나요?

W: 음, 그건 수학에 취약한 학생들이 더 잘하는 학생들과 한자리에 앉아서 그들로부터 배우는 동아리예요. 전 기하학과 미적분학에 어려움을 겪고 있는 신입생들을 도와줬고요.

M: 이 일에 좋은 경험인 것 같네요... 학생이 면접을 보러 가면 Mayfield 고등학교 측에 문의해 볼 수 있을 거예요.

W: 네, 반드시 기억해둘게요! 하지만, 만약을 위해서, 다른 선택권도 알아봐야 할 것 같아요. 다른 어떤 게 가능한가요?

M: 어디 보자... 또 다른 아르바이트 자리가 몇 개 있는데, 여기 하나 Tucker 가에 위치한, Watering Hole이라고 불리는 주점 종업원 일이에요. 시간도 나쁘지 않고... 바쁜 야간에는 팁이 꽤 괜찮을 것 같은데요.

W: 그 일은 안 될 것 같아요. 거기에 가 봤는데, 밤이 깊어질수록 사람들이 난폭해지는 경향이 있거든요, 무슨 말인지 아실 거예요.

M: 이해해요. 흠... 자, 여기 학생이 관심 있을 만한 항목이 하나 더 있어요. 도서관 보조원이에요... 책을 정리하고, 손님을 도와주고, 그런 것들 말이죠... 유일한 문제는 도서관이 네 명의 보조원에게 업무를 분배하기로 해서, 업무량이 꽤 적다는 거예요.

W: 저, 그 일은 제 여름 학기 등록금을 마련하기에는 충분치 않을 것 같아요... 지금으로서는 그냥 그 개별 지도 자리만 알아봐야 할 것 같네요.

[4-6]
Listen to a conversation between a student and a university bookstore employee.

M: Hello. I need a list of the required textbooks for, um . . . let me check . . . Biology 203. Uh, Introduction to Genetics.

W: Sure. Let me print it off for you . . . Um, you know that this information is on our website, right? You can search for books by course number.

M: Yeah. 04 I printed the list out this morning because . . . well, because I knew I'd be coming here to buy them . . . and then I forgot the list. Uh, sorry if it's a bother . . .

W: Oh, it's no problem. Here you go . . . You'll need, um, three books, and they're all in the biology section.

M: Thanks. One more question . . . Where are the used books? I don't see them.

W: Um, we don't actually carry used books anymore. Just new ones . . .

M: What? New textbooks are really expensive . . . Lots of students try to save money by . . . you know . . . by buying secondhand books. Why did the policy change?

W: Well, a couple of reasons. Q5 First of all, the sale of used textbooks was, um, hurting the bookstore financially.

M: Really? I just assumed that you made a profit each time a used book was sold . . .

W: Sure, but selling them resulted in a large number of unsold new textbooks. They just sit as, um, dead stock in the store taking up space. Eventually we have to ship them back to the publishers . . . and they charge us a return fee for each book.

M: Hmm . . . I hadn't considered that. But surely the benefit to students outweighs these money concerns.

W: Well, that's why we continued selling used books for so long. It saved students money, so we were willing to, uh . . . to sustain a certain amount of loss. But we realized this practice caused problems for students as well.

M: Um, I don't get it . . . in what way?

W: Q6 Well, new versions of textbooks are released almost every year . . . and these are the ones professors tend to use in class.

M: That's true.

W: So when a student buys a used textbook, it's likely it'll be the wrong edition. And when the student realizes this and comes back to buy a new edition, well . . . we don't allow returns on used books. So the student ends up buying the book twice . . .

M: I see . . . That makes sense. Anyway, um, I'm going to check online to see if I can get these books any cheaper. If not, I'll be back tomorrow.

W: OK . . . Good luck and let me know if you need more help.

Now get ready to answer the questions. You may use your notes to help you answer.

4. Why does the student visit the bookstore?
5. What problems did selling used books cause?
6. What does the employee say about new editions of books?

M: 안녕하세요. 필수 교과서 목록이 필요해서요, 음... 확인해 볼게요... 생물학 203을 위한 거요. 어, 유전학 입문 수업이에요.

W: 물론이죠. 인쇄해드릴게요... 음, 이 정보가 우리 웹사이트에 있다는 걸 알고 있을 거예요, 그렇죠? 강의 번호로 책을 검색할 수 있잖아요.

M: 네. 오늘 아침에 목록을 인쇄했어요... 음, 제가 책을 사러 여기 올 걸 알고 있었으니까요... 그리고 나서 프린터에서 목록을 깜빡 잊고 안 가져왔어요. 어, 귀찮게 했다면 죄송해요...

W: 오, 천만에요. 여기 있어요... 학생은, 음, 책 세 권이 필요하고, 그것들은 모두 생물학 구역에 있네요.

M: 감사합니다. 질문이 하나 더 있어요... 중고 책은 어디에 있나요? 그것들이 안 보여서요.

W: 음, 사실 우리는 더는 중고 책을 취급하지 않아요. 오직 새 책만 취급하죠...

M: 뭐라고요? 새 교과서는 정말로 비싼데요... 많은 학생이... 그러니까... 중고 책을 사서 돈을 절약하려고 해요. 규정이 왜 바뀌었죠?

W: 음, 몇 가지 이유가 있어요. 우선, 중고 책 판매는, 음, 서점에 재정적으로 손해를 입혔어요.

M: 정말이요? 저는 중고 책이 팔릴 때마다 이윤을 낼 거라고만 생각했어요...

W: 맞아요, 하지만 중고 책을 파는 것은 많은 수의 새 교과서들이 팔리지 않게 했어요. 그것들은 그저, 음, 팔다 남은 상품으로 가게에서 공간만 차지하고 있거든요. 결국 우리는 그것들을 출판업자들에게 돌려보내야 하는데... 그들은 우리에게 책마다 반납 수수료를 청구하죠.

M: 흠... 그건 생각해 본 적이 없네요. 하지만 분명히 학생들의 이익이 돈과 관련한 문제보다 더 클 텐데요...

W: 음, 그게 우리가 오랫동안 중고 책을 계속 팔았던 이유예요. 그건 학생들의 돈을 절약해주었고, 우리는 기꺼이, 어... 일정량의 손실

을 입으려고 했죠. 하지만 우리는 이 관행이 학생들에게도 문제를 유발한다는 걸 알게 됐어요.

M: 음, 이해가 안 돼요... 어떤 식으로요?

W: 음, 교과서의 개정판은 거의 매년 발매되죠... 그리고 이것들은 바로 교수님들이 수업 시간에 사용하는 경향이 있는 것들이고요.

M: 사실이에요.

W: 그래서 어떤 학생이 중고 교과서를 살 때, 그건 잘못된 판일 수도 있어요. 그리고 그 학생이 이걸 깨닫고 새로운 판을 사러 돌아오면, 음... 우리는 중고 책의 반품을 허용하지 않죠. 그래서 그 학생은 결국 그 책을 두 번 사게 되는 거예요...

M: 그렇군요... 이해가 가요. 어쨌든, 음, 저는 이 책들을 온라인으로 조금이라도 싸게 살 수 있는지 확인하러 가 볼게요. 싸게 팔지 않는다면, 책을 사러 내일 다시 올 거예요.

W: 그래요... 행운을 빌고, 도움이 더 필요하면 말씀하세요.

[7-9]
Listen to part of a lecture in an environmental science class.

All right, let's get started. Q7 In the last class, we defined what a renewable energy source is. And just to make sure we're on the same page, let's briefly review what it is. Basically, it's an energy supply that comes from an existing source that can be replenished in a short period of time—water, the sun, wind, geothermal heat, and . . . biomass. Q7 Let's discuss sun and wind in more detail. But before we do that, let's just think about this: why do we continue to use fuel and nuclear power when renewable sources exist? Well . . . for one, renewable sources aren't easy to use. Q8 And another reason is they aren't reliable. In fact, the availability of renewable sources often depends on the weather. Anyway . . . you know how a solar panel works, right? Greece is one country that uses a lot of solar panels. Some might say that's not surprising because the sun always shines in Greece. Well . . . not always. Some parts of Greece don't get enough sun. The cells in the solar panel collect solar energy, so there's always some stored power for when the sun sets. But on very cloudy or rainy days, solar panels can't collect energy. This means that even in naturally sunny areas, a secondary source of power is needed. So sunlight isn't always the most efficient means of generating power. Even in places that are sunny, it's sometimes cloudy or rainy. OK, let's move on. You've all seen windmills, but this is different. Farms, electric companies, and even factories use wind turbines for energy. Obviously, these areas are windy. Q9 That's the nice thing about wind turbines—as long as there's wind, these machines are capable of producing energy. And just how strong are these turbines? Well, quite surprisingly, just one of these mechanisms can create about five megawatts of power. By the way, a single megawatt can power about 200 homes. I can only say they're really ugly, though! And I'm not the only one who feels that way. The major drawback to using turbines is that they're a source of visual pollution.

Now get ready to answer the questions. You may use your notes to help you answer.

7. What is the discussion mainly about?
8. What is one reason that renewable energy sources are not widely used?
9. According to the discussion, what are two advantages of wind turbines?

좋아요, 시작합시다. 지난 강의에서, 우리는 재생 에너지 자원이 무엇인지를 정의했어요. 그리고 모두 여기까지 이해했는지 확인하기 위해, 그게 무엇인지 간단하게 복습해 봅시다. 기본적으로, 그것은 짧은 기간 내에 다시 채워질 수 있는 현존하는 자원으로부터 오는 에너지 공급인데요, 물, 태양, 바람, 지열, 그리고... 바이오매스 말이죠. 태양과 바람에 대해 더 자세히 논의해 봅시다. 하지만 그러기 전에, 이것에 대해 생각해 보세요. 재생 자원이 존재하는데 우리는 왜 계속 연료와 원자력을 쓰는 걸까요? 음... 한 가지 이유는, 재생 자원은 사용하기 쉽지 않다는 거예요. 그리고 또 다른 이유는 그것들이 신뢰할 만하지 않다는 것입니다. 사실, 재생 자원의 이용 가능성은 보통 날씨에 달려 있거든요. 어쨌든... 여러분은 태양 전지판이 어떻게 작동하는지 알고 있어요, 그렇죠? 그리스는 태양 전지판을 많이 사용하는 나라예요. 어떤 사람들은 그리스엔 항상 태양이 비추기 때문에 그건 놀라운 일이 아니라고 말할 수도 있겠죠. 음... 항상 그렇지는 않습니다. 그리스의 일부 지역들은 햇빛을 충분히 받지 못하거든요. 태양 전지판의 전지들이 태양 에너지를 모아서, 해가 졌을 때도 항상 저장된 전력이 좀 있어요. 하지만 구름이 많이 끼거나 비가 오는 날에는, 태양 전지판이 에너지를 모을 수 없죠. 이는 자연적으로 햇빛이 많이 드는 지역에서조차, 2차적인 전력 자원이 필요하다는 것을 뜻해요. 그래서 햇빛이 항상 전력을 생산하는 가장 효율적인 방법은 아니라는 거죠. 햇빛이 잘 드는 곳도, 때로는 구름이 끼고 비가 오니까요.

좋아요, 계속 이야기해 봅시다. 여러분 모두 풍차를 본 적이 있을 텐데요, 이건 다른데요. 농장, 전기 회사, 그리고 공장에서도 에너지를 위해 풍력 터빈을 사용해요. 당연히, 이런 곳에는 바람이 많이 불죠. 그게 풍력 터빈의 좋은 점이에요, 바람이 있는 한, 이 기계들이 에너지를 생산할 수 있다는 것 말이죠. 그럼 이 터빈들은 얼마나 강할까요? 음, 꽤 놀랍게도, 이 기계 하나만으로도 500만 와트의 전력을 만들 수 있어요. 덧붙여 말하자면, 100만 와트는 200가구 정도에 전력을 공급할 수 있죠. 하지만, 제가 말할 수 있는 건 그것들이 정말 못생겼다는 거예요! 그리고 이렇게 느끼는 건 저뿐만이 아닙니다. 터빈을 사용하는 것의 주요 단점은 이것들이 시각적인 오염의 원천이라는 것이거든요.

[10-12]
Listen to part of a lecture in a film class.

OK . . . By now you should all be familiar with the early motion picture devices and their inventors . . . Q10 Today we're going to shift focus and examine film audiences with regard to their socioeconomic status. The, um, type of people who watched films changed significantly during the early years of the industry . . . and this was related to the places where movies were shown. When moving pictures were first introduced, the industry was quite different. There were no movie theaters like we have today. Um, films were played in a variety of settings . . . like fairs, traveling exhibitions, and museums. The type of people in the audience depended largely on the kind of event. But at the beginning of the 20th century, permanent theaters were established. Known as nickelodeons, these theaters included a number of individual viewing devices that showed a collection of short films . . . Um, the entire program usually lasted for about 30 minutes. A visitor would insert a coin in a slot and watch the films in private. Q11 As nickelodeons were inexpensive, they tended to attract working-class people. These people also appreciated the casual atmosphere of the nickelodeon. In fact, nickelodeons were often referred to as the poor man's theater. . . As you might expect, this made them unappealing to people of higher social status. However, this attitude changed in later years. For one thing, some upper-class people developed an interest in watching films and demanded that more respectable venues be constructed. In addition, movies were becoming longer, and it was a challenge to sit through a long film in a cheaply built nickelodeon. This led to the development of movie palaces that were similar to concert halls and playhouses . . . Um, movie palaces were large enough to accommodate several hundred people. Q12 They had comfortable seats and fancy decorations. Some even had full orchestras that played music along with the films. Most importantly, the atmosphere was very formal, and there were staff members who kept the theaters clean and orderly. Furthermore, since these theaters were aimed at wealthier people, the price of admission was much higher than that of a nickelodeon. As a result, few working-class people could afford to visit these establishments . . . Movie palaces dominated until the middle of the 20th century, when they were replaced by modern theaters. What's interesting is that theaters today are places where people of all levels of wealth and status mix. Watching movies has become a shared experience that cuts across social boundaries.

Now get ready to answer the questions. You may use your notes to help you answer.

10. What is the main purpose of the lecture?

11. According to the professor, why were nickelodeons popular with members of the working class?
12. What does the professor say about movie palaces?

자... 이제는 여러분 모두 초기 영화 장치와 그것들의 발명가들을 잘 알 거예요... 오늘은 초점을 바꿔서 영화 관객들의 사회 경제적인 지위에 관해 살펴볼 겁니다. 그, 음, 영화를 보는 사람들의 유형은 영화 산업의 초반 몇 년 동안 상당히 변화했어요... 그리고 이는 영화가 상영된 장소들과 관계가 있었죠.

영화가 처음 소개됐을 때, 그 산업은 상당히 달랐습니다. 오늘날 우리가 가지고 있는 것과 같은 영화관이 없었죠. 음, 영화는 다양한 장소에서 상영되었어요... 박람회, 이동 전시회, 그리고 박물관 같은 곳에서요. 관객들의 유형은 주로 행사의 종류에 달려있었습니다. 그러나 20세기 초에, 상설 영화관들이 세워졌습니다. 5센트 극장이라고 알려진, 이러한 영화관들은 단편 영화 모음을 상영하는 많은 개별적인 감상 장치들을 포함하고 있었죠... 음, 전체 프로그램은 보통 약 30분 동안 지속됐습니다. 방문객은 구멍에 동전을 넣고 다른 사람이 없는 데서 영화를 봤어요. 5센트 극장들은 저렴했기 때문에, 노동자 계급의 사람들을 끌어모으는 경향이 있었죠. 이러한 사람들 또한 5센트 극장의 격식을 차리지 않는 분위기를 환영했고요. 사실, 5센트 극장들은 흔히 가난한 사람의 영화관이라고 불렸습니다... 여러분이 예상할 수 있듯이, 이는 5센트 극장을 더 높은 사회적 지위의 사람들에게 매력적이지 못한 곳으로 만들었죠.

그러나, 이 태도는 그 후 몇 년 동안 변했습니다. 첫째로, 일부 상류 계급 사람들은 영화 보는 것에 대한 흥미를 붙였고 더 훌륭한 장소들이 세워질 것을 요구했거든요. 게다가, 영화는 더 길어지고 있었고, 저렴하게 지어진 5센트 극장에서 긴 영화를 끝까지 앉아서 보는 것은 힘든 일이었죠. 이는 공연장이나 극장과 비슷한 영화 전당의 발전으로 이어졌습니다... 음, 영화 전당은 수백 명의 사람을 수용할 수 있을 만큼 충분히 컸어요. 그것들은 편안한 좌석과 화려한 장식을 가지고 있었죠. 심지어 일부는 영화와 함께 곡을 연주하는 완전한 관현악단을 가지고 있기도 했어요. 가장 중요하게, 분위기는 매우 격식을 차리고 있었고, 영화관을 깨끗하고 질서 있게 유지하는 직원들이 있었죠. 그뿐만 아니라, 이러한 영화관들은 더 부유한 사람들을 목표로 한 것이었기 때문에, 입장료는 5센트 극장의 것보다 훨씬 더 높았습니다. 결과적으로, 이러한 시설을 방문할 여유가 되는 노동자 계급 사람들은 거의 없었죠... 영화 전당들은 20세기 중반까지는 우세했어요, 그것들이 현대식 영화관에 의해 대체된 시기까지요. 흥미로운 것은 오늘날의 영화관들은 모든 부와 신분 계층의 사람들이 어울리는 장소라는 거예요. 영화를 보는 것은 사회적인 경계를 가로지르며 공유되는 경험이 된 것이죠.

HACKERS TEST

p.60

1. (B) Main Purpose/Topic	2. (B) Detail	3. (D) Detail
4. (A) Detail	5. (B), (C) Detail	6. (C) Main Purpose/Topic
7. (A) Detail	8. (C) Detail	9. (B), (C) Detail
10. (B) Detail	11. (B) Detail	12. (C) Main Purpose/Topic
13. (D) Detail	14. (A) Detail	15. (D) Detail
16. (A), (B), (D) Detail	17. (C) Detail	18. (D) Main Purpose/Topic
19. (A), (B), (E) Detail	20. (A) Detail	21. (B), (D) Detail
22. (A) Detail	23. (D) Main Purpose/Topic	24. (C) Detail
25. (C) Detail	26. (B) Detail	27. (A), (D) Detail
28. (D) Detail	29. (D) Main Purpose/Topic	30. (B), (C) Detail
31. (A) Detail	32. (B) Detail	33. (C) Detail
34. (D) Detail		

[1-5]
Listen to a conversation between a student and a professor.

S: Hi, Professor Jenkins. Can I talk to you for a few minutes?
P: Well, hi, James. Sure. Is everything going OK these days?
S: Yeah, I'm really busy with all my classes, but I'm enjoying them.

P: That's good to hear. How did you like the paintings we looked at last class? The ones from the Cubists . . .

S: I really liked them. They really force you to think about the perspective and the way we see everyday objects.

P: Indeed. So, James, did you come by to discuss anything specific or just to have a chat?

S: Well, Professor Jenkins, Q1 I actually came by because I wanted to talk to you about my major. I'm a bit unsure whether I should major in art history or business.

P: Q2 As your art history professor, I think you know I'm a bit biased. But, hmm, it's really interesting that you're trying to decide between, uh, art history and business. I had the same dilemma when I was a college student. Well, when we get right down to it, it's really quite simple . . . which one do you like more?

S: Well, Q3 I've been interested in business since I was in high school. I had to visit a local business for a school project, and I got really inspired by the CEO there. He took a few minutes to talk to me about what his job was like, and it made me want to go in the same direction.

P: It's nice to have a role model like that.

S: I think so, too. Plus, studying business makes it easier for me to get a good job after graduating. But you know, Q4 since I started taking your class and Professor Wheaton's course in Renaissance art, I've become very interested in the field. I definitely enjoy my art history classes more than my business ones this semester. So I'm starting to wonder if I should change my major . . . maybe business isn't for me.

P: My opinion is that you should do what you enjoy, and besides, there are plenty of opportunities for those with art history degrees. Working at a gallery, becoming an art consultant, writing art critiques . . .

S: Yeah, you're right.

P: You know . . . if you really can't decide, you could always do a double major. Have you considered that?

S: Never! It would be an awful lot of work.

P: Well, it's what I wound up doing. Yeah, it was a lot of hard work, and took devotion, but it was worth it in the end.

S: Really? So you think it's a good idea to double major?

P: Well, it was highly beneficial for me. Q5 I got to explore my more, um, imaginative, creative side by studying art . . . and at the same time I honed my analytical and strategic thinking in my business classes.

S: Yeah, I see your point. It does sound appealing . . . not to mention useful.

P: You ought to give it some serious thought.

S: I really appreciate your advice. It does seem like a great idea, though I really have to take some time to look at the pros and cons. I'll let you know what I decide, Professor Jenkins. Thanks so much!

P: Good luck with your choice, James, and definitely let me know what you decide!

Now get ready to answer the questions. You may use your notes to help you answer.

1. Why does the student go to see the professor?
2. What does the professor say about majoring in art history?
3. What does the student say about the CEO he met?
4. Why does the student want to major in art history?
5. According to the professor, what are two benefits she received from having a double major?

S: 안녕하세요, Jenkins 교수님. 저와 몇 분만 이야기하실 수 있으신가요?

P: 음, 안녕, James. 물론이지. 요즘 잘 지내고 있니?

S: 네, 모든 수업 때문에 정말 바쁘지만, 즐겁게 하고 있어요.

P: 그렇다니 잘됐구나. 지난 수업에서 보았던 그림들은 어땠니? 입체파의 그림들 말이야...

S: 정말 좋았어요. 그것들은 정말로 관점과 일상적인 사물들을 바라보는 방법에 대해서 생각하게 하거든요.

P: 정말 그렇지. 자, James, 뭔가 구체적인 것에 대해 논의하러 왔니 아니면 그냥 이야기를 나누러 왔니?

S: 음, Jenkins 교수님, 사실 제 전공에 관해 이야기하고 싶어서 왔어요. 미술사를 전공해야 할지 경영학을 전공해야 할지 잘 모르겠거든요.

P: 네 미술사 교수로서, 내가 편향된다는 걸 너도 알 텐데. 하지만, 흠, 네가, 어, 미술사와 경영학 중에서 선택하려 한다니 정말 흥미롭구나. 나도 대학생 때 같은 고민을 했었거든. 음, 본론으로 들어가자면, 사실 그건 아주 간단하단다... 네가 더 좋아하는 게 어떤 거니?

S: 음, 저는 고등학생 때부터 경영학에 관심이 있었어요. 학교 과제로 지역의 한 기업을 방문했는데, 그곳의 최고 경영자에게 정말로 영감을 받았었거든요. 그는 몇 분 동안 제게 자신의 일이 어떤지 말해주었고, 저는 그와 같은 방향으로 가고 싶다고 생각하게 되었어요.

P: 그런 역할 모델을 갖는다는 건 좋은 일이지.

S: 저도 그렇게 생각해요. 게다가, 경영학을 공부하면 졸업 후 더 쉽게 좋은 직업을 구할 수 있어요. 하지만 그러니까, 제가 교수님의 수업과 Wheaton 교수님의 르네상스 예술 수업을 듣기 시작한 이후로, 이 분야에 매우 관심을 갖게 되었거든요. 이번 학기에 저는 확실히 경영학 수업보다 미술사 수업을 즐기고 있어요. 그래서 전공을 바꿔야 할지 고민하기 시작했고요... 아마도 경영학은 저와 맞지 않는 것 같아요.

P: 나는 네가 즐기는 것을 해야 한다고 생각해. 게다가, 미술사 학위를 가진 사람들에게도 많은 기회가 있단다. 미술관에서 일하거나, 아트 컨설턴트가 되거나, 미술 평론을 쓰거나...

S: 네, 맞아요.

P: 그러니까... 만약 네가 정말로 결정하지 못하겠다면, 복수 전공을 할 수도 있지. 그건 생각해 봤니?

S: 전혀요! 그건 해야 할 일이 엄청나게 많을 거예요.

P: 음, 내가 결국 그렇게 하게 되었지. 그래, 힘든 일이 아주 많았고, 전념이 필요했지만, 결과적으로는 그만한 가치가 있었어.

S: 정말요? 그럼 복수 전공하는 게 좋은 방안이라고 생각하세요?

P: 음, 내게는 아주 유익했단다. 미술을 공부하면서 나의 더, 음, 창의적이고, 창조적인 측면을 탐구할 수 있었거든... 그리고 동시에 경영학 수업에서는 분석적이고 전략적인 사고를 길렀지.

S: 네, 무슨 말씀인지 알겠어요. 매력적으로 들리네요... 유용한 건 말할 필요도 없고요.

P: 그것에 대해 한 번 진지하게 생각해 보렴.

S: 조언 정말 감사해요. 좋은 생각인 것 같아요, 장단점을 살펴보는 시간이 분명 필요하기는 하지만요. 제가 어떤 결정을 하는지 알려드릴게요, Jenkins 교수님. 정말 감사합니다!

P: 네 선택에 행운을 빌게, James, 그리고 무엇을 결정했는지 꼭 알려주렴!

어휘

Cubist[kjú:bist] 입체파   perspective[pərspéktiv] 관점   specific[spisífik] 구체적인   biased[báiəst] 편향된
inspire[inspáiər] 영감을 주다   critique[krití:k] 평론   awful[ɔ́:fəl] 엄청나게   wind up 결국 ~하게 되다   devotion[divóuʃən] 전념
beneficial[bènəfíʃəl] 유익한   imaginative[imǽdʒənətiv] 창의적인   hone[houn] 기르다   analytical[æ̀nəlítikəl] 분석적인
strategic[strətí:dʒik] 전략적인   appealing[əpí:liŋ] 매력적인   pros and cons 장단점

[6-11]

Listen to part of a lecture in a biology class.

P: As I was saying, the chimpanzees of Africa are divided into three distinct groups. Eastern and central chimpanzees live mainly in tropical rainforests, while western chimpanzees inhabit savannas . . . which are, uh, grassy ecosystems with few trees. Q6 To adapt to life in the savanna, western chimpanzees have developed a number of unique behavioral traits . . . Let's examine a few of them now.

So . . . uh, when discussing the behavior of chimpanzees, food availability is a significant factor . . . Um, [Q7] these primates can digest both animal proteins and plant fibers, but they have a strong preference for fruits and leaves . . . Now, uh, because fruits and leaves are readily available in tropical rainforests, the chimpanzees living here eat only small quantities of meat and insects.

[Q8] The savanna is much more challenging. This type of area . . . well, it receives less annual rainfall and has long seasonal dry periods. As a result, fruits and other edible plants are rare and only obtainable at certain times of the year. This means that western chimpanzees must make an effort to locate other sources of food. And they have met this challenge in, well . . . in almost a human way. They have become very proficient at using tools . . .

S1: Um, I saw a documentary film about this . . . Don't they catch ants using long pieces of grass?

P: Well, that activity is common to all types of chimpanzees . . . but those in the savanna do it more often because insects are a larger part of their diet. They also engage in two unique forms of tool use . . . [Q9] These chimpanzees have been observed using stones to crack open nuts. They carry rocks with them to places where there are nuts . . . so you know, this indicates planning. The other thing they do is create weapons to hunt other animals. Uh, they sharpen the ends of long pieces of wood with their teeth, and then use these to kill tiny animals that sleep in holes in tree trunks. In short, the lack of an easily accessible, year-round food source has forced western chimpanzees to develop some very innovative strategies to survive. Now, dealing with the hot African climate is also more difficult in the savanna. Daytime temperatures are extremely high . . . but unlike the chimpanzees in tropical rain forests, western chimpanzees do not live under a thick cover of leaves and branches that provide shade. So they have very little protection from the sun. Obviously this poses a serious problem for animals that must spend hours each day searching for food. Once again, the western chimpanzees have come up with a few solutions. [Q10] First, they make use of the caves that are common in the region. They gather in these caves during the hottest part of the day to avoid the sun. Um, they will also take long naps to conserve energy. To do this, they must adjust their schedules to be more active in the early mornings and evenings. And if the moon is full enough to provide sufficient light, they will even search for food at night. OK . . . another thing I wanted to mention is that western chimpanzees have been observed sitting in pools of water . . . Yes?

S2: [Q11] Excuse me, but . . . uh, aren't chimpanzees scared of water? I seem to remember reading somewhere that they avoid crossing even shallow streams whenever possible.

P: Well, that's true of most chimpanzees . . . But, surprisingly, the chimpanzees that live in the savanna will seek out fairly deep pools when it gets too hot. And they will submerge themselves entirely to cool down, acting, like, well . . . like a group of people at the local swimming pool on a summer day.

Now get ready to answer the questions. You may use your notes to help you answer.

6. What is the main topic of the lecture?
7. What does the professor say about the diet of chimpanzees?
8. Why is finding food more challenging for western chimpanzees?
9. According to the professor, what are two examples of tool use specific to western chimpanzees?
10. How do chimpanzees in the savanna avoid the sun?
11. Why is it noteworthy that western chimpanzees go into pools of water?

P: 제가 이야기하던 것처럼, 아프리카의 침팬지들은 세 개의 별개 집단으로 나뉩니다. 동부와 중앙의 침팬지들은 주로 열대 우림에 사는 반면, 서부 침팬지들은 대초원에 서식하는데요... 그곳은, 어, 나무가 거의 없는 풀로 덮인 생태계죠. 대초원에서의 삶에 적응하기 위해, 서부 침팬지들은 여러 가지 독특한 행동적 특성을 발달시켜 왔어요... 이제 그것들 중 몇몇을 살펴봅시다.

자... 어, 침팬지의 행동을 논의할 때, 식량 입수 가능성은 중요한 요인입니다... 음, 이 영장류는 동물 단백질과 식물 섬유를 모두 소화할 수 있지만, 과일과 나뭇잎에 대한 강한 선호를 가지고 있죠... 자, 어, 과일과 나뭇잎은 열대 우림에서 손쉽게 구할 수 있기 때문에, 여기에 사는 침팬지들은 오직 적은 양의 고기와 곤충을 먹습니다.

대초원은 훨씬 더 힘듭니다. 이러한 종류의 지역은... 음, 연간 강수량이 적으며 길고 주기적인 건기를 가지고 있거든요. 결과적으로, 과일과 다른 식용 식물들은 드물고 연중 특정 시기에만 구할 수 있습니다. 이는 서부 침팬지들이 다른 식량 출처를 찾아내기 위해 노력해야 한다는 것을 의미하죠. 그리고 그들은 이 어려움에 대처해왔어요, 음... 거의 인간의 방식으로요. 도구를 사용하는 데 매우 능숙해진 거죠...

S1: 음, 이에 관한 다큐멘터리 영화를 봤어요... 그들은 기다란 풀 조각을 사용해서 개미를 잡지 않나요?

P: 음, 그 활동은 모든 종류의 침팬지들에게 공통적인 거예요... 하지만 대초원에 사는 침팬지들은 그들의 식사에서 곤충이 더 큰 부분을 차지하기 때문에 이를 더 자주 하는 것이죠. 그들은 또한 두 가지 독특한 형태의 도구 사용에 관여합니다... 이러한 침팬지들은 견과류를 부수어 열기 위해 돌을 사용하는 것으로 관찰되어 왔어요. 그들은 견과류가 있는 장소로 돌을 가지고 가요... 그러니까, 이것은 계획을 나타내는 겁니다. 그들이 하는 또 다른 것은 다른 동물들을 사냥하기 위한 무기를 만드는 거예요. 어, 그들은 이빨로 기다란 나무 조각의 끝을 날카롭게 해서, 이것들을 나무 줄기의 구멍에서 자는 작은 동물들을 죽이는 데 이용하죠. 요컨대, 쉽게 구할 수 있고, 연중 계속되는 식량 출처의 부족은 서부 침팬지들이 생존하기 위한 매우 획기적인 몇 가지 전략들을 발달시키도록 만든 거예요.

자, 대초원에서는 더운 아프리카 기후에 대처하는 것 또한 더욱 어렵습니다. 낮 온도가 극도로 높거든요... 하지만 열대 우림의 침팬지들과 달리, 서부 침팬지들은 그늘을 제공하는 나뭇잎과 가지의 두꺼운 초목 밑에서 살지 않죠. 그래서 그들은 태양으로부터 정말 거의 보호받지 못합니다. 분명히 이것은 매일 몇 시간씩 식량을 찾는 데 보내야 하는 동물들에게 심각한 문제를 야기해요. 한 번 더, 서부 침팬지들은 몇몇 해결책을 찾아냈습니다. 첫째로, 그들은 그 지역에서 흔한 동굴을 이용해요. 그들은 태양을 피하려고 하루의 가장 더운 시간 동안 이러한 동굴에 모입니다. 음, 또한 그들은 에너지를 보존하기 위해 긴 낮잠을 잘 거예요. 이렇게 하려면, 이른 아침과 저녁에 더 활동적이도록 그들의 일정을 조정해야 하죠. 그리고 달이 충분한 빛을 제공할 수 있을 만큼 찼을 때에는, 밤에도 식량을 찾을 겁니다.

좋아요... 언급하고 싶었던 또 다른 것은 서부 침팬지들이 물웅덩이에 앉아있는 것이 관찰되었다는 거예요... 네?

S2: 죄송해요, 하지만... 어, 침팬지들은 물을 무서워하지 않나요? 어디선가 그들이 가능하다면 심지어 얕은 물줄기를 건너는 것조차 꺼린다고 읽은 기억이 있어요.

P: 음, 침팬지 대부분에게는 그게 사실입니다... 하지만, 놀랍게도, 대초원에 사는 침팬지들은 너무 더워지면 꽤 깊은 웅덩이를 찾을 거예요. 그리고 그들 자신을 식히기 위해 완전히 잠수할 겁니다, 마치, 음... 여름의 어느날 지역 수영장에 있는 사람들 무리처럼 행동하면서 말이죠.

어휘

tropical rainforest 열대 우림   savanna[səvǽnə] (아열대 지방의) 대초원   grassy[grǽsi] 풀로 덮인
ecosystem[ékousìstəm] 생태계   availability[əvèiləbíləti] (입수) 가능성   primate[práimeit] 영장류   plant fiber 식물 섬유
annual rainfall 연간 강수량   seasonal[síːzənl] 주기적인   dry period 건기   edible[édəbl] 식용의   locate[lóukeit] 찾아내다
proficient[prəfíʃənt] 능숙한   engage in ~에 관여하다   trunk[trʌŋk] 줄기   year round 연중 계속되는
come up with ~을 찾아내다   submerge[səbmə́ːrdʒ] 잠수하다

[12-17]
Listen to part of a lecture in a music class.

P: Okay, let's turn now to opera . . . As most of you probably know, this musical tradition developed in the 16th century. It includes theatrical elements such as, um, acting, costumes, and stage scenery. ^{Q12} I want to look at the career of one Italian composer in particular . . . uh, Gioachino Antonio Rossini. He managed to achieve a high level of professional success at a young age . . .

Born in 1792, Rossini's career in music seemed almost inevitable because his father was a musician and his mother was a singer. In fact, Rossini started training quite young. By the age of six, he was performing with his father's musical group. Recognizing his talent, Rossini's parents sent him to Angelo Tesei, a prominent music teacher. Rossini thrived under Tesei's instruction. [Q13] When he was just 12, Rossini composed his first pieces of music . . . um, six sonatas over a period of three days. This would be an impressive feat for an experienced composer . . . never mind an adolescent boy.

Now, this brought Rossini a lot of attention. He was soon asked to compose the music for an opera called *Demetrio e Polibio*. [Q14] But Rossini faced a difficult task because the text for *Demetrio e Polibio* was given to him in sections . . .

S1: Excuse me, but . . . what do you mean by, um . . . sections?

P: Well, he was provided with a few pages of text at a time. Um, usually the lyrics and stage directions for an opera are written before the music. But that wasn't the case here . . . The text was still being written when Rossini started. This meant that he had to compose much of the music without knowing how the story would end. Yet despite this challenge, the resulting opera was well received by critics.

After composing his first opera, Rossini studied under a teacher named Cavedagni for several years. This period had the most profound impact on Rossini's development as a composer, but probably not for the reasons you would guess. [Q15] Um, Cavedagni was, how should I say it . . . rigid. He felt that there were many rules that a composer must learn, and he tried to force Rossini to follow them. This did not sit well with Rossini, who responded by adopting a, well . . . a more flexible approach.

S1: It sounds like he was a bit of a rebel . . .

P: That's one way of putting it . . . The end result was that Rossini developed a very innovative style. [Q16] For example, he often used the same melodies over and over to build tension. He also incorporated the rhythms of, um, Italian folk music. But his greatest break with tradition was that he made music the focus of his operas . . . Uh, most composers felt that the vocals were more important.

Over the next decade or so, Rossini wrote many operas, but he earned his place in music history with *The Barber of Seville* . . . a romantic comedy produced in 1816. [Q17] This opera was based on a stage play by Pierre Beaumarchais that was already very popular in Europe. So there was a lot of public interest in this opera before it was even performed . . . Yes?

S2: Um, are you saying that Rossini shouldn't be given credit for the success of *The Barber of Seville*?

P: That isn't the impression I meant to give . . . Uh, *The Barber of Seville* includes many of the innovations I mentioned earlier. It showcased Rossini's skill as a composer like no other piece. As a result, the opera was a hit with contemporary audiences and is now considered one of the greatest operas of all time. Rossini became a household name in Europe. In fact, some claim that he was more famous than Beethoven . . .

Now get ready to answer the questions. You may use your notes to help you answer.

12. What is the lecture mainly about?
13. According to the professor, what was Rossini's first significant accomplishment as a composer?
14. What does the professor say about *Demetrio e Polibio*?
15. How did studying with Cavedagni influence Rossini?
16. According to the professor, what are the key aspects of Rossini's style?

17. Why was there early public interest in *The Barber of Seville*?

P: 좋아요, 이제 오페라로 넘어가 봅시다... 아마 여러분 대다수가 알고 있듯이, 이 음악적 양식은 16세기에 발달했습니다. 그것은, 음, 연기, 분장, 그리고 무대 장치와 같은 연극적 요소를 포함했어요. 특히 한 이탈리아 작곡가의 이력을 살펴보고 싶습니다... 어, 조아키노 안토니오 로시니죠. 그는 어린 나이에 높은 수준의 전문가로서의 성공을 성취해냈어요...

1792년에 태어나서, 아버지는 음악가였고 어머니는 가수였기 때문에 로시니의 음악 분야로의 진로는 거의 필연적으로 보였어요. 실제로, 로시니는 꽤 어릴 때 교육받기 시작했죠. 여섯 살 즈음에는, 아버지의 악단과 연주하고 있었어요. 그의 재능을 알아보고, 로시니의 부모는 그를 유명한 음악 선생님, 안젤로 테세이에게 보냈어요. 로시니는 테세이의 가르침 아래에서 잘 성장했죠. 로시니는 겨우 12살이었을 때, 첫 번째 음악 작품을 작곡했어요... 음, 3일이라는 기간 동안 여섯 개의 소나타를 썼죠. 이는 경험이 풍부한 작곡가에게도 인상적인 위업이었을 거예요... 청소년에게는 말할 것도 없죠.

자, 이는 로시니에게 많은 관심을 가져다주었습니다. 그는 곧 '데메트리오와 폴리비오'라고 불리는 오페라를 위한 음악을 작곡해 달라고 요청받았어요. 하지만 '데메트리오와 폴리비오'의 원고가 그에게 부분부분 전달되었기 때문에 로시니는 어려운 과업을 마주하게 되었죠.

S1: 죄송하지만... 음... 부분부분이라는 게 무슨 뜻이죠?

P: 자, 그는 한 번에 몇 쪽의 원고를 받았어요. 음, 보통 오페라의 가사와 무대 지시는 음악 이전에 쓰이죠. 하지만 여기서는 그렇지 않았어요... 로시니가 시작했을 때 원고가 여전히 쓰이는 중이었거든요. 이는 로시니가 그 이야기가 어떻게 끝나는지 모르는 채 많은 음악을 작곡해야 했다는 것을 의미했죠. 하지만 이러한 문제에도 불구하고, 결과적으로 오페라는 비평가들에 의해 좋은 평가를 받았어요.

첫 번째 오페라를 작곡한 뒤, 로시니는 몇 년 동안 카베이다니라는 선생님 밑에서 공부했습니다. 이 기간은 작곡가로서 로시니의 성장에 가장 지대한 영향을 주었지만, 아마 여러분이 짐작하는 이유 때문은 아닐 거예요. 음, 카베이다니는, 어떻게 말해야 할까요... 융통성이 없었어요. 그는 작곡가가 익혀야 하는 많은 규칙들이 있다고 생각했고, 로시니에게 그것들을 따르도록 강요하려고 했어요. 이는 로시니와 어울리지 않았고, 로시니는, 음... 더 유연한 접근을 받아들이는 식으로 반응했어요.

S1: 그가 좀 반항적인 사람이었던 것처럼 들리네요...

P: 그렇게 말할 수도 있겠죠... 최종 결과는 로시니가 매우 획기적인 양식을 발전시켰다는 거예요. 예를 들어, 그는 종종 긴장감을 만들어내기 위해 똑같은 선율을 반복해서 사용했어요. 그는 또한, 음, 이탈리아 민요의 리듬을 결합했죠. 하지만 그가 전통을 가장 크게 깨뜨린 부분은 음악을 오페라의 중심으로 만들었다는 거예요... 어, 대부분의 작곡가는 가창이 더 중요하다고 생각했거든요. 향후 10여 년 동안, 로시니는 많은 오페라를 썼지만, 음악사에서 그의 지위는 '세비야의 이발사'로 얻었습니다... 1816년에 만들어진 로맨틱 코미디죠. 이 오페라는 유럽에서 이미 굉장히 유명했던 피에르 보마르셰의 무대극을 바탕으로 했어요. 그래서 심지어 그것이 공연되기도 전에 많은 대중의 관심이 있었죠... 네?

S2: 음, 로시니가 '세비야의 이발사'의 성공에 대해 인정받지 못했어야만 했다고 말씀하시는 건가요?

P: 그건 제가 전하려고 한 생각이 아닙니다... 어, '세비야의 이발사'는 제가 앞서 언급했던 획기적인 많은 것들을 포함했어요. 이는 작곡가로서 로시니의 남다른 기술을 소개했죠. 결과적으로, 그 오페라는 당대의 관객들에게 큰 인기를 끌었고 지금은 전례 없는 가장 위대한 오페라 중 하나로 여겨집니다. 로시니는 유럽에서 누구나 아는 이름이 되었어요. 실제로, 어떤 사람들은 그가 베토벤보다도 유명하다고 주장하죠...

어휘
tradition[trədíʃən] (예술 등의) 양식   costume[kástju:m] 분장   stage scenery 무대 장치   inevitable[inévətəbl] 필연적인   prominent[prámənənt] 유명한   thrive[θraiv] 잘 성장하다   text[tekst] 원고   section[sékʃən] 부분   profound[prəfáund] 지대한   rigid[rídʒid] 융통성이 없는   sit well with ~와 어울리다   rebel[rébəl] 반항적인 사람   incorporate[inkɔ́ːrpərèit] 결합하다   folk music 민요   vocal[vóukəl] 가창   showcase[ʃóukèis] 소개하다   contemporary[kəntémpərèri] 당대의   all time 전례 없는   household[háushòuld] 누구나 아는

[18-22]
Listen to a conversation between a student and a professor.

S: Good morning, Professor Blum. Do you have a few minutes?
P: Uh, Sam Porter, right? You were in my classical composition class last semester.
S: That's right. I'm, uh, surprised you remember me. It was a large class.

P: Oh, I make it a point to memorize all of my students' names. Especially those who are music majors. I have a meeting soon, but I can spare a few minutes to chat. What can I do for you?

S: Well . . . My friend John is in your class on Italian opera this semester. He is really enjoying it . . .

P: That's good to hear. I, um, actually just started teaching that class last semester, so positive feedback from students is always appreciated.

S: The thing is . . . he mentioned that the class would be attending an opera at the Harborview Arts Center on, uh, April 11.

P: Yes . . . We will be watching *La Traviata*, which, as I am sure you know, is one of Verdi's most famous works. We've been talking about 19th-century operas, and it will be a great opportunity for the class to hear one live, so I'm looking forward to it.

S: Actually, it is one of my favorite operas. I have wanted to see it performed for a long time now. [Q18] This brings me to the reason I wanted to speak with you. I was, uh, wondering if you had any extra tickets. It would really mean a lot to me if I could attend the opera with your class.

P: I'd really like to help you out . . . It's pretty rare to find a student with such a passion for opera. However, it's just not possible. [Q19] First, I—well, I don't have any extra tickets. I was only given a restricted number . . . and the university has certain policies about who can participate in field trips . . .

S: Really? What do you mean?

P: Well, [Q19] only enrolled students are allowed to take part . . . it's a liability issue. They'll grant exceptions on a case-by-case basis, though. So, [Q19] if a student from outside the class wanted to participate, he or she would've had to request special permission to attend. I'm afraid the deadline for that has passed . . . the department sent out a notice to all students about it.

S: Oh, I must've missed it . . . But I'd really like to see this opera.

P: Have you considered buying your own ticket? You could even try to get a seat in the same area as the other students.

S: Well . . . this is kind of embarrassing, but I can't afford one. Even the cheapest seats are over $150. [Q20] I don't have a part-time job right now, so my money is really limited.

P: Uh, what about volunteering at the arts center? I know they make use of student volunteers . . . [Q21] Volunteers help out writing concert brochures and monthly music newsletters, or assist with seating audience members before concerts . . . and you are majoring in music, so they would be glad to have you. Volunteers get free passes to the performances.

S: [Q22] Um, I'm not sure. I have a busy course load this semester . . .

P: It would only be for a few hours a week. Not a bad deal, in my opinion.

S: You're right. I'll stop by there this Saturday to get some more information. Thanks!

P: I'm glad I could help.

Now get ready to answer the questions. You may use your notes to help you answer.

18. Why does the student visit the professor?
19. According to the professor, why is it impossible for the student to participate in the field trip?
20. Why does the student have very little money right now?
21. According to the professor, what kinds of tasks do volunteers do at the arts center?
22. According to the conversation, why is the student uncertain about volunteering?

S: 좋은 아침입니다, Blum 교수님. 잠시 시간 있으신가요?
P: 어, Sam Porter, 맞지? 지난 학기에 내 고전음악 작곡 수업을 들었었지.
S: 맞아요. 저는, 어, 교수님께서 저를 기억하시다니 놀랍네요. 규모가 큰 수업이었잖아요.

P: 오, 나는 모든 학생의 이름을 반드시 기억한단다. 특히 음악 전공인 학생들은 말이야. 곧 회의가 있지만, 몇 분 정도 이야기할 시간은 낼 수 있단다. 무엇을 도와줄까?

S: 음... 제 친구 John이 이번 학기에 교수님의 이탈리아 오페라 수업을 들어요. 그는 그 수업을 정말 좋아하고 있어요...

P: 그렇다니 다행이구나. 나는, 음, 사실 지난 학기에 그 수업을 가르치기 시작해서, 학생들의 긍정적인 피드백은 늘 고마워한단다.

S: 실은... 제 친구가 그 수업에서 Harborview 아트센터로 오페라를 보러 간다고 하던데요, 어, 4월 11일에요.

P: 그래... 우리는 '라 트라비아타'를 볼 거야, 그건, 너도 분명 알겠지만, 베르디의 가장 유명한 작품 중 하나지. 19세기 오페라에 대한 이야기를 해서, 수업을 듣는 학생들이 실황으로 그 공연을 본다면 멋진 경험이 될 거야, 그래서 기대하고 있단다.

S: 사실, 그건 제가 가장 좋아하는 오페라 중 하나예요. 지금까지 오랫동안 그 공연을 보고 싶었어요. 그게 바로 제가 교수님과 이야기하고 싶었던 이유고요. 저는, 어, 교수님께서 여분의 표를 갖고 계시는지 궁금했거든요. 제가 교수님 수업의 학생들과 함께 오페라를 볼 수 있다면 정말로 큰 의미가 있을 거예요.

P: 나도 정말로 도와주고 싶구나... 오페라에 그만한 열정을 보이는 학생을 보는 건 꽤 드문 일이니까. 하지만, 그게 가능하지가 않단다. 우선, 음, 나는 여분의 표가 없어. 한정된 수만 받았지... 그리고 대학은 누가 현장 학습에 참여할 수 있는지에 대해 분명한 방침을 가지고 있단다.

S: 정말요? 그게 무슨 말씀이세요?

P: 음, 오로지 등록된 학생들만 참가하도록 허락된다는 거야... 책임에 대한 문제이지. 하지만, 그들은 사례에 따라 예외를 허용할 거란다. 그래서, 만약 수업을 듣지 않는 학생이 참가하길 원한다면, 그 학생은 참가를 위한 특별 허가를 요청해야 해. 유감이지만 그것에 대한 마감 기한이 지났단다... 학부가 모든 학생에게 그것에 대한 공지를 발송했었거든.

S: 오, 제가 놓친 게 분명해요... 하지만 저는 정말로 이 오페라를 보고 싶어요.

P: 네가 직접 표를 사는 건 생각해 봤니? 다른 학생들과 같은 구역의 자리를 구할 수도 있을 텐데.

S: 음... 이건 좀 부끄럽지만, 저는 표를 살 여유가 없어요. 심지어 가장 저렴한 자리의 가격도 150달러가 넘잖아요. 지금은 아르바이트를 하고 있지 않아서, 정말로 돈이 많지 않거든요.

P: 어, 아트센터에서 자원봉사하는 건 어떠니? 그들이 학생 자원봉사자를 쓴다고 알고 있는데... 자원봉사자들은 콘서트 책자와 월간 음악 회보를 쓰는 걸 돕거나, 연주회 전에 관객들에게 자리를 안내하지... 그리고 넌 음악을 전공하고 있으니까, 그들이 널 반길 거야. 자원봉사자들은 공연의 무료 입장권을 받는단다.

S: 음, 잘 모르겠어요. 이번 학기에는 수업 분량이 많아서 바쁘거든요...

P: 그건 일주일에 몇 시간이면 될 거야. 내 생각에, 나쁜 조건은 아니란다.

S: 교수님 말씀이 맞아요. 이번 주 토요일에 그곳에 들러서 좀 더 정보를 얻어 볼게요. 감사합니다!

P: 도와줄 수 있어서 기쁘구나.

어휘

composition[kàmpəzíʃən] 작곡 make it a point to 반드시 ~하다 spare[spɛər] (시간·돈 등을) 내다
appreciate[əpríːʃièit] 고마워하다 extra[ékstrə] 여분의 restricted[ristríktid] 한정된 field trip 현장 학습
enroll[inróul] 등록하다 liability[làiəbíləti] 책임 exception[iksépʃən] 예외 permission[pərmíʃən] 허가
limited[límitid] 많지 않은 brochure[brouʃúər] (안내·광고용) 책자 newsletter[njúːzlètər] 회보 free pass 무료 입장권

[23-28]

Listen to a talk on beavers' decision making.

P: Good afternoon, everyone. ᑫ²³ Today, I'd like to talk about decisions. Decision making is a part of our everyday life, right? I mean, you made a decision to come to class today, a decision as to what you ate, and a decision about what clothes you're wearing. Here's the question I want to ask, though: is decision making a purely human capability, or can animals do it too? ᑫ²³ To narrow things down a bit, let's focus on the behavior of beavers.

Why did I choose beavers to look at? Put simply, because they make dams. Dam making is a highly complex behavior that allows beavers to build a dwelling that's protected from predators and provides them with safe access to food sources. ᑫ²⁴ Dams cause a stream or river to flood, and the beaver lives in a shelter called a lodge in the middle of the flooded region that develops. They make their dams primarily from trees, and if you've ever seen a picture of a beaver before, you can guess how they do it—they use those giant teeth of theirs to gnaw away at the tree's trunk until it falls, and then they cut it up and drag it back, or float it downstream, to the place they're building the dam. We can already see that there's a decision to be made . . . ^Q25 the beaver has to decide which trees to cut down and which ones to leave. They have to consider tree size, distance to the tree, ease of transport, the tree location's exposure to predators . . . lots of variables. Beavers like aspens, willows, and pines, but that could be a genetically programmed preference.

In terms of selecting a specific tree, though . . . well, there was an experiment done a few years ago that dealt with this. A controlled environment was set up where there was a small group of three trees relatively nearby and a large, single tree quite a bit of distance away . . . maybe three or four times farther away than the close ones. What would you do in this situation? Let's take a look at the pros and cons. ^Q26 If the beaver chooses the closer trees, it limits the danger of predators because the beavers can quickly jump in the water to avoid them, since the predators typically can't swim. ^Q27 Going far away from their lodge—their home—exposes them to more danger. Also, we can think of energy expenditure. A beaver is going to use up much more energy trying to drag a huge tree across a large distance than it would by chopping down and carrying three small ones. It seems obvious to me which decision to make, yet the beavers in the experiment always went for the single tree. I'm not sure why—it's likely a result of genetic programming.

S: ^Q28 But don't beavers build their dams at night? Doesn't that put them in danger of predators?
P: Right. Think about which animals hunt beavers . . . wolves, coyotes, wolverines . . . these are all nocturnal animals. They're awake at night. And if they're awake, chances are they are hunting. This goes to show us again that beavers do what they are programmed to do and don't actually think, even if a behavior appears complex. If they could, they'd likely build their dams during the day and rest at night, nodding off to sleep in their island-like lodges.

Now get ready to answer the questions. You may use your notes to help you answer.

23. What does the professor mainly discuss?
24. According to the lecture, what purpose does a dam serve?
25. According to the lecture, what is true of beavers when finding dam-building materials?
26. What does the professor say about the beaver's predators?
27. What are two disadvantages of beavers choosing the far tree in the experiment?
28. What do beavers and their predators have in common?

P: 안녕하세요, 여러분. 오늘은, 결정에 대해 이야기하고 싶어요. 결정을 내리는 것은 우리 일상생활의 한 부분입니다, 그렇죠? 내 말은, 여러분은 오늘 수업에 오기로 결정했고, 먹은 것에 대한 결정, 그리고 입고 있는 옷에 대한 결정을 내렸어요. 하지만, 제가 하고 싶은 질문은 이것입니다. 결정을 내리는 것은 순전히 인간의 능력일까요, 아니면 동물들도 할 수 있을까요? 내용을 좀 좁히기 위해, 비버들의 행동에 초점을 맞춰 봅시다.

제가 왜 비버를 살펴보자고 선택했을까요? 간단히 말하자면, 그들이 댐을 만들기 때문이죠. 댐을 만드는 것은 비버들이 포식동물들로부터 보호되고 식량 자원으로의 안전한 길을 제공하는 주거지를 만들 수 있도록 하는 아주 복잡한 행동입니다. 댐은 시내나 강이 넘치도록 하며, 비버들은 확장하는 침수 지역의 중간에 있으며 오두막이라고 불리는 은신처에 살아요. 비버들은 그들의 댐을 주로 나무로 만들어요, 그리고 여러분이 앞서 비버의 사진을 본 적 있다면, 그들이 어떻게 하는지 추측할 수 있을 텐데요, 비버들은 그들의 거대한 이빨을 사용하여 나무가 무너질 때까지 그루터기를 갉아대서, 그것을 잘라서 끌고 가거나, 하류로 떠내려가게 해서, 그들이 댐을 짓고 있는 장소로 보내요. 우리는 여기서 이미 결정해야 할 것이 있다는 걸 알 수 있어요... 비버는 어떤 나무를 자르고 어떤 걸 남겨둘지 결정해야 해요. 나무의 크기, 나무까지의 거리, 운송의 편리함, 나무의 위치가 포식동물에게 노출되는지... 많은 변수들을 고려해야 하죠. 비버들은 미루나무, 버드나무, 그리고 소나무를 좋아하지만, 그건 유전적으로 정해진 선호일 수도 있어요.

하지만, 특정 나무를 선택하는 것에 있어서... 음, 몇 년 전에 이것을 다룬 실험이 있었어요. 통제된 환경이 만들어졌는데 이곳에는 비교적 가까운 곳에 있는 작은 나무 세 그루와 커다란, 한 그루의 나무가 조금 먼 곳에 있었죠... 아마 가까운 것보다 3배나 4배 더 먼 곳에 있었을 거예요. 여러분이라면 이 상황에서 어떻게 하겠어요? 장단점을 살펴보죠. 만약 비버가 가까운 나무를 선택한다면, 포식동물들은 보통 수영을 못하기 때문에, 비버는 그들을 피하기 위해 빨리 물 속으로 뛰어들 수 있으므로 포식동물들의 위험이 적을 거예요. 그들의 집인 오두막에서 멀리 가는 것은 더 많은 위험에 노출시키죠. 또한, 우리는 에너지 소비도 생각할 수 있어요. 비버는 작은 나무 세 그루를 베어 운반하는 것보다 커다란 나무 한 그루를 먼 거리에 걸쳐 끌고 오는 데 훨씬 더 많은 에너지를 사용하게 돼요. 저에게는 어떤 결정을 내려야 할지 명확한데, 이 실험에서 비버들은 항상 하나의 나무만을 선택했어요. 왜 그런지는 모르겠는데, 유전적으로 정해져 있는 결과일 확률이 크죠.

S: 하지만 비버들은 밤에 댐을 짓지 않나요? 그건 비버를 포식동물의 위험에 빠뜨리는 거 아닌가요?

P: 맞아요. 어떤 동물들이 비버를 사냥하는지 생각해 보세요... 늑대, 코요테, 오소리... 이들은 모두 야행성 동물이에요. 밤에 깨어 있죠. 그리고 만약 이들이 깨어 있다면, 사냥을 하고 있을 확률이 커요. 이것은 비버들이 정해져 있는 대로 행동하고 사실 생각을 하지 않는다는 걸 다시 보여주죠, 비록 행동이 복잡해 보이더라도요. 할 수 있다면, 그들은 낮 동안에 댐을 짓고 밤에는 쉬겠죠, 섬 같은 오두막에서 꾸벅꾸벅 졸면서요.

어휘

dwelling[dwélin] 주거지　predator[prédətər] 포식동물　shelter[ʃéltər] 은신처　lodge[lɑdʒ] 오두막
gnaw away at ~을 갉아대다　trunk[trʌŋk] (나무의) 그루터기　variable[vέəriəbl] 변수　aspen[ǽspən] 미루나무
willow[wílou] 버드나무　pine[pain] 소나무　genetically[dʒənétikəli] 유전적으로　programmed[próugræmd] 정해진
preference[préfərəns] 선호　pros and cons 장단점　expenditure[ikspéndi.tʃər] 소비　chop down 베다
wolverine[wùlvərí:n] 오소리　nocturnal[nɑktə́:rnl] 야행성의　nod off to sleep 꾸벅꾸벅 졸다

[29-34]
Listen to part of a lecture from an art history class. The professor is discussing Renaissance art.

I'd like to pick up where we left off yesterday . . . um, the visual arts in Renaissance Europe. Um, there were various painting techniques used during this period. Of course, oil painting is probably the most famous . . . ^{Q29} but I want to start with another type of painting . . . the fresco. This technique isn't used much these days, so you might not be familiar with it. Just so you know the basics, let me briefly outline the process. It starts with putting wet plaster on the wall . . . and, um, plaster was basically a mixture of sand, water, and lime at this time. Next, the artist applies water-based paint to the plaster. When paint is applied to plaster, a chemical reaction occurs. This causes the paint to bond with the plaster. ^{Q30} The paint actually becomes, uh, part of the wall rather than just covering it. As a result, it is very difficult to fix any mistakes . . . the paint can't just be wiped off or painted over. Another challenge is that the color of the paint changes significantly as the plaster dries . . . Um, so an artist can't be sure what a section of the painting will look like until it is finished.

Despite these disadvantages, Renaissance artists used the fresco technique to create many stunning works of art. And while the styles of these paintings vary greatly, they all share a couple of key features. Uh, let's take a look at an example . . . Michelangelo's large paintings on the ceiling of the Sistine Chapel are the most well-known frescoes, but my personal favorite is Raphael's *The School of Athens*. ^{Q31} Um, the majority of frescoes from this period deal with religious themes. But *The School of Athens* is different. It's not a religious scene . . . it depicts over 20 scholars from ancient Greece and Rome standing together in a room . . . people like, uh, Plato and Aristotle.

Here . . . let me put a picture up on the screen. I'm sure the first thing that strikes you is the bright, contrasting colors. I mean, just look at the robes the figures are wearing . . . most of them are bright green, red, blue, or yellow. These are the colors that were typically used in Renaissance frescoes. There's a practical reason for this. ^{Q32} You see, the lime in plaster is corrosive . . . It can actually destroy many of the natural pigments that Renaissance artists used to make their paints. But the pigments that produce the colors I just mentioned are not affected by lime. Now, since the paint was immediately absorbed by the plaster . . . well, this meant that the artist couldn't really blend different colors together. So each part of the plaster was usually painted only one color. ^{Q33} That's why the transitions between the colors in this painting are so sudden. Again, look at the robes . . . There's none of the gradual blending you'd see in an oil painting.

OK . . . another thing about this fresco is that many of the people seem to have, um . . . I guess you could say dark, intense eyes. This is because Raphael took advantage of the fact that he was painting on wet plaster. ^{Q34} He used his brush to kind of . . . um . . . to press down on the plaster whenever he painted someone's eyes. So they appear deeper and, uh, more distinct than the rest of the face. This was a common practice when painting a fresco. Artists often did this to create a three-dimensional effect that added emphasis. For example, some painters would push the plaster down around an important figure . . . Uh, this caused the person to stand out more prominently than the other parts of the painting . . .

Now get ready to answer the questions. You may use your notes to help you answer.

29. What is the main topic of the lecture?
30. What are the disadvantages of the fresco method?
31. What distinguishes *The School of Athens* from other Renaissance frescoes?
32. Why were only certain colors used when painting a fresco?
33. What does the professor say about the color transitions in *The School of Athens*?
34. How did artists make certain elements of a fresco more noticeable?

어제 우리가 멈췄던 부분부터 계속하고 싶군요... 음, 르네상스 유럽에서의 시각 예술 말이에요. 음, 이 시기 동안 사용된 다양한 화법이 있었어요. 물론, 아마도 유화가 가장 유명하겠죠... 하지만 또 다른 종류의 그림으로 시작해 보고 싶군요... 프레스코화 말이죠. 오늘날에는 이 화법이 많이 사용되지 않아서, 여러분은 이것에 익숙하지 않을 수도 있어요. 여러분들이 기초를 알 수 있도록, 그 과정의 개요를 간단하게 서술해 볼게요. 그건 덜 마른 석고 반죽을 벽에 바르는 것으로 시작합니다... 그리고, 음, 기본적으로 이 시기에 석고 반죽은 모래, 물, 그리고 석회의 혼합물이었죠. 다음으로, 화가는 수성 물감을 석고 반죽에 바릅니다. 물감이 석고 반죽에 발라지면, 화학 반응이 일어나요. 이는 물감이 석고 반죽과 결합되도록 하죠. 실제로 물감은, 어, 그저 벽을 덮기보다는 벽의 일부가 돼요. 결과적으로, 어떠한 실수라도 고치기 매우 어렵죠... 물감은 단지 닦이거나 덧칠될 수 없으니까요. 또 다른 문제는 석고 반죽이 마르면서 물감의 색깔이 상당히 변한다는 거예요... 음, 그래서 화가는 끝날 때까지 그림의 일부가 어떻게 보일지 확신할 수 없죠.

이러한 단점에도 불구하고, 르네상스 화가들은 많은 훌륭한 미술 작품을 만들어내기 위해 프레스코 화법을 사용했어요. 그리고 이러한 그림들의 방식이 서로 크게 달랐음에도 불구하고, 그것들은 모두 몇 가지 주요한 특징을 공통으로 가지고 있었죠. 어, 예를 하나 살펴봅시다... 시스티나 성당 천장에 있는 미켈란젤로의 커다란 그림들이 가장 잘 알려진 프레스코화인데, 제가 개인적으로 좋아하는 것은 라파엘의 '아테네 학당'입니다. 음, 이 시기의 프레스코화 대다수는 종교적인 주제를 다뤄요. 하지만 '아테네 학당'은 다르죠. 그건 종교적인 장면이 아니에요... 그건 고대 그리스와 로마의 20명 넘는 학자들이 한 공간에 함께 서 있는 것을 묘사하거든요... 어, 플라톤과 아리스토텔레스 같은 사람들 말이죠.

여기... 화면에 그림 하나를 띄워 볼게요. 가장 먼저 여러분의 주의를 끈 것이 밝고, 대비를 이루는 색깔들일 거라고 확신합니다. 제 말은, 인물들이 입고 있는 예복을 좀 보세요... 그것들 대부분은 밝은 초록색, 빨간색, 파란색, 또는 노란색입니다. 이는 르네상스 프레스코화에서 전형적으로 사용되었던 색깔들이에요. 여기에는 실질적인 이유가 하나 있죠. 그러니까, 석고 반죽 안의 석회가 부식을 일으켰거든요... 그건 실제로 르네상스 화가들이 그들의 물감을 만드는 데 사용했던 많은 천연 색소들을 훼손할 수 있었어요. 하지만 제가 방금 언급했던 색깔들을 만들어내는 색소는 석회의 영향을 받지 않습니다. 자, 물감은 석고 반죽에 즉시 흡수됐기 때문에... 음, 이는 화가가 사실상 다른 색깔들을 함께 혼합할 수 없다는 것을 의미했어요. 그래서 석고 반죽의 각 부분은 보통 오직 한 가지의 색깔로 칠해졌습니다. 그게 바로 이 그림에서 색깔 간의 변화가 굉장히 갑작스러운 이유입니다. 다시, 예복을 보세요... 여러분들이 유화에서 볼 수 있는 점진적인 혼합이 없죠.

좋아요... 이 프레스코화에 관한 또 다른 점은 많은 사람들이, 음... 어둡고, 짙다고 말할 수 있는 눈을 가지고 있는 것처럼 보인다는 거예요. 이는 라파엘이 그가 덜 마른 석고 반죽 위에 그림을 그리고 있다는 사실을 이용했기 때문이죠. 그는 누군가의 눈을 그릴 때마다 붓을... 음... 석고 반죽 위를 누르는 식으로 사용했어요. 그래서 그것들은 얼굴의 나머지보다 더 깊고, 어, 더 뚜렷하게 나타나죠. 이는 프레스코화를 그릴 때 흔한 관습이었습니다. 화가들은 종종 강조를 더하는 입체적인 효과를 만들어내기 위해 이렇게 했죠. 예를 들어, 일부 화가들은 중요한 인물 주위의 석고 반죽을 내리눌렀습니다... 어, 이는 그 사람이 그림의 다른 부분보다 더 두드러지게 눈에 띄도록 했거든요...

어휘

fresco[fréskou] 프레스코화 outline[àutláin] 개요를 서술하다 plaster[plǽstər] 석고 반죽 lime[laim] 석회 apply[əplái] 바르다
water-based[wɔ́:tərbèist] 수성의 wipe off 닦다 paint over 덧칠을 하다 stunning[stʌ́niŋ] 훌륭한
strike[straik] 주의를 끌다 contrasting[kəntrǽstiŋ] 대비를 이루는 robe[roub] 예복 corrosive[kəróusiv] 부식을 일으키는
pigment[pígmənt] 색소 transition[trænzíʃən] 변화 intense[inténs] 짙은 take advantage of ~을 이용하다
three-dimensional[θrì:diménʃənl] 입체적인 stand out 눈에 띄다

CHAPTER 03 Function & Attitude

* 각 문제에 대한 정답단서는 지문에 보라색으로 표시되어 있습니다.

문제 공략하기
p.77

W: 안녕하세요, 어... 제 과제 중 하나가, 음, 특이하고 오래된 책에 관해 보고서를 작성하는 거예요. 그래서 제가 사용할 만한 좋은 것이 있나요?

M: 특이하고 오래된 책이라... 어디 보자... 오, 한 권 있네요. 요리책이요.

W: 농담하시는 거죠! 그러니까... 조리법이요? 하지만, 음... 그 책으로 제가 뭘 할 수 있나요? 제 말은, 그건 그저 조리법이잖아요.

M: 그게, 이건 그냥 오래된 요리책이 아니에요. 이 책에 있는 조리법과 작가가 그것들을 설명하는 방법이 옛 문화를 많이 보여주고 있거든요.

W: 오, 작가가 조리법에 대해 무언가를 말하는군요... 음, 그럼, 자료를 충분히 제공하겠네요. 며칠 동안 그 책을 빌려가야겠어요.

M: 미안하지만, 그렇게는 안 돼요. 우리 도서관의 방침은, 이 문제라면, 다른 도서관에서도 그러겠지만, 이용자들이 오래되고, 희귀한 책들은 도서관에서만 볼 수 있다는 거예요.

HACKERS PRACTICE
p.78

1. (D) Function & Attitude	2. (C) Function & Attitude	3. (A) Function & Attitude
4. (D) Main Purpose/Topic	5. (B) Function & Attitude	6. (A) Function & Attitude
7. (C) Main Purpose/Topic	8. (D) Function & Attitude	9. (A), (D) Detail
10. (B) Main Purpose/Topic	11. (C) Function & Attitude	12. (A), (D) Detail

[1-3]

Listen to a conversation between a student and an employee at the university fitness center.

M: Hi. Uh, I'd like to use the gym for a few hours.

W: OK . . . I assume you're a student here?

M: Actually, no. I attend an out-of-state school. I'm visiting my family for the last few weeks of the summer vacation. Q1 Could I get a . . . you know . . . a visitor pass?

W: Sure. I'll just need to see some ID.

M: Oh . . . ID. I didn't even think about that. Um, the thing is . . . I lost my wallet.

W: Really? That's too bad. The same thing happened to my friend, and . . . well, it was a real hassle.

M: You can say that again. So, I, um . . . obviously don't have an ID right now.

W: I'm really sorry, but there isn't much I can do. The university has really strict rules about using the gym . . . It's a matter of security.

M: I can't believe this . . . It just doesn't seem fair.

W: You'll hear no argument from me. But I'm just an employee . . . I have to follow the policy.

M: I know . . . It's not your fault. Q2 But this is really frustrating. Um, this gym is really close to my parents' house, and I heard it has excellent facilities. I'm hoping to join the volleyball team next semester, so I need to stay fit.

W: That's understandable . . . I was an athlete in my university days as well. Um, I don't suppose you have a copy of your ID?

M: A copy?

W: Um, some people scan their ID in case they lose it. I could issue you a visitor pass if I had a copy of your ID, I guess.

M: Hmm . . . I wish I'd thought of that before. Any other ideas?

W: Let me see . . . Do you know anyone who attends this university?

M: Actually, my friend is a student here. Uh, he's the one who recommended this gym to me . . .

W: 03 Well, he could sign you in as a guest. The only thing is that both of you would have to use the gym at the same time.

M: At the same time? I don't know . . . I like to work out pretty early in the day, and my friend . . . Um, he's not really a morning person. It'd be kind of inconvenient.

W: This is the only way I can think of for you to use the gym, though . . .

M: I guess you have a point . . . I'll call my friend and see if I can figure something out. Thanks for taking the time to give me some options.

W: No problem . . . I just wish I could've done more.

Now get ready to answer the questions. You may use your notes to help you answer.

Listen again to part of the conversation. Then answer the question.

M: Could I get a . . . you know . . . a visitor pass?

W: Sure. I'll just need to see some ID.

M: Oh . . . ID. I didn't even think about that. Um, the thing is . . . I lost my wallet.

1. What does the student mean when he says this:
   W: Oh . . . ID.

Listen again to part of the conversation. Then answer the question.

M: But this is really frustrating. Um, this gym is really close to my parents' house, and I heard it has excellent facilities. I'm hoping to join the volleyball team next semester, so I need to stay fit.

W: That's understandable . . . I was an athlete in my university days as well.

2. What does the employee mean when she says this:
   W: That's understandable . . .

Listen again to part of the conversation. Then answer the question.

W: Well, he could sign you in as a guest. The only thing is that both of you would have to use the gym at the same time.

M: At the same time? I don't know . . . I like to work out pretty early in the day, and my friend . . . Um, he's not really a morning person. It'd be kind of inconvenient.

3. Why does the student say this:
   M: I don't know . . .

M: 안녕하세요. 어, 체육관을 몇 시간만 사용하고 싶은데요.

W: 네... 여기 학생이시죠?

M: 사실, 아니에요. 저는 다른 주의 대학에 다녀요. 여름 방학 몇 주 동안 가족을 방문하는 중이에요. 제가... 그러니까... 방문객 출입증을 얻을 수 있을까요?

W: 물론이죠. 신분증만 확인하면 돼요.

M: 오... 신분증이요. 그것에 대해서는 생각도 못 했네요. 음, 문제는... 제가 지갑을 잃어버렸어요.

W: 정말이요? 그것참 안됐네요. 제 친구한테 똑같은 일이 있었는데... 음, 그건 정말 번거로운 상황이었죠.

M: 전적으로 동의해요. 그래서, 저는, 음... 당연히 지금 당장 신분증을 가지고 있지 않아요.

W: 정말 죄송하지만, 제가 해줄 수 있는 게 없네요. 우리 대학은 체육관 사용에 관해 매우 엄격한 규칙을 가지고 있거든요... 보안 문제 라서요.

M: 말도 안 돼요... 이건 타당하지 않아 보이는데요.

W: 일리가 있다고 생각해요. 하지만 저는 직원일 뿐이라... 규정을 따라야 해요.

M: 알아요... 당신 잘못이 아니에요. 하지만 이건 정말 불만스럽네요. 음, 이 체육관은 저희 부모님 집과 정말 가깝고, 훌륭한 시설들을 가지고 있다고 들었거든요. 저는 다음 학기에 배구팀에 가입하고 싶어서 체력관리를 해야 하고요.

W: 이해할 만하군요... 저도 대학 시절 운동선수였거든요. 음, 신분증 사본을 가지고 있지는 않죠?

M: 사본이요?

W: 음, 어떤 사람들은 신분증을 잃어버릴 때를 대비해서 그것을 스캔하죠. 제 생각에, 신분증 사본이 있다면 방문객 출입증을 발급해 드릴 수 있을 것 같아서요.

M: 흠... 제가 이전에 그 생각을 했다면 좋았을 텐데요. 다른 방안은 없나요?

W: 어디 보자... 이 대학에 다니는 누구든 아는 사람이 있나요?

M: 사실, 제 친구가 여기 학생이에요. 어, 그가 바로 제게 이 체육관을 추천해준 친구거든요...

W: 음, 그가 학생을 손님으로 가입시켜줄 수 있어요. 한 가지 문제는 둘이 동시에 체육관을 사용해야 한다는 거죠.

M: 동시에요? 잘 모르겠네요... 저는 낮에 꽤 일찍 운동하는 걸 좋아하는데, 제 친구는... 음, 아침형 인간이 아니거든요. 그건 좀 불편 할 것 같네요.

W: 하지만 이게 제가 생각할 수 있는 학생이 체육관을 사용할 유일한 방법이에요...

M: 일리가 있는 것 같아요... 친구에게 전화해서 뭐든 알아낼 수 있을지 봐야겠어요. 제게 몇 가지 방안을 주시느라 시간 내주셔서 감 사합니다.

W: 천만에요... 제가 더 도울 수 있었다면 좋았을 거예요.

[4-6]

Listen to a conversation in a registrar's office.

W: Hello! How may I help you today?

M: ^{Q4} I came to pay my tuition. I have a check here for the balance left on my account.

W: OK, then give me just a minute to pull up your record. Can I have your student ID, please?

M: Oh, yeah, here you go.

W: Mr. Jameson? It seems that the balance of your payment, which is, uh, half the tuition, was due last week.

M: Yeah, I know. I was waiting for the check from my parents to come, and I didn't get it until this morning.

W: But the registrar's office has strict guidelines regarding payment of fees. And ^{Q5} since your dues weren't paid in full by last week's deadline, your registration has been canceled. After making the final payment today, you can register for classes again. Does that make sense?

M: Yeah, I understand, but that puts me in a real bind. It's so late in the registration process now that if I try to sign up for the classes again, they'll definitely be full. And two of the required courses for my major are only offered once a year. That means I'd have to wait two whole semesters before enrolling in those courses again.

W: That's all the more reason to make sure your payments are received on time . . . or if for some reason you can't meet the deadline, you would need to negotiate a payment plan with the college treasurer's office . . . but before the deadline, not after. At this point, you have only one option. You need to make an appointment to see your advisor.

M: What good will that do? I mean, if a class is full, shouldn't I try to convince the professor of that course to let me in?

W: You could definitely try that route, but usually advisors have an easier time convincing professors to let students into classes when they are full. Your advisor is sort of, well, your mediator. In any case, it may be the only hope you have to get the classes you want.

M: Hmm . . . OK, I will make an appointment with him today. Now, let's see . . . so after I make this payment, I'll be able to register for classes again, right?

W: Let me just record your payment right now . . . there you go! Good as new!

M: All right. Thanks for your help.

W: Q6 For future purposes, you should concentrate on paying your bills on time . . . especially when it comes to tuition fees.

M: You aren't kidding!

Now get ready to answer the questions. You may use your notes to help you answer.

4. Why does the student visit the registrar's office?

Listen again to part of the conversation. Then answer the question.

W: . . . since your dues weren't paid in full by last week's deadline, your registration has been canceled. After making the final payment today, you can register for classes again. Does that make sense?

5. Why does the woman say this:
   W: Does that make sense?

Listen again to part of the conversation. Then answer the question.

W: For future purposes, you should concentrate on paying your bills on time . . . especially when it comes to tuition fees.

M: You aren't kidding!

6. Why does the man say this:
   M: You aren't kidding!

W: 안녕하세요! 오늘 어떻게 도와드릴까요?

M: 수업료를 내러 왔어요. 제 계정에 있는 잔액을 낼 수표를 여기 가져왔습니다.

W: 네, 그럼 학생의 기록을 잠시 찾아볼게요. 학생증 좀 줄래요?

M: 오, 네, 여기 있어요.

W: Jameson 씨? 학생의 납부금 잔액, 그러니까, 어, 수업료 절반의, 납부 기한이 지난주까지였어요.

M: 네, 알고 있어요. 부모님께서 보내주신 수표가 오기를 기다리고 있었는데, 오늘 아침까지 받지 못했거든요.

W: 하지만 학적과는 수업료 납부에 관해 엄격한 정책을 가지고 있어요. 그리고 학생의 수업료가 지난주 마감 기한까지 완전히 납부되지 않아서, 등록이 취소되었고요. 오늘 마지막 금액을 납부한 후, 다시 수업에 등록할 수 있어요. 이해되나요?

M: 네, 이해돼요, 하지만 그건 저를 정말 곤란한 상황에 놓이게 하네요. 이제 등록 일정상 너무 늦어서 제가 수업에 다시 등록하려고 하면, 분명히 다 찼을 거예요. 그리고 제 전공 필수 과목 중 두 개는 일 년에 오직 한 번만 제공돼요. 그건 제가 이 수업들에 다시 등록하려면 두 학기 전체를 기다려야 한다는 뜻이고요.

W: 그러니까 납부금이 제때 도착하는지 더 확실히 했어야죠... 혹은 어떠한 이유로 마감 기한을 못 맞춘다면, 학교의 회계과 직원과 납부 계획을 조정해야 하는 거고요... 하지만 마감 기한 전에요, 그 후가 아니라. 이 시점에서는, 한 가지 방법밖에 없어요. 지도 교수님과 만날 약속을 해야 해요.

M: 그게 어떤 도움이 될까요? 제 말은, 수업이 다 찼다면, 들어가기 위해서 그 수업의 교수님을 설득하려고 해야 하는 것 아닌가요?

W: 물론 그런 방법도 시도해 볼 수 있겠지만, 보통 지도 교수님은 수업이 다 찼어도 학생들이 그것을 들을 수 있도록 그 교수님을 더

쉽게 설득할 수 있거든요. 학생의 지도 교수님은 일종의 음, 중재인이라고 할 수 있죠. 어쨌든, 이건 학생이 원하는 수업을 들을 수 있는 유일한 희망일 수 있어요.

M: 흠... 네, 오늘 지도 교수님과 약속을 잡을게요. 이제, 어디 보자... 그래서 수업료를 납부하면, 다시 수업에 등록할 수 있는 거죠, 그렇죠?

W: 학생의 납부 내역을 지금 바로 기록할게요... 됐어요! 감쪽같아요!

M: 좋아요. 도와주셔서 감사합니다.

W: 앞으로는, 납부금을 제때 내는 것에 신경 쓰도록 하세요... 특히 수업료에 관해서는요.

M: 물론이죠!

[7-9]
Listen to part of a lecture from an archaeology class.

P: Since the late 18th century, approximately 400 stone balls have been discovered in Scotland . . . Um, they're anywhere from 3,000 to 5,000 years old. ⁰⁷ A number of theories have been presented to explain the function of these objects . . . and this morning we'll consider a couple of these.
First, though, let me put a few pictures up on the screen. As you can see, these artifacts are all about the same size . . . What makes them unique is that they have elaborate spirals and rings carved into their surface . . . Yes?

S1: Um, actually, I'm surprised they're so detailed. They're thousands of years old, right? It must have taken a long time to make them . . . especially with primitive tools . . .

P: That's a good point . . . Some experts believe each took about 100 hours to produce. And of course, this leads to the question . . . what were they used for? ⁰⁸ One theory is that these balls functioned as weights on early scales. Um, this is based on the fact that they're all roughly the same size . . . 7 centimeters in diameter. But, uh, most scholars find this idea unlikely. I mean, why put so much effort into making something that just served as a weight? A more likely explanation is that these objects were part of a weapon. Um, is anyone familiar with a bola?

S2: Yeah . . . Isn't that a type of throwing weapon? It came up in another class I'm taking . . .

P: Right . . . Basically, stone or metal balls are fastened to the ends of a long rope. If this is thrown at an animal, it will wrap around the animal's neck or legs. Now, one piece of evidence to support this theory is the shape of the stone balls. ⁰⁹ They aren't perfect spheres . . . They actually have deep lines cut into them. So it wouldn't have been difficult to tie leather ropes around them. In addition, the artifacts are decorated with intricate patterns. This is another point in favor of the weapon theory. Ancient hunters often had very elaborate weapons . . . This helped to indicate their status as skillful hunters.
But, well . . . this argument has a major weakness. Um, prized possessions such as weapons were usually placed in tombs. But the stone balls have never been found at a gravesite. So the exact purpose of the stone balls remains a mystery . . .

Now get ready to answer the questions. You may use your notes to help you answer.

7. What is the lecture mainly about?

Listen again to part of the lecture. Then answer the question.

P: One theory is that these balls functioned as weights on early scales. Um, this is based on the fact that they're all roughly the same size . . . 7 centimeters in diameter. But, uh, most scholars find this idea unlikely. I mean, why put so much effort into making something that just served as a weight?

8. Why does the professor say this:

P: I mean, why put so much effort into making something that just served as a weight?

9. Why is it likely that the stone balls were part of a weapon?

P: 18세기 후반부터, 스코틀랜드에서 약 400개의 석구가 발견되었어요... 음, 그것들은 3,000년에서 5,000년 전 사이의 것이었습니다. 이 물건의 기능을 설명하기 위해 많은 이론이 제시되었고요... 그리고 오늘 오전에는 이 중 몇 개를 고찰해 볼 거예요.

하지만, 먼저, 화면에 사진 몇 장을 띄워 볼게요. 여러분이 볼 수 있듯이, 이 공예품들은 거의 모두 같은 크기입니다... 그것들을 특별하게 만드는 것은 표면에 새겨진 정교한 나선과 고리 모양을 가지고 있다는 것이죠... 네?

S1: 음, 사실, 저는 그것들이 굉장히 정밀하다는 데 놀랐어요. 수천 년 된 것들이잖아요, 맞죠? 그것들을 만드는 데 틀림없이 오랜 시간이 걸렸을 거예요... 특히 원시 도구를 가지고서는요...

P: 좋은 지적이에요... 일부 전문가들은 각각을 만들어내는 데 약 100시간이 걸렸을 거라고 생각하죠. 그리고 물론, 이것은 바로 이 질문으로 이어집니다... 그것들이 어디에 쓰였을까요? 한 이론은 이 구들이 초기 저울의 추로써 기능했다는 것입니다. 음, 이는 그것 모두가 거의 같은 크기라는 사실에 근거하죠... 지름 7cm 말이에요. 하지만, 어, 학자 대부분은 이 발상이 믿기 힘들다고 생각해요. 제 말은, 겨우 추로 쓰이는 무언가를 만드는 데 왜 그렇게 많은 노력을 들였겠어요? 더 그럴듯한 설명은 이 물건들이 무기의 일부였다는 것이죠. 음, 볼라를 알고 있는 사람 있나요?

S2: 네... 던지는 무기의 한 종류 아닌가요? 제가 듣고 있는 다른 수업에서 나왔었거든요...

P: 맞아요... 기본적으로, 돌이나 금속 구가 기다란 밧줄 끝에 단단히 고정돼요. 이게 동물에게 던져지면, 동물의 목이나 다리 주변을 휘감죠. 자, 이 이론을 뒷받침하는 한 가지 증거는 석구의 모양이에요. 그것들은 완벽한 구가 아니거든요... 실제로는 새겨진 깊은 선들을 가지고 있죠. 그래서 그것들 주위에 가죽 밧줄을 매는 것은 어렵지 않았을 거예요. 게다가, 그 공예품은 복잡한 무늬로 장식되어 있어요. 이는 무기 이론을 지지하는 또 다른 점이죠. 고대 사냥꾼들은 보통 매우 정교한 무기를 가지고 있었거든요... 이는 솜씨 좋은 사냥꾼으로서 그들의 지위를 보여주는 것을 도왔고요.

하지만, 음... 이 주장은 중대한 약점을 가지고 있어요. 음, 무기와 같은 소중한 소유물들은 보통 무덤에 놓여있었거든요. 그런데 석구들은 묘지에서 발견된 적이 전혀 없었어요. 따라서 석구의 정확한 목적은 수수께끼로 남아있죠...

[10-12]
Listen to part of a lecture in a biology class.

P: By now, you all know that the tiny organisms known as zooplankton are an important part of the ocean's food chain . . . Um, at the bottom of the chain are marine plants that convert sunlight into energy. Zooplankton eat these plants. In turn, they are eaten by larger creatures like fish and whales. Q10 Let's look more closely at the zooplankton's diet and, specifically, the daily journey it makes to search for food.

Um, some types of zooplankton can find food near their underwater habitats . . . they don't have to look far. But for some varieties . . . a little less than 50 percent . . . they need to go up to the ocean's surface to get food . . . a migration, in other words. This is because there is a large supply of the microorganisms they feed on at the surface. So after the sun sets, these types of zooplankton travel from the ocean's depths to the surface. At dawn, they return to deep water. Q11 Over a 24-hour period, they migrate about a kilometer. Yes?

S1: I don't mean to interrupt, but, um . . . Did you say a kilometer? That doesn't seem far enough to be called a migration . . .

P: Well, remember that zooplankton are small . . . just a few millimeters in length. For a creature that size, a kilometer is a long way to go . . . In addition, water feels very different for these tiny creatures. Because of their small size in relation to the ocean, they experience strong resistance from the water. Uh, it feels like a thick, sticky soup to them. This means that it takes a lot of effort to swim through it. Luckily for them, they've developed a number of ways to do this. ^{Q12} Some use their legs to push themselves against the water . . . it almost looks like they're walking. Others have body parts that they flap like wings. Still others pull themselves through the water using their antennae.

S2: Um, but what about ocean currents? Aren't zooplankton too small to swim against currents?

P: Well, yes, that's true. But this isn't a serious problem. See, ocean currents move side-to-side, while zooplankton swim upwards. So, even as the currents push them in one direction, the zooplankton can continue to make progress toward the surface. Now, when making the return trip to the bottom, they simply let themselves sink . . . Despite their small size, zooplankton are denser than seawater, so they naturally tend to sink. And often, because they've just eaten, they sink faster than they would otherwise . . .

Now get ready to answer the questions. You may use your notes to help you answer.

10. What is the lecture mainly about?

Listen again to part of the lecture. Then answer the question.

P: Over a 24-hour period, they migrate about a kilometer. Yes?

S1: I don't mean to interrupt, but, um . . . Did you say a kilometer? That doesn't seem far enough to be called a migration . . .

11. What does the student mean when she says this:
    S1: Did you say a kilometer?

12. According to the professor, how do zooplankton move through water?

P: 이제, 여러분 모두는 동물성 플랑크톤이라고 알려진 아주 작은 생물이 해양 먹이 사슬의 중요한 부분이라는 것을 알 텐데요... 음, 사슬의 맨 아래에는 햇빛을 에너지로 바꾸는 해상 식물이 있어요. 동물성 플랑크톤은 이 식물들을 먹죠. 다음으로, 그것들은 물고기와 고래 같은 더 커다란 생물들에게 먹힙니다. 동물성 플랑크톤의 식생활과, 특히, 그것이 먹이를 찾기 위해 떠나는 매일의 여정을 더 면밀하게 살펴봅시다.
음, 동물성 플랑크톤의 일부 종류는 그들의 수중 서식지 근처에서 먹이를 찾을 수 있어요... 멀리서 찾을 필요가 없죠. 하지만 일부 종류에게는... 50퍼센트가 좀 안 되는데요... 그들은 먹이를 얻기 위해 해수면으로 올라가야 해요... 다시 말해서, 이동이죠. 이는 그들이 먹고 사는 다량의 미생물이 수면에 있기 때문이에요. 그래서 해가 지고 나면, 이러한 종류의 동물성 플랑크톤은 해양의 밑바닥에서 표면까지 이동합니다. 새벽에는, 깊은 수중으로 돌아가죠. 24시간이라는 기간 동안, 그들은 약 1km를 이동하는 거예요. 네?

S1: 방해하려는 것은 아니지만요, 음... 1km라고 말씀하셨나요? 그건 이동이라고 불릴 만큼 먼 것으로 보이지는 않는데요...

P: 음, 동물성 플랑크톤은 작다는 것을 기억하세요... 길이가 겨우 몇 mm죠. 그 크기의 생물에게, 1km는 가기에 오래 걸리는 길이입니다... 게다가, 이 작은 생물들에게 물은 매우 다르게 느껴지죠. 해양에 비해 작은 그들의 크기 때문에, 그들은 물로부터 강한 저항력을 겪습니다. 어, 그들에게 바다는 걸쭉하고, 끈적거리는 수프처럼 느껴지죠. 이는 그 사이를 헤엄쳐가는 데 많은 노력이 든다는 것을 의미하고요. 다행히도, 그들은 이를 위한 많은 방법을 발전시켜 왔습니다. 일부는 그들 자신을 물로부터 밀어내기 위해 다리를 사용해요... 거의 걷고 있는 것처럼 보이죠. 다른 일부는 그들이 날개처럼 펄럭거리는 신체 부분을 가지고 있습니다. 게다가 또 다른 일부는 그들의 더듬이를 사용해서 물을 헤쳐나가죠.

S2: 음, 하지만 해류는요? 동물성 플랑크톤은 해류를 거슬러 헤엄치기에 너무 작지 않나요?

P: 음, 네, 맞아요. 하지만 심각한 문제는 아닙니다. 보세요, 동물성 플랑크톤은 위쪽으로 헤엄치는 반면에, 해류는 좌우로 움직이니까요. 그래서, 해류가 그들을 한쪽 방향으로 밀어낼지라도, 동물성 플랑크톤은 계속해서 수면 쪽으로 전진할 수 있는 거죠. 자, 바닥으로 돌아오는 여정을 할 때, 그들은 그저 그들 스스로가 가라앉게 합니다... 작은 크기에도 불구하고, 동물성 플랑크톤은 바닷물보다 밀도가 높아서, 자연스럽게 가라앉는 경향이 있거든요. 그리고 종종, 그들은 막 배를 채웠기 때문에, 그렇지 않았을 때보다 더 빠르게 가라앉는 거죠...

HACKERS TEST

p.82

1. (C) Main Purpose/Topic	2. (D) Function & Attitude	3. (D) Detail
4. (D) Detail	5. (A) Function & Attitude	6. (D) Main Purpose/Topic
7. (A), (B), (D) Detail	8. (C) Function & Attitude	9. (B) Function & Attitude
10. (B) Detail	11. (A) Function & Attitude	12. (A) Main Purpose/Topic
13. (D) Function & Attitude	14. (A), (D), (E) Detail	15. (B) Detail
16. (D) Detail	17. (D) Function & Attitude	18. (D) Main Purpose/Topic
19. (C) Function & Attitude	20. (A), (D) Detail	21. (B) Detail
22. (A) Function & Attitude	23. (A) Main Purpose/Topic	24. (D) Function & Attitude
25. (C) Detail	26. (D) Detail	27. (A) Function & Attitude
28. (A) Function & Attitude	29. (C) Main Purpose/Topic	30. (A) Function & Attitude
31. (D) Function & Attitude	32. (D) Detail	33. (A) Detail
34. (C) Function & Attitude		

[1-5]

Listen to a conversation between a student and a professor.

S: Professor Canes? Are you busy right now?

P: Oh, hi there, Jess! Not at all . . . Come right on in.

S: Thanks. Sorry for barging in on you like this.

P: It's not a problem. So what's up?

S: Q1 Oh, well, I came to talk about a presentation I'm preparing for the film festival that starts in two weeks. The, uh, the nominating committee selected me as the key student speaker.

P: Q2 Well now, that's quite an honor! Congratulations! Q1/Q2 So what are you doing your presentation on?

S: Isn't that the question of the day!

P: All right . . . well, what are you considering? You must have given it some thought . . .

S: You might think this is far-fetched, but what I'd really like to give it on is the relationship between film and literature. Actually, I'm really interested in this topic, and I—I heard that you gave a seminar on this topic before as part of your comparative literature course, so I thought that, uh . . . perhaps you could point me in the direction of some good references.

P: Uh-huh. Q3 OK, first off, the topic is a bit too broad. Have you thought about what you want to focus on? Like, is there a specific time period? And what type of literature or movie genre are you particularly interested in?

S: Actually, I'm not really particular about the time period . . . Q4 I just wanted to compare the similarities between film and literature . . . at least, uh, where storytelling is concerned.

P: Q5 I see, I see . . . and what purpose would such a comparison serve? I mean, why are you making a comparison in the first place?

S: Well, I have an idea. If we compare film and literature in terms of storytelling, and if both of them make use of the same techniques . . . then the definition of each art form is, well, open to debate. It brings up questions like, you know, what is film . . . and how influential is film?

P: Now you're onto something . . . but it still sounds pretty complex to me. Anyhow, what you might want to do is fine-tune your theory a bit and then come up with one or two comparisons.

I would even suggest limiting the topic further; for example . . . a single story from literature . . . and a single film.

S: That's a start, anyway, but, uh, could you recommend any readings or films to look at that might back up my theory? It'll save me a lot of time in the library.

P: Sure, I don't see why not. I'd start with Eisenstein's article, "Evolution of Cinematography." It gives a pretty thorough overview of the film industry's effect on literature during the late 20th century. I'd also take some time to look over J. Robertson's article on literary definitions and terminologies. He's quite a master when it comes to describing the precise function of terms.

S: Great! You've given me some excellent starting points. I think I'll be able to manage by myself from here. But just in case I have any more questions, could I . . .

P: Certainly. Don't ever be afraid to stop by for a chat. I know how easy it is to get stuck, or to run out of ideas.

S: Thanks, Professor Canes! I appreciate it!

Now get ready to answer the questions. You may use your notes to help you answer.

1. What is the conversation mainly about?

Listen again to part of the conversation. Then answer the question.

P: Well now, that's quite an honor! Congratulations! So what are you doing your presentation on?
S: Isn't that the question of the day!

2. Why does the student say this:
   S: Isn't that the question of the day!

3. What does the professor suggest the student do?
4. What paper does the student want to present at the film festival?

Listen again to part of the conversation. Then answer the question.

P: I see, I see . . . and what purpose would such a comparison serve? I mean, why are you making a comparison in the first place?
S: Well, I have an idea. If we compare film and literature in terms of storytelling, and if both of them make use of the same techniques . . . then the definition of each art form is, well, open to debate. It brings up questions like, you know, what is film . . . and how influential is film?
P: Now you're onto something . . .

5. What does the professor mean when he says this:
   P: Now you're onto something . . .

S: Canes 교수님? 지금 바쁘신가요?
P: 오, 안녕, Jess! 전혀 바쁘지 않단다... 어서 들어오렴.
S: 감사합니다. 이렇게 갑자기 찾아와서 죄송해요.
P: 괜찮아. 그래서 무슨 일이니?
S: 오, 음, 2주 후에 시작하는 영화 축제를 위해 제가 준비하고 있는 발표에 대해 이야기하고 싶어서 왔어요. 그, 어, 선정 위원회가 저를 주요 학생 연설자로 선출했거든요.
P: 자 그렇다면, 그건 꽤 영광이구나! 축하한다! 그래서 무엇에 대해 발표할 거니?
S: 바로 그게 문제 아니겠어요!
P: 그렇구나... 음, 넌 무엇을 고려하고 있니? 그것에 대해 좀 생각해 봤을 텐데...

S: 이게 억지스럽다고 생각하실지 모르지만, 제가 정말 발표하고 싶은 것은 영화와 문학의 관계예요. 사실, 저는 이 주제에 대해 아주 관심이 많아요, 그리고 저, 저는 교수님께서 예전에 비교문학 수업의 일부로 이 주제에 대한 세미나를 하셨다고 들었어요. 그래서 저는, 어... 아마도 교수님께서 저에게 좋은 참고자료들을 알려주실 수 있을 거라고 생각했죠.

P: 그렇구나. 자, 우선, 주제가 다소 너무 광범위해. 무엇에 초점을 맞추고 싶은지 생각해 봤니? 그러니까, 특정 시대가 있니? 그리고 어떤 종류의 문학이나 영화 장르에 특별히 관심이 있는 거니?

S: 사실, 저에게 시대는 그리 중요하지 않아요... 저는 그냥 영화와 문학의 유사점을 비교하고 싶었거든요... 최소한, 어, 이야기 전달과 관련된 부분 말이에요.

P: 그래, 그렇구나... 그럼 그런 비교가 어떤 목적을 갖고 있니? 내 말은, 애당초 왜 비교를 하려고 하는 거지?

S: 음, 제 생각은 이래요. 만약 우리가 이야기 전달의 관점에서 영화와 문학을 비교하고, 둘 다 같은 기법을 사용한다면... 그럼 각 예술 형식의 정의는, 음, 논쟁의 여지가 있죠. 그러니까, 그건 질문을 제기해요, 무엇이 영화이고... 영화가 얼마나 영향력이 있는지와 같은 것 말이에요?

P: 이제 네가 뭔가에 도달할 것 같구나... 하지만 내게는 여전히 다소 복잡하게 들리는데. 어쨌든, 너는 네 이론을 약간 다듬고 나서 한두 개의 비교 점을 찾는 게 좋겠어. 주제를 더 제한하는 것을 권하고 싶구나, 예를 들어... 문학에서의 하나의 이야기나... 한 개의 영화 말이지.

S: 그게 시작이겠네요, 어쨌든, 하지만, 어, 제 이론을 뒷받침할 수 있는 어떤 책이나 영화를 추천해주실 수 있으세요? 제가 도서관에서 보내는 시간을 상당히 줄일 수 있을 거예요.

P: 물론이야, 안 될 이유가 없지. 에이젠슈타인의 기사, '영화 촬영법의 발달'로 시작하는 게 좋을 거야. 그건 20세기 후반 동안 영화 산업이 문학에 끼친 영향에 대해 꽤 면밀한 개관을 보여주거든. 또한 J. 로버트슨의 문학적 정의와 용어들에 대한 기사도 시간을 좀 내서 검토해 보렴. 그는 용어의 명확한 기능을 설명하는 데 있어서 대가나 다름없단다.

S: 좋아요! 몇 가지 훌륭한 출발점을 알려주셨어요. 여기서부터는 저 혼자서도 잘 해나갈 수 있을 것 같아요. 하지만 만약에 질문이 더 생긴다면, 제가...

P: 물론이지. 잠깐 이야기하러 들리는 걸 절대 어려워하지 말거라. 난관에 봉착하거나, 아이디어가 바닥나는 게 얼마나 쉬운지 나도 잘 알거든.

S: 고맙습니다, Canes 교수님! 감사합니다!

어휘
barge in on 갑자기 찾아오다   nominating committee 선정 위원회   far-fetched [fáːrfétʃt] 억지스러운
in terms of ~의 관점에서   make use of ~을 사용하다   definition [dèfəníʃən] 정의   fine-tune [fàintʃúːn] 다듬다
evolution [èvəlúːʃən] 발달   cinematography [sìnəmətágrəfi] 영화 촬영법   thorough [θə́ːrou] 면밀한
overview [óuvərvjùː] 개관   terminology [tə̀ːrmənálədʒi] 용어   precise [prisáis] 명확한   manage [mǽnidʒ] 잘 해나가다
get stuck 난관에 봉착하다   run out of ~이 바닥나다

[6-11]
Listen to part of a lecture in an economics class.

P: There is a good chance that a company will experience a problem that reduces profits or even, um, threatens its existence. ^{Q6} So it's important for management to know how to respond to these situations . . . how to, uh, deal with a crisis, in other words. And the most important part of this process takes place long before the crisis happens . . . I'm talking about contingency planning.

So . . . what exactly is contingency planning? Well, it is when a company decides how to respond to a specific problem in advance. ^{Q7} That way, it won't waste a lot of time scrambling around when disaster strikes. And, with a contingency plan, the company is more likely to do the right thing . . . Um, it's hard to figure out the best course of action when you are, well . . . in the middle of a crisis. And, of course, a good contingency plan can minimize financial losses . . . ^{Q8} Now, contingency planning can be divided into three specific stages. The first of these is risk assessment. What do you think I mean by this? Jake?

S1: Uh . . . risk assessment? I'm not sure . . . Maybe it has to do with the, um, the potential problems different types of companies experience? I mean, a chemical manufacturer would be more concerned about an environmental disaster than, say, a publishing company.

P: You've got it . . . and that's a great example. A company should determine which risks it faces. It also has to figure out which of these will have serious consequences. Um, there's no point in making elaborate preparations for minor problems, right?

The next thing is to create a detailed plan to deal with the crisis. What resources are required? What specific actions must be taken? Things like that . . . Q9 Another task that must be accomplished during this planning stage is setting up the crisis response team. Management must assign employees and make sure they know their roles. I can't stress enough how important it is to do this before a problem occurs . . . Um, a crisis can't be managed if nobody involved knows what to do or who to report to . . .

So, the threat has been identified and the plan is made . . . Job done, right? Well . . . not quite. Q10 The final step is something called maintenance. What this means is that a contingency plan must be periodically reviewed and revised . . . Um, this is usually done on an annual basis. Now . . . why do you think this is necessary?

S2: Well . . . You mentioned that employees are assigned to the crisis response team when the plan is created. But . . . um, people quit their jobs, right? So I guess this has to be taken into account . . .

P: Good . . . the plan has to be updated due to personnel changes. But that's not the entire story . . . Other circumstances can change as well. Um, new technologies, new laws . . . Almost anything can affect the viability of a plan. So it must be kept up-to-date . . . Yes?

S1: Um, I was just wondering . . . How effective are contingency plans in real-world situations? They sound good in theory . . . but do they really work?

P: They are incredibly effective . . . Um, a recent case with a mining company is a good example. When a shaft at one of its mines collapsed, several workers were trapped underground. Fortunately, this was a risk the company had anticipated . . . so it had a, uh . . . a contingency plan in place. There was a response team ready to go, and it had all of the, um, equipment needed to perform a rescue. Q11 The result? The miners were brought to the surface in less than 24 hours. It didn't even take a full day! Uh, these situations often drag on for several days while preparations are being made.

Now get ready to answer the questions. You may use your notes to help you answer.

6. What is the lecture mainly about?
7. According to the professor, what are the benefits of contingency planning?

Listen again to part of the lecture. Then answer the question.

P: Now, contingency planning can be divided into three specific stages. The first of these is risk assessment. What do you think I mean by this? Jake?

S1: Uh . . . risk assessment? I'm not sure . . . Maybe it has to do with the, um, the potential problems different types of companies experience?

8. What does the student mean when he says this:
   S1: Uh . . . risk assessment?

9. What is the professor's attitude toward a crisis response team?
10. What is the final stage of the contingency planning process?

Listen again to part of the lecture. Then answer the question.

P: The result? The miners were brought to the surface in less than 24 hours. It didn't even take a full day! Uh, these situations often drag on for several days while preparations are being made.

11. Why does the professor say this:
   P: It didn't even take a full day!

P: 회사가 이윤을 감소시키거나 심지어, 음, 그것의 존재를 위협하는 문제를 겪을 가능성은 큽니다. 따라서 경영진이 이러한 상황에 어떻게 대응하는지를 아는 것은 중요해요... 다시 말해서, 어떻게, 어, 위기에 대처하는지를 말이죠. 그리고 이 과정의 가장 중요한 부분은 위기가 발생하기 한참 전에 일어납니다... 저는 긴급 사태 대책에 관해 이야기하고 있는 거예요.
   자... 긴급 사태 대책이란 정확히 무엇일까요? 음, 그것은 회사가 특정한 문제에 어떻게 대응할지를 사전에 결정하는 것이에요. 그렇게 하면, 재해가 발생했을 때 급히 서두르느라 많은 시간을 낭비하지는 않을 겁니다. 그리고, 긴급 사태 대책으로, 회사는 적절한 행동을 할 가능성이 더 크죠... 음, 최선의 행동 방침을 생각해내는 것은 어렵잖아요, 음... 위기의 한가운데에 있다면 말이에요. 그리고, 물론, 훌륭한 긴급 사태 대책은 재정적인 손실을 최소화시킬 수 있겠죠...
   자, 긴급 사태 대책은 구체적인 세 단계로 나뉠 수 있어요. 이 중 첫 번째는 위험 평가입니다. 이게 무슨 뜻이라고 생각하나요? Jake?

S1: 어... 위험 평가요? 잘 모르겠어요... 아마도 그건, 음, 서로 다른 종류의 회사들이 겪는 잠재적인 문제와 관계있지 않나요? 제 말은, 화학 물질 제조사는 환경 재해에 대해, 이를테면, 출판사보다는 더 걱정할 것 같아서요.

P: 맞았어요... 그리고 그건 훌륭한 예시네요. 회사는 그것이 직면할 위험을 알아내야 합니다. 또한 이 중 어떤 것이 심각한 결과를 가지고 있을지 생각해내야 해요. 음, 가벼운 문제에 공을 들인 대책을 마련하는 것은 의미가 없잖아요, 그렇죠?
   다음은 위기에 대응할 상세한 대책을 만드는 거예요. 어떤 자원이 요구되는가? 어떤 구체적인 조치가 취해져야 하는가? 이런 것들 말이죠... 이 대책 단계 동안 완수되어야 하는 또 다른 과제는 위기 대응팀을 마련하는 거예요. 경영진은 직원들을 배정하고 그들이 자신의 역할을 확실하게 알도록 해야 합니다. 이것을 문제가 발생하기 전에 하는 것이 얼마나 중요한지 아무리 강조해도 지나치지 않아요... 음, 관련된 사람 중 그 누구도 뭘 해야 하는지 혹은 누구에게 보고해야 하는지를 알지 못하면 위기는 처리될 수 없거든요...
   자, 위험이 확인되고 대책이 세워지면... 일이 끝났네요, 그렇죠? 음... 완전히는 아니에요. 마지막 단계는 유지라고 불리는 것입니다. 이것이 의미하는 것은 긴급 사태 대책이 주기적으로 검토되고 수정되어야 한다는 거예요... 음, 이는 보통 연간 기준으로 행해집니다. 자... 이것이 왜 필요하다고 생각하나요?

S2: 음... 교수님께서는 대책이 만들어지면 직원들이 위기 대응팀에 배정된다고 말씀하셨잖아요. 그런데... 음, 사람들은 직장을 그만둬요, 그렇죠? 그래서 저는 이것이 고려되어야 한다고 생각했어요...

P: 좋아요... 대책은 직원 변화 때문에 갱신되어야 하겠죠. 하지만 그것이 전부는 아닙니다... 다른 상황들 또한 바뀔 수 있으니까요. 음, 새로운 기술, 새로운 법... 거의 모든 것이 대책의 실행 가능성에 영향을 미칠 수 있어요. 그래서 그것은 최신 정보에 근거하도록 유지되어야 하고요... 네?

S1: 음, 그냥 궁금해서요... 현실 세계의 상황에 긴급 사태 대책이 얼마나 효과적인가요? 이론상으로는 괜찮게 들리는데... 정말로 효과가 있나요?

P: 그것들은 믿을 수 없을 정도로 효과적이에요... 음, 최근 한 광산업 회사의 경우가 좋은 예입니다. 광산 중 하나의 수직갱도가 붕괴했을 때, 몇몇 노동자들이 지하에 갇혔어요. 다행히도, 이것은 회사가 예상했던 위험이었죠... 그래서 회사는, 어... 긴급 사태 대책을 위한 준비가 돼 있었어요. 준비된 대응팀이 있었고, 음, 구조를 수행하는 데 필요한 모든 장비를 가지고 있었죠. 결과요? 광부들은 24시간 안에 지면으로 인도되었습니다. 심지어 꼬박 하루도 걸리지 않았어요! 어, 이러한 상황은 대책이 마련되는 동안 보통 며칠간 계속되곤 하거든요.

어휘

management[mǽnidʒmənt] 경영진 contingency planning 긴급 사태 대책 scramble[skrǽmbl] 급히 서두르다
strike[straik] 발생하다 course of action 행동 방침 manufacturer[mæ̀njufǽktʃərər] 제조사 determine[ditə́ːrmin] 알아내다
elaborate[ilǽbərət] 공을 들인 assign[əsáin] 배정하다 maintenance[méintənəns] 유지 take into account ~을 고려하다
personnel[pə̀ːrsənél] 직원의 viability[vàiəbíləti] 실행 가능성 up-to-date[ʌ̀ptədéit] 최신 정보에 근거한 shaft[ʃæft] 수직갱도
in place ~을 위한 준비가 되어 있는 drag on 계속되다

[12-17]

Listen to part of a lecture on astronomy.

As you know, Saturn is one of the most recognizable objects in the solar system. Its elegant rings are unlike anything else we've seen. What a lot of people probably don't realize, though, is that . . . Saturn holds the distinction of having more moons than any other planet. So, what are these moons like? Well, that's a tricky question, because they are so diverse . . . but one classification, albeit a rough one, is between regular satellite and irregular satellite. Moons in the first group are characterized by prograde orbits . . . um, orbits that are counterclockwise when you view it from the north pole of the planet. Also, the angle or inclination of these orbits against Saturn's equatorial plane is not very high. Irregular satellites, on the other hand, have orbits that are farther from Saturn. Their inclinations are higher, and some have retrograde orbits . . . orbits that go in a direction opposite to the rotation of the planet. Q12 Today, we'll focus on regular satellites, particularly Titan and Dione, and discuss their unique characteristics.

So, what's so special about Titan? To start with, it's over 5,000 kilometers in diameter and accounts for 96 percent of the estimated mass of all of Saturn's moons combined! Just to compare, it's even larger than the planet Mercury. Other attributes that set it apart are its similarities to Earth.

Q13/Q14 For example, Earth and Titan have the only nitrogen-rich atmospheres in the entire solar system. Q13 This finding has fueled speculation that Titan might have the building blocks to sustain life. Personally, I don't think it's too far-fetched, do you? Anyway, a thick layer of gases allows dense clouds to form, which protect the atmosphere from much of the Sun's radiation. Q14 Yet, any solar energy that gets through the protective layer produces a faint greenhouse effect. The similarities with Earth do not stop there. Q14 The presence of wind as well as rain and surface liquid—probably in the form of liquid methane and ethane—continually erode the surface of Titan so that rivers, valleys, and dunes have formed.

Now let's talk about Dione . . . Dione is the second largest of Saturn's moons. Its terrain is heavily cratered, and it has an extensive network of depressions and fractures, suggesting that there may have been some tectonic activity on Dione in the past . . . Q15 But what's interesting is the presence of what is called "wispy terrain", um, streaks that are transparent and don't conceal the physical features beneath . . . that's why they were called wispy. On December 13, 2004, the Cassini spacecraft flew by Dione and discovered that the wisps were actually bright cliffs of ice that may have been brought on by the moon's tectonic features—some of these cliffs were several hundred meters high! Another characteristic of Dione is that the fractures and wispy terrain are mostly located on the moon's trailing hemisphere—the hemisphere that faces away from the direction of Dione's motion. Q16 Usually, these features are found on the leading hemisphere, so some scientists believe Dione was spun around when a huge meteor or debris crashed onto its surface. However, no one is positive about why this unusual phenomenon exists. Q17 No doubt, we'll learn a lot more about Saturn's moons as NASA's Cassini spacecraft probes further and further.

Now get ready to answer the questions. You may use your notes to help you answer.

12. What is the professor mainly discussing?

Listen again to part of the lecture. Then answer the question.

P: For example, Earth and Titan have the only nitrogen-rich atmospheres in the entire solar system. This finding has fueled speculation that Titan might have the building blocks to sustain life. Personally, I don't think it's too far-fetched, do you?

13. Why does the professor say this:
    P: Personally, I don't think it's too far-fetched, do you?

14. According to the professor, what are three ways in which Titan is similar to the Earth?
15. What does the professor say about Dione's terrain?
16. What do some researchers suppose about Dione?
17. What is the professor's opinion about research on Saturn's moons?

여러분도 알다시피, 토성은 태양계에서 가장 잘 알아볼 수 있는 물체 중 하나예요. 그것의 멋진 고리들은 우리가 봐온 그 어떤 것과도 다릅니다. 하지만, 아마도 많은 사람이 깨닫지 못하는 것은, 바로... 토성이 다른 어떤 행성보다 많은 위성을 가지는 특징이 있다는 점이에요. 그럼, 이 위성들은 어떨까요? 자, 그건 까다로운 질문이에요, 왜냐하면 그것들은 너무나도 다양하기 때문이죠... 하지만 한 가지 분류법은, 비록 개략적이지만, 규칙 위성과 불규칙 위성입니다. 첫 번째 그룹의 위성들은 순행 궤도라는 특징이 있어요... 음, 행성의 북극에서 볼 때 반시계방향의 궤도죠. 또한, 토성의 적도면에 대한 이 궤도의 각이나 경사는 그리 크지 않습니다. 반면에, 불규칙 위성은, 토성으로부터 더 먼 궤도를 가지고 있어요. 그것들의 경사는 더 크고, 일부는 역행 궤도를 가지고 있습니다... 행성의 자전과 반대 방향으로 가는 궤도죠. 오늘, 우리는 규칙 위성, 특히 타이탄과 디오네에 초점을 맞춰서, 그것들의 독특한 특징에 관해 논의할 것입니다.

그럼, 타이탄의 특별한 점은 무엇일까요? 우선, 그것의 지름은 5,000km가 넘고, 토성의 모든 위성의 추정된 질량을 합친 것의 96퍼센트를 차지합니다! 비교하자면, 그것은 행성인 수성보다도 커요. 그것을 특별하게 하는 다른 특성은 지구와의 유사성입니다. 예를 들면, 지구와 타이탄은 태양계 전체에서 유일하게 질소가 풍부한 대기를 가지고 있어요. 이 발견은 타이탄이 생명체가 존재하게 하는 구성 요소를 가지고 있을지도 모른다는 추측을 부추겼죠. 개인적으로, 저는 그게 아주 설득력이 없다고는 생각하지 않아요, 여러분은 어떤가요? 어쨌든, 두꺼운 기체층이 짙은 구름을 형성하게 하는데, 그 구름은 상당량의 태양 복사광으로부터 대기를 보호합니다. 그러나, 보호층을 통과한 모든 태양 에너지는 약한 온실효과를 만들어내요. 지구와의 유사성은 여기서 그치지 않습니다. 아마도 액체 메탄과 에탄의 형태일 비와 지표수뿐만 아니라 바람의 존재도 타이탄의 지표면을 계속 침식시켜서 강, 계곡, 그리고 모래 언덕이 형성되어 왔기 때문이죠.

이제 디오네에 대해 이야기해 봅시다... 디오네는 토성의 위성 중 두 번째로 커요. 그것의 지형은 심하게 파여 있고, 광범위한 망의 함몰과 균열이 있는데, 이것은 과거에 디오네에서 어떤 지각 운동이 있었을지도 모른다는 것을 암시합니다... 하지만 흥미로운 것은, '희미한 지형'이라고 불리는 것이 있다는 건데, 음, 이것은 투명해서 아래에 있는 지형들을 가리지 않는 선이에요... 그것이 바로 희미하다고 불리는 이유죠. 2004년, 12월 13일, 카시니 우주선은 디오네로 비행했고 이 선들이 실은 위성의 지질 구조적인 특징에 의해 생겼을지도 모르는 밝은 얼음 절벽이라는 것을 밝혀냈는데, 일부 절벽은 높이가 수백 미터였어요! 디오네의 또 다른 특징은 균열과 희미한 지형이 대부분 쫓아가는 반구, 즉 디오네가 움직이는 방향에서 반대쪽을 향하는 반구에 있다는 것이죠. 보통, 이러한 특징들은 이끄는 반구에서 나타나거든요, 그래서 어떤 과학자들은 거대한 유성이나 잔해가 디오네의 표면에 충돌했을 때, 그것의 방향이 바뀌었을 것이라고 생각합니다. 그러나, 왜 이런 특이한 현상이 존재하는지는 아무도 확신할 수 없어요. 물론, 우리는 나사의 카시니 우주선이 더 탐색하면 할수록 토성의 위성들에 대해 더 많이 알 수 있게 되겠죠.

어휘

classification[klæ̀səfikéiʃən] 분류법　albeit[ɔːlbíːit] 비록 ~이지만　prograde[próugrèid] 순행의
counterclockwise[kàuntərklákwàiz] 반시계방향의　inclination[ìnklənéiʃən] 경사　equatorial plane 적도면
retrograde[rétrəgrèid] 역행의　account for ~을 차지하다　mass[mæs] 질량　fuel[fjuːəl] 부추기다　building block 구성 요소
sustain[səstéin] 존재하게 하다　far-fetched 설득력이 없는　radiation[rèidiéiʃən] 복사광　dune[djuːn] 모래 언덕
terrain[təréin] 지형　depression[dipréʃən] 함몰　fracture[frǽktʃər] 균열　tectonic[tektánik] 지각의　wispy[wíspi] 희미한
streak[striːk] 선　transparent[trænspɛ́ərənt] 투명한　physical feature 지형　wisp[wisp] 선　trail[treil] 쫓아가다
hemisphere[hémisfìər] 반구　face away 반대쪽을 향하다　meteor[míːtiər] 유성　debris[dəbríː] 잔해　probe[proub] 탐색하다

[18-22]
Listen to a conversation between an academic advisor and a student.

S: Professor Boyle? Could I talk to you for a second?

P: Sure. Come on in. You're the student who shifted to mass communications, uh . . . Melody Woods, right?

S: Right. [Q18] Um, I need your advice. Since you're my counselor and all, I thought you could help me pick an elective for this semester. See, the one I wanted is already full. You know, Strategic Media with Dr. Willis?

P: Yes, Dr. Willis. He's an excellent professor, but anyhow . . . aren't you only a sophomore? That course is designed for upperclassmen, and, well, I'm assuming you haven't completed all the prerequisites yet . . .

S: [Q19/Q20] Um, the woman at the registrar's office said I could take journalism electives in place of my general electives, and since I have two elective requirements this year, I thought I could go for the journalism electives instead.

P: [Q19] That's doubtful. The thing with journalism electives is that the requirements for these subjects are generally pretty stringent. That's the reason journalism majors need Introduction to Reporting or Journalism 201 before they're allowed to take an elective like Strategic Media.

S: What if I take Features Writing? It's a journalism elective and is probably not as difficult as Strategic Media . . . you know, something a sophomore like me could probably handle.

P: Uh, Professor Meyer—he's the one offering Features Writing this semester—well, he might not be crazy about the idea of letting a sophomore into his class.

S: So what do you suggest I do?

P: Since introductory courses are required anyway, your best bet would be to take that course this semester . . . and then go for Features Writing next semester.

S: Is it, like, possible for me to take both the introductory course and the Features Writing together? See, [Q20] I don't want to waste time taking electives that are not related to my major . . . also, that way I'd be killing two birds with one stone, so to speak.

P: I think that would all depend on Professor Meyer. He may require you to have some experience in writing features articles. Have you worked for a school paper, perhaps?

S: I did, yes. In my freshman year here . . . I contributed to the university paper.

P: [Q22] Oh, good! So what was writing for the university paper like for you?

S: To be honest, I got a lot out of it, but it took a lot out of me as well . . . you know, here at university, not only do they expect you to write quality stuff, they also want you to meet strict deadlines.

P: OK. Well . . . you might want to see Professor Meyer, then, and let him know about your experience with the school paper. Just one thing, though . . . [Q21] Professor Meyer is known to be very strict. Then again, he genuinely cares about his students, which is why he really pushes them to do their best.

P: I don't really mind doing a lot of hard work. Besides, if I'm going to work in the industry one day, I'd better get used to it, I suppose. Newspapers make their reporters work hard, so I expect the training to be just as tough. Thanks for the advice, Professor Boyle.

Now get ready to answer the questions. You may use your notes to help you answer.

18. Why does the student talk to the professor?

Listen again to part of the conversation. Then answer the questions.

S: Um, the woman at the registrar's office said I could take journalism electives in place of my general electives, and since I have two elective requirements this year, I thought I could go for the journalism electives instead.

P: That's doubtful. The thing with journalism electives is that the requirements for these subjects are generally pretty stringent.

19. Why does the professor say this:
    P: That's doubtful.

20. According to the conversation, what are two reasons the student gives for choosing an elective in journalism?

21. What does the professor say about studying under Professor Meyer?

Listen again to part of the conversation. Then answer the question.

P: Oh, good! So what was writing for the university paper like for you?
S: To be honest, I got a lot out of it, but it took a lot out of me as well . . . you know, here at university, not only do they expect you to write quality stuff, they also want you to meet strict deadlines.

22. What does the student mean when she says this:
    S: To be honest, I got a lot out of it, but it took a lot out of me as well . . .

S: Boyle 교수님? 잠시 이야기 좀 나눌 수 있을까요?
P: 물론이지. 들어오렴. 네가 대중 매체로 전공을 바꾼 학생, 어... Melody Woods지, 그렇지?
S: 맞아요. 음, 교수님의 조언이 필요해요. 교수님께서는 제 지도 교수님이시고 하니까, 이번 학기 선택 과목을 고르는 것을 도와주실 수 있으리라 생각했어요. 저, 제가 듣고 싶은 수업은 이미 다 찾았어요. 그러니까, Willis 박사님의 전략 미디어 수업이요?
P: 그래, Willis 박사님. 훌륭한 교수님이시지, 그런데 어쨌든... 넌 아직 2학년이지 않니? 그 수업은 상급생들을 위해 개설된 거야, 그리고, 음, 난 네가 아직 모든 선수 과목들을 끝내지 않았으리라 생각하는데...
S: 음, 학적과의 여직원이 일반 선택 과목 대신 언론학 선택 과목을 들을 수 있다고 했어요. 그리고 전 올해 필수 선택 과목을 두 개 들어야 하기 때문에, 대신 언론학 선택 과목을 들을 수 있을 것이라 생각했고요.
P: 그건 불확실하단다. 문제는 언론학 선택 과목들은 일반적으로 필수 요건이 꽤 엄격하다는 거야. 그게 바로 언론학 전공자들이 전략 미디어와 같은 선택 과목을 들을 수 있게 되기 전에 보도 입문이나 언론 201을 수강해야 하는 이유지.
S: 제가 만약 기사 작성을 듣는다면 어떻게 되나요? 그건 언론학 선택 과목이고 아마 전략 미디어만큼 어렵지 않을 거예요... 그러니까, 저 같은 2학년이 충분히 다룰 수 있는 것이잖아요.
P: 어, Meyer 교수님이, 그분께서 이번 학기에 기사 작성을 담당하시는데, 음, 그분은 2학년이 그 수업에 들어간다는 것에 대해 그리 좋아하지 않으실 것 같구나.
S: 그러면 저는 어떻게 해야 할까요?
P: 어쨌든 입문 수업들은 필수이기 때문에, 이번 학기에 그 수업을 듣고... 그러고 나서 다음 학기에 기사 작성을 듣는 것이 최선의 방법일 것 같아.
S: 그럼, 그러니까, 입문 수업과 기사 작성을 함께 수강하는 것이 가능할까요? 그게, 저는 제 전공과 관련 없는 선택 과목을 들으면서 시간을 낭비하고 싶지 않거든요... 또, 그렇게 하면 소위 말해, 두 마리 토끼를 잡을 수 있잖아요.
P: 그건 모두 Meyer 교수님께 달려있을 거야. 그는 네게 특집 기사 작성 경험이 있어야 한다고 하실지도 몰라. 혹시, 학교 신문과 관련한 일을 한 적 있니?
S: 네, 있어요. 여기 1학년 때... 대학교 신문에 기고했었어요.
P: 오, 좋구나! 그래서 대학교 신문에 기고하는 건 너에게 어땠니?
S: 솔직히 말해서, 많은 것을 배웠지만, 힘도 많이 들었어요... 그러니까, 이런 대학교에서는, 질 높은 것을 쓰길 기대할 뿐만 아니라, 엄격한 마감 기한을 맞추길 원하잖아요.
P: 그래. 음... 그럼, Meyer 교수님을 만나보고, 학교 신문과 관련된 너의 경험에 대해 알려드리렴. 다만, 한 가지... Meyer 교수님은 아주 엄하기로 알려져 있단다. 한편으로는, 진심으로 학생들을 보살피고, 그래서 사실은 그들이 최선을 다하도록 만드시는 거야.
S: 힘든 일을 많이 해야 하는 것은 정말 괜찮아요. 게다가, 제가 언젠가 이 업계에서 일할 거라면, 익숙해지는 게 좋을 것 같거든요. 신문사는 기자들에게 일을 많이 하게 해서, 그만큼 훈련도 힘들 거라고 예상하고 있어요. 조언 감사합니다, Boyle 교수님.

shift[ʃift] 바꾸다 mass communications 대중 매체 counselor[káunsələr] 지도 교수 elective[iléktiv] 선택 과목
strategic[strətíːdʒik] 전략의 sophomore[sáfəmɔ̀ːr] 2학년 upperclassman[ʌ̀pərklǽsmən] 상급생
assume[əsúːm] 생각하다 registrar's office 학적과 general[dʒénərəl] 일반의
requirement[rikwáiərmənt] 필수 과목, 필수 요건 doubtful[dáutfəl] 불확실한 stringent[stríndʒənt] 엄격한
introduction[intrədʌ́kʃən] 입문 reporting[ripɔ́ːrtiŋ] 보도 feature[fíːtʃər] 기사, 특집 article[áːrtikl] 기사
contribute[kəntríbjuːt] 기고하다 genuinely[dʒénjuinli] 진심으로

[23-28]
Listen to part of a talk on art history.

P: Realist art began in France in the 1850s, but ^Q23 today we're going to talk about an American realist painter, Andrew Wyeth, whose name has become synonymous with the realist movement. ^Q24 Wyeth was exposed to art at a young age because . . . you see, his father, N.C. Wyeth, who was an accomplished painter and illustrator of books, taught Andrew many painting techniques. I'm sure he wouldn't have done that if he didn't think his son had talent. It sort of goes without saying that the tips paid off because we all know Andrew grew up to be one of America's most renowned artists.

A lot of Andrew's early work gained enough attention to be sold to dealers, but it was through his painting *Christina's World* that he received his greatest fame. I'm pretty sure most of you have seen it at some point, maybe in a book or on TV. Anyway, the painting is of a woman named Christina who is sitting in a grassy meadow and looking toward a house. It's, um . . . it's known for its literal depiction of a country landscape. ^Q25 You know, the style itself really couldn't have been more different from what was popular in art circles in those days . . . because by the mid-twentieth century, abstract expressionism had really taken off in New York City. So, um, it might not surprise you to hear that Wyeth's art was polarizing.

On the positive side, some critics praised what they saw as his revolutionary vision. This might sound contradictory. How can realism be revolutionary, right? Well, what they saw in Wyeth was a rebel against the incessant change and trends associated with modern art. Maybe more than anything, though, they respected how Wyeth could paint a landscape with photographic precision while instilling the painting with a deep and sincere emotional quality. The American people as a whole must have felt this way because Wyeth became very famous during his lifetime.

Despite all the praise, Wyeth certainly attracted his share of negative attention, too. Much of it, um, centered on the belief that he had added nothing new, or worse, had actually gone backwards. What I mean by that is regardless of his skill, they thought he contributed nothing more to the world of art than pretty pictures. This sentiment became particularly strong in the 1950s and 1960s when the influence of artists like Jackson Pollock took hold of the art world, but that's for another class . . . Ahem . . . so even though Wyeth's works were highly regarded among the public, many artists and experts refused to give Wyeth any credit. ^Q26 They went so far as to call his work old-fashioned, claiming that it was completely out of step with the times. ^Q27 To give you an idea of how strongly some people felt about it, a curator in a well-known New York museum refused to participate in an exhibit just because it included some of Wyeth's works!

S: Wow. That curator must have felt silly in hindsight.

P: You can say that again! What I think is especially interesting is that Wyeth had to live with this controversy his whole life. Even at the time of his death, the debate about his relevance was still raging. [Q28] I suppose from a purely practical perspective, though, the issue is pointless now; when some of an artist's paintings have sold for millions of dollars at auctions, that artist must have done something right.

Now get ready to answer the questions. You may use your notes to help you answer.

23. What is the talk mainly about?

Listen again to part of the lecture. Then answer the question.

P: Wyeth was exposed to art at a young age because . . . you see, his father, N.C. Wyeth, who was an accomplished painter and illustrator of books, taught Andrew many painting techniques. I'm sure he wouldn't have done that if he didn't think his son had talent.

24. What does the professor mean when he says this:
   P: I'm sure he wouldn't have done that if he didn't think his son had talent.

25. What does the professor say about *Christina's World*?
26. According to the professor, why were many artists and critics unwilling to give Wyeth's art any acclaim?

Listen again to part of the lecture. Then answer the question.

P: To give you an idea of how strongly some people felt about it, a curator in a well-known New York museum refused to participate in an exhibit just because it included some of Wyeth's works!
S: Wow. That curator must have felt silly in hindsight.

27. Why does the student say this:
   S: Wow. That curator must have felt silly in hindsight.

28. What is the professor's opinion of the controversy surrounding Wyeth's work?

P: 사실주의 미술은 1850년대에 프랑스에서 시작했지만, 오늘 우리는 미국의 사실주의 화가, 앤드루 와이어스에 대해 이야기할 겁니다, 그의 이름은 사실주의 운동과 같은 뜻을 의미하는 게 되었죠. 와이어스는 어린 나이에 미술에 노출되었는데... 그러니까, 뛰어난 화가이자 책의 삽화가였던, 아버지 N.C. 와이어스가 앤드루에게 많은 회화 기술을 가르쳤기 때문이죠. 아들이 재능이 없다고 생각했으면 그러지 않았을 거라고 확신해요. 그 예측이 성공했다는 것은 두말할 나위가 없는데 우리 모두 앤드루가 미국에서 가장 유명한 미술가 중 한 명으로 성장했다는 것을 알기 때문이죠.
앤드루의 초기 작품 중 다수가 미술상들에게 팔릴 만큼 충분한 관심을 얻었지만, 그가 가장 큰 명성을 얻게 된 것은 그의 작품 '크리스티나의 세계'를 통해서였어요. 여러분 대부분이 아마 책이나 텔레비전에서, 언젠가 그것을 분명 봤을 거예요. 어쨌든, 이 그림은 풀로 덮힌 초원에 앉아서 집을 바라보고 있는 크리스티나라는 이름의 여성이죠. 그것은, 음... 시골 풍경을 그대로 묘사한 것으로 알려졌어요. 그런데, 양식 자체로는 당시 미술계에서 인기 있었던 것과 완전히 달랐습니다... 20세기 중반에는, 추상적 표현주의가 뉴욕에서 굉장히 인기를 얻고 있었으니까요. 그래서, 음, 와이어스의 그림이 사람들을 대립시켰다는 것이 놀랍지 않을 거예요.
긍정적인 측면에서, 일부 평론가들은 그들이 본 것을 혁명적인 시각이라고 칭찬했어요. 이는 모순적으로 들릴 수도 있겠죠. 사실주의가 어떻게 혁명적일 수 있겠어요, 그렇죠? 음, 그들이 와이어스에게서 본 것은 현대 미술과 관련된 끊임없는 변화와 추세에 대한 저항이었던 거예요. 하지만, 무엇보다도, 그들은 와이어스가 그림에 깊고 진실한 감적적 특성을 불어넣으면서도 사진으로 찍은 듯한 정확성으로 풍경을 그릴 수 있었다는 점을 존경했죠. 와이어스가 살아 생전에 아주 유명해졌기 때문에 전반적인 미국인들이 이렇게 느꼈음이 분명해요.
이 모든 칭찬에도 불구하고, 와이어스는 분명 부정적인 반응도 불러일으켰죠. 그것의 대부분은, 음, 그가 새로운 것은 하나도 보태지 않았고, 더 나쁘게는, 사실상 퇴보했다는 믿음에 초점을 맞추고 있었어요. 제 말은 그의 기술에도 불구하고, 그들은 그가 미술계에 기여한 것이 예쁜 사진에 불과하다고 생각했다는 거예요. 이러한 정서는 잭슨 폴락과 같은 미술가들의 영향력이 미술계를 장악

했던 1950년대와 1960년대에 특히 강했는데, 그건 다른 시간에 다루고... 으흠... 그래서 와이어스의 작품이 대중 사이에서는 높이 평가되었음에도 불구하고, 다수의 미술가들과 전문가들은 와이어스를 인정하기 거부했어요. 그들은 그의 작품이 시대와 전혀 맞지 않다고 주장하며, 구식이라고까지 말했죠. 일부 사람들이 그것에 대해 얼마나 강력하게 느꼈는지를 보여주자면, 뉴욕의 한 유명 미술관의 큐레이터는 단지 와이어스의 일부 작품이 포함됐다는 이유로 전시회에 참가하기를 거부하기도 했어요!

S: 와. 그 큐레이터는 돌이켜 보았을 때 분명 어리석었다는 기분이 들었겠네요.

P: 바로 그렇죠! 내가 특히 흥미롭다고 여기는 것은 와이어스가 평생 이러한 논란을 가지고 살아야만 했다는 거예요. 그가 사망하는 순간조차, 여전히 그의 타당성에 대한 논쟁이 맹렬하게 계속되었거든요. 하지만, 순전히 현실적인 관점에서 보자면, 그 논쟁은 이제 의미가 없어 보여요. 한 미술가의 그림 일부가 경매에서 수백만 달러에 팔린다면, 그 미술가는 무언가 제대로 된 일을 한 것임이 분명하니까요.

어휘

synonymous[sinánəməs] 같은 뜻을 의미하는 expose[ikspóuz] 노출하다 accomplished[əkámpliʃt] 뛰어난
go without saying 두말할 나위가 없다 tip[tip] 예측 pay off 성공하다 renowned[rináund] 유명한
meadow[médou] 초원 abstract[æbstrǽkt] 추상적인 expressionism[ikspréʃənìzm] 표현주의
polarize[póuləràiz] (사람들을) 대립시키다 contradictory[kàntrədíktəri] 모순적인 rebel[rébəl] 저항
incessant[insésnt] 끊임없는 instill[instíl] 불어넣다 contribute[kəntríbjuːt] 기여하다 sentiment[séntəmənt] 정서
out of step with ~과 맞지 않는 in hindsight 돌이켜 보았을 때 controversy[kántrəvəːrsi] 논란 relevance[réləvəns] 타당성
rage[reidʒ] 맹렬하게 계속되다

[29-34]
Listen to part of a lecture on psychology.

Hello, class. I'd like to start by talking about an experiment called the Sally-Anne test. A psychologist puts on a skit for a group of children using two dolls, Sally and Anne. Sally is shown playing with a marble and then putting it away in her toy box before leaving. Then Anne comes in and plays with the marble, but puts it away in her basket. Anne goes away, Sally comes back, and the psychologist asks the children, "Where do you think Sally will look for the marble?"
Q30 Three-year-olds without a theory of mind, that is, without an understanding that others have their own mental states, desires, intents, and beliefs, will probably answer, "in Anne's basket." Children closer to the age of four, or those who have developed a theory of mind, will likely say, "in her box." I urge those of you with suitable research subjects at home to give it a try.
We're not going to talk about children today, though. Q29 Many scientists think some animals have a theory of mind as well. So today . . . we'll limit our discussion to vervet monkeys because research involving this South African monkey is often cited. In particular, scientists observe vervet monkeys because they sometimes sound false alarm calls, and scientists want to know—is this intentional? Because if it is, it would seem to support the idea that vervet monkeys have a theory of mind.
Q31 Two primate researchers at the University of Pennsylvania, Cheney and Seyfarth, once witnessed a low-ranking vervet monkey giving an alarm call when a new monkey approached the group. The low-ranking part is important, because Q32 alarms are generally only sounded by animals high up in the social hierarchy. No predators were around, but the alarm call still made all the other monkeys climb up into trees and hide. Now, some animal psychologists use this observation to speculate that the alarm-calling monkey's intent was to make its social rank appear higher than it actually was to the new monkey for the purpose of gaining a subordinate. Q33 The researchers argued that the alarm-calling monkey was able to put itself in the shoes of the other monkey and understand the effect a false alarm would have on its perception. What would this argument suggest? Simply that vervet monkeys have a theory of mind, that they can distinguish

between reality and the perception of others.

I'd like to point out, however, that the problem with using such anecdotal evidence is that it's so hard to prove. Other psychologists refute the claims made by Cheney and Seyfarth by referring to other experiments involving vervet monkeys. In these experiments, certain monkeys continuously made false alarm calls. They kept doing it until they were eventually ignored by the entire group. The newcomer, too, would eventually figure out what's going on. In the end, maybe the presence of the new monkey had no bearing on the false alarm call being made. It could be an unintentional behavior, you know, something that indicates the monkey suffers from some sort of impairment or mental deficiency.

This just goes to show you that scientists may interpret the same situation differently. It's difficult, if not impossible, to conduct psychological experiments on animals in the wild, so something like the Sally-Anne test is impossible to conduct on the monkeys. Observation and induction are all scientists can rely upon. [Q34] I don't think either side offers overwhelming evidence regarding a theory of mind in animals, so I'll leave it up to all of you to decide which explanation you prefer.

Now get ready to answer the questions. You may use your notes to help you answer.

29. What is the main topic of the lecture?

Listen again to part of the lecture. Then answer the question.

P: Three-year-olds without a theory of mind, that is, without an understanding that others have their own mental states, desires, intents, and beliefs, will probably answer, "in Anne's basket." Children closer to the age of four, or those who have developed a theory of mind, will likely say, "in her box." I urge those of you with suitable research subjects at home to give it a try.

30. Why does the professor say this:
    P: I urge those of you with suitable research subjects at home to give it a try.

Listen again to part of the lecture. Then answer the question.

P: Two primate researchers at the University of Pennsylvania, Cheney and Seyfarth, once witnessed a low-ranking vervet monkey giving an alarm call when a new monkey approached the group. The low-ranking part is important . . .

31. Why does the professor say this:
    P: The low-ranking part is important . . .

32. What does the professor say about vervet monkey alarm calls?
33. According to the professor, what is a reason some scientists believe that vervet monkeys have a theory of mind?
34. What is the professor's attitude concerning a theory of mind in animals?

안녕하세요, 여러분. 저는 샐리-앤 테스트라고 불리는 실험에 대해 이야기하면서 시작하고 싶어요. 한 심리학자는 샐리와 앤이라고 이름 붙인 두 인형을 사용하여 어린이들을 위한 토막극을 꾸몄어요. 샐리는 구슬을 가지고 논 뒤 나가기 전에 그것을 자신의 장난감 상자에 넣습니다. 그런 다음 앤이 들어와서 그 구슬을 가지고 놀죠, 하지만 그것을 자신의 바구니에 넣습니다. 앤이 나가고, 샐리가 다시 돌아오면, 심리학자는 어린이들에게, "너희는 샐리가 그 구슬을 어디서 찾아볼 거라 생각하니?"라고 묻습니다. 마음 이론이 없는, 즉, 다른 사람들이 그들만의 정신 상태, 욕구, 의도, 그리고 신념이 있다는 것에 대한 이해가 없는 3세의 어린이들은 아마 "앤의 바구니 안이요."라고 대답할 것입니다. 4세에 가까운 어린이들, 혹은 마음 이론이 발달한 어린이들은, "자신의 상자 안이요."라고 대답할 확률이 크죠. 여러분 중 집에 적당한 연구 대상이 있는 사람은 한 번 시도해 보길 권합니다.

하지만, 오늘 우리는 어린이들에 관해 이야기하지 않을 거예요. 많은 과학자들은 일부 동물들도 마음 이론을 가지고 있다고 생각합니다. 그래서 오늘은 우리의 논의를 버빗 원숭이에 제한할 거예요, 왜냐하면 이 남아프리카 원숭이에 대한 연구는 종종 인용되거든요. 특히, 과학자들은 버빗 원숭이가 가끔 가짜 경고음을 내기 때문에 그들을 관찰해요, 과학자들은 알고 싶어 합니다, 그게 의도적인 걸까요? 만약 그렇다면, 이건 버빗 원숭이가 마음 이론을 가지고 있다는 의견을 지지하는 것처럼 보일 테니까요.

펜실베이니아 대학교의 두 영장류 연구원, 체니와 세이파스는, 언젠가 새로운 원숭이 한 마리가 무리에 접근하자 하위 계급의 버빗 원숭이가 경고음을 내는 것을 목격했어요. 하위 계급 부분이 중요해요, 왜냐하면 경고음은 보통 사회적 계급이 높은 동물들만 내거든요. 주변에 아무 포식 동물도 없었지만, 그럼에도 불구하고 그 경고음은 다른 모든 원숭이들이 나무 위로 올라가서 숨게 했어요. 자, 몇몇 동물 심리학자들은 이 관찰을 이용해 경고음을 낸 원숭이의 목적이 부하를 얻기 위해 새로운 원숭이에게 자신의 사회적 지위가 높은 것처럼 보이게 하는 것이라고 추측했어요. 연구원들은 경고음을 내는 원숭이가 다른 원숭이의 입장에 서서 가짜 경고음이 다른 원숭이의 인식에 미치는 영향을 이해할 수 있다고 주장했습니다. 이 주장이 무엇을 제시하는 걸까요? 간단히 버빗 원숭이들은 마음 이론을 가지고 있고, 그들은 현실과 다른 이들의 인식 사이를 구별할 수 있다는 거죠.

하지만, 이러한 일화적인 증거를 사용하는 것의 문제점은 증명하기가 아주 어렵다는 것을 지적하고 싶습니다. 다른 심리학자들은 버빗 원숭이와 관련한 다른 실험들을 언급하면서 체니와 세이파스가 내세웠던 주장을 반박합니다. 그 실험들에서, 어떤 원숭이들은 계속해서 가짜 경고음을 냈습니다. 그들은 끝내 집단 전체에게 무시당할 때까지 계속 그랬어요. 새로운 원숭이가 또한, 무슨 일이 일어나고 있는지 마침내 알아챘습니다. 결국, 새로운 원숭이의 존재는 어쩌면 가짜 경고음을 내는 것과 관련이 없었을 수도 있습니다. 그건 의도적이지 않은 행동일 수 있어요, 그러니까, 그 원숭이가 일종의 장애나 지능 장애를 겪고 있다는 걸 나타내는 것일 수도 있겠죠.

이는 과학자들이 같은 상황을 다르게 해석할 수도 있다는 것을 보여줍니다. 야생의 동물들에게 심리학적인 실험을 하는 것은, 불가능하지는 않더라도, 어려워요, 그래서 샐리-앤 테스트 같은 것을 원숭이에게 실행하는 건 불가능하죠. 과학자들이 의지할 수 있는 건 관찰과 귀납뿐이니까요. 제 생각에는 둘 중 어느 것도 동물의 마음 이론에 대한 강력한 증거를 제시하지 못해요. 그래서 어떠한 설명이 더 좋은지는 여러분 모두가 직접 고르게 놔둘게요.

어휘

put on ~을 꾸미다   skit[skit] 토막극   marble[mɑːrbl] 구슬   desire[dizáiər] 욕구   intent[intént] 의도   urge[əːrdʒ] 권하다
suitable[súːtəbl] 적당한   vervet monkey 버빗 원숭이   cite[sait] 인용하다   alarm call 경고음   intentional[inténʃənl] 의도적인
low-ranking[lòuræŋkiŋ] 하위 계급의   speculate[spékjulèit] 추측하다   subordinate[səbɔ́ːrdənət] 부하
put oneself in the shoes of ~의 입장에 서다   perception[pərsépʃən] 인식   anecdotal[ænikdóutl] 일화적인
refute[rifjúːt] 반박하다   have no bearing on ~과 관련이 없다   impairment[impέərmənt] 장애   mental deficiency 지능 장애
induction[indʌ́kʃən] 귀납   overwhelming[òuvərhwélmiŋ] 강력한

*각 문제에 대한 정답단서는 지문에 보라색으로 표시되어 있습니다.

문제 공략하기
p.100

자, 우주 탐사기, 마리너 10호가, 수성을 3번 탐사하고 2,700장 정도의 사진을 찍었습니다. 1965년에, 과학자들은 수성이 5일 정도의 오차를 두고, 59일마다 자전하는 것을 계산해냈어요. 그러나, 마리너 10호는 자전이 0.0005일의 오차를 두고, 실제로는 58.846일에 한 번씩 일어난다는 것을 밝혀낼 수 있었습니다.

자... 마리너 10호가 밝혀낸 또 다른 점은 수성이 지구의 자기장보다 약 100배 약한 자기장을 갖고 있다는 것입니다. 흥미로운 점은... 행성이 자기장을 가지려면, 부분적으로 용해된 핵이 있어야 하는데, 즉, 액화된 금속이나 액화된 암석이어야 하는 것이죠. 고체 핵은 자기장을 만들 수 없거든요. 과학자들은 수성의 핵이 한때 액화된 철이었지만, 이 모든 몇십억 년 동안 그것이 차가워지고 고체화되었다고 추정했습니다. 하지만, 마리너 10호는 자기장을 탐지해냈어요, 약한 것이기는 했지만요.

지적하고 싶은 또 다른 점은... 달과 수성 모두 극한의 온도를 가진다는 것이에요... 수성의 온도는 밤에 섭씨 영하 170도까지 내려가고 낮에는 섭씨 350도로 올라가는데, 달의 온도는 영하 100도에서 340도까지 오르내립니다. 그 둘 사이의 유일한 큰 차이점은 밀도입니다. 달의 더 낮은 밀도는 그 행성이 대부분 용암류로 인한 화성암으로 구성되어 있음을 알려주지만, 수성의 더 높은 밀도는 그것이 철로 된 핵을 가지고 있음을 의미하죠.

HACKERS PRACTICE
p.102

1. (C) Main Purpose/Topic
2. Connecting Contents I

	Included	Not Included
Easier access to online publications		✓
Improved organization of the website	✓	
Additional options for book reservations		✓
An enhanced search function	✓	

3. (B) Detail   4. (B) Main Purpose/Topic
5. Connecting Contents I

Step 1	Provide schedule and route information
Step 2	Recalculate the travel costs
Step 3	Arrange an inspection of the bicycles

6. (D) Detail   7. (C) Main Purpose/Topic   8. (A) Detail
9. Connecting Contents I

	Yes	No
A number of misleading hints are given.	✓	
Two detectives compete to solve a crime.		✓
A perceptive and eccentric detective solves the crime.	✓	
The story revolves around a crime and a criminal.	✓	
Several people are directly responsible for the crime.		✓

10. (B) Main Purpose/Topic

[1-3]

Listen to a conversation between a student and a librarian.

W: Hi. I have a problem . . . It's about a book that, uh, my professor recommended for an assignment.

M: OK. What exactly is the issue?

W: [Q1] When I search for the book in the library's online catalogue, the system shows its status as, um, "repair" . . . I've never seen this before . . . so I'm not sure what it means. Can you let me know what's going on?

M: Oh . . . That just means that the book has been pulled from the shelves to be . . . well, to be repaired. Let me double-check for you, though. What's the, uh, title of the book?

W: Um, it's *Arctic Gold* . . . by Max Pearson.

M: Give me a minute . . . OK, here it is. The spine is damaged and the front cover needs to be replaced. It's in pretty rough shape.

W: I guess that makes sense. It's a really old book. Um, the computer system sure gives a lot of information about the status of a book now . . .

M: Yeah . . . It was recently upgraded . . . At the beginning of the semester, actually. There are many new features.

W: I noticed that the system had improved. The previous version had . . . um, it had some problems.

M: I agree . . . [Q2] Lots of students have commented on the additional search options. They say it's much easier to do their research now.

W: Right . . . And the new website is really great. The old one was hard to navigate . . . The new setup makes more sense and is more orderly.

M: I'm glad you like it.

W: I'm not really sure what to do now, though. My professor is insistent that I use that book. He seems to think it will provide me with, um, important insights into the topic. My deadline is May 10th . . . That's just two weeks away.

M: May 10th? Well, you're in luck, then. The book will be back in the library on May 5th. That should still give you enough time to write the paper.

W: Hmm . . . It'll be a little tight, but I think I can get it done.

M: [Q3] OK . . . Why don't I reserve the book for you now, and you can, uh, pick it up as soon as it goes back into circulation? The library will send you a notification by email.

W: That's great. Thank you so much for your help. I was worried I'd have to . . . um, you know . . . ask my professor for an extension.

M: You're welcome. Enjoy the rest of your day.

Now get ready to answer the questions. You may use your notes to help you answer.

1. What is the student's problem?
2. What improvements are included in the updated computer system? Indicate whether each of the following is included.
3. What does the librarian offer to do for the student?

W: 안녕하세요. 문제가 하나 있어서요... 그건, 어, 제 교수님께서 과제를 위해 추천해주신 책에 관한 거예요.

M: 그렇군요. 문제가 정확히 뭔가요?

W: 도서관의 온라인 목록에서 그 책을 찾으면, 시스템은 그것의 상태를, 음, '수선'이라고 나타내요... 전에는 이런 걸 본 적이 없어서... 그게 무슨 뜻인지 모르겠어요. 무슨 일인지 알려주실 수 있나요?

M: 오... 그건 단지 그 책이... 음, 수선되기 위해 선반에서 빠져있다는 걸 뜻하는 거예요. 하지만, 한 번 더 확인해 볼게요. 책의 제목이, 어, 뭐죠?

W: 음, 'Arctic Gold'예요... 맥스 피어슨이 쓴 거요.

M: 잠시만요... 네, 여기 있어요. 책의 등이 훼손됐고 앞표지가 교체되어야 하네요. 그건 꽤 거친 상태거든요.

W: 이해가 될 것 같아요. 그건 정말 오래된 책이니까요. 음, 이제 전산 시스템이 책의 상태에 관해 정말로 많은 정보를 주네요...

M: 네... 최근에 개선됐죠... 사실, 이번 학기 초예요. 많은 새로운 기능이 있어요.

W: 시스템이 개선되었다는 건 알아챘어요. 이전 버전은... 문제가 좀 있었잖아요.

M: 그렇죠... 많은 학생이 추가적인 검색 옵션에 대해 언급했어요. 그들은 이제 조사를 하기가 훨씬 더 쉬워졌다고 말하더군요.

W: 맞아요... 그리고 새로운 웹사이트는 정말로 훌륭해요. 예전 것은 웹사이트에서 여기저기 찾기가 힘들었거든요... 새로운 구성이 이해가 더 잘 되고 더 정돈되어 있더라고요.

M: 마음에 든다니 기쁘네요.

W: 하지만, 저는 이제 정말로 어떻게 해야 할지 모르겠네요. 교수님은 제가 그 책을 사용해야 한다고 주장하시거든요. 그는 그 책이 제게, 음, 그 주제에 관한 중요한 통찰력을 줄 거라고 생각하시는 것 같아요. 기한이 5월 10일인데... 2주밖에 안 남았어요.

M: 5월 10일이요? 음, 그렇다면, 학생은 운이 좋군요. 그 책은 5월 5일에 도서관에 반납될 거예요. 그건 아직 학생이 보고서를 쓸 충분한 시간을 주겠죠.

W: 흠... 조금 빠듯할 것 같지만, 마칠 수 있을 것 같아요.

M: 그래요... 지금 제가 학생을 위해 책을 예약하고, 그게 다시 유통되자마자, 어, 가져가는 건 어때요? 도서관에서 이메일로 알림을 보내줄 거예요.

W: 좋아요. 도와주셔서 정말 감사합니다. 교수님께... 음, 그러니까... 연장을 요청해야 할까 봐 걱정했거든요.

M: 천만에요. 남은 하루 잘 보내세요.

[4-6]
Listen to a conversation between a student and an employee in the Student Activity Center.

W: Hi. Um, I'm in charge of organizing a trip for my club . . .

M: OK. Which club is it?

W: Oh, it's the architecture club . . . We're planning to visit the, uh, Pacific Heights neighborhood of San Francisco later this month. There are some excellent examples of Victorian style houses there . . .

M: That sounds fun . . . I grew up near there. It's a beautiful area.

W: Yeah, I'm looking forward to it. 04 Our trip was approved last month, but we, um . . . we want to make a last-minute adjustment to our travel plans. I, uh, wasn't sure if I had to notify the university or not . . .

M: Well, it depends. Can you be more specific?

W: Sure. We were originally going to rent a bus to take us. But, um . . . the club's vice president suggested that we go by bicycle instead.

M: By bicycle?

W: Right. She said the trip should only take about three hours each way. And lots of club members like the idea . . .

M: I see . . . This means some paperwork for you, unfortunately.

W: That's what I was afraid of . . .

M: Yeah . . . Um, significant changes to a club's travel plans have to get approved. Don't worry, though . . . The process is, um . . . fairly straightforward.

W: What does it involve?

M: Q5 Well, the first thing you need to do is submit a new travel itinerary . . . You know, one that includes your departure and arrival times, the, uh, route you plan to take . . . things like that. I have the form here if you want to fill it out now.

W: OK. Thanks.

M: It should take about a day to process the itinerary. Q5 Assuming there are no problems, you'll then need to create an updated budget. Um, you won't be spending money on the bus anymore, but maybe there will be . . . you know . . . other expenses.

W: I can ask the club treasurer about that . . . He'll have all the information.

M: Good. Q5 The final step is to get the bicycles for the trip, um, certified.

W: Certified? What do you mean?

M: They need to be checked to make sure that there are no mechanical problems. Q6 It's a new university regulation. There was an incident last year involving a cycling trip taken by another club. Two of the members were injured.

W: OK . . . Um, where exactly can I do this?

M: The bike shop on campus . . . Don't worry . . . you won't be charged because this is an official club trip. I'll give you the necessary forms once we've approved your new budget.

W: Oh, that doesn't sound too hard.

Now get ready to answer the questions. You may use your notes to help you answer.

4. Why does the student visit the Student Activity Center?

5. The employee explains the steps in the process for getting a change in travel plans approved. Put the steps listed below in the correct order.

6. Why did the university recently introduce a new regulation regarding cycling trips?

W: 안녕하세요. 음, 저는 제 동아리의 여행 준비를 담당하고 있는데요...

M: 그렇군요. 무슨 동아리죠?

W: 오, 건축학 동아리예요... 저희는 이번 달 말에, 어, 샌프란시스코의 Pacific Heights 지역에 가려고 계획 중이에요. 거기에는 빅토리아 양식 가옥의 훌륭한 본보기들이 좀 있거든요.

M: 재미있을 것 같네요... 저는 거기 근처에서 자랐거든요. 아름다운 지역이죠.

W: 네, 기대하고 있어요. 여행은 지난달에 승인됐는데, 저희는, 음... 여행 계획에 막바지 수정을 하고 싶어서요. 제가, 어, 학교에 알려야 하는지 아닌지를 확실히 모르겠더라고요.

M: 음, 그건 때에 따라 달라요. 좀 더 구체적으로 말해줄래요?

W: 물론이죠. 원래는 저희를 데려다줄 버스 한 대를 빌리려고 했어요. 그런데, 음... 동아리 부회장이 그 대신에 자전거로 갈 것을 제안했죠.

M: 자전거로요?

W: 네. 그녀는 여행이 편도로 약 3시간밖에 걸리지 않을 거라고 말했어요. 그리고 많은 동아리 회원이 그 제안을 마음에 들어 해요...

M: 그렇군요... 유감스럽게도, 이건 학생이 서류 작업을 좀 해야 한다는 의미네요.

W: 그게 바로 제가 염려했던 거예요...

M: 네... 음, 동아리 여행 계획의 중요한 변경사항들은 승인을 받아야 하거든요. 하지만, 걱정하지 마세요... 그 과정은, 음... 꽤 간단해요.

W: 그건 무엇을 수반하나요?

M: 음, 학생이 해야 할 첫 번째는 새로운 여행 일정을 제출하는 거예요... 그러니까, 출발시각과 도착시각, 그, 어, 가기로 계획한 경로... 그런 것들을 포함한 거 말이에요. 지금 기재하고 싶다면 여기 서식이 있어요.

W: 좋아요. 고맙습니다.

M: 일정을 처리하는 데 약 하루가 걸릴 거예요. 문제가 없다고 가정하면, 학생은 새로운 예산을 짜야겠죠. 음, 더는 버스에 돈을 쓰지 않겠지만, 아마... 그러니까... 다른 비용이 들 수도 있잖아요.

W: 동아리 회계 담당자에게 그것에 관해 물어볼 수 있겠어요... 그가 모든 정보를 가지고 있을 거예요.

M: 좋아요. 마지막 단계는 여행을 위한 자전거들을 증명받는 거예요.

W: 증명받는다고요? 무슨 말씀이죠?

M: 기계적인 문제가 없다는 것을 확실히 하기 위해 자전거들을 점검받아야 해요. 그건 학교의 새로운 규정이죠. 작년에 다른 동아리의 자전거 여행과 관련된 사고가 있었거든요. 회원 두 명이 다쳤었어요.

W: 그렇군요... 음, 정확히 어디에서 이걸 할 수 있나요?

M: 교내 자전거 가게에서요... 걱정하지 말아요... 이건 공식적인 동아리 여행이니까 요금이 청구되지 않을 거예요. 일단 우리가 학생의 새 예산을 승인하고 나면 필요한 서식을 줄게요.

W: 오, 그건 너무 어렵게 들리지는 않네요.

[7-9]

Listen to part of a lecture on literature. The professor is discussing a detective novel.

P: As part of our series of discussions on Victorian novels, [Q7] we'll be discussing an 1868 work of fiction written by Wilkie Collins. It's called *The Moonstone*, and it's considered the first full-length detective novel. Maybe you can tell me what you thought of the book . . . as a whole, I mean.

S: I thought the way Collins told the story . . . you know, through the characters themselves . . . I found it unique.

P: Right. It's actually an old-fashioned technique for narration. But this isn't really what I wanted to go into.
Earlier, I mentioned that *The Moonstone* is considered the first full-length detective novel.
[Q9] *The Moonstone* contains all the characteristics of a typical modern English detective novel: a large number of suspects . . . several false clues meant to mislead the reader . . . and a crime that's being investigated, of course. In the case of *The Moonstone*, an extremely valuable diamond was stolen. [Q9] But what makes *The Moonstone* noteworthy is that it was the first work of detective fiction to have an undisclosed and significant crime and criminal at the center of its plot. And another thing . . . [Q8] the character that did the investigating in the novel, Sergeant Cuff, is considered the prototype of the detective hero in English fiction.
Sergeant Cuff isn't actually the main character of the novel. By now, you know that an heiress named Rachel and her suitor, Franklin, are at the center of the plot. But just so we understand why Cuff is important in our study of modern detective novels, let's examine him a bit more closely. In many detective novels, you'll find someone who represents the amateur detective. It could be an unskilled investigator . . . or the inept local police. In *The Moonstone*, the incompetent person is the police superintendent. [Q9] In contrast, we have the . . . extremely perceptive, very civilized, professional investigator who is a bit eccentric. Can you recall what Cuff's deductions were? He reasoned that the thief had to have been someone close to the victim, right? But he went one step further. He—he deduced that the thief had not actually stolen the diamond. You do remember reading that part?
Now, let's think about Sir Arthur Conan Doyle's Sherlock Holmes. Sergeant Cuff is the forerunner of the great Sherlock Holmes. Cuff used critical thinking skills and reasoning power

just as Holmes did. And he was every bit a gentleman as Holmes was. And like Holmes, Cuff had his, um . . . eccentricities.

Now get ready to answer the questions. You may use your notes to help you answer.

7. What does the professor mainly discuss?
8. What does the professor say about Sergeant Cuff?
9. In the lecture, the professor describes typical characteristics of modern detective fiction novels. Indicate whether each of the following is a characteristic.

P: 빅토리아 시대 소설에 관한 토론의 일환으로, 윌키 콜린스가 쓴 1868년도의 소설 작품에 관해 논의할 거예요. 제목은 '월장석'이고, 최초의 장편 탐정소설이라고 여겨지죠. 여러분이 이 책에 대해 어떻게 생각했는지 이야기해 볼 수 있겠네요... 제 말은, 전반적으로 말입니다.

S: 저는 콜린스가 이야기를 들려주는 방법... 그러니까, 등장인물 각각을 통해서 말이에요... 이것이 독특하다고 생각했어요.

P: 맞아요. 실제로 그건 이야기를 풀어나가는 옛날식 방법이죠. 그러나 사실 이건 제가 살펴보고자 했던 것은 아닙니다.
앞서, 저는 '월장석'이 첫 장편 탐정소설로 여겨진다고 언급했었죠. '월장석'은 전형적인 현대 영국 탐정소설의 특징을 모두 포함하고 있습니다. 많은 용의자들... 독자를 속이려는 여러 가지 거짓 단서들... 그리고 물론, 수사되고 있는 범죄 말이죠. '월장석'의 경우에는, 엄청나게 값비싼 다이아몬드가 도난당합니다. 하지만 '월장석'을 주목할 만하게 하는 것은 줄거리의 중심에 밝혀지지 않은 심각한 범죄와 범죄자가 있는 최초의 탐정소설이라는 것입니다. 그리고 또 한 가지는... 이 소설에서 조사를 하는 인물인 커프 경사가 영국 소설의 탐정 영웅 시초로 여겨진다는 점이고요.
사실 커프 경사가 이 소설의 주인공은 아니죠. 지금쯤, 여러분은 상속녀인 레이첼과 그녀의 애인 프랭클린이 이 줄거리의 중심에 있다는 것을 알 거예요. 하지만 왜 커프가 현대 탐정소설 연구에 중요한지 이해하기 위해, 그를 조금 더 자세히 탐구해 봅시다. 많은 탐정소설에는, 아마추어 탐정을 상징하는 누군가가 있을 거예요. 미숙한 수사관이나... 또는 서투른 지역 경관일 수 있죠. '월장석'에서, 그 무능한 인물은 경찰 서장입니다. 반대로, 대단히 통찰력 있고, 굉장히 교양 있으며, 전문적이긴 하나 다소 괴짜인... 수사관이 등장합니다. 커프의 추리가 무엇이었는지 기억하나요? 그는 도둑이 희생자와 가까운 사람임이 틀림없다고 추리했었죠, 그렇죠? 그러나 그는 한 단계 더 나아갔죠. 그는, 그 도둑이 사실 다이아몬드를 훔치지 않았다고 추리해냈어요. 그 부분을 읽었던 것이 기억나죠?
자, 아서 코난 도일 경의 셜록 홈스에 관해 생각해 봅시다. 커프 경사는 그 위대한 셜록 홈스의 전신입니다. 커프는 홈스가 그랬듯이 비판적 사고 능력과 추리력을 사용했습니다. 그리고 그는 전적으로 홈스와 같은 신사였고요. 그리고 홈스처럼, 커프는 그의, 음... 괴팍함을 지니고 있었죠.

[10-12]
Listen to part of a lecture in an archaeology class.

So, there are a number of technologies available to modern archaeologists. For example, muon-detectors, which are installed at sites that researchers believe contain ancient ruins. They're used to detect buried buildings. Q10 But to locate such sites in the first place, archaeologists must rely on other technologies like LIDAR . . .
The name LIDAR comes from the words *light* and *radar*. Like radar, LIDAR measures the distances to solid objects. But instead of using radio waves, it uses light waves produced by a laser. Using LIDAR, archaeologists can create three-dimensional maps of an area. Here's how it works. Q11 First, a LIDAR unit is attached to a low-flying aircraft. Then, from the air, the LIDAR unit emits light to objects on the ground. Next, it measures the time it takes for the light to travel to the object and back. This information is entered into a computer to determine the distance to the object, as well as the object's height above the ground. To ensure the accuracy of these measurements, the computer must then compare this data to other information. Uh, planes constantly shift while in flight and the computer corrects for these movements. Anyway, to continue, the entire process is

repeated over a large area to gather data about multiple objects. Finally, all of the data is combined to produce a three-dimensional map.

How is this useful? Well, looking at a three-dimensional map makes it easier to detect patterns on the ground. Archaeologists can clearly distinguish between natural objects, such as rocks and trees, and man-made structures like buildings and roads. Let me give you an example. In Cambodia, archaeologists had spent years looking for the lost city of Mahendraparvata. The clues they found indicated that the city was in one part of the country, but they faced a few, um, challenges. The site was covered in thick jungle and contained other hazards. By attaching LIDAR systems to helicopters, they were able to explore the area safely from the air. Q12 Within a week, they had a detailed map that showed where ancient buildings had been located. A week! This achievement would have been impossible without LIDAR. It just goes to show how much, um . . . how much archaeologists have benefited from the development of new technologies . . .

Now get ready to answer the questions. You may use your notes to help you answer.

10. What is the lecture mainly about?
11. In the lecture, the professor explains the sequence of steps used to create a three-dimensional map of an area. Put the steps listed below in the correct order.

Listen again to part of the lecture. Then answer the question.

P: Within a week, they had a detailed map that showed where ancient buildings had been located. A week! This achievement would have been impossible without LIDAR.

12. Why does the professor say this:
    P: A week!

자, 현대 고고학자들이 이용할 수 있는 많은 기술들이 있습니다. 예를 들어, 뮤온 탐지기 말이죠, 연구원들이 고대 유적을 포함하고 있다고 생각하는 장소에 설치되는 것 말이에요. 그것들은 파묻힌 건물들을 감지하는 데 사용됩니다. 하지만 먼저 그러한 장소들의 정확한 위치를 찾아내기 위해, 고고학자들은 LIDAR와 같은 다른 장비에 의존해야 합니다...

LIDAR라는 이름은 '빛'과 '레이더'라는 단어에서 나왔어요. 레이더처럼, LIDAR는 고형 물체까지의 거리를 측정합니다. 하지만 전파를 사용하는 대신, 레이저에서 만들어진 광파를 사용하죠. LIDAR를 이용해서, 고고학자들은 한 지역의 3차원 지도를 만들어낼 수 있어요. 이게 그것이 작동하는 방법입니다... 먼저 LIDAR 장치가 저공 비행 항공기에 부착됩니다. 그 후, LIDAR 장치가 대기에서 지상에 있는 물체로 광선을 방출하죠. 다음으로, 그것은 광선이 물체까지 갔다가 되돌아오는 데 걸리는 시간을 측정합니다. 이 정보는 지상에서의 물체의 높이뿐만 아니라, 물체까지의 거리를 알아내기 위해 컴퓨터에 입력돼요. 이러한 측정의 정확성을 보장하기 위해, 그 후 컴퓨터는 이 자료를 반드시 그 밖에 다른 정보와 비교해야 합니다. 어, 항공기는 비행 중에 끊임없이 이동하고, 컴퓨터는 이러한 움직임을 바로잡거든요... 어쨌든, 계속하자면, 전체 과정은 다수의 물체에 대한 자료를 수집하기 위해 넓은 지역에 걸쳐 반복됩니다. 마침내, 모든 자료는 3차원 지도를 만들어내기 위해 결합되죠...

이것이 어떻게 유용할까요? 음, 3차원 지도를 보는 것은 지면의 형태를 감지하는 것을 더 쉽게 해줍니다. 고고학자들은 바위와 나무 같은 자연물과, 건물과 도로 같은 인공 구조물을 분명하게 구별할 수 있어요. 예를 하나 들어 볼게요. 캄보디아에서, 고고학자들은 잃어버린 도시 마헨드라파르바타를 찾는 데 몇 년을 보냈어요... 그들이 찾아낸 단서는 그 도시가 캄보디아의 한 부분이었다는 것을 보여줬지만, 그들은 몇 가지, 음, 문제에 직면했다. 그 장소는 빽빽한 밀림으로 덮여있었고 다른 위험 요소들을 가지고 있었거든요. LIDAR 장치를 헬리콥터에 부착함으로써, 그들은 그 지역을 공중에서 안전하게 탐험할 수 있었어요. 일주일 내에, 고대 건물들이 정확히 어디에 있었는지를 보여주는 상세한 지도를 갖게 됐어요. 일주일이요! 이 업적은 LIDAR가 없이는 불가능했을 거예요. 그것은, 음... 새로운 기술의 발달로 고고학자들이 얼마나 많은 이득을 받아왔는지를 보여줬죠...

HACKERS TEST

p.106

1. (C) Main Purpose/Topic   2. (C) Detail   3. (B) Detail
4. (C) Function & Attitude
5. Connecting Contents I

	Suggested	Not Suggested
Consult with another professor	√	
Search for relevant websites	√	
Review a unit in the textbook		√
Get texts from the library	√	

6. (B) Main Purpose/Topic   7. (A) Detail
8. (B) Connecting Contents I

Step 1	Transportation routes project from the CBD.
Step 2	Factories are built along roads and railway lines.
Step 3	Residential areas form in relation to industrial areas.

9. (B) Function & Attitude   10. (A), (B), (D) Detail   11. (D) Detail
12. (C) Main Purpose/Topic   13. (A), (D) Detail   14. (A) Detail
15. (D) Function & Attitude   16. (A) Function & Attitude
17. Connecting Contents I

	Yes	No
It is divided into multiple channels.	√	
It has extremely high banks.		√
It includes unstable islands.	√	
It contains little sediment.		√
It experiences regular floods.	√	

18. (B) Main Purpose/Topic   19. (A) Function & Attitude   20. (B) Detail
21. (B) Detail
22. Connecting Contents I

	Suggested	Not Suggested
Search for an item online	√	
Visit a different bookstore	√	
Borrow the book from the library		√
Visit the university's storage unit		√
Ask the professor if he will order more books	√	

23. (C) Main Purpose/Topic   24. (C) Function & Attitude   25. (C) Detail
26. Connecting Contents I

	Yes	No
They altered the forms of many letters.	√	
They eliminated most of the vowels.		√
They combined a few of the consonants.		√
They created some additional symbols.	√	

27. (A) Detail   28. (A), (D) Detail   29. (C) Main Purpose/Topic
30. (D) Detail   31. (C) Function & Attitude

Step 1	Dust and gas combine in outer space.
Step 2	An object increases significantly in mass.
Step 3	The accumulation of matter stops.

33. (B) Detail   34. (A) Function & Attitude

[1-5]

Listen to a conversation between a student and a professor.

S: Hi, Professor Jennings. I hope I'm not bothering you.

P: It's, uh, Sally, right?

S: Q1 Right. Um, I'm really struggling with my presentation topic. It's the, uh . . . the law of diminishing returns.

P: I'm not surprised. It's a complex concept. That's why I gave everyone a list of supplemental readings. Uh, you read those articles, right?

S: Of course, but . . . um, I still feel a little lost. I was hoping you could go over it with me.

P: OK. I provided a basic definition of this economic principle in class. Do you remember what it was?

S: Q2 Well, the law of diminishing returns has to do with, um . . . the factors of production . . .

P: Right. And these can be almost anything . . . It depends on the circumstances. In the case of a farm . . . seeds, land, and, uh, fertilizer are the factors of production. But in, say, a factory, you'd be dealing with something else. Go on . . .

S: Um, let me think . . . OK, when, uh, only one factor is increased, and the others remain constant, then, well . . . at a certain point production will decrease. But that's what confuses me. I don't really understand why this would lead to lower overall output.

P: Ah . . . I see the problem. You're confused about a key element of this law. Just to be clear, Q3 increasing only one factor will not cause overall output to, well . . . to decline. It will rise. But each time you do this, the resulting increase in production will be smaller. Eventually, the extra output will not be worth the cost of the additional input.

S: I guess that makes sense. But still . . . It's just so abstract. I'm having trouble understanding what it means in practical terms.

P: Well, let's look at an example then . . . Imagine that you are in charge of the university cafeteria. If the number of customers increased, how would you deal with it?

S: Um, bring in more workers, I suppose.

P: That's what most people would do . . . And it would initially result in a significant boost in production. Uh, more workers means more meals . . . Now, say you just kept adding new employees . . . and you didn't install new kitchen equipment or, I don't know . . . purchase larger quantities of ingredients. You only increased one factor of production, in other words . . . What do you think would happen?

S: Um, the workers would probably slow down a bit.

P: Exactly. Workers would be wasting a lot of time . . . you know, getting in each other's way and so on. Q4 Overall output would continue to increase a bit as new workers were added, but not enough to justify their wages. Does that make sense?

S: Hmm . . . I think I have a lot of work to do for my presentation. This is really complicated.

P: Q5 Well, there might be some good resources online. And I can recommend a few books for you that, um . . . that should be available at the library.

S: That would be very helpful . . .

P: Oh, I almost forgot . . . Professor Wilkins has written several articles on this topic. Maybe you could ask him about other sources of information. I'm sure he'd be glad to help.

S: Thanks. I'll do that now.

Now get ready to answer the questions. You may use your notes to help you answer.

1. Why does the student go to see the professor?
2. What does the professor say about the factors of production?
3. According to the professor, what is an important aspect of the law of diminishing returns?

Listen again to part of the conversation. Then answer the question.

P: Overall output would continue to increase a bit as new workers were added, but not enough to justify their wages. Does that make sense?

S: Hmm . . . I think I have a lot of work to do for my presentation. This is really complicated.

4. What does the student mean when she says this:
   S: Hmm . . . I think I have a lot of work to do for my presentation.

5. The professor suggests several ways for the student to learn more about a law of economics. Indicate whether each of the following is included.

S: 안녕하세요, Jennings 교수님. 제가 교수님을 귀찮게 하는 게 아니었으면 좋겠네요.

P: 어, Sally, 맞지?

S: 맞아요. 음, 제 발표 주제로 정말 고심하는 중이에요. 그게, 어... 수확체감의 법칙 말이에요.

P: 놀랍지 않구나. 그건 복잡한 개념이지. 그게 바로 내가 모두에게 추가적인 읽기 자료 목록을 나눠준 이유란다. 어, 그 논문들을 읽었을 텐데, 그렇지?

S: 물론이죠, 하지만... 음, 저는 여전히 잘 이해할 수가 없어요. 교수님께서 그걸 저와 함께 검토해주시길 바라고 있었어요.

P: 그렇구나. 내가 수업 시간에 이 경제 원리의 기본적인 정의를 내렸지. 그게 뭐였는지 기억하니?

S: 음, 수확체감의 법칙은, 음... 생산 요소와 관련이 있다는 거요...

P: 맞아. 그리고 요소는 거의 무엇이든 될 수 있단다... 상황에 의해 결정되지. 농장의 경우에는... 씨앗, 땅, 그리고, 어, 비료가 생산 요소란다. 하지만, 가령, 공장에서는, 다른 무언가를 다룰 수도 있겠지. 계속해 보렴...

S: 음, 생각해 볼게요... 네, 어, 오직 한 가지 요소만 증가하고, 나머지 요소들은 계속 변함없을 때, 그러면, 음... 어떤 지점에서 생산량이 감소할 거예요. 하지만 그게 바로 저를 혼란스럽게 하는 거예요. 저는 왜 이게 전체적으로 낮은 생산량으로 이어지는지 정말 이해가 안 가요.

P: 아... 문제가 뭔지 알겠구나. 너는 이 법칙의 주요 원리에 대해 혼동한 거야. 분명히 하자면, 한 가지 요소만을 증가시키는 것이 전반적인 생산량을, 음... 감소하게 하지는 않을 거야. 생산량은 증가하지. 하지만 이렇게 할 때마다, 결과적인 생산량의 증가는 더 적을 거란다. 결국, 여분의 생산량이 추가적인 투입의 비용을 정당화하지 못하게 되지.

S: 이해가 가는 것 같아요. 하지만 아직도... 그건 그저 너무 추상적이에요. 저는 그게 현실적인 조건에서 무엇을 뜻하는지 이해하기가 힘들어요.

P: 음, 그렇다면 예를 하나 들어 보자... 네가 교내 식당을 담당하고 있다고 상상해 보렴. 만약 손님 수가 증가한다면, 너는 그것에 어떻게 대응할 것 같니?

S: 음, 제 생각에는, 더 많은 직원을 들여오겠지요.

P: 그게 대부분의 사람이 하는 일일 거야... 그리고 처음에는 그게 상당한 생산량의 증가를 일으키겠지. 어, 더 많은 직원은 더 많은 음식을 의미하니까... 자, 네가 계속해서 새로운 직원만 추가한다고 생각해 보자... 그리고 새 주방 장비를 설치하지 않거나, 글쎄... 더 많은 양의 재료를 구매하지 않는다든지. 다시 말해서, 오직 하나의 생산 요소만 증가시키는 거지... 그럼 무슨 일이 일어날 거라고 생각하니?

S: 아마도 직원들이 조금 느긋해지겠죠.

P: 정확해. 직원들은 많은 시간을 낭비하겠지... 그러니까, 서로에게 방해되는 등등 말이야. 새 직원들이 추가됨에 따라 전체적인 생산량은 계속해서 조금씩 증가하겠지만, 그들의 임금을 정당화할 만큼 충분하지는 않겠지. 이해가 가니?

S: 흠... 발표를 위해서 할 일이 많은 것 같아요. 이건 정말 복잡하네요.

P: 음, 온라인에 좋은 자료가 좀 있을지도 몰라. 그리고 내가, 음... 도서관에서 이용할 수 있을 책 몇 권을 추천해줄 수도 있단다.

S: 그건 정말 도움이 될 것 같아요...

P: 오, 하마터면 잊어버릴 뻔했네... Wilkins 교수가 이 주제에 대해 논문 몇 개를 썼단다. 아마 너는 그에게 다른 정보 자료에 관해 물어볼 수도 있겠구나. 그는 기꺼이 도와줄 거야.

S: 감사합니다. 지금 여쭤 볼게요.

어휘

struggle with ~으로 고심하다   diminishing returns 수확체감   supplemental[sÀpləméntl] 추가적인   lost[lɔːst] 이해할 수 없는
go over 검토하다   provide a definition 정의를 내리다   have to do with ~과 관련이 있다   production[prədʎkʃən] 생산, 생산량
fertilizer[fɔ́ːrtəlàizər] 비료   constant[kánstənt] 변함없는   element[éləmənt] 원리   output[áutpùt] 생산량
abstract[æbstrǽkt] 추상적인   practical[prǽktikəl] 현실적인   term[təːrm] 조건   deal with ~에 대응하다   boost[buːst] 증가
equipment[ikwípmənt] 장비   ingredient[ingríːdiənt] 재료

[6-11]
Listen to part of a lecture in a sociology class.

P: This week, Ꮭᵁ⁶ we're looking at urbanization models . . . um, theories that explain the internal structures of cities. You've already learned about the ring model proposed by Ernest Burgess from the assigned reading. But there are a couple of more recent ones I'd like to consider . . .
So, as the reading explained, the ring model divides a city into five ring-shaped areas with a central business district, or CBD, in the middle. The two rings closest to the center include, um, factories and businesses. The other three rings are made up of homes . . . and these, uh, homes are more expensive the further away you get from the CBD. Q7 Well, this model was criticized because it didn't match how cities are really organized . . . This led Homer Hoyt to develop the sector model.
Now, Hoyt agreed with Burgess about the CBD. But he argued that the rest of a city doesn't fit into these neat, ring-shaped patterns. Instead, cities include irregularly shaped areas called sectors . . . In Hoyt's model, industrial, commercial, and residential areas form separate sectors. And the locations of these sectors are determined by the city's transportation routes.

S1: I get it. Um, if I owned a factory, then . . . well, I'd want my business to be near a major road or something so I could move my goods more easily.

P: Yes . . . that's a perfect example. And this is how Hoyt explained the urbanization process . . . Q8 First, major transportation routes . . . uh, roads and railway lines . . . are built extending from the city center. Then the industrial areas form along these. Finally, the development of residential areas is determined by . . . um, by where these factories have been built.
Working-class neighborhoods are found on the edges of the industrial sectors. Wealthier neighborhoods are located as far as possible from the factories . . .

S2: Q9 So what I'm hearing is . . . According to Hoyt, a city is organized like a sliced pie? Is that right? The different sectors kind of extend from the, uh, CBD like knife marks in a pie?

P: Well, the sectors aren't uniform in shape or size . . . but that's the general idea. However, some people felt that Hoyt's model didn't describe actual cities any better than the ring model. They argued that the problem was that Hoyt placed too much of an emphasis on the CBD . . . He thought that the CBD was the focal point of the entire city. To address this issue, Chancy

Harris and Edward Ullman proposed the multiple nuclei model . . .

S1: Uh, nuclei? Isn't that the middle part of a, um . . . a cell?

P: Right. And that's how Harris and Ullman viewed a city . . . ^{Q10} as a collection of distinct areas that form around key institutions . . . the nuclei, in other words. They argued that cities have many centers . . . each with a different function. And the centers develop independently of the CBD, so they can be located almost anywhere in a city. OK, I can see some blank looks out there. Take our university, for example . . . what's nearby?

S2: Um, coffee shops, bookstores . . . lots of cheap restaurants . . . things like that.

P: Good . . . These are places that provide students with what they need. The university is the basis of this entire area of the city. Certain types of businesses are attracted to the area because of the university, while others stay away . . . And this happens everywhere in the city. And, of course, the types of businesses in these centers determine what kinds of residential neighborhoods form nearby. ^{Q11} So the main benefit of the multiple nuclei model is its flexibility . . . Unlike the others we've discussed, this way of describing the process of urbanization can be applied to any city . . .

Now get ready to answer the questions. You may use your notes to help you answer.

6. What is the lecture mainly about?
7. What does the professor say about the ring model?
8. In the lecture, the professor explains the steps in the urbanization process according to Hoyt. Put the steps listed below in the correct order.

Listen again to part of the lecture. Then answer the question.

S2: So what I'm hearing is . . . According to Hoyt, a city is organized like a sliced pie? Is that right? The different sectors kind of extend from the, uh, CBD like knife marks in a pie?

P: Well, the sectors aren't uniform in shape or size . . . but that's the general idea.

9. What does the student mean when he says this:
   S2: So what I'm hearing is . . .

10. What are key elements of the multiple nuclei model?
11. According to the professor, what is an advantage of the multiple nuclei model?

P: 이번 주에, 우리는 도시화 모형들을 살펴보고 있어요... 음, 도시의 내부 구조를 설명하는 이론 말이에요. 여러분은 배정된 읽기 자료에서 어니스트 버제스에 의해 제시된 원 모형에 대해 이미 배웠어요. 하지만 제가 고려하고 싶은 두 가지의 더 최근 이론들이 있습니다...
    자, 읽기 자료가 설명했던 것처럼, 원 모형은 하나의 도시를 중앙에 중심 산업 구역, 또는 CBD를 가진 다섯 개의 원 모양으로 된 구역으로 나눕니다. 중심에 가장 가까운 두 개의 원은, 음, 공장과 사업체를 포함합니다. 나머지 세 개의 원들은 주택들로 구성되어 있죠... 그리고 어, 주택들은 CBD에서 멀리 갈수록 더 비쌉니다. 음, 이 모형은 실제로 도시가 구성된 방식과 일치하지 않았기 때문에 비판받았어요... 이는 호머 호이트가 부문 모형을 개발하도록 이끌었죠.
    자, 호이트는 CBD에 관해서는 버제스에 동의했어요. 하지만 그는 도시의 나머지가 이 깔끔한, 원 모양의 양식에 들어맞지 않는다고 주장했습니다. 그보다는, 도시는 부문이라고 불리는 불규칙적으로 형성된 지역들을 포함하죠... 호이트의 모형에서, 산업, 상업, 그리고 주거 지역은 별개의 부문을 형성합니다. 그리고 이 부문들의 위치는 도시의 교통 경로에 의해 결정되고요.

S1: 이해했어요. 음, 제가 만약 공장을 하나 소유하고 있다면, 그럼... 음, 상품을 더 쉽게 옮길 수 있도록 제 사업체가 주요 도로나 뭐 그런 것 근처에 있기를 원할 것 같아요.

P: 네... 그건 완벽한 예시입니다. 그리고 이게 바로 호이트가 도시화 과정을 설명한 방법이죠... 첫째로, 주요 교통 경로가... 어, 도로와 철도 선이... 도시 중심으로부터 확장되며 지어져요. 그리고 나서 산업 구역들이 이를 따라 형성하죠. 마침내, 주거 지역의 발

달이... 음, 이러한 공장들이 어디에 지어졌는지에 따라 결정됩니다. 노동층 주민들은 산업 구역의 가장자리에서 발견돼요. 더 부유한 주민들은 공장으로부터 가능한 한 멀리 위치합니다...

S2: 그러니까 제가 듣기로는... 호이트에 따르면, 도시가 잘린 파이처럼 구성되어 있다는 거네요? 맞나요? 서로 다른 부문들이, 어, 파이에 난 칼자국처럼 CBD로부터 연장되는 뭐 그런 건가요?

P: 음, 부문들은 모양이나 크기가 일정하지는 않아요... 하지만 그것이 일반적인 개념입니다. 그런데, 몇몇 사람들은 호이트의 모형이 실제 도시를 원 모형보다 조금이라도 더 낫게 설명하지는 못했다고 생각했어요. 그들은 호이트가 CBD를 너무 크게 강조한 것이 문제라고 주장했죠... 호이트는 CBD가 전체 도시의 중심점이라고 생각했거든요. 이 문제를 해결하기 위해, 챈시 해리스와 에드워드 울만은 다핵 모형을 제시했습니다...

S1: 어, 핵이요? 그건, 어... 세포의 중심 부분 아닌가요?

P: 맞아요. 그리고 그게 해리스와 울만이 도시를 본 방식이죠... 주요 기관... 다시 말해서, 핵 주위에 형성된 별개 지역들의 집단으로요. 그들은 도시가 많은 중심을 가지고 있고... 각각은 다른 기능을 가진다고 주장했어요. 그리고 그 중심들은 CBD와 독립적으로 발달하므로, 도시의 거의 어느 곳에나 위치할 수 있다고 했죠. 자, 멍한 표정들이 몇 보이는군요. 예로, 우리 대학교를 들어 봅시다... 근처에 뭐가 있죠?

S2: 음, 커피숍, 서점... 많은 저렴한 식당... 그런 것들이요.

P: 맞아요... 이런 것들은 학생들에게 그들이 필요로 하는 것을 제공하는 장소입니다. 대학교는 이 도시 전체 지역의 기반이고요. 특정 종류의 사업체들은 대학교 때문에 이 지역에 끌리는 반면, 다른 것들은 떨어져 있어요... 그리고 이것은 도시 어디에서나 발생합니다. 또한, 물론, 이러한 중심에 있는 사업체들의 종류는 인근에 형성되는 주거 지역의 종류를 결정하죠. 따라서 다핵 모형의 주된 장점은 유연성입니다... 우리가 논의했던 다른 것들과 달리, 도시화 과정을 설명하는 이러한 방식은 어느 도시에나 적용될 수 있으니까요...

어휘

urbanization[ə̀:rbənizéiʃən] 도시화　district[dístrikt] 구역　business[bíznis] 사업체　sector[séktər] 부문
commercial[kəmə́:rʃəl] 상업의　residential[rèzədénʃəl] 주거의　neighborhood[néibərhùd] 주민, 지역
uniform[júːnəfɔ̀:rm] 일정한　place emphasis on ~을 강조하다　nuclei[njúːkliài] 핵(nucleus의 복수형)
institution[ìnstətjúːʃən] 기관　flexibility[flèksəbíləti] 유연성　apply[əplái] 적용하다

[12-17]
Listen to part of a lecture in a geology class.

P: By now, the role of vegetation in keeping the banks of rivers stable should be pretty clear. Um, without plants . . . specifically without their roots to hold the soil around rivers in place, most rivers wouldn't stay on fixed paths. But it's important to note that ^Q12 there are a number of natural events that can alter the shape of a river . . . such as flooding. For the rest of the class, we're going to look at this more closely.

A flood occurs when a river overflows its banks . . . um, in other words, the water rises so high that it spills out over the sides. This normally happens when too much water enters the river. How often this occurs is determined by a couple of factors. ^Q13 One is whether a region experiences significant rises in precipitation at different points in the year . . . like spring or summer. Another is the type of rock and soil found in the land around a river. If this material can absorb a lot of water . . . well, then floods are less common. If not, the risk of floods is high.

So how do floods affect the shape of a river? Of course, when the water overflows, the river becomes wider . . . but this is just a temporary change. However, floods can also alter a river system permanently . . . For example, a river channel can become deeper over time. Does anyone know why this happens?

S1: Well, the water moves more quickly during a flood, right? So maybe it . . . I don't know . . . maybe it digs out the bottom of the river?

P: I can see how that would make sense . . . but, well . . . it's not what happens. ^Q14 In fact, a river channel gets deeper because sediments are deposited around it. You see, whenever a river overflows, it leaves soil and rock on the land beside it. Each time this happens, the land on either side of the river becomes a little higher . . . Um, these raised areas of land are called levees. In extreme cases, the sides of the river can become significantly higher than the surrounding land. And this means that the river channel is much deeper. Now . . . Oh, do you have a question?

S2: ^Q15 Um, do the levees ever get high enough to actually prevent flooding?

P: They can, in fact . . . Um, sometimes years can pass without a flood happening. But if there's an unusually large amount of snow or rain one year . . . Well, it's almost as if the levee doesn't exist. The water just goes right over it. In some cases, the force of the moving water can also destroy these natural barriers . . .

Now, if a region regularly experiences such massive floods, well . . . the appearance of the river can change dramatically. ^Q16 The Jamuna River in Bangladesh is a good example of this phenomenon. I've researched this river system extensively, and . . . uh, it's fascinating. There's always something new to observe. Take a look at this picture . . . What's the first thing you notice?

S1: It seems like a bunch of individual streams rather than one big . . . you know . . . one big river.

P: Good . . . ^Q17 That's because repeated flooding has caused many new channels to form. Uh, the river floods seasonally. You see, as the excess water moves downstream, it carries large amounts of sediment. This leads to the creation of islands that split up the river into different streams. Um, you should note that these islands aren't necessarily permanent . . . Some increase in size every year, while others are destroyed by subsequent floods. In addition, the floodwaters can break down the riverbanks, creating new paths for the water to follow. The end result is a complex network of connected waterways.

Now get ready to answer the questions. You may use your notes to help you answer.

12. What is the main topic of the lecture?
13. What are the factors that determine the frequency of floods in a river system?
14. What happens during flooding to cause a river channel to become deeper?

Listen again to part of the lecture. Then answer the question.

S2: Um, do the levees ever get high enough to actually prevent flooding?

P: They can, in fact . . . Um, sometimes years can pass without a flood happening. But if there's an unusually large amount of snow or rain one year . . . Well, it's almost as if the levee doesn't exist. The water just goes right over it.

15. What does the professor mean when she says this:
    P: Well, it's almost as if the levee doesn't exist.

16. What is the professor's opinion of the Jamuna River?

17. In the lecture, the professor describes several characteristics of the Jamuna River. Indicate whether each of the following is a characteristic.

P: 이제는, 강의 둑을 안정적으로 유지하는 것에 있어서 식물의 역할은 꽤 명확할 거예요. 음, 식물 없이는... 특히 강 주변의 토양을 제자리에 붙들고 있는 식물의 뿌리 없이는, 강 대부분은 고정된 경로로 유지되지 못할 겁니다. 하지만 강의 모양을 바꿀 수 있는 많은 자연 현상이 있다는 것에 주목하는 것이 중요해요... 홍수 같은 것 말이죠. 나머지 수업 시간 동안에는, 이를 더 면밀하게 살

펴볼 것입니다.

홍수는 강이 둑을 범람했을 때 일어납니다... 음, 다시 말해, 수면이 너무 높아져서 측면으로 넘쳐 흐르는 거죠. 이는 보통 너무 많은 물이 강으로 들어올 때 발생해요. 홍수가 얼마나 자주 일어나는지는 두 가지 요소에 의해 결정됩니다. 하나는 한 지역이 연중 서로 다른 시점에 강우량의 상당한 상승을 경험하느냐 입니다... 봄이나 여름처럼요. 다른 하나는 강 주변의 토지에서 발견되는 바위와 토양의 종류입니다. 만약 이 물질이 많은 물을 흡수할 수 있다면... 음, 그러면 홍수가 덜 흔하겠죠. 그렇지 않다면, 홍수의 위험이 크고요.

그래서 홍수가 어떻게 강의 모양에 영향을 미칠까요? 물론, 물이 범람하면, 강이 더 넓어지지만... 이는 일시적인 변화일 뿐이에요. 하지만, 홍수는 강의 체계를 영구적으로 바꿀 수도 있죠... 예를 들어, 수로가 시간이 지나면서 더 깊어질 수 있어요. 왜 이렇게 되는지 아는 사람 있나요?

S1: 음, 물은 홍수 중에 더 빠르게 움직이잖아요, 그렇죠? 그래서 아마도... 잘 모르겠지만... 어쩌면 강의 바닥을 파내는 건가요?

P: 말이 되기는 하네요... 하지만, 음... 발생하는 일은 그게 아닙니다. 사실, 수로는 그것 주변에 침전물이 퇴적되기 때문에 깊어지는 거예요. 보세요, 강은 범람할 때마다, 그 옆의 토지에 토양과 바위를 남겨요. 이게 발생할 때마다, 강둑은 조금씩 높아지는 거죠... 음, 토지의 이 상승된 지역은 제방이라고 불려요. 극단적인 경우에는, 강의 양 측면이 주위의 토지보다 상당히 높아지는 거죠. 그리고 이는 수로가 훨씬 더 깊다는 것을 의미하고요. 자... 오, 질문이 있나요?

S2: 음, 제방이 실제로 홍수를 예방할 수 있을 만큼 높아지나요?

P: 사실, 그럴 수 있어요... 음, 가끔은 홍수 발생 없이 몇 년이 지나갈 수도 있죠. 하지만 한 해에 비정상적으로 많은 양의 눈이나 비가 내리면... 음, 그건 마치 제방이 거의 존재하지 않는 것과 같아요. 물은 그저 그 바로 위로 흐르거든요. 어떤 경우에는, 움직이는 물의 힘 또한 이러한 자연 장벽을 파괴할 수 있습니다...

자, 만약 한 지역이 이렇게 거대한 홍수를 주기적으로 겪는다면, 음... 강의 모습은 극적으로 변할 수 있어요. 방글라데시에 있는 야무나 강은 이 현상의 좋은 예시입니다. 저는 이 강의 체계를 광범위하게 조사해왔어요, 그리고... 어, 그것은 대단히 흥미롭습니다. 언제나 관찰할 새로운 무언가가 있거든요. 이 사진을 한 번 보세요... 가장 먼저 보이는 것이 무엇인가요?

S1: 그건 하나의 큰... 그러니까... 하나의 큰 강이라기보다는 다수의 개별적인 개울 같아 보여요.

P: 맞아요... 그건 반복된 홍수가 많은 새로운 수로를 형성하도록 했기 때문이죠. 어, 강은 주기적으로 범람해요. 그러니까, 과잉수가 하류로 이동하면서, 많은 양의 침전물을 실어 나른 거죠. 이는 강을 서로 다른 개울로 나누는 섬들의 생성으로 이어집니다. 음, 이 섬들이 반드시 영구적인 것은 아니라는 것에 주목해야 해요... 일부는 매년 크기가 증가하는 반면, 다른 것들은 차후의 홍수로 인해 파괴됩니다. 게다가, 홍수로 불어난 물은 흘러갈 새로운 경로를 만들면서, 강둑을 부술 수도 있습니다. 최종 결과는 연결된 수로들의 복잡한 망이죠.

어휘

vegetation[vèdʒətéiʃən] 식물　bank[bæŋk] (강의) 둑　in place 제자리에　alter[ɔ́:ltər] 바꾸다　overflow[òuvərflóu] 범람하다
spill out 넘쳐 흐르다　rainfall[réinfɔ̀:l] 강우량　river channel 수로　dig out ~을 파내다　sediment[sédəmənt] 침전물
deposit[dipázit] 퇴적시키다　levee[lévi] 제방　barrier[bǽriər] 장벽　extensively[iksténsivli] 광범위하게　stream[stri:m] 개울
downstream[dàunstí:m] 하류

[18-22]
Listen to a conversation between a bookstore attendant and a student.

M: Excuse me, do you work here?

W: Yes. Can I help you with something?

M: Yes, um . . . at least I hope you can . . .

W: Well, I'll try to help you in any way I can.

M: [Q19] Here's the thing. I need to buy a textbook for Political Science 101—Professor Taylor's class.

W: Hmm . . . I know which textbook you're talking about, since it's a really popular course among freshmen, but we ordered copies for the beginning of the semester . . . and that was two months ago!

M: Uh, yeah, I realize that it's kind of late in the semester . . . [Q18] but I recently lost my book, and I need to replace it right away. Can you please help me find a copy?

W: Let me check the computer . . . *Introduction to Political Science*, right? I'm really sorry, but I'm afraid we don't have any copies of that textbook left.

M: Oh no! I was worried about that. Q20 I really need that book because final exams are coming up! What can I do to get a copy? Would it be possible to order it through you? It's not like it's gone out of print in the last couple of months, has it? There must be a few copies left.

W: Actually, we don't order books on an individual basis. However, there is a slight possibility that there are some extras in our storage facility. Let's see . . . Q21 Nope, it looks like the warehouse doesn't have that title listed—and the thing is, it's very unlikely that we'll be getting any more in before the end of the semester . . . But there are still a couple of other options. Q22 First, it's possible that the professor who's in charge of your class may decide to order more textbooks. I'm not sure when or if that's actually going to happen, though. You might want to check with him.

M: I see.

W: Q22 The other thing you might want to try is . . . well, there's another bookstore across campus that may have what you're looking for. It's quite a bit smaller than our store, so the selection isn't that big. But since fewer students go there—and your book is fairly common—they might still have copies of it. Again, I can't make promises, but you can try.

M: OK, I'll look into that possibility as well.

W: Q22 Lastly, I suggest that you check that website—Used Books Online. It's a community of students and teachers, and they buy and sell used books at really low prices. Like I said, yours is a popular one, so chances are you'll find a used copy.

M: That looks promising . . . What's the address of that website?

W: Here, let me write it down. It's www.usedbooksonline.org. I believe you'll have to make an account first. It's free, of course. You'll need your student ID number to sign up. After you register, you can start buying and selling used books. And if all else fails, you may have to borrow one from a classmate and make copies or something. It's not the most convenient option, but at least you'd have the material.

M: Yeah, that's a good point. I hadn't thought of that . . . Thanks for all your help!

Now get ready to answer the questions. You may use your notes to help you answer.

18. Why does the man visit the bookstore?

Listen again to part of the conversation. Then answer the question.

M: Here's the thing. I need to buy a textbook for Political Science 101—Professor Taylor's class.

W: Hmm . . . I know which textbook you're talking about, since it's a really popular course among freshmen, but we ordered copies for the beginning of the semester . . . and that was two months ago!

19. What does the woman mean when she says this:
    W: . . . and that was two months ago!

20. Why does the man need to order the book?
21. What does the woman say about the textbook?
22. The bookstore clerk suggests what the man should do. Indicate whether each of the following is a suggestion.

M: 실례합니다. 여기서 일하시나요?
W: 네. 무엇을 도와드릴까요?

M: 네, 음... 도와주실 수만 있다면 좋겠네요...

W: 음, 제가 할 수 있는 한 도와드리려고 해 볼게요.

M: 그게 말이죠. 저는 정치학 101의 교과서를 사야 해요, Taylor 교수님의 수업이죠.

W: 흠... 학생이 어떤 교과서를 말하는 건지 알겠어요, 그건 1학년들 사이에서 매우 인기 있는 수업이니까요, 그런데 우리는 학기 초에 책을 주문했었어요... 그리고 그건 2개월 전이었고요!

M: 어, 네, 이제 거의 학기 말인 건 아는데... 제가 최근에 책을 잃어버려서, 당장 다시 사야 하거든요. 그 책 구하는 걸 도와주실 수 있나요?

W: 컴퓨터를 확인해 볼게요... '정치학 개론', 맞죠? 정말 유감이지만, 그 교과서는 남은 게 하나도 없네요.

M: 오, 안 돼요! 그걸 걱정했었어요. 기말고사가 다가오고 있어서 그 책이 정말 필요해요! 그 책을 구하려면 어떻게 해야 하죠? 당신을 통해서 주문하는 게 가능할까요? 지난 몇 달간 절판되거나 그런 건 아니겠죠, 그렇죠? 분명히 몇 권이라도 남아 있을 거예요.

W: 사실, 우린 개인 단위로 책을 주문하지 않아요. 하지만, 우리 보관 시설에 여분 몇 권이 남아 있을 가능성은 좀 있어요. 어디 보자... 아니네요, 창고 목록에는 그 제목이 없는 것 같아요. 그리고 문제는, 학기 말까지 더 주문하지 않을 것 같다는 거예요... 하지만 아직 몇 가지 다른 방법이 있어요. 첫째로, 학생의 수업을 담당하시는 교수님께서 교과서를 더 주문하기로 결정하실 수도 있죠. 하지만, 그게 언제가 될지, 혹은 정말로 그렇게 될지는 잘 모르겠어요. 학생이 교수님께 확인해 볼 수 있겠네요.

M: 알겠습니다.

W: 학생이 해 볼 수 있는 또 다른 방법은... 음, 학교 건너편에 학생이 찾고 있는 것을 가지고 있을 수도 있는 다른 서점이 있어요. 우리 가게보다는 좀 많이 작아서, 선택할 수 있는 게 그리 많진 않아요. 하지만 그 가게에 찾아가는 학생 수가 더 적고, 학생이 찾는 책은 꽤 흔하기 때문에, 아직 몇 권 가지고 있을 수도 있어요. 다시 말하는데, 장담할 수는 없지만, 시도해 볼 수 있겠죠.

M: 네, 그 가능성도 살펴볼게요.

W: 마지막으로, 온라인 중고 서적 웹사이트를 확인해 보라고 제안할게요. 그곳은 학생들과 교사들의 커뮤니티인데, 정말 낮은 가격에 중고책을 사고 팔아요. 말했듯이, 학생이 찾는 책은 인기 있는 것이라서, 중고책을 찾을 가능성이 있어요.

M: 그거 가능성이 있어 보이네요... 그 웹사이트의 주소가 뭔가요?

W: 여기요, 제가 적어 줄게요. www.usedbooksonline.org예요. 먼저 계정을 하나 만들어야 할 거예요. 물론, 무료이고요. 등록하려면 학생증 번호가 필요할 거예요. 등록하고 나면, 중고책을 사고 팔기 시작할 수 있어요. 그리고 만약 모든 방법이 실패하면, 반 친구에게 책을 빌려서 복사하거나 해야겠네요. 가장 편리한 방법은 아니지만, 적어도 그 자료를 얻을 수는 있잖아요.

M: 네, 맞는 말이네요. 그건 생각해 보지 않았어요... 도와주셔서 정말 감사합니다!

어휘

political science 정치학 freshman[fréʃmən] 1학년 go out of print (서적이) 절판되다 storage facility 보관 시설
warehouse[wɛ́ərhàus] 창고 in charge of ~을 담당하는 fairly[fɛ́ərli] 꽤 used copy 중고책
promising[prámisiŋ] 가능성이 있는 account[əkáunt] 계정 register[rédʒistər] 등록하다

[23-28]
Listen to part of a lecture in a history class.

P: I'd like to expand on something I mentioned earlier . . . um, cultural diffusion. Q23 Like I said, this is the process by which ideas move from one cultural group to another over long periods of time. This typically occurs as a result of trade or war. For the rest of the class, we are going to discuss a famous example of this . . . the development and spread of the Latin alphabet. Before we get into this though, I should probably point out that the Latin alphabet is the one we use today. It's a phonetic language . . . meaning that each of the 26 letters represents a specific sound. Some letters can even represent more than one. Q24 For example, the pronunciation of a vowel changes if there is an *e* at the end of the word. Like *tap* and *tape* . . . Of course, these are English words. In, say, French or German, the letters would stand for slightly different sounds. But the basic principle still applies.

So, where did this versatile writing system originate? Q25 Well, it can be traced back to the Phoenicians . . . a group of people from the Middle East. They were one of the first to develop a writing system based on symbols for specific sounds. Prior to this, individual symbols were usually used to express entire words or concepts. Anyway, the superiority of the Phoenician system was recognized by the Greeks, who adopted it in the 8th century BC and, uh, modified it to suit their own language.

S1: Um, the Greeks modified the Phoenician alphabet? What exactly did they have to change?

P: [Q26] Well, they changed the shapes of many of the symbols. Uh, the ancient Greek letters are similar to modern ones. [Q26] But they also added quite a few new letters. You see, the Phoenician alphabet didn't include special vowel symbols . . . um, some letters were both consonants and vowels. The Greeks created new symbols for each.
[Q27] Now, during this same period, Greek traders were establishing colonies on the Italian peninsula. As a result, variations of the Greek alphabet came to be used by the different groups that inhabited this region. And when the Romans rose to power a few centuries later, they adopted the writing system of one of these earlier civilizations. Of course, the Romans made a few minor changes . . . uh, for example, they added the letter *g*, and eventually *y* and *z* as well. But their most important contribution was to spread this alphabet as they expanded their empire. Um, Latin was used for all government records and trade documents, so people in conquered territories tried to learn how to read and write in this language . . .

S2: But, uh, the Roman Empire eventually collapsed, right? Why did this writing system continue to be used?

P: A couple of reasons, actually . . . [Q28] First of all, Latin was used by Church officials in Europe for centuries. Um, this allowed them to communicate with each other easily, even if they had different native languages. The other reason is the flexibility of the Latin alphabet . . . These letters can express almost any sound. So medieval scholars in Europe found it easy to apply this writing system to their own languages.

Now get ready to answer the questions. You may use your notes to help you answer.

23. What is the lecture mainly about?

Listen again to part of the lecture. Then answer the question.

P: For example, the pronunciation of a vowel changes if there is an *e* at the end of the word. Like *tap* and *tape* . . . Of course, these are English words. In, say, French or German, the letters would stand for slightly different sounds. But the basic principle still applies.

24. Why does the professor say this:
    P: Of course, these are English words.

25. What was unusual about the symbols of the Phoenician writing system?
26. In the lecture, the professor explains the changes made by the Greeks to the Phoenician alphabet. Indicate whether each of the following is a change.
27. How did the Greek writing system spread to Italy?
28. Why was the Latin alphabet still used after the end of the Roman Empire?

P: 제가 앞서 말한 것에 대해 부연 설명하고 싶군요... 음, 문화적 확산이요. 말했듯이, 이것은 생각들이 오랜 기간에 걸쳐 한 문화 집단에서 다른 집단으로 이동하는 거예요. 이는 일반적으로 무역이나 전쟁의 결과로 일어납니다. 나머지 수업 시간 동안에는, 이것의 유명한 예시에 관해 논의할 거예요... 로마자의 발전과 전파에 대해서요.
하지만 시작하기 전에, 로마자는 오늘날 우리가 사용하는 것이라는 점을 언급해야겠군요. 그것은 음성 언어인데요... 26개 문자 각각이 특정한 소리를 나타낸다는 것을 의미하죠. 일부 문자는 심지어 하나 이상의 소리를 의미할 수 있습니다. 예를 들어, 단어의 끝에 'e'가 있다면 모음의 발음이 바뀝니다. '탭'과 '테이프'처럼요... 물론, 이것들은 영어 단어입니다. 예를 들어, 프랑스어나 독일어에서는, 이 문자들이 약간 다른 소리를 나타낼 거예요. 하지만 기본적인 원리는 여전히 적용되죠.

자, 이 만능 문자 체계는 어디에서 유래했을까요? 음, 이것의 기원은 페니키아인까지 거슬러 올라갑니다... 중동에서 온 사람들의 집단이죠. 그들은 특정 소리의 기호에 기반을 둔 문자 체계를 맨 처음 발명한 사람들 중 하나였습니다. 이전에는, 각각 기호들이 일반적으로 전체 단어나 개념을 표현하는 데 사용되곤 했거든요. 어쨌든, 페니키아 체계의 우월성은 그리스인들에 의해 인정받았죠, 이들은 그것을 기원전 8세기에 차용하고, 어, 그들 자신의 언어에 맞도록 수정했어요.

S1: 음, 그리스인들이 페니키아 문자를 수정했다고요? 그들은 정확히 무엇을 바꿔야 했나요?

P: 음, 그들은 많은 기호의 모양을 바꿨어요. 어, 고대 그리스 문자는 현대 문자와 비슷해요. 하지만 그들은 또한 상당수의 문자들을 더하기도 했죠. 보세요, 페니키아 문자는 특별한 모음 기호를 포함하지 않았어요... 음, 일부 문자들은 자음이자 모음이었죠. 그리스인들은 각각을 위한 새로운 기호를 만들었어요.

자, 같은 기간 동안, 그리스 상인들은 이탈리아 반도에 식민지를 설립하고 있었어요. 그 결과, 이 지역에 살던 다른 집단들에 의해 그리스 문자의 변형이 사용되기 시작했죠. 그리고 로마 사람들이 몇 세기 후 권세를 얻었을 때, 그들은 이러한 초기 문명의 문자 체계 중 하나를 차용했습니다. 물론, 로마 사람들은 몇 가지 작은 변화를 주었죠... 어, 예를 들어, 그들은 문자 'g'를 더했어요, 그리고 마침내 'y'와 'z'도요. 하지만 가장 중요한 기여는 그들이 제국을 확장함에 따라 이 문자를 확산시킨 것이었습니다. 음, 로마어는 모든 정부 기록이나 무역 문서에 사용되었고, 정복된 영토의 사람들은 이 언어를 읽고 쓰는 법을 배우려고 했죠.

S1: 그런데, 어, 로마 제국은 결국 무너졌잖아요, 맞죠? 왜 이 문자 체계가 계속해서 사용됐나요?

P: 사실, 두 가지 이유가 있습니다... 첫째로, 로마어는 수 세기 동안 유럽의 교회 당국자들에 의해 사용되었어요. 음, 이는 그들이 서로 다른 모국어를 가지고 있었음에도 불구하고, 쉽게 의사소통할 수 있게 해주었습니다. 또 다른 이유는 로마자의 유연성인데요... 이 문자들은 거의 어떤 소리라도 표현할 수 있어요. 그래서 유럽의 중세 학자들은 이 문자 체계를 그들 자신의 언어에 적용하는 것이 쉽다고 생각했죠.

어휘

diffusion[difjúːʒən] 확산 spread[spred] 전파 Latin alphabet 로마자 phonetic[fənétik] 음성의 stand for ~을 나타내다
versatile[vɔ́ːrsətl] 만능의 originate[ərídʒənèit] 유래하다 trace back to 기원이 ~까지 거슬러 올라가다 adopt[ədápt] 차용하다
colony[káləni] 식민지 peninsula[pənínsjulə] 반도 variation[vɛ̀əriéiʃən] 변형 rise to power 권세를 얻다
conquer[káŋkər] 정복하다 collapse[kəlǽps] 무너지다 official[əfíʃəl] 당국자 native language 모국어

[29-34]
Listen to part of a lecture from an astronomy course.

P: When you hear the word *star*, you probably think of something like the Sun. A massive ball of gas that produces huge amounts of energy. Q29 Well, there are actually many different types of stars. For the rest of the class, I want to focus on brown dwarfs. Um, this type of star is, well . . . It has some features that may surprise you.

Q30 First of all, brown dwarfs are only a little larger than Jupiter, which is the largest planet in the solar system. This means that they are much smaller than other types of stars. However, there is a great deal of variation among brown dwarfs in terms of mass . . . um, the amount of matter they contain. Some are about 13 times the mass of Jupiter, while others are almost 80 times more massive than this planet. So . . . they are about the same size as a large planet, but they include more matter . . . this means that brown dwarfs are much denser than planets. Q31 Now, does anyone want to guess what else distinguishes brown dwarfs from planets?

S1: Well, they're stars, right? So, clearly, they emit a lot more energy than a planet . . .

P: You got it. You see, as matter is compressed . . . or made denser, in other words . . . it becomes hotter. So brown dwarfs do release some energy out into space . . . mostly in the form of infrared radiation, or heat. It's important to note, though, that the amount of energy a brown dwarf produces is tiny compared to that of regular stars. Most brown dwarfs are about one-sixth as hot as the Sun, and many are much cooler. In fact, some are only as warm as an oven used to bake bread . . .

S1: Um, I assume this is because a regular star has a greater mass than a brown dwarf?

P: Right. And this is a direct result of the brown dwarf formation process. Um, in fact, the initial stages are the same for all types of stars . . . [Q32] An object called a protostar is created when gravity causes dust and gas in space to join together. Over time, the protostar collects more matter, causing its mass to grow. If it becomes massive enough . . . nuclear fusion will occur. This is the main source of energy in most stars. But in the case of a brown dwarf, matter stops being added before this happens. The protostar never gains enough mass to start a nuclear reaction . . . So I guess you could say that brown dwarfs are failed stars. They have a mass greater than that of planets but significantly less than that of other stars. Yes?

S2: I was just wondering . . . How common are brown dwarfs? I mean, it sounds like they form under a very specific set of circumstances. So they must be pretty rare.

P: To be honest, no one knows for certain. [Q33] You need to keep in mind that because they generate such small amounts of energy, they are incredibly difficult to detect with telescopes. It was only in 1988 that the first brown dwarf was spotted. So everyone just assumed that they weren't common. But as technology improves, more and more of these stars are being observed. This has caused some astronomers to reconsider. [Q34] One recent estimate states that there are over 70 billion brown dwarfs in our galaxy alone. This is just speculation, though. I'm a little skeptical, honestly . . . I wouldn't take it too seriously at this point . . . Unless further research supports it, of course.

Now get ready to answer the questions. You may use your notes to help you answer.

29. What is the lecture mainly about?
30. What does the professor say about the size of a brown dwarf?

Listen again to part of the lecture. Then answer the question.

P: Now, does anyone want to guess what else distinguishes brown dwarfs from planets?
S1: Well, they're stars, right? So, clearly, they emit a lot more energy than a planet . . .
P: You got it. You see, as matter is compressed . . . or made denser, in other words . . . it becomes hotter.

31. Why does the student say this:
    S1: Well, they're stars, right?

32. In the lecture, the professor explains the steps in the formation process of a brown dwarf. Put the steps listed below in the correct order.

33. According to the professor, why are brown dwarfs difficult to detect with telescopes?

34. What is the professor's attitude toward the recent estimate about the number of brown dwarfs?

P: '항성'이라는 단어를 들으면, 여러분은 아마 태양과 같은 것을 떠올리겠죠. 엄청난 양의 에너지를 만들어내는 거대한 가스 덩어리 말이에요. 음, 사실 서로 다른 많은 종류의 항성이 존재합니다. 나머지 수업 시간 동안에는, 갈색 왜성에 초점을 맞추고 싶군요. 음, 이 종류의 항성은, 저... 여러분들을 놀라게 할 몇 가지 특징을 가지고 있죠.
우선, 갈색 왜성은 태양계에서 가장 큰 행성인 목성보다 조금 더 클 뿐입니다. 이는 그것들이 다른 종류의 항성들보다 훨씬 더 작다는 것을 의미하죠. 그러나, 질량 측면에서 갈색 왜성들 사이에는 많은 차이가 있습니다... 음, 그것들이 함유한 물질의 양 말이에요. 일부는 목성 질량의 약 13배이지만, 다른 몇몇은 이 행성보다 거의 80배만큼 더 거대해요. 그래서... 그것들은 하나의 커다란 행성과 거의 같은 크기이지만, 더 많은 물질을 포함하는 거죠... 이는 갈색 왜성이 행성보다 훨씬 밀도가 높다는 것을 의미하고요. 자, 이밖에 또 무엇이 갈색 왜성을 행성으로부터 구별하는지 추측해 보고 싶은 사람 있나요?

S1: 음, 그것들은 항성이잖아요, 그렇죠? 그래서, 분명히, 행성보다 훨씬 더 많은 에너지를 방출하겠죠...

P: 맞췄어요. 그러니까, 물질이 압축되면서... 다시 말해, 밀도가 높아지면서... 그건 더 뜨거워지죠. 그래서 갈색 왜성은 에너지 일부를 우주로 방출해요... 주로 적외선, 혹은 열의 형태로요. 하지만, 갈색 왜성이 만들어내는 에너지의 양은 일반 항성의 에너지양과 비교했을 때 매우 적다는 데 주목하는 것이 중요합니다. 갈색 왜성 대부분은 태양의 약 6분의 1만큼 뜨거워요, 그리고 많은 갈색 왜성은 훨씬 더 차갑죠. 실제로, 일부는 빵을 구울 때 사용되는 오븐 정도로만 따뜻할 뿐이에요...

S1: 음, 저는 이게 일반 항성이 갈색 왜성보다 더 큰 질량을 가지고 있기 때문이라고 생각하는데요?

P: 맞아요. 그리고 이것은 갈색 왜성 형성 과정의 직접적인 결과예요. 음, 사실, 모든 종류의 항성의 초기 단계는 같습니다... 중력이 우주에 있는 먼지와 가스를 합쳐지게 하면 원시성이라고 불리는 물체가 만들어지죠. 시간이 지나면서, 원시성은 그것의 질량이 커지도록 하면서, 더 많은 물질을 모아요. 그것이 충분히 거대해지면... 핵융합이 일어날 거예요. 이는 대부분 항성의 주요 에너지 원입니다. 하지만 갈색 왜성의 경우, 물질은 이것이 발생하기 전에 더해지는 것을 멈춰요. 원시성은 핵반응을 시작하기에 충분한 질량을 절대로 얻지 못하죠... 그러니까 갈색 왜성이 실패한 항성이라고 말할 수도 있겠군요. 그것들은 행성의 질량보다 훨씬 크지만 다른 항성들의 질량보다는 상당히 적은 질량을 가지고 있으니까요. 네?

S2: 그냥 궁금해서요... 갈색 왜성이 얼마나 흔한가요? 제 말은, 그것들이 아주 특수한 일련의 상황에서만 형성하는 것처럼 들려서요. 그래서 그것들은 굉장히 드물 것 같은데요.

P: 솔직히 말하자면, 아무도 확실히 알지 못해요. 그것들이 그토록 적은 양의 에너지를 발생시키기 때문에, 망원경으로 발견하기가 엄청나게 힘들다는 것을 명심할 필요가 있어요. 첫 번째 갈색 왜성이 발견된 것은 겨우 1988년이에요. 그래서 모든 사람들이 단지 그것들은 흔하지 않다고 가정했죠. 하지만 기술이 향상될수록, 점점 더 많은 이 항성들이 관찰되고 있어요. 이는 일부 천문학자들이 다시 생각하도록 만들어왔습니다. 최근의 한 가지 견해는 우리 은하에만 700조가 넘는 갈색 왜성이 존재한다고 말합니다. 하지만, 이는 그저 추측일 뿐이죠. 솔직히, 저는 약간 회의적입니다... 현시점에서는 이것을 너무 진지하게 받아들이지 않을 거예요... 물론, 그 이상의 연구가 이를 뒷받침한다면 모를까 말이죠.

어휘

star[stɑːr] 항성 brown dwarf 갈색 왜성 Jupiter[dʒúːpətər] 목성 planet[plǽnit] 행성 variation[vὲəriéiʃən] 차이
compress[kəmprés] 압축하다 infrared radiation 적외선 protostar[próutoustàːr] 원시성 nuclear fusion 핵융합
spot[spɑt] 발견하다 astronomer[əstránəmər] 천문학자 estimate[éstəmət] 견해 speculation[spèkjuléiʃən] 추측
skeptical[sképtikəl] 회의적인

CHAPTER 05 Connecting Contents II

• 각 문제에 대한 정답단서는 지문에 보라색으로 표시되어 있습니다.

문제 공략하기

p.123

P: 오늘은 로마인들이 이름 지은 행성에 관해 이야기하고 싶습니다... 수성이라는 행성이죠. 음, 여러분들이 수성에 대해 알고 있는 것을 이야기해 보세요.

S: 그건 태양에 가장 가까워요.

P: 맞아요. 또 다른 내용이 있나요?

S: 제 생각에 그건 우리 달과 같은 크기예요... 아니면 그건 명왕성인가요?

P: 처음에 말한 게 맞아요, 우리 달 말이에요. 어, 또 다른 의견 있나요? 더 없나요? 좋아요, 음, 바로 저의 요점이군요. 많은 행성들이 굉장히 자세히 논의되어왔지만, 교사 대부분은 수성이 지구의 달과 색깔, 표면적, 그리고 대기가 부족하다는 점이 꽤 비슷하다는 것만 알고 있기 때문에 수성에 대해 대충 지나가는 경향이 있죠. 자, 수성에 대한 정보가 그렇게 많지 않은 한 가지 이유는...

HACKERS PRACTICE

p.124

1. **(B)** Main Purpose/Topic	2. **(C)** Detail	3. **(C)** Connecting Contents II
4. **(C)** Main Purpose/Topic	5. **(B)** Detail	6. **(A)** Connecting Contents II
7. **(C)** Main Purpose/Topic	8. **(C)** Connecting Contents II	9. **(D)** Connecting Contents II
10. **(D)** Main Purpose/Topic	11. **(D)** Connecting Contents II	12. **(D)** Detail

[1-3]

Listen to a conversation between a professor and a student.

S: Professor Sanderson?

P: Yes?

S: My name is Marc Tate . . . Um, I'm not one of your students, but a friend . . . uh . . . my friend recommended that I talk to you. She's in your history of theater class.

P: Well, now I'm curious . . . What's on your mind?

S: Q1 Um, I was hoping you could recommend a club for me to join. I'm . . . well, I'm really interested in acting. When I was in high school, I performed in several plays. I'd like to give it a try again.

P: I see . . . The obvious choice is the drama club, of course. Um, this club receives a lot of support from the university, so it is able to put on a big performance each semester. The last show was particularly impressive.

S: That was my original plan . . . Q2 But when I applied, I was . . . well, I was rejected. I guess membership is limited to theater majors. I'm an English major . . .

P: Oh, I forgot about that policy.

S: Yeah . . . I'm not very happy about it. Anyway, I'm not sure what other options there are on campus.

P: Hmm . . . If you just want the chance to participate in a play, I have a suggestion. The acting class I teach will be performing a play next month. Q3 Um, we could use some extra bodies . . .

S: What do you mean?

P: Well, the play includes a scene on a train . . . We need a few more people to play . . . um, to play the passengers. It might be an interesting experience for you.

S: Um, I appreciate the offer, but I don't just want to be an extra. I'd really like a speaking role.

P: Maybe you should talk to Professor Cooper. Uh, his office is just down the hall. He mentioned to me the other day that he is planning to hold a series of, um, acting workshops. And these will be open to non-theater majors . . .

S: Really? Um, what exactly will these workshops involve?

P: From my understanding, the group will meet twice a week and, uh . . . will act out scenes from a variety of different plays.

S: So I'd get a chance to try out a bunch of different roles?

P: Sure. But don't get me wrong . . . these aren't going to be, um, elaborate stage productions. There won't be any costumes . . . or even an audience.

S: I get that . . . but it still sounds like I'd learn a lot. I'm going to talk to Professor Cooper now. Thanks!

Now get ready to answer the questions. You may use your notes to help you answer.

1. Why does the student visit the professor?
2. What does the student say about the drama club?
3. Why does the professor mention a scene on a train?

S: Sanderson 교수님?

P: 네?

S: 제 이름은 Marc Tate입니다... 음, 제가 교수님의 반 학생 중 한 명은 아니지만, 한 친구가... 어... 제 친구가 교수님과 이야기해 보라고 추천해줬어요. 그녀는 교수님의 연극의 역사 수업을 듣거든요.

P: 음, 이제 궁금해지는군요... 무슨 일인가요?

S: 음, 교수님께서 제가 가입할 동아리를 추천해주셨으면 해서요. 저는... 음, 정말로 연기에 관심이 많거든요. 고등학교 시절에는, 여러 연극에서 공연을 하기도 했어요. 다시 한 번 해 보고 싶어서요.

P: 그렇군요... 물론, 명백한 선택은 연극 동아리죠. 음, 이 동아리는 대학으로부터 많은 후원을 받아서, 학기마다 큰 공연을 상연할 수 있거든요. 지난번 공연은 특히 인상적이었고요.

S: 그게 제 원래 계획이었어요... 하지만 제가 지원했을 때, 저는... 음, 거절당했어요. 회원 자격이 연극 전공자들에게만 한정되어 있나 봐요. 저는 영어 전공자거든요...

P: 오, 내가 그 규정을 깜박했군요.

S: 네... 그것에 기분이 좋지는 않아요. 어쨌든, 학교 내에 다른 어떤 선택권이 있는지 잘 모르겠어요.

P: 흠... 만약 학생이 단지 연극에 참여할 기회를 원하는 거라면, 한 가지 제안이 있어요. 내가 가르치는 연극반이 다음 달에 공연을 할 거예요. 음, 단역을 좀 쓸 수 있을 것 같군요...

S: 무슨 말씀이신가요?

P: 음, 그 연극은 기차에서의 장면을 하나 포함하고 있는데... 우리는... 음, 승객 역할을 해줄 몇 사람이 더 필요해요. 학생에게 흥미로운 경험이 될 수도 있어요.

S: 음, 제안은 감사드리지만, 단지 단역이 되고 싶지는 않아요. 대사가 있는 역할을 정말 하고 싶거든요.

P: 아마 Cooper 교수와 이야기해 봐야 할 것 같네요. 어, 그의 연구실은 바로 복도 끝에 있어요. 얼마 전에 그가 내게 일련의, 음, 연기 워크숍을 개최할 계획이라고 말했거든요. 그리고 워크숍은 연기 전공이 아닌 학생들에게도 개방될 거고요...

S: 정말이요? 음, 이 워크숍은 정확히 무엇을 포함하고 있나요?

P: 내가 아는 바로는, 그 모임은 일주일에 두 번씩 만나고, 어... 서로 다른 다양한 연극의 장면들을 연출할 거예요.

S: 그러면 제가 많은 다른 역할을 해 볼 기회를 얻을 수 있겠네요?

P: 물론이죠. 하지만 오해하지는 말아요... 이것들은, 음, 정교한 연극 작품은 아닐 거니까요. 의상이나... 관중조차도 없을 거예요.

S: 그렇군요... 하지만 여전히 제가 많이 배울 것처럼 들리네요. 지금 가서 Cooper 교수님과 이야기해 볼게요. 감사합니다!

[4-6]
Listen to a conversation between a student and an employee at the Campus Security Office.

W: Hi. I've, uh, got a bit of a problem . . .

M: OK. What's going on?

W: Well, it's about my laptop . . .

M: Was it stolen?

W: No, that's not it. [04] Um, I left my laptop in the, uh, common room of my old dorm at the end of last semester. I didn't even realize it was missing until I had been home for a few days. I, uh, called the dorm supervisor a couple of times, but he said my laptop hadn't been turned in. Um, he suggested that I stop by this office when I returned from vacation.

M: I see. Let me check the system. Nope . . . No laptops have been brought in over the summer. I'm really sorry.

W: In that case, do you have any ideas on how to track down my laptop? I already have assignments coming up for some of my classes. Um, I have an essay due next week, in fact. I'm a history major, so I have to write a lot of papers. My grades are going to suffer if I don't have my own computer.

M: Well, there are a couple things you can try.

W: Like what?

M: Well, the first thing I would do is visit the, um, Facilities Management Office . . .

W: The Facilities Management Office? Where's that?

M: It's in the basement of the administration building. Um, it has its own lost and found. Maybe someone dropped off your laptop there.

W: [05] I don't think many students even know that the, uh, Facilities Management Office exists . . . It doesn't seem very likely that someone would . . . um . . . would take my laptop there rather than here.

M: That might be true, but you should check anyway. And if it's not there, you could still try something else . . .

W: What did you have in mind?

M: [06] Well, you could take advantage of the university's online community. You know, make a post with a description of your laptop and your, um, contact information. A lot of students access the website regularly . . . There's a chance that the person who found it will reply.

W: But I assume if someone had found my laptop, it would have been, well . . . it would've been turned in by now . . .

M: It's hard to say . . . The person who has it may not know where to take it . . . or might just be too busy to bother. It could be sitting in someone's dorm room right now.

W: That's true. I hadn't considered that.

M: There's no guarantee, of course, but it's worth a try.

W: You're right . . . Thank you so much. You've been really helpful.

Now get ready to answer the questions. You may use your notes to help you answer.

4. Why does the student visit the campus security office?
5. What does the student say about the Facilities Management Office?
6. Why does the employee discuss the university's online community?

W: 안녕하세요. 제가, 어, 문제가 좀 있어서요...
M: 네. 무슨 일이죠?

W: 음, 제 노트북 컴퓨터에 관한 건데요...

M: 도난당했나요?

W: 아뇨, 그건 아니에요. 음, 제가 지난 학기 말에, 어, 제 예전 기숙사 휴게실에 노트북 컴퓨터를 뒀거든요. 심지어 집에 간지 며칠이 됐을 때까지 그게 없어진 줄도 몰랐어요. 제가, 어, 기숙사 관리인에게 몇 번 전화를 걸었지만, 그분은 제 노트북 컴퓨터가 반납되지 않았다고 말씀하셨어요. 음, 방학이 끝나고 돌아오면 이 사무실에 들르라고 제안하셨고요.

M: 그렇군요. 확인해 볼게요. 아뇨... 여름 동안 들어온 노트북 컴퓨터는 없네요. 정말 유감이에요.

W: 그렇다면, 노트북 컴퓨터를 찾을 수 있는 방법에 대한 어떤 생각이 있으신가요? 이미 다가오는 몇몇 수업의 과제들이 있어요. 음, 사실, 다음 주에 예정되어있는 과제가 하나 있거든요. 저는 역사 전공자라서, 많은 보고서를 작성해야 해요. 저만의 컴퓨터가 없으면 성적이 나빠질 거예요.

M: 음, 학생이 해 볼 수 있는 것들이 몇 가지 있어요.

W: 예를 들면요?

M: 음, 저라면 첫 번째로 했을 일은, 음, 시설 관리 사무소에 찾아가는 거예요...

W: 시설 관리 사무소요? 그게 어디에 있죠?

M: 행정관 지하에 있어요. 음, 그곳엔 자체 분실물 보관소가 있죠. 아마 누군가가 학생의 노트북 컴퓨터를 거기에 가져다 놓았을 수도 있어요.

W: 많은 학생들이, 어, 시설 관리 사무소가 존재한다는 것조차 알고 있을 것 같지 않은데요... 누군가가... 음... 여기 대신 그곳으로 제 노트북 컴퓨터를 가져갔을 것 같지 않아요.

M: 그럴지도 모르지만, 어쨌든 확인해 보는 것이 좋을 거예요. 그리고 만약 거기에 없다면, 여전히 다른 무언가를 해 볼 수 있고요...

W: 생각해둔 것이 있으신가요?

M: 음, 대학의 온라인 커뮤니티를 이용할 수 있어요. 그러니까, 노트북 컴퓨터에 대한 설명과 학생의, 음, 연락처를 포함한 게시글을 작성해 봐요. 많은 학생들이 그 웹사이트에 꾸준히 접속하니까요... 그것을 발견한 사람이 연락할 가능성이 있잖아요.

W: 하지만 만약 누군가 제 노트북 컴퓨터를 찾았다면, 그건, 음... 지금쯤 반납되었을 거예요...

M: 뭐라 말하기가 어렵네요... 그것을 가지고 있는 사람이 어디로 가져가야 할지 모를 수도 있죠... 아니면 신경 쓰기엔 그저 너무 바빴을 수도 있고요. 지금 누군가의 기숙사 방에 있을 수도 있잖아요.

W: 맞아요. 그건 생각해 보지 않았네요.

M: 물론, 보장은 없지만, 시도해 볼만은 하죠.

W: 맞는 말이네요... 정말 감사합니다. 많은 도움이 되었어요.

[7-9]
Listen to part of a lecture on history.

During the reign of Charles I, the theater had flourished in England . . . Q8 but after the civil war, the Puritans—the hardcore Protestants of the land—banned it. They were very strict, and this showed in the laws and restrictions they made. However, when the English, Scottish, and Irish monarchies were reinstated a decade later during the Restoration, the theater was restored as well. Now, plays under Charles II—particularly the comedies—were extremely coarse. The playwrights had to give the spectators what they wanted . . . and they wanted vulgar. This changed when theater became more accessible to both women and the middle class . . . the comedies became softer, and this marked the birth of sentimental comedy.

Q7 We need to consider the philosophical viewpoint from which sentimental comedies were written. During the early 18th century, audiences were more conservative, so plays were designed to appeal to their sense of moral righteousness. Why the shift? For one, there was a demographic change in England—more women and a larger middle class, as I mentioned earlier. And it also had a lot to do with the enthroning of William III and Mary, who both disliked theater in general, and immorality and profanity on the theater stage in particular. So the typical sentimental comedy involved middle-class characters who faced some sort of moral trial or tribulation and eventually were able to overcome their weaknesses and rediscover their innate virtues. The earlier

Restoration comedies didn't have that moral base.

Q9 A good example of the transition between Restoration comedies and sentimental comedies was the play *Love's Last Shift* by Colley Cibber. It's considered the first example of a sentimental comedy, but it also has an element of the immorality that audiences of the era had come to expect. It tells the story of a husband, Loveless, who leaves London for a 10-year stint abroad, most of which was spent in bars. His wife knew about his exploits. Upon his return to London, she dressed up as another woman and seduced him. He was unaware of her true identity until she confessed. Loveless was so struck by her faithfulness that he immediately changed his ways and became a devoted husband. The final, climactic scene was written to elicit an emotional reaction from the crowd. In fact, most audiences of the time were moved to tears by the final scene.

Now get ready to answer the questions. You may use your notes to help you answer.

7. What is the lecture mainly about?
8. Why does the professor mention the Puritans?
9. Why does the professor discuss Cibber's play *Love's Last Shift*?

찰스 1세의 통치 동안, 영국에서 연극이 번성했습니다... 하지만 내전 후, 그 나라의 강경 신교도인들인 청교도인들이 그것을 금지했어요. 그들은 아주 엄격했고, 이는 그들이 만든 법과 규제에서 보여집니다. 하지만, 10년 후 왕정 복고 시대 동안 영국, 스코틀랜드, 그리고 아일랜드의 군주들이 복위되자, 연극 또한 부활했습니다. 자, 찰스 2세 치하의 연극, 특히 희극은 극도로 외설적이었습니다. 극작가들은 관객들에게 그들이 원하는 것을 줘야 했어요... 그리고 그들은 저속한 걸 원했죠. 이는 연극이 여성과 중산층 모두에게 더 접근할 수 있게 되었을 때 변화했습니다... 희극은 더 부드러워졌고, 이는 감상희극 출현의 전조였습니다.

우리는 감상희극이 쓰여진 철학적인 관점을 고려할 필요가 있어요. 18세기 초기에, 관객들은 더욱 보수적이어서, 연극은 그들의 도덕적 올바름에 대한 감각에 호소하도록 구성되었어요. 왜 이런 변화가 있었을까요? 첫째로, 영국에 인구통계학적 변화가 있었어요, 앞서 말한 것처럼, 더 많은 여성과 더 큰 중산층 말이에요. 또한 연극 자체와, 부도덕성 그리고 연극 무대에서의 모독을 특히 싫어했던, 윌리엄 3세와 메리가 왕위에 오른 것과 많은 관련이 있었어요. 그래서 전형적인 감상희극은 어떤 도덕적 시련이나 동요를 마주하고 결국 그들의 약점을 극복하며 천성적 미덕을 되찾을 수 있었던 중산층 인물들을 포함합니다. 이전 왕정 복고 시대의 희극은 이 도덕적 기반을 가지고 있지 않았죠.

왕정 복고 시대의 희극과 감상희극 사이의 전환을 나타내는 좋은 예는 콜리 시버의 '사랑의 마지막 계교'라는 연극입니다. 그것은 감상희극의 첫 번째 예로 여겨지는데, 그 시대의 관객들이 기대하게 되었던 부도덕의 요소 또한 가지고 있어요. 그것은 런던을 떠나 10년의 기간 동안 해외에서 지내며, 대부분의 시간을 술집에서 보낸, 러브리스라는 남편에 대한 이야기입니다. 그의 아내는 그의 행적에 대해 알고 있었어요. 그가 런던으로 돌아오자마자, 그녀는 다른 여자처럼 옷을 입고 그를 유혹했어요. 그는 그녀가 고백하기 전까지 그녀의 진짜 정체를 몰랐죠. 러브리스는 그녀의 충실함에 너무나도 놀라서 즉시 그의 태도를 바꾸고 헌신적인 남편으로 변했어요. 마지막, 절정의 장면은 관중들로부터 감정적인 반응을 이끌어내기 위해 쓰였죠. 사실, 그 시대의 관객 대부분은 마지막 장면에 감동을 받아 눈물을 흘렸습니다.

[10-12]
Listen to part of a lecture in an astronomy class.

P: Is everyone ready? We're getting into the, uh, outer planets of the solar system . . . the so-called gas giants. Um, some of you have expressed interest in Saturn, especially its rings. We'll get to that eventually, but this afternoon, Q10 we'll talk about Uranus, starting with how it was discovered.

Uranus is the 7th planet in our solar system. It was officially discovered in 1781 . . . Um, there are actually earlier observations of Uranus. For example, an astronomer named John Flamsteed spotted it six times in 1690. But Uranus had always been mistaken for a star . . . In fact, it was listed in star catalogs as 34 Tauri.

Now, it was an English astronomer . . . his name was, um, William Herschel . . . that first noticed something odd about the star . . . He saw that 34 Tauri seemed to be moving more quickly than other stars . . . Now, remember what I told you about the movement of stars?

S1: ^{Q11} Um, yeah . . . Most of them are so far away . . . so they appear to move very slowly . . .

P: Right . . . It's like looking at ships on the horizon . . . Objects that are nearer to us appear to be moving faster than objects that are further away, despite moving at the same speed. It's an illusion created by distance . . . Anyway, Herschel initially thought 34 Tauri was a comet based on its movement. However, it didn't leave a trail of ice and dust . . . the most obvious sign of a comet . . . so 34 Tauri clearly wasn't one. Other astronomers had similar doubts and began tracking its movement. That's when they realized that it was orbiting the Sun. From this, they concluded that 34 Tauri was actually a planet.

Because Herschel was the first to notice that 34 Tauri wasn't a star, he got the honor of naming it. He called it George's Star after Great Britain's King George III.

S2: Um . . . why didn't he name it like the other planets, after Roman gods and goddesses?

P: Well, ^{Q12} he believed the name would allow people in the future to know when the planet had been discovered. Basically, it would, you know, indicate that Uranus was discovered during the time of King George III . . . But, um, many in the scientific community disagreed. The Americans were at war with Britain at the time and, well, they objected pretty strongly to the name. Eventually, it was decided that the planet should be called Uranus, after the Greek god of the sky.

Now get ready to answer the questions. You may use your notes to help you answer.

10. What is the main topic of the lecture?
11. Why does the professor mention ships on the horizon?
12. According to the professor, why did Herschel name the new planet George's Star?

P: 모두 준비됐나요? 우리는, 어, 태양계의 외행성을 시작해 볼 거예요... 이른바 가스상 거대 혹성이라고 불리는 것들이죠. 음, 여러분 중 일부는 토성에 흥미를 보인 적이 있을 거예요, 특히 그것의 고리에 대해서요. 결국 그것에 이르게 될 테지만, 오늘 오후에는, 천왕성에 관해 이야기해 보도록 하죠, 그것이 어떻게 발견되었는지로 시작하면서요.

천왕성은 우리 태양계의 일곱 번째 행성이에요. 그것은 공식적으로 1781년에 발견됐죠... 음, 사실 더 이른 천왕성의 관찰이 있어요. 예를 들어, 1690년에 존 플램스티드라는 한 천문학자는 그것을 여섯 번 발견했죠. 하지만 천왕성은 항상 항성으로 오인되어 왔습니다... 실제로, 그것은 34 Tauri로 성표에 포함되어 있었고요.

자, 이 항성에 대해 뭔가 이상한 것을 처음으로 알아챈 사람은 영국의 천문학자였습니다... 그의 이름은, 음, 윌리엄 허셜이었죠... 그는 34 Tauri가 다른 항성들보다 더 빠르게 움직이고 있는 것처럼 보인다는 걸 목격했어요... 자, 항성의 움직임에 대해 제가 이야기했던 것을 기억하나요?

S1: 음, 네... 그들 대부분은 정말 멀리에 있어서... 매우 느리게 움직이는 것처럼 보인다고요...

P: 맞아요... 그건 지평선에 있는 배를 보는 것과 같아요... 우리에게 더 가까이 있는 물체는 멀리 떨어져 있는 물체보다 더 빨리 움직이는 것처럼 보이죠, 같은 속도로 움직이고 있음에도 불구하고요. 그건 거리에 의해 만들어진 착각입니다... 어쨌든, 처음에 허셜은 34 Tauri의 움직임에 근거해서 그것이 혜성이라고 생각했어요. 하지만, 그것은 얼음과 먼지 자국을 남기지 않았죠... 혜성의 가장 명백한 표시를요... 그래서 34 Tauri는 분명 혜성이 아니었어요. 다른 천문학자들도 비슷한 의문을 가졌고 그것의 움직임을 추적하기 시작했습니다. 그것이 바로 그들이 34 Tauri가 태양의 궤도를 돌고 있다는 것을 깨달은 시점이었죠. 이로부터, 그들은 34 Tauri가 실제로 행성이라는 결론을 내렸어요.

34 Tauri가 항성이 아니라는 것을 알아챈 사람은 허셜이 처음이었기 때문에, 그는 그것의 이름을 짓는 영예를 얻게 됐어요. 그는 영국 국왕 조지 3세의 이름을 따서 그것을 조지의 항성이라고 불렀죠.

S2: 음... 왜 그가 그것을 다른 행성들처럼, 로마의 신과 여신들의 이름을 따서 명명하지 않았나요?

P: 음, 그는 그 이름이 미래의 사람들에게 그 행성이 발견된 시기를 알게 해줄 거라고 믿었어요. 기본적으로, 그것은, 그러니까, 천왕성이 국왕 조지 3세 시기 동안에 발견되었다는 것을 나타낼 수 있을 테니까요... 하지만, 음, 과학계의 많은 사람들이 이의를 제기

했어요. 미국인들은 그 당시 영국과 전쟁 중이었고, 음, 이 이름을 매우 강력하게 반대했죠. 결국, 그 행성은 천왕성이라고 불려야 한다고 결정됐어요. 그리스 하늘의 신의 이름을 따서요.

HACKERS TEST

1. (B) Main Purpose/Topic
2. (C) Function & Attitude
3. (C) Detail
4. (B), (D) Detail
5. (A) Connecting Contents II
6. (B) Main Purpose/Topic
7. (C) Function & Attitude
8. (D) Detail
9. (C) Connecting Contents II
10. (C), (D) Detail
11. (C) Detail
12. (D) Main Purpose/Topic
13. (B), (C) Detail
14. (A) Detail
15. (D) Connecting Contents II
16. (A) Detail
17. (B) Function & Attitude
18. (B) Main Purpose/Topic
19. (B) Detail
20. (A) Connecting Contents II
21. (D) Detail
22. (D) Connecting Contents II
23. (C) Main Purpose/Topic
24. (A) Connecting Contents II
25. (D) Detail
26. Connecting Contents I

Step 1	A material is heated and pressurized.
Step 2	A gas is filtered to get rid of contaminants.
Step 3	An element is added to a gas to cause a reaction.
Step 4	A gas is allowed to cool and become a liquid.

27. (A), (C), (D) Detail
28. (C) Function & Attitude
29. (B) Main Purpose/Topic
30. (A) Detail
31. (B) Connecting Contents II
32. (A), (C) Detail
33. (D) Connecting Contents II
34. (A) Function & Attitude

[1-5]
Listen to a conversation between a student and a student center employee.

W: Um, hello . . . I'm here to speak with the person in charge of the, uh, volunteer programs for students.

M: Yes, that's me. I'm Bob Hill.

W: I'm Lina Jones, and, um, I'm a music student. Q1 I'm looking for volunteer opportunities related to music. You see, the music department awards students, um, extra credit for volunteering if it has to do with music . . . and I thought that this center might have a few ideas . . .

M: OK . . . Did you have anything particular in mind?

W: Well, I was thinking I could give, uh, piano lessons or something . . .

M: Let's see . . . Would you be interested in teaching children? Clearview Community Center is expanding its after-school program for middle school students, and it needs more instructors.

W: That sounds perfect! Could you give me more details?

M: Q2 Well, the main thing is you'd have to be able to commit to being there from . . . um . . . 3:30 to 5 p.m. on Tuesdays and Thursdays.

W: Oh . . . did you say Tuesdays and Thursdays? That might be tricky . . .

M: What's the problem?

W: Hmm . . . it's not ideal since I've got a class on Thursdays that runs from 4 to 6 p.m. I'm totally free on Tuesdays, though.

M: I'm afraid instructors need to be available on both days. Uh, maybe you should put it off until next semester, then. . .

W: Um . . . [Q3] I was hoping to get this extra credit as soon as possible. Right now, my course load is pretty manageable, but next semester . . . It's hard to say. I'll be in my fourth year, and my classes will probably be more demanding. I'm not sure if I will have the time and, um, energy for volunteering. And won't they have found a piano instructor by then anyway?

M: You never know. They've had trouble getting qualified instructors. I mean, a lot of people have expressed interest in teaching music, but very few of them have the skills required for the job.

W: I don't know. . . I was really hoping to volunteer this semester.

M: Well, there may be another opportunity that might interest you . . . [Q4] Fairfield General Hospital is trying to organize some, uh, music performances for charity . . . The goal is to raise money for the children's care center.

W: That could be really interesting.

M: Also, [Q4] I think the schedule is pretty flexible at this point . . . They haven't decided when to hold the performances, so you may be able to ask them to work around your classes.

W: All right, I think I will ask them. How can I apply?

M: You can just call and request to speak to the hospital's fundraising director. Let me see . . . Her name is, uh, Molly Hines. She'll want to interview you first, and she'll probably ask you for a few work references. She'll want to hear you play as well . . . You should prepare some pieces of music to perform for her.

W: OK . . . I'll do that.

M: Before you go . . . You may also want to let the other students in your program know about these opportunities . . . both at the community center and the, uh, hospital.

W: [Q5] I'm actually meeting my study group later today . . . at least a handful of them would be interested . . . I mean, if practicing for our upcoming concert isn't taking up too much of their time. In any case, I'll let them know.

M: Excellent. And I hope things go well with your application.

W: I do, too. Thanks again for your help.

Now get ready to answer the questions. You may use your notes to help you answer.

1. Why does the student visit the student center?

Listen again to part of the conversation. Then answer the question.

M: Well, the main thing is you'd have to be able to commit to being there from . . . um . . . 3:30 to 5 p.m. on Tuesdays and Thursdays.

W: Oh . . . did you say Tuesdays and Thursdays? That might be tricky . . .

2. What does the student mean when she says this:
   W: Oh . . . did you say Tuesdays and Thursdays?

3. Why is the student unwilling to volunteer at Clearview Community Center next semester?

4. What does the employee say about the hospital's music performances?

5. Why does the student mention her study group?

W: 음, 안녕하세요... 저는, 어, 학생들을 위한 자원봉사 프로그램을 담당하고 계신 분과 이야기하러 왔어요.

M: 네, 접니다. Bob Hill이에요.

W: 저는 Lina Jones입니다, 음, 음악과 학생이고요. 음악 관련 자원봉사 기회를 찾고 있어요. 그러니까, 음악학부는 학생들에게, 음,

음악과 관련된 일이라면 자원봉사에 대해 추가 학점을 수여하거든요... 그리고 이곳이 몇 가지 제안을 가지고 있을 거라고 생각했어요...

M: 그렇군요... 특별히 생각했던 것이라도 있나요?

W: 음, 저는 제가, 어, 피아노 수업 같은 것을 할 수 있을 거라 생각했었어요.

M: 어디 보자... 아이들을 가르치는 일에 관심이 있나요? Clearview 지역 문화 회관이 중학생들을 위한 방과 후 프로그램을 확대하고 있어서, 더 많은 강사가 필요하거든요.

W: 완벽하네요! 세부 사항을 좀 더 알려주실래요?

M: 음, 중요한 것은 학생이... 음... 화요일과 목요일마다 오후 3시 30분부터 5시까지를 그곳에 있는 데 할당할 수 있어야 해요.

W: 오... 화요일과 목요일이라고 하셨나요? 그건 좀 곤란하겠는데요...

M: 무슨 문제가 있나요?

W: 흠... 목요일마다 오후 4시부터 6시까지 진행되는 수업이 있어서 그건 알맞지 않네요. 하지만 화요일에는 완전히 한가해요.

M: 안타깝지만 강사는 이틀 모두 가능해야 해요. 어, 그러면 아마 다음 학기까지 미뤄야겠네요...

W: 음... 저는 가능한 한 빨리 이 추가 학점을 얻길 바라고 있었어요. 지금은, 제 수업량이 꽤 감당할 만하지만, 다음 학기에는... 예측할 수 없어요. 저는 4학년이 될 거라서, 수업은 아마 더 부담이 커질 거예요. 자원봉사 활동을 위한 시간과, 음, 기운이 있을지 잘 모르겠어요. 그리고 어쨌든 그때쯤이면 피아노 강사를 찾지 않았겠어요?

M: 그건 모르는 일이죠. 그들은 자격을 갖춘 강사를 찾는 데 어려움을 겪어왔거든요. 제 말은, 많은 사람이 음악을 가르치는 것에 관심을 보여왔지만, 업무를 위해 요구되는 기술을 가지고 있는 사람은 오직 몇 명뿐이죠.

W: 잘 모르겠네요... 정말로 이번 학기에 자원봉사를 하고 싶었거든요.

M: 음, 학생의 관심을 끌 만한 또 다른 기회가 있을지도 몰라요... Fairfield 종합병원이 어떤, 어, 자선 음악회를 조직하려 하고 있어요... 목표는 어린이 병동을 위한 기금을 모으는 거고요.

W: 그거 아주 흥미로운데요.

M: 또, 제 생각에 현재로써는 일정이 꽤 융통성 있어요... 아직 공연을 언제 개최할지 결정하지 않았으니, 학생의 수업 일정을 피해서 일할 수 있도록 요청할 수 있을 거예요.

W: 좋아요, 제가 요청해 보도록 할게요. 어떻게 지원하면 되죠?

M: 그냥 전화해서 병원의 모금 행사 책임자와 이야기하게 해달라고 요청하면 돼요. 어디 보자... 그녀의 이름은, 어, Molly Hines네요. 먼저 학생을 인터뷰하길 원할 텐데, 몇 개의 추천서를 요구할 수도 있어요. 학생이 연주하는 것도 들어보길 원할 거예요... 그녀를 위해 연주할 몇 곡을 준비하는 게 좋겠네요.

W: 네. 그렇게 할게요.

M: 가기 전에... 학생 과의 다른 학생들에게 이 기회에 대해 알려주는 게 좋겠어요... 지역 문화 회관과, 어, 병원에서의 기회 둘 다요.

W: 사실 오늘 늦게 스터디 모임과 만나요... 그들 중 적어도 소수는 관심 있어 할 거예요... 제 말은, 다가오는 공연을 위한 연습이 그들의 시간을 너무 많이 차지하지 않는다면 말이죠. 어쨌든, 그들에게 알릴게요.

M: 훌륭하군요. 그리고 학생의 지원이 잘 되길 바랍니다.

W: 저도요. 도와주셔서 다시 한 번 감사합니다.

어휘

award[əwɔ́ːrd] 수여하다   credit[krédit] 학점   have to do with ~와 관련되다   instructor[instrʌ́ktər] 강사
commit to ~에 할당하다   tricky[tríki] 곤란한   put off 미루다   manageable[mǽnidʒəbl] 감당할 만한
demanding[dimǽndiŋ] 부담이 큰   qualified[kwɑ́ləfàid] 자격을 갖춘   charity[tʃǽrəti] 자선   work around ~을 피해서 일하다

[6-11]

Listen to part of a talk on the circadian rhythm.

I'd like to start off by asking if you've ever gone on a long trip, perhaps to some place several time zones away . . . or if you've ever held a job on the graveyard shift. Well, the reason I ask has to do with my lecture today on the circadian rhythm. The human circadian rhythm is based on a 24-hour cycle, and any interruption to this rhythm, such as the ones I just mentioned, would have an impact on the body. 07 A person could have sleep problems or become depressed and anxious. But I'm getting ahead of myself. Let's take a closer look at just what the circadian rhythm is.

Q8 Essentially, what this rhythm does is it helps stabilize the timing of our bodily functions. The sleep cycle, body temperature, blood pressure, brainwave activity, hormone and digestive secretions—all of these operate according to a 24-hour cycle. So as long as this rhythm stays on cue, an individual will generally experience physical and mental well-being.

Q6 But what happens when the rhythm goes out of sync? And how does it go out of sync? Well, let me deal with the second question first. OK . . . there are two aspects that control the circadian rhythm. One is internal. The body has a circadian pacemaker, or what many people call a biological clock. It's a section of the brain known as the suprachiasmatic nucleus or SCN. Now, the SCN adjusts itself to the 24-hour light-dark cycle. So if the SCN is dependent on the intervals of daytime and nighttime, what would happen if a person were blind? Well, the SCN would get confused, so to speak. Q9 A blind person may have a couple of nights when he sleeps well and then a couple of nights when he doesn't. What this tells us is the SCN cannot, on its own, establish a normal circadian rhythm. A second aspect is needed to help the circadian rhythm function properly. This involves the external cues the SCN needs to make the necessary adjustments.

So what are these external cues? Well, they're environmental cues, specifically, light. Temperature also plays a role, but it doesn't have the same impact that light does. The circadian rhythm resets itself to the 24-hour day as it is exposed to either sunlight or darkness. The morning sun will cue the body to produce certain hormones and neurotransmitters that increase blood pressure and body temperature. It's these little changes that'll get the body going for daytime activities. At sunset, however, the body begins to produce melatonin and the blood pressure goes down. And as the evening hours wear on, the body continues to wind down. It is, in effect, preparing for nighttime sleep. Q10 So how is this cycle broken? Well, actually, very easily. A long-distance trip, a nighttime job, putting off your bedtime for hours because you have an important exam.

This brings me back to the first question. What happens when the cycle goes out of sync? Well, if you continue to subject your body to a routine that goes against your body clock, it will simply go out of balance. It will begin to produce chemicals and hormones in the wrong quantities and at the wrong time. Your mood and sleep problems will get worse. Q11 Those who work on the night shift are prone to physical and mental abnormalities. Our world today depends on round-the-clock workers, especially in the fields of medicine, agriculture, transportation, heavy manufacturing, and the service industries. This translates to millions of people with circadian rhythm-related health problems. So . . . medical people have come to see the importance of the circadian rhythm where health is concerned.

Now get ready to answer the questions. You may use your notes to help you answer.

6. What does the professor mainly discuss?

Listen again to part of the lecture. Then answer the question.

P: A person could have sleep problems or become depressed and anxious. But I'm getting ahead of myself. Let's take a closer look at just what the circadian rhythm is.

7. What does the professor mean when he says this:
   P: But I'm getting ahead of myself.

8. According to the professor, what major role does the circadian rhythm play?
9. Why does the professor discuss a blind person?

10. According to the professor, what are two ways the circadian rhythm can be disrupted?
11. What point does the professor make when he refers to round-the-clock workers?

시차가 몇 시간 나는 곳으로, 장거리 여행을 하거나... 야간 근무 일을 해 본 적이 있는지 질문하면서 강의를 시작하고 싶군요. 음, 이 질문을 하는 이유는 생체리듬에 관한 오늘 강의와 관련이 있습니다. 인간의 생체리듬은 24시간 주기에 바탕을 두고 있으며, 앞서 얘기했던 경우들처럼, 이 리듬이 방해를 받으면, 신체에 영향을 줍니다. 수면장애가 오거나 우울하고 불안해질 수 있죠. 하지만 제가 앞서 나가고 있군요. 생체리듬이 무엇인지 좀 더 자세히 살펴봅시다.

기본적으로, 이 리듬이 하는 일은 신체기능의 시간 조절을 안정시켜주는 것입니다. 수면 주기, 체온, 혈압, 뇌파 활동, 호르몬과 소화액 분비, 이 모든 것들이 24시간 주기에 따라 작용해요. 따라서 이 리듬이 정상적으로 유지되는 한, 인간은 대개 신체 및 정신적 건강을 누리게 되죠.

그러나 이 리듬의 조화가 깨지면 어떤 현상이 발생할까요? 그리고 그것은 어떻게 깨질까요? 음, 두 번째 질문에 대해 먼저 논의해 보죠. 자... 생체리듬을 조절하는 두 가지 요인이 있어요. 첫 번째는 체내 요인입니다. 신체는 생체 조절 기관, 또는 많은 사람들이 생체시계라고도 부르는 것을 가지고 있어요. 그것은 시신경교차상부핵 혹은 SCN으로 알려진 뇌의 한 부분입니다. 자, SCN은 낮과 밤의 24시간 주기에 스스로 적응합니다. 그럼 만약 SCN이 낮 시간과 밤 시간의 간격에 좌우된다면... 시각장애인에게는 어떤 일이 일어날까요? 음, 그러니까, SCN은 혼란에 빠질 거예요. 시각장애인은 며칠 간은 밤에 잠을 잘 자지만, 또 다른 며칠 간은 잘 자지 못하기도 할 겁니다. 이를 통해 SCN은, 그 자체만으로, 정상적인 생체리듬을 조성하지 못한다는 것을 알 수 있어요. 생체리듬이 제대로 기능하는 것을 돕는 데에는 또 다른 요인이 필요하죠. 이것은 SCN이 필수적으로 조절해야 하는 외부 자극을 수반합니다.

그렇다면 이러한 외부 자극은 무엇일까요? 음, 환경적인 자극입니다, 특히, 빛이죠. 온도도 역할을 하지만, 빛이 미치는 영향만큼은 아닙니다. 생체리듬은 햇빛이나 어둠에 노출되면 스스로를 다시 하루 24시간에 맞춥니다. 아침 햇살은 혈압과 체온을 높이는 특정 호르몬과 신경전달물질을 생성하도록 신체에 신호를 보내요. 이러한 작은 변화들이 바로 신체가 낮 동안의 활동을 시작하도록 해주는 것이죠. 그러나, 해 질 무렵이면, 신체는 멜라토닌을 생성하기 시작하고 혈압은 내려갑니다. 그리고 저녁 시간이 지나면서, 신체는 계속해서 긴장을 풀죠. 그건, 사실상, 밤에 자기 위한 준비를 하는 거예요. 그러면 이 주기가 어떻게 깨질까요? 음, 사실, 아주 쉽습니다. 장거리 여행, 야간 근무, 중요한 시험이 있어서 취침 시간을 미루는 것으로요.

이는 다시 첫 번째 질문으로 돌아가게 하네요. 생체주기의 조화가 깨지면 어떠한 현상이 발생할까요? 음, 몸의 생체시계에 어긋나는 일과를 계속 유지하면, 그것은 쉽게 균형을 잃게 됩니다. 그것은 적절하지 않은 때에 적절하지 않은 양의 화학물질과 호르몬을 생성하게 돼요. 기분은 더 나빠지고 수면장애는 더 심해집니다. 야간 근무를 하는 사람들은 신체적이고 정신적인 이상을 겪게 되기 쉬워요. 현대 사회는 밤낮으로 일하는 사람들, 특히 의학, 농업, 운송, 중장비 제조업, 그리고 서비스 분야의 사람들에게 의지합니다. 이것은 생체리듬과 관련된 건강 문제를 가진 사람들이 수백만 명이라는 것을 뜻하죠. 그래서... 의학 계통 사람들은 건강에 있어서 생체리듬의 중요성을 깨닫게 되었어요.

어휘

graveyard shift 야간 근무 circadian rhythm 생체리듬 depressed[diprést] 우울한 anxious[ǽŋkʃəs] 불안한
stabilize[stéibəlàiz] 안정시키다 digestive[didʒéstiv] 소화의 secretion[sikríːʃən] 분비 out of sync 조화가 깨진
pacemaker[péismèikər] 조절 기관 suprachiasmatic nucleus 시신경교차상부핵 cue[kjuː] 자극; 신호를 보내다
neurotransmitter[njùəroutrǽnsmítər] 신경전달물질 go against 어긋나다 abnormality[æ̀bnɔːrmǽləti] 이상
round-the-clock[ràundðəklák] 밤낮으로 일하는

[12-17]
Listen to part of a lecture in an architecture class.

Q12 Today, I'll be discussing a phenomenon that grew out of the need to conserve energy. In the past few decades, quite a number of airtight buildings were constructed—actually, they continue to be constructed. What we'll be looking at is how these buildings make people sick. Yes, that's the phenomenon—these buildings make people sick. You may have heard of the ailment . . . sick building syndrome, or SBS for short. Seems like an apt name . . .
Well, initial studies on airtight buildings showed that building owners could save substantially on heating and cooling energy costs—as much as 37 percent . . . Now, that's a lot of money. So naturally more than a few showed interest in having this type of building constructed. By the

1970s, it became a requirement in some states for buildings to be airtight. This was the government's bid to conserve fuel.

So, people in the construction field began devising ways to make these structures more airtight. I'll talk about just two approaches. Q13 One involves wrapping the building—the sealed polyethylene approach. Basically, sealed polyethylene is inserted between the insulating materials and the interior finish materials. But that's not all. On the outside, building paper, or "housewrap," is used to form a moisture barrier. Now, I guess not many of you have ever seen building paper. It's a very heavy and durable paper that has been coated or laminated to make it resistant to water. It's very good at insulating, so you can see how it would make a building airtight. A second approach is the airtight drywall method, which necessitates the laying of gypsum boards against the foundation, roof, and walls of a building. Gypsum is actually a common mineral that is used to make cement and plaster.

So, building owners began to enjoy energy savings. The government was able to reduce fuel consumption. But in the 1970s, doctors saw a sharp increase in the number of people with headaches, respiratory problems, dizziness, fatigue, eye irritations, nausea . . . Q14 It took a while—in fact, several years—to trace these symptoms to their source. The doctors discovered that people who lived or worked in certain buildings became sick. But when they left these buildings, their symptoms disappeared! This is why it took so long to figure out what was going on . . .

Well, medical researchers ascertained that the problem with these buildings was the flow of air, or, rather, the lack of it. You see, when you seal a building or change its air flow, air may not move as freely. Q15 Contaminants are found in any building, you know, the paint on the walls, wooden decorations coated with varnish, poisonous emissions from photocopiers and computers, uh, damp walls and floors that may have molds and fungi, and even perfume—I could go on and on. You see, Q16 when temperatures rise to about 20 degrees Celsius, volatile organic compounds, or VOCs, are emitted as vapors and gases from both solids and liquids that may be present in a room. And these vapors and gases are toxic and hazardous to health. Well, think of these gases in an airtight building, and you'll understand why people were getting sick. The most common symptoms that people experience are respiratory. A runny nose and a chronic cough are the milder symptoms. The worst is real respiratory distress, and for asthma sufferers, full-blown asthma fits.

So it's not surprising that with the construction of so many airtight buildings, more and more people began taking sick leaves. The World Health Organization has estimated that the loss due to absenteeism from sick building ailments amounts to about $100 billion a year. Q17 So sure, the government was looking to save energy, but I guess these folks didn't realize that those savings would be wiped out by employee absenteeism, medical costs, reduced productivity, and decreased company earnings.

Now get ready to answer the questions. You may use your notes to help you answer.

12. What is the talk mainly about?
13. What are two aspects of the sealed polyethylene approach?
14. According to the professor, why did doctors take years to discover the reason for the sharp increase in health ailments in the 1970s?
15. How does the professor clarify her point about contaminants found in any building?
16. What does the professor say about solids and liquids in a room?
17. What is the professor's opinion of the government's solution to save on energy costs?

오늘은, 에너지를 보존하려는 필요성에서 시작된 현상에 관해 논의하겠습니다. 지난 몇 십 년간, 수많은 밀폐형 건물들이 세워졌어요, 사실, 계속해서 세워지고 있죠. 우리가 알아볼 것은 이런 건물들이 사람들을 병들게 하는 방식입니다. 네, 그게 그 현상이에요, 이 건물들이 사람들을 병들게 하는 것 말이죠. 그 질환에 대해 들어 봤을 거예요... 건물 질환 증후군, 혹은 줄여서 SBS 말이에요. 매우 적절한 이름인 것 같네요...

음, 밀폐형 건물에 관한 초기 연구는 건물 소유주들이 냉난방 에너지 경비를 상당히 절약할 수 있었다는 것을 보여줬습니다, 37퍼센트만큼이나요... 자, 이건 상당한 비용이죠. 그래서 자연스럽게 적지 않은 사람들이 이 유형의 건물을 세우는 데 관심을 보였어요. 1970년대가 되자, 일부 주에서 건물이 밀폐형인 것은 필수조건이 되었습니다. 이는 연료를 절약하려는 정부의 노력이었죠.

그래서, 건설 분야의 사람들은 이러한 건축물들을 더 밀폐형으로 만드는 방법을 고안하기 시작했습니다. 두 가지 방법에 대해서만 이야기할 거예요. 하나는 건물을 감싸는 것인데, 밀봉된 폴리에틸렌 방식이에요. 기본적으로, 밀봉된 폴리에틸렌이 단열재와 내부 마감재 사이에 삽입되죠. 그러나 이게 다가 아닙니다. 외부에는, 습기 차단 벽을 만들기 위해 방습지, 혹은 "주택 포장재"가 사용되었어요. 자, 여러분 중 대다수가 방습지를 본 적이 없을 것이라 생각해요. 그것은 물에 대한 저항력을 만들기 위해 코팅되거나 얇은 판을 씌운 아주 무겁고 오래 지속되는 종이예요. 그것은 단열을 아주 잘해서, 여러분은 그것이 어떻게 건물을 밀폐형이 되도록 하는지 알 수 있을 거예요. 두 번째 방법은 건물의 토대, 지붕, 그리고 벽에 석고 판을 동반하는, 밀폐 건식 벽체 기법입니다. 석고는 사실 시멘트나 회반죽을 만드는 데 사용되는 일반적인 광물이에요.

그래서, 건물 소유주들은 에너지 절약을 즐기기 시작했어요. 정부는 연료 소비를 줄일 수 있었죠. 그러나 1970년대에, 의사들은 두통, 호흡 장애, 현기증, 피로, 눈의 염증, 구역질 증상을 가진 사람들의 숫자가 급격히 증가하는 것을 보았습니다... 이러한 증상들의 원인을 밝혀내기까지는 조금, 사실, 몇 년이 걸렸죠. 의사들은 특정한 건물에서 살거나 근무했던 사람들이 병에 걸렸다는 것을 발견했어요. 하지만 그들이 이 건물에서 나오면, 증상이 사라졌고요! 이게 바로 무슨 일이 일어나고 있는지 알아내는 데 그렇게 오랜 시간이 걸린 이유입니다...

음, 의학 연구원들은 이러한 건물의 문제가 공기의 흐름이라는 것을 알아냈습니다, 또는, 오히려, 공기 흐름의 부족 때문이었죠. 그러니까, 건물을 밀봉하거나 건물 내 공기의 흐름을 바꾸면, 공기는 자유롭게 이동하지 못합니다. 오염 물질은 어느 빌딩에서나 발견돼요, 그러니까, 벽의 페인트, 니스로 칠해진 목제 장식, 복사기와 컴퓨터로부터의 유독한 배출물, 어, 곰팡이와 균류가 있을 수도 있는 눅눅한 벽과 바닥, 그리고 심지어 향수도, 계속해서 나열할 수 있죠. 그러니까, 온도가 섭씨 20도쯤으로 올라가면, 방에 있을 수 있는 고체와 액체로부터 휘발성 유기 화합물, 또는 VOC가 증기와 가스의 형태로 방출됩니다. 그리고 이러한 증기와 가스는 독성이 있으며 건강에 해롭죠. 음, 밀폐형 건물 안에 있는 이러한 가스를 생각해 보세요, 그러면 사람들이 병에 걸린 이유를 이해하게 될 거예요. 사람들이 경험하는 가장 일반적인 증상은 호흡기와 관련되어 있습니다. 콧물과 만성적인 기침은 보다 가벼운 증상이에요. 가장 심한 것은 진정한 호흡 곤란, 그리고 천식 환자들에게는, 악화된 천식 발작입니다.

그래서 정말 많은 밀폐형 건물들의 건설과 함께, 점점 더 많은 사람들이 병가를 내기 시작한 것은 놀라운 일이 아닙니다. 세계보건기구는 건물 질환으로 인한 결근의 손실이 연간 거의 천억 달러에 달한다고 추정했어요. 그래서 물론, 정부는 에너지를 절약하려는 거였지만, 그들은 그런 절약이 직원들의 결근, 의료비용, 감소된 생산성, 그리고 감소된 회사의 소득 때문에 없어질 거라는 것을 알지 못했을 거예요.

어휘

conserve[kənsə́:rv] 보존하다 airtight[ɛ́ərtàit] 밀폐형의 ailment[éilmənt] 질환 sick building syndrome 건물 질환 증후군
sealed[si:ld] 밀봉된 insulating[ínsəlèitiŋ] 단열의 building paper 방습지 laminate[lǽmənèit] 얇은 판을 씌우다
necessitate[nəsésətèit] 동반하다 gypsum[dʒípsəm] 석고 plaster[plǽstər] 회반죽
respiratory[réspərətɔ̀:ri] 호흡의, 호흡기와 관련된 dizziness[dízinis] 현기증 irritation[ìrətéiʃən] 염증 nausea[nɔ́:ziə] 구역질
ascertain[æ̀sərtéin] 알아내다 contaminant[kəntǽmənənt] 오염 물질 varnish[vɑ́:rniʃ] 니스 damp[dæmp] 눅눅한
mold[mould] 곰팡이 fungi[fʌ́ndʒai] 균류(fungus의 복수형) volatile[vɑ́lətl] 휘발성의 chronic[krɑ́nik] 만성적인
asthma[ǽzmə] 천식 full-blown[fùlblóun] 악화된 fit[fit] 발작 sick leave 병가 absenteeism[æ̀bsəntí:izm] 결근
amount[əmáunt] ~에 달하다

[18-22]
Listen to a conversation between a student and a professor.

S: Hi there. I'm looking for, uh, Professor Riteman?

P: Yes? Are you from one of my classes?

S: Not exactly . . . I'm Emily . . . I'm, um, a third-year psychology student, and I'm interested in your class about Freud.

P: Great! That class is always popular. It fills up quickly every year.

S: Q18 That is sort of why I'm here, actually. I was hoping that you would let me, well . . . let me audit the course. Um, I should explain . . . Originally, I tried to register for the class online, but the system wouldn't let me . . . I realized afterward that it was because I didn't take the prerequisite class about, uh, modern psychology.

P: Oh, that's too bad. Q19 But, you know, the course will be offered next semester, too, so you can complete the prerequisite in the meantime and sign up then . . .

S: I'm not sure I can wait . . . Q20 You see, I'm really interested in Freud, and I'm planning on writing an undergraduate thesis on him next year . . . So I really need to take the course now.

P: I'm sorry, but auditing doesn't sound like a good idea. My course isn't for beginners . . . It builds on the concepts from the modern psychology course. You could get, um, overwhelmed if you don't have that knowledge.

S: Hmm . . . How about if I review the concepts on my own? I could catch up that way, I think . . .

P: That's a lot of material for you to cover independently . . .

S: I know I could do it. I'd really appreciate it if you gave me a chance.

P: Well . . . all right, I'll allow you to audit the course . . . but there is one condition.

S: Sure, what is it?

P: Well, I need you to take the course seriously. I had a problem related to this with another student who audited one of my courses. Q21 There will be a lot of class discussions based on readings . . . and, um, I expect you to be prepared. That means reading the assigned material and actively contributing to the discussions. The students are meant to learn as much from each other as from me.

S: Of course. You've done me a huge favor, and I'm, um . . . I'm really grateful . . . Um, I wonder if I could ask just one more thing.

P: What is it?

S: Well, I'm probably going to focus my thesis topic on Freud's dream theories . . . I think it's fascinating how he viewed our dreams as a way for our unconscious mind to, uh, express itself . . . Um, would you meet with me at the end of the semester to give feedback on my paper's outline? Just to be clear . . . you wouldn't need to read anything extensive . . . It'd just be a brief conversation about, you know, if my outline is workable or not.

P: I can't guarantee anything now. Q22 The end of the semester is a busy period for me. I'll be interviewing and hiring research assistants for the psychology department's summer research program. And we're expanding the program, so it's going to be an even bigger commitment. Anyway, if I can spare some time to review your outline, I will.

S: OK . . . I will talk to you about this again near the end of the semester. Once again, thanks so much.

Now get ready to answer the questions. You may use your notes to help you answer.

18. Why does the student go to see the professor?
19. What does the professor say about the course on Freud?
20. Why does the student mention an undergraduate thesis?
21. What condition does the professor put on the student's attendance in his class?
22. Why does the professor mention the psychology department's summer research program?

S: 안녕하세요. 저는, 어, Riteman 교수님을 찾고 있는데요?
P: 네? 제 수업 중 하나를 듣는 학생인가요?

S: 그건 아니에요... 저는 Emily입니다... 저는, 음, 심리학과 3학년 학생이고, 프로이트에 관한 교수님의 수업에 관심이 있어요.

P: 좋네요! 그 수업은 언제나 인기가 많아요. 매년 빨리 차죠.

S: 사실, 그게 제가 여기 온 일종의 이유예요. 교수님께서 제가, 음... 그 수업을 청강할 수 있도록 해주시길 바라고 있었거든요. 음, 설명해드리는 게 좋겠네요... 원래는, 온라인으로 그 강의를 신청하려고 했는데, 시스템이 허용하지 않더라고요... 제가, 어, 현대 심리학에 관한 선수 과목을 듣지 않았기 때문이라는 것을 나중에 깨달았죠.

P: 오, 안타깝네요. 하지만, 그러니까, 그 강의는 다음 학기에도 제공될 테니, 그동안 선수 과목을 수료하고 그때 신청할 수 있어요...

S: 제가 기다릴 수 있을지 모르겠어요... 그러니까, 저는 프로이트에 정말 관심이 있어서, 내년에 그에 관한 학부 논문을 쓸 예정이거든요... 그래서 정말로 지금 이 강의를 들어야 해요.

P: 미안하지만, 청강이 좋은 생각 같지는 않네요. 내 강의는 입문자를 위한 것이 아니거든요... 그건 현대 심리학 강의의 개념들로부터 발전되는 것이니까요. 학생은, 음, 그 지식이 없으면 난처해질 수도 있어요.

S: 흠... 제가 그 개념들을 스스로 복습한다면요? 제 생각에, 그렇게 하면 따라잡을 수 있을 것 같은데요...

P: 학생이 혼자서 다루기엔 많은 내용일 텐데요...

S: 제가 할 수 있다는 걸 알아요. 저에게 기회를 주신다면 정말 감사하겠습니다.

P: 음... 좋아요, 그 강의를 청강하도록 허락할게요... 하지만 조건이 하나 있어요.

S: 물론이죠, 그게 무엇인가요?

P: 음, 강의에 진지하게 임해주었으면 해요. 제 강의 중 하나를 청강했던 또 다른 학생과 이와 관련된 문제가 있었거든요. 읽기 자료에 기반한 많은 토론이 있을 거고... 음, 학생이 준비돼 있었으면 해요. 그건 주어진 자료를 읽고 적극적으로 토론에 기여하는 것을 의미하죠. 학생들은 저에게서 배우는 것만큼 서로에게서도 배울 예정이거든요.

S: 물론이죠, 교수님께서 큰 호의를 베풀어주셨고, 저는 음... 정말 감사드려요... 음, 한 가지만 더 여쭤봐도 되는지 궁금해요.

P: 뭔데요?

S: 음, 저는 아마 제 논문 주제로 프로이트의 꿈 이론들에 초점을 맞출 거예요... 저는 그가 꿈을 우리의 무의식이, 어, 그 스스로를 표현하는 방법으로 바라본 것이 흥미롭다고 생각하거든요... 음, 학기 말에 저와 만나서 제 논문의 개요에 대해 의견을 주실 수 있으신가요? 분명히 말하자면... 교수님께서 상세한 것을 읽어주실 필요는 없을 거예요... 그건 단지, 그러니까, 제 개요가 실행 가능한지 아닌지에 관한 간단한 대화일 거예요.

P: 지금은 아무것도 보장할 수가 없네요. 학기 말은 제게 바쁜 시기거든요. 심리학부의 여름 연구 프로그램을 위한 연구 조교들을 면접하고 고용하고 있을 거예요. 그리고 그 프로그램을 확장하고 있어서, 심지어 더 큰 책무가 될 거고요. 어쨌든, 만약 학생의 개요를 검토할 시간을 낼 수 있다면, 그렇게 할게요.

S: 네... 이것에 대해서는 학기 말쯤 다시 말씀드릴게요. 다시 한 번 정말 감사합니다.

어휘

audit[ɔ́ːdit] (수업을) 청강하다 prerequisite[priːrékwəzit] 선수의; 선수 과목 undergraduate[ʌ̀ndərgrǽdʒuət] 학부의
thesis[θíːsis] 논문 get overwhelmed 난처해지다 catch up 따라잡다 condition[kəndíʃən] 조건
unconscious mind 무의식 feedback[fíːdbæk] 의견 extensive[iksténsiv] 상세한 workable[wɔ́ːrkəbl] 실행 가능한
commitment[kəmítmənt] 책무

[23-28]

Listen to part of a lecture in an environmental science class.

P: Now, I'm sure many of you are familiar with the concept of peak oil. Um, this is the idea that at some time in the future, the amount of oil available to us will begin to decline. Q23 Obviously, people are concerned about this and want to prepare for it . . . so there has been research into the production of synthetic fuel. Today you're going to learn about one way that this substance is made.

The process I'm referring to is called the Fischer-Tropsch method. Q24 Um, it was developed in 1925 . . . but it wasn't used until World War II. The German government didn't have enough fuel for its armed forces, so it . . . well, it decided to make use of this process. The Fischer-Tropsch method involves the conversion of the carbon in organic material into either gasoline or diesel. Q25 Coal and natural gas were used initially . . . but in recent years, it has become common to use biomass instead. Now . . .

S1: Excuse me, professor, but . . . uh, what do you mean by biomass? I'm not familiar with that term . . .

P: Ah . . . I guess I should explain. Um, in the broadest sense, biomass is simply the remains of organisms. [Q25] But in the context of energy production, this term is used to refer to plant material, like wood or agricultural waste products. I should probably point out that some farmers have actually started growing crops solely for conversion into fuel. Uh, corn is a good example of this . . .

Anyway, let's take a look at the Fischer-Tropsch method in detail. How does this process work? [Q26] Well, the first step is to expose the organic material to heat and pressure. This causes it to break down into two gasses . . . carbon monoxide and hydrogen. Um, this mixture of gasses is called syngas. [Q26] OK . . . next, the syngas is filtered to remove any chemical impurities. After that, a catalyst is added . . . What do you think I mean by this?

S2: Um, a catalyst is just something that causes change, right? So I assume you're talking about some sort of material that, uh, alters the syngas . . .

P: Exactly . . . [Q26] the catalyst is a chemical element such as iron that triggers a chemical reaction in the syngas . . . Depending on the catalyst used, the molecules in the syngas will combine in different ways . . . and this determines the type of synthetic fuel that will eventually be produced. [Q26] The final stage of the process involves cooling the syngas so that it becomes a liquid. [Q27] The end result is a synthetic form of gasoline or diesel that produces very little pollution when burned . . . which is obviously a significant advantage. Yes?

S2: Um, is that because the, uh, impurities were removed?

P: To some extent . . . Um, getting rid of toxic substances during the production process definitely results in a fuel that is cleaner when it burns. But that's not the whole story. The main reason this fuel causes so little pollution is the materials it's made from. Um, they contain few pollutants . . . [Q27] And, of course, another major advantage is that plant matter is renewable . . . so we will never run out of synthetic fuel. I should also point out that this fuel is compatible with existing gasoline and diesel engines . . . Um, any car can use it. [Q28] But synthetic fuel isn't going to start appearing at gas stations any time soon. It has one major drawback . . . It's very expensive to make. Unless researchers come up with a less costly production process . . . well, let's just say that synthetic fuel won't be widely used until this happens.

Now get ready to answer the questions. You may use your notes to help you answer.

23. What is the main topic of the lecture?
24. Why does the professor mention the German government?
25. According to the professor, what is synthetic fuel commonly made from?
26. In the lecture, the professor explains the sequence of steps involved in the production of synthetic fuels. Put the steps listed below in the correct order.
27. What are the advantages of synthetic fuel?

Listen again to part of the lecture. Then answer the question.

P: But synthetic fuel isn't going to start appearing at gas stations any time soon. It has one major drawback . . . It's very expensive to make. Unless researchers come up with a less costly production process . . . well, let's just say that synthetic fuel won't be widely used until this happens.

28. Why does the professor say this:
P: But synthetic fuel isn't going to start appearing at gas stations any time soon.

P: 자, 여러분 대부분이 피크 오일의 개념에 익숙할 거라고 확신합니다. 음, 미래의 어떤 시점에, 우리가 이용 가능한 석유의 양이 감소하기 시작할 거라는 개념이죠. 분명히, 사람들은 이에 대해 염려하고 그것에 대비하기 원합니다... 그래서 합성 연료 생산에 관한 연구가 있어왔죠. 오늘 여러분은 이 물질이 만들어지는 한 가지 방법에 대해 배울 거예요.
제가 말하고 있는 공정은 피셔-트로프슈법이라고 불립니다. 음, 이것은 1925년에 개발되었죠... 하지만 제2차 세계 대전 때까지는 사용되지 않았습니다. 독일 정부는 군대를 위한 충분한 연료가 없었어요, 그래서... 음, 이 공정을 이용하기로 결정한 거예요. 피셔-트로프슈법은 유기 물질에 들어있는 탄소를 휘발유나 디젤로 전환하는 것을 포함합니다. 처음에는 석탄과 천연가스가 사용되었지만... 최근 몇 년간, 대신 바이오매스를 사용하는 것이 흔해졌죠. 자...
S1: 죄송해요, 교수님, 그런데... 어, 바이오매스는 무슨 뜻이에요? 저는 그 용어에 익숙하지 않아서...
P: 아... 설명해야겠네요. 음, 가장 넓은 의미에서, 바이오매스는 단순히 유기체의 유해입니다. 하지만 에너지 생성의 맥락에서, 이 용어는 식물성 소재를 지칭하는 데 사용되죠, 나무나 농업 폐기물 같은 거요. 일부 농부들이 실제로 오로지 연료로의 전환을 위한 농작물들을 기르기 시작했다는 것을 언급하는 것이 좋겠군요. 어, 옥수수가 이것의 좋은 예시죠...
어쨌든, 피셔-트로프슈법에 대해 자세히 살펴봅시다. 이 공정이 어떻게 작동될까요? 음, 첫 번째 단계는 유기 물질을 열과 압력에 노출시키는 것입니다. 이는 그것이 두 가지 가스로 분해되도록 하죠... 일산화탄소와 수소로요. 음, 이 가스의 혼합물은 합성가스라고 불립니다. 자... 다음으로, 합성가스는 모든 화학 불순물들을 제거하기 위해 여과됩니다. 그 후, 촉매제가 더해져요... 이게 무슨 뜻이라고 생각하나요?
S2: 음, 촉매제는 단지 변화를 야기하는 어떤 것이잖아요, 맞죠? 그렇다면 교수님이, 어, 합성가스를 변화시키는 어떤 물질에 대해 말씀하고 계신다고 생각해요...
P: 정확해요... 촉매제는 합성가스에 화학 반응을 유발하는 철과 같은 화학 성분이죠... 사용되는 촉매제에 따라, 합성가스의 분자는 다른 방식으로 결합할 거예요... 그리고 이것이 마침내 생산되는 합성 연료의 종류를 결정하죠. 공정의 마지막 단계는 합성가스가 액체가 되도록 식히는 것을 포함합니다. 최종 결과는 태웠을 때 매우 적은 공해를 생산하는 합성 형태의 휘발유나 디젤이에요... 이는 분명 상당한 장점이죠. 네?
S2: 음, 그건, 어, 불순물이 제거됐기 때문인가요?
P: 어느 정도는요... 음, 생산 과정 동안 독성 물질을 제거하는 것은 분명히 탈 때 더 깨끗한 연료가 되게 하죠. 하지만 그것이 전부는 아닙니다. 이 연료가 그렇게 적은 공해를 야기하는 주된 이유는 그것이 만들어진 원료 때문이에요. 음, 그것들은 오염 물질을 거의 함유하고 있지 않거든요... 그리고, 물론, 또 다른 주요 장점은 식물성 물질이 재생 가능하다는 거예요... 그래서 우린 절대로 합성 연료가 부족하지 않을 거예요. 이 연료가 현재 사용되는 휘발유와 디젤 엔진에 호환된다는 것 또한 언급해야겠군요... 음, 어떤 자동차든지 그것을 사용할 수 있어요. 하지만 합성 연료가 곧장 주유소에서 보이기 시작하지는 않을 겁니다. 한 가지 중요한 문제점이 있거든요... 만들기가 굉장히 비싸다는 거죠. 연구원들이 비용이 덜 드는 생산 과정을 찾아내지 않는다면... 음, 그때까지는 합성 연료가 널리 사용되지는 않을 거라고만 말해둘게요.

어휘
synthetic fuel 합성 연료 armed forces 군대 make use of ~을 이용하다 conversion[kənvə́ːrʒən] 전환
gasoline[ɡǽsəliːn] 휘발유 remains[riméinz] 유해 waste product 폐기물 break down into ~으로 분해하다
carbon monoxide 일산화탄소 syngas[síngæs] 합성 가스 filter[fíltər] 여과하다 impurity[impjúərəti] 불순물
catalyst[kǽtəlist] 촉매제 molecule[máləkjùːl] 분자 renewable[rinjúːəbl] 재생 가능한 compatible[kəmpǽtəbl] 호환되는
any time soon 곧장 drawback[drɔ́ːbæ̀k] 문제점

[29-34]
Listen to part of a talk on literature.

Q30 Back in the 20th century—well, that's not so long ago—um, one of the most important reading skills was extensive reading, that is, reading to, uh, determine the overall meaning of a written work. The text was supposed to have a single meaning, or theme, if you will, and the reader's goal was to grasp that one meaning. Well, you and I know that we don't always read to extract the meaning of a text. That's not always our goal. Q29 So what I want to do today is to . . . focus on two aspects of reading, the aesthetic and the functional, and as you might have guessed, these aspects have something to do with what our purpose is when we read literature.

Now, Q31 there's nothing nicer than curling up in an armchair to read a book, right? I hope I'm not speaking for myself. There was a time when the American public was truly a reading public. Well, that's essentially what the aesthetic aspect is. Q31/Q32 People read a book to enjoy it. When you're into what you're reading, you become much more aware of what you're experiencing as you read. The reading event evokes ideas, feelings, associations, memories of perhaps similar experiences . . . the values you have and how these are challenged or, or affirmed by what you're reading.

Q32 Whatever the reader brings to the reading is as important as what is contained in the text. You're exploring the work and yourself.

The functional aspect, on the other hand, is, shall we say, more practical. The objective of the reader is to take away certain pieces of information that can be used . . . that might provide a logical way to solve a problem or answer a question. Uh, let's say you have a pop quiz on history, and you need to know the causes of the American Civil War. Well, you open your textbook to those pages that will give you the information you need. You might underline what those causes are in your textbook. So the difference between this aspect and the aesthetic aspect is, you're not . . . caught up in what you're reading. It's not an emotional or sensational experience for you. Here's a question for you. Q33 Is it possible to read a work of literature having, as your purpose, both aspects? Um, let's look at the children's book *Good-Night, Owl!* by Pat Hutchins. It has a pretty simple plot. During the daytime, the protagonist, an owl, can't sleep because the other animals in the forest are making a real racket. The owl gets so annoyed that when the animals fall asleep at night, it starts screeching so that they wake up and aren't able to get a good night's sleep. If you're reading this book to a group of small children, what might be a good way to turn the event into an aesthetic experience? Q34 Um, you might get the kids to imitate the sounds the animals make. The children can really get into that. Have any of you seen this book? The author uses onomatopoeia to help children pick up the sounds the animals make and how noisy these sounds are, like the "crunch, crunch" of chipmunks eating acorns. Very young children love to imitate sounds like that.

Now, what about the functional? Well, to help children understand the setting of the story, the reader might describe or draw the owl's habitat. That way, the kids can understand how come all these animals live together in one place. Q33 So it's entirely possible, isn't it, to satisfy both aspects when you're reading a work of literature.

Now get ready to answer the questions. You may use your notes to help you answer.

29. What is the lecture mainly about?
30. What does the professor say about extensive reading?
31. Why does the professor mention "curling up in an armchair to read a book"?
32. According to the professor, what are two characteristics of the aesthetic aspect of reading?
33. Why does the professor talk about Pat Hutchins' *Good-Night, Owl!*?

Listen again to part of the lecture. Then answer the question.

P: Um, you might get the kids to imitate the sounds the animals make. The children can really get into that. Have any of you seen this book? The author uses onomatopoeia to help children pick up the sounds the animals make and how noisy these sounds are, like the "crunch, crunch" of chipmunks eating acorns. Very young children love to imitate sounds like that.

34. Why does the professor say this:
P: Have any of you seen this book?

지난 20세기에, 음, 그리 오래되진 않았죠, 음, 가장 중요한 독서 방법 중 하나는 광범위한 독서였어요, 즉, 어, 쓰인 작품의 전반적인 의미를 판단하기 위한 것 말이에요. 글은 하나의 의미, 또는, 말하자면, 주제를 가지도록 되어있었고, 독자의 목표는 그 하나의 의미를 이해하는 것이었죠. 음, 여러분과 저는 우리가 항상 글의 의미를 발췌하기 위해 읽는 건 아니라는 것을 알아요. 그게 항상 우리의 목표인 것은 아니죠. 그래서 오늘 제가 하고 싶은 것은... 독서의 두 가지 측면에 초점을 맞추는 거예요, 심미적이고 기능적으로요, 그리고 여러분이 아마 짐작했듯이, 이러한 측면들은 문학을 읽을 때 우리의 목적이 무엇인가와 관련되어 있습니다.

자, 안락의자에서 책을 읽으려고 웅크리고 앉는 것보다 좋은 건 없어요, 그렇죠? 저만 그렇게 느끼는 게 아니길 바랄게요. 미국 대중이 진정으로 독서하는 대중이었던 적이 있었죠. 음, 이게 기본적으로 심미적인 측면이에요. 사람들은 즐기기 위해 책을 읽어요. 여러분이 읽고 있는 것에 빠져 있을 때, 읽으면서 경험하는 것들에 대해 더 잘 알 수 있게 돼요. 독서라는 일은 생각, 감정, 연관, 아마도 비슷한 경험들의 기억들을 불러일으키죠... 읽고 있는 것에 의해 여러분이 가진 가치관과 그것들이 어떻게 도전을 받는지나, 확신을 받는지도 말이에요. 독자가 독서로 가지고 오는 게 무엇이든 그 글에 담겨있는 것만큼 중요해요. 작품과 자기 자신을 탐구하고 있는 거니까요.

반면, 기능적인 측면은, 더 실용적이라고 말할 수 있어요. 독자의 목적은 사용될 수 있는 특정 정보의 조각들을 가져가는 거예요... 그건 문제를 해결하거나 질문에 답하기 위한 논리적인 방법을 제공할 수도 있죠. 어, 역사 시간에 쪽지 시험이 있고, 여러분은 미국 남북전쟁의 원인을 알 필요가 있다고 합시다. 음, 여러분은 교과서에서 여러분이 필요한 정보를 제공할 페이지를 펴겠죠. 교과서에 있는 그 원인들에 밑줄을 그을 수도 있을 거예요. 그래서 이러한 측면과 심미적인 측면의 차이점은, 여러분이... 읽고 있는 것에 사로잡혀 있지 않다는 거예요. 이건 여러분에게 감정적이거나 감성적인 경험이 아니죠.

여기 질문이 있어요. 여러분의 목적대로, 두 가지 측면을 가지고 하나의 문학 작품을 읽는 것이 가능할까요? 음, 팻 허친스의 어린이 책 'Good-Night, Owl!'을 봅시다. 그것은 꽤 간단한 줄거리를 가지고 있어요. 낮 시간 동안, 주인공인 부엉이는, 숲 속의 다른 동물들이 정말 큰 소음을 만들어서 잘 수가 없어요. 그 부엉이는 너무 화가 나서 밤에 동물들이 잠들었을 때, 그들이 깨어나고 밤잠을 제대로 이룰 수 없게 비명을 지르기 시작합니다. 만약 여러분이 이 책을 어린 아이들 몇 명에게 읽어준다면, 이 일을 심미적인 경험으로 바꿀 수 있는 좋은 방법은 무엇일까요? 음, 여러분은 동물들이 내는 소리를 아이들이 따라하게 할 수도 있겠죠. 어린이들은 그것에 아주 집중할 거예요. 이 책을 본 사람이 있나요? 작가는 의성법을 사용하여 동물들이 내는 소리와 그 소리들이 얼마나 시끄러운지를 어린이들이 이해할 수 있도록 합니다, 도토리를 먹는 줄다람쥐들의 '오도독, 오도독'하는 소리처럼. 매우 어린 아이들은 그런 소리를 따라 하는 것을 아주 좋아하죠.

자, 기능적으로요? 음, 어린이들이 그 이야기의 배경을 이해하는 것을 돕기 위해, 독자는 부엉이의 서식지를 묘사하거나 설명할 수 있어요. 이렇게 함으로써, 아이들은 이 많은 동물들이 어떻게 한 공간에서 같이 살 수 있는지 이해할 수 있겠죠. 그래서 문학 작품을 읽을 때 두 가지 측면을 모두 만족시키는 것은 전적으로 가능한 것입니다.

어휘

extensive[iksténsiv] 광범위한 extract[ikstrǽkt] 발췌하다 aesthetic[esθétik] 심미적인 curl up 웅크리고 앉다
armchair[ɑ́ːrmtʃɛ̀ər] 안락의자 evoke[ivóuk] 불러일으키다 association[əsòusiéiʃən] 연관 affirm[əfə́ːrm] 확신하다
Civil War 남북전쟁 underline[ʌ̀ndərláin] 밑줄을 긋다 protagonist[proutǽgənist] 주인공 racket[rǽkit] 큰 소음
annoyed[ənɔ́id] 화가 난 screech[skriːtʃ] 비명을 지르다 onomatopoeia[ɑ̀nəmæ̀təpíːə] 의성법 pick up 이해하다
crunch[krʌntʃ] 오도독 소리 chipmunk[tʃípmʌŋk] 줄다람쥐 acorn[éikɔːrn] 도토리

* 각 문제에 대한 정답단서는 지문에 보라색으로 표시되어 있습니다.

문제 공략하기 p.145

마리너 10호가 밝혀낸 또 다른 점은 수성이 지구의 자기장보다 약 100배 약한 자기장을 가지고 있다는 것입니다. 흥미로운 점은... 행성이 자기장을 가지려면, 부분적으로 용해된 핵이 있어야 한다는 거예요, 즉, 액화된 금속이나 액화된 암석 말이죠. 고체 핵은 자기장을 만들 수 없거든요. 과학자들은 수성의 핵이 한 때 액화된 철이었지만, 이 모든 몇십억 년 동안 그것이 차가워지고 고체화되었다고 추정했습니다. 하지만, 마리너 10호는 자기장을 탐지해냈죠, 약한 것이기는 했지만요.

HACKERS PRACTICE p.146

1. (C) Main Purpose/Topic   2. (D) Inference   3. (A) Detail
4. (A), (B) Main Purpose/Topic   5. (D) Inference   6. (A) Inference
7. (B) Main Purpose/Topic   8. (C) Inference   9. (D) Connecting Contents II
10. (B) Main Purpose/Topic
11. Connecting Contents I

	Computer Art	Painting
Encourage risk taking	✓	
Uses numerous strokes with a handheld implement		✓
Provides instant results when settings are altered	✓	
Is guided by reflections and emotions.		✓

12. (D) Inference

[1-3]
Listen to a conversation between a teaching assistant and a student.

M: Hi, Ms. Stevens. Is Professor Platt in?

W: Oh, hi, Jeff. No, he's not in right now. I'm afraid you'll have to try back later or make an appointment.

M: I guess it could wait, but ᑫ1 I really need some information about my coursework.

W: Well, I may be able to help you with that. I have all the manuals here . . . and besides, I know quite a bit about the course requirements.

M: Well . . . ᑫ1 I–I've been thinking of taking a marketing class at another university.

W: Doesn't our university offer all the courses that business and marketing majors need?

M: Well, Northwestern University has this really excellent tie-up where business and marketing students have a sort of an internship at Raiders, Inc. It's like an education within an education.

W: Oh, yeah . . . I read about that. It was in a column in the magazine *Business Smart*—how one student had a breakthrough idea that gave him a very lucrative career in marketing. Is that the reason you're interested in taking the marketing course at Northwestern?

M: What? Oh, you mean like . . . having a lucrative career? No, that's not why. I just need hands-on experience in a real business setting.

W: Right. I'm sure you'll have no problem enrolling at Northwestern and taking your other units here. Uh . . . the procedure is actually pretty simple. You need an approval form to take a course at another university. I think you need to include the course description at Northwestern for Professor Platt to make sure that it meets university curriculum requirements.

M: OK, simple enough.

W: ⁰² And after you get Professor Platt's signature, go back to academic affairs for their signature, and then submit the form to the registrar.

M: Well, that's not too bad.

W: One more thing, though. ⁰³ After you complete the course at Northwestern, you'll need to have them send a transcript to our university. That way, you can be sure that the grade for that course will be recorded.

M: OK . . . Thanks for all this information. But actually, I'd still like to see Professor Platt because I want his advice on the matter. So . . . is it possible for me to see him sometime this afternoon?

W: Um . . . he's at a meeting right now and he won't be in for another two hours. He does have a half-hour window starting at 3:30.

M: Great! Could you tell him I'll be dropping in at that time?

W: Sure will, Jeff.

Now get ready to answer the questions. You may use your notes to help you answer.

1. Why does the man go to the professor's office?

Listen again to part of the conversation. Then answer the question.

W: And after you get Professor Platt's signature, go back to academic affairs for their signature, and then submit the form to the registrar.

M: Well, that's not too bad.

2. What does the student imply when he says this:
   M: Well, that's not too bad.

3. What does the woman suggest the man do to get credit for the marketing course?

M: 안녕하세요, Stevens 씨. Platt 교수님 계신가요?

W: 오, 안녕, Jeff. 아니, 지금 안 계신단다. 나중에 다시 오거나 약속을 잡아야 할 것 같구나.

M: 미룰 수 있을 것 같지만, 제 교과 학습에 대한 정보가 정말 필요한데요.

W: 음, 그거라면 내가 도와줄 수도 있을 거야. 여기 모든 안내책자를 가지고 있고... 게다가, 나는 교과 필수 요건에 대해서 꽤 알고 있거든.

M: 음... 저, 저는 다른 대학교에서 마케팅 수업을 듣는 걸 생각해 보고 있었어요.

W: 우리 대학교도 경영과 마케팅 전공자들이 필요로 하는 모든 과목을 제공하고 있지 않니?

M: 음, Northwestern 대학교에는 경영과 마케팅 전공 학생들이 Raiders 주식회사에서 인턴십 같은 것을 할 수 있는 정말 좋은 협력 제도가 있거든요. 교육 내의 교육인 셈이죠.

W: 오, 그래... 나도 그것에 대해 읽었단다. 'Business Smart' 잡지의 기고란에 나왔었어, 한 학생이 마케팅 분야에서 돈을 아주 많이 버는 직업을 얻게 해준 기발한 아이디어를 어떻게 가졌는지에 관한 것이었지. 그게 Northwestern 대학교의 마케팅 수업을 듣는 것에 관심을 갖게 된 이유니?

M: 네? 오, 그 말씀은... 돈을 많이 버는 직업 말씀이세요? 아니요, 그 때문은 아니에요. 저는 그냥 실제 비즈니스 환경에서의 실무 경험이 필요해서요.

W: 그렇구나. Northwestern에 등록하고 다른 수업은 여기서 듣는 건 문제없을 거라고 확신해. 어... 절차도 사실 꽤 간단하지. 다른 대학교 수업을 들을 수 있는 승인서가 필요하단다. 그 수업이 대학교 이수과정 요건을 충족시킨다는 것을 Platt 교수님이 확인하실 수 있도록 Northwestern의 수업 소개서를 포함해야 할 거야.

M: 네, 꽤 간단하네요.

W: 그리고 Platt 교수님의 서명을 받은 후, 교무처에 가서 서명을 받고, 그 다음 학적 담당 사무원에게 그 서류를 제출하면 돼.

M: 음, 일이 많지는 않군요.

W: 하지만, 한 가지가 더 있어. Northwestern에서 수업을 마친 후, 그쪽에서 네 성적 증명서를 우리 대학교로 보내도록 해야 해. 그래야, 그 수업의 성적이 기록되는 것을 확인할 수 있으니까.

M: 알겠습니다... 이 모든 정보를 주셔서 감사해요. 그런데 사실, 이 문제에 대해 Platt 교수님의 조언을 듣고 싶어서 여전히 교수님을 뵙고 싶어요. 그래서... 오늘 오후에 교수님을 뵐 수 있을까요?

W: 음... 지금 회의 중이셔서 2시간 이내에는 안 계실 거야. 교수님은 3시 30분부터 30분 정도 빈 시간이 있으셔.

M: 좋아요! 그 시간에 제가 방문할 거라고 교수께 전해주시겠어요?

W: 물론 그럴게, Jeff.

[4-6]

Listen to a conversation between a professor and a student.

S: Hi, Professor Dupuis. Um, are you busy?

P: Hello, Colin. I've got a few minutes. What do you need?

S: Um, it's about my midterm grade. I got a C, and, well . . . I'm pretty disappointed. To be honest, I was exhausted when I wrote it . . . Uh, I had a lot of exams that week. ^{Q4} I was hoping I could take a, um . . . a makeup test to improve my grade.

P: I'm sorry, but I can't let you take a makeup exam just because you were tired. Um, you should focus on your essay now. If you do well, you can still get a good grade in the class. Have you decided what to write about yet?

S: ^{Q4} Actually, that's another reason I came here today. I wasn't sure what to write about. I was thinking about picking an animal and discussing its, uh . . . its sleeping habits . . . but I wondered if this was too narrow topic . . .

P: I see . . . Um, instead of focusing on a particular species, why don't you choose one of the sleep-wake cycles and, uh, discuss it in detail? Like how some animals are nocturnal . . .

S: Nocturnal? You mean the animals that sleep during the day but are awake at night?

P: Exactly.

S: ^{Q5} Hmm . . . Maybe I could talk about the physical traits of nocturnal animals. Like night vision . . .

P: Well, that's one way to go. But, um, I have a suggestion . . . What about discussing the advantages of being nocturnal?

S: Advantages? Oh, do you mean like avoiding predators? I know that some rodent species are nocturnal because the birds that hunt them are . . . uh, they're more active during the day.

P: Right . . . That's a benefit. But this isn't a perfect strategy. It doesn't necessarily mean that the animal will avoid being attacked. For example, the hawk will occasionally hunt at dusk . . . and this means that it can sometimes . . . you know . . . catch nocturnal rodents out in the open. But this sleeping pattern is still a significant advantage for many prey species.

S: So, predator avoidance . . . Anything else I should consider?

P: ^{Q6} Another thing is many species that live in the desert are nocturnal. They spend the day in underground shelters and come out at night to, um, search for food . . .

S: I get it . . . Being nocturnal is an advantage because it prevents animals from overheating during the day.

P: Well, it's actually more to do with water conservation. [Q6] There is limited water in a desert ecosystem . . . um, much less than in other types. So desert organisms have to take extra care to retain the moisture in their bodies. This won't happen if they're running around in the hot sun.

S: Wow . . . you've given me some great ideas. Thanks!

Now get ready to answer the questions. You may use your notes to help you answer.

4. Why does the student go to see the professor?

Listen again to part of the conversation. Then answer the question.

S: Hmm . . . Maybe I could talk about the physical traits of nocturnal animals. Like night vision . . .
P: Well, that's one way to go. But, um, I have a suggestion . . . What about discussing the advantages of being nocturnal?

5. What can be inferred about the professor when she says this:
   P: Well, that's one way to go. But, um, I have a suggestion . . .

6. What does the professor imply about desert animals?

S: 안녕하세요, Dupuis 교수님. 음, 바쁘신가요?
P: 안녕, Colin. 잠깐 시간이 있단다. 필요한 게 뭐니?
S: 음, 중간고사 성적에 관한 건데요. 저는 C를 받았어요. 그리고, 음... 꽤 실망스럽고요. 솔직히, 시험을 볼 때 정말 지쳐있었거든요... 어, 그 주에 시험이 많았어요. 제 성적을 향상시키기 위해, 음... 재시험을 볼 수 있었으면 했어요.
P: 미안하지만, 단지 네가 피곤했다는 이유로 재시험을 보도록 허락해줄 수는 없단다. 음, 이제는 네 보고서에 집중해야 할 것 같은데. 네가 잘한다면, 이 수업에서 여전히 좋은 점수를 받을 수 있으니까. 무엇에 대해 쓸지 이미 결정했니?
S: 사실, 그게 제가 오늘 여기에 온 또 다른 이유예요. 무엇에 대해 쓸지 확실하지 않았거든요. 동물 하나를 골라서 그것의, 어... 수면 습관을 논할까 생각 중이었어요... 하지만 이게 너무 좁은 주제가 아닌가 해서요...
P: 그렇구나... 음, 특정 종에 초점을 맞추는 대신, 수면 각성 주기 중 하나를 골라서, 어, 그것을 자세히 논하는 건 어떠니? 예를 들면, 몇몇 동물들이 야행성인 것에 관해 말이야...
S: 야행성이요? 낮에는 자고 밤에는 깨어있는 동물들 말씀이세요?
P: 바로 그거야.
S: 흠... 아마도 야행성 동물들의 신체적 특징에 대해 이야기해 볼 수 있겠네요. 야간 시력처럼요...
P: 음, 그것도 하나의 방법이지. 하지만, 음, 제안을 하나 하자면... 야행성인 것의 장점들을 논하는 것이 어떻겠니?
S: 장점들이요? 오, 포식 동물을 피하는 것과 같이 말이요? 저는 몇몇 설치류 종들이 야행성이라는 걸 알아요, 왜냐하면 그들을 사냥하는 새들이... 어, 낮에 더 활동적이니까요.
P: 맞아... 그것은 한 가지 장점이지. 하지만 이게 완벽한 전략은 아니란다. 그게 그 동물이 공격당하는 걸 반드시 피할 거라는 뜻은 아니거든. 예를 들면, 매는 종종 해 질 무렵에 사냥한단다... 그리고 이건 매가 때때로... 그러니까... 야행성인 설치류를 공공연하게 잡을 수 있다는 의미지. 하지만 이 수면 양식은 여전히 많은 피식자 종들에게 엄청난 장점이란다.
S: 그럼, 포식자 회피라는 거죠... 제가 고려해야 할 다른 것이 있을까요?
P: 또 다른 것으로는 사막에 사는 많은 종이 야행성이라는 거야. 그들은 지하에 있는 은신처에서 낮을 보내고 밤에, 음, 음식을 찾기 위해 나온단다...
S: 알겠어요... 야행성인 것은 동물들이 낮 동안 과열되는 것을 방지해주기 때문에 장점이 되는군요.
P: 음, 그것은 사실 수분 보존과 더 관련이 있단다. 사막 생태계에는 물이 한정되어 있지... 음, 다른 종류의 생태계보다 훨씬 적어. 그래서 사막 생물들은 그들 몸속에 있는 수분을 유지하기 위해 특히 더 주의해야만 한단다. 만약 그들이 뜨거운 태양 아래에서 뛰어다닌다면 이렇게 되지 않겠지.
S: 와... 훌륭한 의견들을 몇 가지 주셨네요. 감사합니다!

[7-9]
Listen to part of a lecture in an engineering class.

P: Airplane designs have changed a lot over the past century or so . . . Just compare the Wright brothers' first plane to any modern one. Q7 But all airplanes rely on the same fundamental laws of physics to fly.
There are two forces that must be considered when designing an airplane . . . thrust and lift. The first is a fairly easy concept to grasp. Thrust is what, um . . . what moves the airplane forward through the air . . .

S1: Um, you mean like the propeller or jet of an airplane?

P: Yes . . . those are the parts of a plane that generate thrust. A propeller pulls the plane, while the jet pushes it. The end result is the same, though . . . The plane goes forward. Yes?

S1: Q8 Um, so thrust determines how fast a plane can travel? I guess engine power is the key to designing a fast aircraft, then . . .

P: Actually, it's more about overcoming wind resistance . . . um, the friction created by its movement through the air. So it must be aerodynamic . . . shaped in such a way that it passes through the air easily. Um, think of how a dolphin's sleek form lets it move swiftly through the water . . . It's the same basic idea. Low-powered yet aerodynamic aircraft can move pretty quickly . . . but not the other way around.
OK . . . let's turn to lift. This is what causes a plane to go up. And it is the wings that create lift . . . Here, look at this picture of the cross section of a typical airplane wing. What do you notice about it?

S2: Well, it's got kind of an unusual shape. There's a, um, prominent curve on the top of the wing . . . near the front.

P: Good eye. Q9 This curved shape is called an airfoil . . . and it's responsible for lift. What's interesting is that scientists in the 1800s discovered the airfoil by studying the wings of, um, birds. Um, bird wings have this same feature. So, how does an airfoil work? Well, as the plane moves forward, air passes along the top and bottom of the wing. But the shape of the wing causes the air above it to move more quickly. And the faster air moves, the less pressure it has. The higher pressure air below the wing pushes up into the lower pressure air . . . and this causes the plane to move upwards as well . . .

Now get ready to answer the questions. You may use your notes to help you answer.

7. What is the main topic of the lecture?

Listen again to part of the lecture. Then answer the question.

S1: Um, so thrust determines how fast a plane can travel? I guess engine power is the key to designing a fast aircraft, then . . .

P: Actually, it's more about overcoming wind resistance . . . um, the friction created by its movement through the air.

8. What does the professor imply when he says this:
   P: Actually, it's more about overcoming wind resistance . . .

9. Why does the professor mention birds?

P: 항공기 설계는 지난 100년쯤 동안 상당히 변화해왔어요... 라이트 형제의 첫 번째 항공기를 현대의 그 어느 항공기와 비교해 보세

요. 하지만 모든 항공기는 비행하기 위한 동일하고 기본적인 물리학 법칙에 의존하죠.

항공기를 설계할 때 고려되어야 하는 두 가지 힘이 있습니다... 추진력과 양력이죠. 첫 번째는 상당히 이해하기 쉬운 개념입니다. 추진력은, 음... 항공기가 공기를 뚫고 앞쪽으로 나아가게 하는 것이죠...

S1: 음, 비행기의 추진기나 제트 엔진 같은 것을 의미하시는 건가요?

P: 네... 그것들은 추진력을 발생시키는 항공기의 부품들이죠. 추진기는 항공기를 끌어당기는 반면에, 제트 엔진은 그것을 밀어냅니다. 하지만, 최종 결과는 같아요... 비행기가 전진하는 거죠. 네?

S1: 음, 그러니까 추진력은 항공기가 얼마나 빨리 이동할 수 있는지를 결정하는 거네요? 그렇다면, 엔진 출력은 빠른 항공기를 설계하는 비결이겠고요...

P: 사실, 그건 바람의 저항을 극복하는 것과 더 관련이 있어요. 음, 공기를 통과하는 항공기의 움직임에 의해 생겨나는 마찰 말이에요. 그래서 항공기는 공기 역학적이어야 합니다... 공기를 쉽게 통과하는 방식으로 만들어져야 하죠. 음, 돌고래의 매끈한 형태가 그것을 재빠르게 물을 헤치며 가도록 해주는 것을 생각해 보세요... 같은 기본 개념입니다. 저출력이지만 공기 역학적인 항공기는 상당히 빠르게 움직일 수 있어요... 하지만 그 반대로는 아니죠.

좋아요... 양력으로 넘어갑시다. 이건 항공기가 올라가도록 하는 것이에요. 그리고 양력을 만들어내는 것은 바로 날개죠... 여기, 전형적인 항공기 날개의 단면도 사진을 보세요. 무엇이 눈에 띄나요?

S2: 음, 그건 좀 색다른 모양인 것 같아요. 음, 날개 위에 돌출된 곡선이 있네요... 앞쪽에요.

P: 관찰력이 훌륭하군요. 이 곡선 모양은 익형이라고 불려요... 그리고 그것은 양력을 책임지죠. 흥미로운 것은 1800년대에 과학자들이 새의, 음, 날개를 연구함으로써 익형을 발견했다는 거예요. 음, 새의 날개는 동일한 특징을 가지고 있거든요. 자, 익형이 어떻게 작동할까요? 음, 비행기가 앞으로 나아갈 때, 공기가 날개의 윗면과 아랫면을 따라 지나갑니다. 하지만 이러한 날개 모양은 위에 있는 공기가 더 빠르게 이동하도록 만들어요. 그리고 공기가 더 빠르게 움직일수록, 그것은 더 낮은 압력을 갖게 되죠. 날개 아래에 있는 압력이 더 높은 공기는 압력이 더 낮은 공기를 밀어올려요... 그리고 이게 비행기 또한 위쪽으로 움직이도록 만드는 겁니다.

[10-12]

Listen to part of a lecture on computer art.

Q10 OK, maybe some of you don't think computer art is in the same league as paintings, you know, like those done by Picasso or Van Gogh, but it has come to be accepted as an expression of artistic creativity. Creativity isn't bound by the implements and materials the artist chooses to use. Obviously, the implements used by a painter and a computer artist are different. An easel, a canvas, and pigment media versus a computer, a monitor, a software program, and a printer. I guess there's no mystery as to how each type of artist produces an image, right? Q11 Now, a painting is made up of possibly thousands of strokes. The electronic surface of the computer, on the other hand, consists of millions of small electronic elements called bits. A computer program can set these bits to form various shades, shapes, and visual images. Q11 Different software programs can change the way the bits are set, and the screen of your monitor gives immediate feedback in full color. The nice thing about these computer programs is . . . they can simulate virtually any tool or type of paint available to the painter.

So programming is essentially a logical process that requires a conscious mind. And because a computer artist uses a program to create an image, computer art can be pretty precise. The painter, however, doesn't go by a logical or step-by-step process when he paints. I'm not saying that traditional painting is less logical. Obviously, a thought process is involved in the creation of art. Uh, frankly, a lot more is involved. The work that a painter does is influenced by the art movement or school that he's associated with. Q11 And a lot of the painter's thoughts and feelings go into the work . . . The painter's hand is much less precise than a software program, isn't it? So whatever he's thinking, whatever he's feeling . . . these are the things that influence his art. One other thing . . . Q11 computer art allows the artist to take more risks than the painter. If a painter suddenly has an inspiration or a new idea while he's painting, he might have to start with a fresh canvas to follow up on that idea, wouldn't he? If he used the same canvas, he would risk destroying what has been completed. ^{Q12} Well, with a computer program, the artist need not face the agony of destroying his work. And that's because a digital image can be saved, changed, and transferred without any loss of information.

Now get ready to answer the questions. You may use your notes to help you answer.

10. What is the main purpose of the talk?
11. The professor describes the features of computer art and painting. Indicate for each type the feature that characterizes them.
12. What does the professor imply about an image on a computer screen?

자, 아마도 여러분 중 몇몇은 컴퓨터 미술이, 그러니까, 피카소나 반 고흐에 의한 그림들과 같은 범주라고 생각하지는 않을 겁니다, 그러나 그것은 예술적인 창조성의 한 가지 표현으로 받아들여지고 있어요. 창조성은 화가가 사용하기로 한 도구와 재료에 결속되지 않죠. 분명, 화가와 컴퓨터 미술가에 의해 사용되는 도구는 완전히 다릅니다. 이젤, 캔버스, 그리고 물감 도구에 대비하여 컴퓨터, 모니터, 소프트웨어 프로그램, 그리고 프린터죠. 각 유형의 미술가가 이미지를 만드는 방법에 대해서는 모르는 게 없을 거예요, 그렇죠? 자, 그림은 수천 번의 획으로 만들어지는 것이 가능합니다. 반면에, 컴퓨터의 전자 화면은 비트라고 불리는 수백만 개의 작은 전자 요소로 구성되죠. 컴퓨터 프로그램은 이 비트들이 다양한 명암, 모양, 그리고 시각적 영상을 만들어내도록 배치합니다. 다양한 소프트웨어 프로그램들은 비트가 배치되는 방법을 바꿀 수 있으며, 모니터 스크린은 즉시 완벽한 색상으로 그 결과를 보여줘요. 이러한 컴퓨터 프로그램의 좋은 점은... 화가가 이용할 수 있는 어떠한 도구나 물감의 종류도 모방할 수 있다는 것입니다.
그래서 프로그래밍은 본질적으로 이성이 요구되는 논리적인 과정이죠. 그리고 컴퓨터 미술가는 이미지를 만들기 위해 프로그램을 사용하기 때문에, 컴퓨터 미술은 상당히 정확할 수 있습니다. 그러나, 화가는 그림을 그릴 때 논리적이거나 단계적인 과정을 거치지 않아요. 전통적인 그림이 덜 논리적이라는 말이 아닙니다. 분명, 미술의 창작에는 사고 과정이 수반되어 있으니까요. 어, 사실, 훨씬 더 많은 것이 수반되어 있죠. 화가가 그린 작품은 그와 관련된 미술 운동이나 학파의 영향을 받습니다. 그리고 화가의 많은 생각과 느낌들이 작품에 녹아들죠... 화가의 손은 소프트웨어 프로그램보다 훨씬 덜 정확합니다, 그렇죠? 그래서 그가 생각하거나 느끼는 게 무엇이든지 간에... 그것들이 그의 미술에 영향을 주는 거죠. 또 한 가지는... 컴퓨터 미술은 화가들에게 더 많은 위험을 감수할 수 있게 한다는 것입니다. 만약 화가가 그림을 그리는 동안 갑자기 어떤 영감이나 새로운 생각이 떠올랐다면, 그는 그 생각을 표현하기 위해 새로운 캔버스에 그리기 시작해야만 해요, 그렇겠죠? 만약 같은 캔버스를 사용한다면, 그는 이미 완성해가는 것을 파기해야 하는 위험을 무릅써야 합니다. 음, 컴퓨터 프로그램을 사용하면, 화가는 자신의 작품을 파기하는 데 고통받을 필요가 없죠. 그리고 그건 디지털 이미지가 정보의 손실 없이 저장되고, 변경되고, 전송될 수 있기 때문입니다.

HACKERS TEST

p.150

1. (D) Main Purpose/Topic	2. (B) Inference	3. (B) Function & Attitude
4. (A), (D) Detail	5. (A) Inference	6. (C) Main Purpose/Topic
7. (B) Connecting Contents II	8. (B) Inference	9. (D) Detail
10. (B) Detail	11. (A) Inference	12. (D) Main Purpose/Topic
13. (B) Connecting Contents II	14. (A), (D), (E) Detail	15. (B) Inference
16. (A) Detail	17. (C) Function & Attitude	18. (C) Main Purpose/Topic
19. (D) Inference	20. (C) Inference	21. (C) Detail
22. (B) Connecting Contents II	23. (B) Main Purpose/Topic	24. (A) Detail
25. (D) Function & Attitude	26. (A) Inference	27. (C) Function & Attitude
28. (A) Connecting Contents II	29. (D) Main Purpose/Topic	30. (C) Inference
31. (A) Detail	32. (A), (C) Detail	33. (D) Function & Attitude
34. (A), (D) Detail		

[1-5]

Listen to a conversation between a professor and a student.

S: Hi, Dr. Hanson. Maurice told me you wanted me to drop by your office at this time, is that right?

P: James! Yes, thanks so much for coming. There's something I really wanted to discuss with you.

S: ^{Q2} Is this about my paper, ma'am?

P: As a matter of fact, it is. Don't look so concerned, James. Your writing was wonderful. The content was most interesting . . . racial tensions in the Andalucia region of southern Spain. But what I really wanted to discuss with you was more like . . . about your writing skills.

S: My writing skills?

P: Yes, James. ^{Q1} I really think you should consider joining the writing club—you know, the one established by the English department a couple years ago. Are you . . . do you know about this club?

S: Well, yes, uh . . . I've seen some of their writings in the campus newspaper. The writers are pretty good, although I can't say that I'm really qualified to judge . . . well, I thought they were pretty good.

P: You can write like that too . . . probably even better!

S: Oh, I don't know about that, Dr. Hanson.

P: No, I'm serious, James. Just hear me out. Let me tell you more about this club. It's made up of students who have been recommended by their professors for their exceptional writing abilities.

S: ^{Q3} But I've never actually enrolled in any writing course, so I can't say for sure that I've got what it takes to be a writer. So, uh, does the club hold regular meetings?

P: They get together twice a week in the evenings, uh, in one of the reading rooms at Memorial Library.

S: Well, that's great and everything, but, uh, what exactly do they do at those meetings?

P: OK, well . . . actually, I've never been to one of their meetings, but ^{Q4} I know for a fact that they discuss both old and new pieces of writing.

S: You mean . . . by other writers?

P: Yes, other writers, but also their own writings . . . and ^{Q4} they sponsor occasional lectures by visiting writing professors.

S: Well . . . the club seems to be pretty well established if they've got professors giving lectures. Just how big is the club now?

P: I believe they currently have a membership of . . . uh . . . I think 17 students. And, oh, yes, I wanted to point out that they receive information about upcoming regional and national seminars on writing . . . as well as writing competitions.

S: Writing competitions? Wow . . . that's really . . . interesting.

P: So . . . the club is just basically meant to create an opportunity for talented young writers to grow.

S: ^{Q5} It really sounds exciting, and I'm glad you think I have what it takes to be a good writer . . . but to be honest with you, I've already got my hands full. I'm presently involved in two organizations, the Anti-Prejudice Forum and the student council, and they—they take up all of my free time. And I've got 21 credits this term.

P: All right, I see. I do understand, but if you do find the time, I'd be happy to recommend you. The offer is always open.

S: Thanks, Dr. Hanson. I'll get back to you about it, but right now I've got to run to Spanish 203 . . .

Now, there's a subject I'm far from exceptional in.

Now get ready to answer the questions. You may use your notes to help you answer.

1. What is the main topic of the conversation?

Listen again to part of the conversation. Then answer the question.

S: Is this about my paper, ma'am?
P: As a matter of fact, it is. Don't look so concerned, James. Your writing was wonderful.

2. What does the professor imply when she says this:
   P: Don't look so concerned, James.

3. How does the student feel about becoming a member of the writing club?
4. According to the conversation, what are two activities the members of the writing club do?

Listen again to part of the conversation. Then answer the question.

S: It really sounds exciting, and I'm glad you think I have what it takes to be a good writer . . . but to be honest with you, I've already got my hands full. I'm presently involved in two organizations, the Anti-Prejudice Forum and the student council, and they—they take up all of my free time. And I've got 21 credits this term.

5. What can be inferred about the student?

S: 안녕하세요, Hanson 박사님. Maurice가 박사님께서 제가 이 시간에 사무실에 들르길 바라신다고 알려주었어요, 맞나요?
P: James! 그래, 와줘서 고맙다. 너와 정말 의논하고 싶은 게 있거든.
S: 제 보고서 말인가요, 박사님?
P: 사실은, 그렇단다. 너무 걱정하지 마, James. 네 작문은 훌륭했어. 내용이 가장 흥미로웠지... 남부 스페인 안달루시아 지역의 인종 갈등 말이야. 하지만 내가 정말 의논하고 싶은 것은... 네 작문 솜씨에 대한 것이란다.
S: 제 작문 솜씨요?
P: 그래, James. 난 네가 작문 동아리에 가입하는 걸 정말 고려해봤으면 해, 그러니까, 몇 년 전 영어 학부에서 설립한 것 말이야. 너는... 이 동아리에 대해서 알고 있니?
S: 음, 네, 어... 그들의 글 몇 개를 학교 신문에서 본 적이 있어요. 작가들은 꽤 훌륭했어요, 제가 판단할 자격이 있다고 말할 수는 없겠지만... 음, 그들이 꽤 훌륭하다고 생각했어요.
P: 너 역시 그렇게 쓸 수 있어... 아마 더 잘 쓸 수도 있을 거야!
S: 오, 그건 잘 모르겠어요, Hanson 박사님.
P: 아니야, 진심이란다, James. 내 말을 들어 보렴. 이 동아리에 대해 더 이야기해줄게. 그건 뛰어난 작문 실력으로 교수들에게 추천받은 학생들로 구성되어 있어.
S: 하지만 전 실제로 어떤 작문 수업도 수강한 적이 없어서, 제가 작가가 되기 위해 필요한 것을 가지고 있다고 확실하게 말할 수 없어요. 그래서, 어, 그 동아리는 정기적인 모임을 갖나요?
P: Memorial 도서관의 열람실 중 한 곳에서, 어, 일주일에 두 번씩 저녁에 모인단다.
S: 음, 그것과 모든 게 괜찮네요, 그렇지만, 어, 그 모임에서 정확히 무엇을 하나요?
P: 그래, 음... 사실, 내가 그 모임에 참석해 본 적은 없지만, 그들이 예전의 글과 새로운 글에 대해 토론한다는 사실은 알고 있어.
S: 그러니까... 다른 작가의 글 말인가요?
P: 그래, 다른 작가의 글, 하지만 그들 스스로의 글에 대해서도 말이야... 그리고 때때로 방문하는 작문 교수님들의 강의를 후원하지.
S: 음... 교수님들의 강의를 듣는다면 그 동아리는 꽤 잘 설립된 것 같은데요. 현재 그 동아리는 규모가 어떤가요?
P: 현재... 어... 17명의 회원이 있다고 알고 있단다. 그리고, 오, 맞아, 그들은 작문 대회뿐만 아니라... 다가오는 지역적이고 전국적인 작문 세미나에 대한 정보 또한 받고 있다는 것을 언급하고 싶구나.

S: 작문 대회요? 와... 그건 정말... 흥미롭네요.

P: 그래서... 그 동아리는 기본적으로 재능있는 젊은 작가들이 성장할 기회를 주는 것에 의미를 두고 있어.

S: 정말 흥미롭게 들리네요, 그리고 박사님께서 제가 좋은 작가가 되기 위해 필요한 것을 가지고 있다고 생각해주셔서 기뻐요... 하지만 솔직히, 전 이미 할 일이 너무 많아요. 현재 두 개의 모임에 가입되어 있는데, 편견에 반대하는 공개 토론회와 학생회요, 그리고 그, 그 모임들은 제 자유시간을 모두 차지하고요. 또 저는 이번 학기에 21학점이나 듣고 있어요.

P: 그래, 알겠다. 이해하지만, 시간을 낼 수 있다면, 너를 추천하고 싶구나. 내 제안은 항상 유효하단다.

S: 감사합니다, Hanson 박사님. 다시 논의하러 오겠습니다만, 지금은 스페인어 203 수업으로 달려가야 해요... 저, 뛰어난 것과는 거리가 먼 과목이죠.

어휘

as a matter of fact 사실은 racial[réiʃəl] 인종의 qualified[kwáləfàid] 자격이 있는 exceptional[iksépʃənl] 뛰어난
reading room 열람실 membership[mémbərʃìp] 회원 point out 언급하다 upcoming[ʌ́pkʌ̀miŋ] 다가오는
regional[rí:dʒənl] 지역적인 prejudice[prédʒudis] 편견 forum[fɔ́ːrəm] 공개 토론회 student council 학생회
take up 차지하다

[6-11]

Listen to part of a lecture on environmental science. The professor is discussing introduced species.

P: I guess it's time. Let's get started. We're going to talk a bit about introduced species. You know, this is actually an important issue in many areas of the world. Um . . . can anyone tell me what an introduced species is?

S: Is it a species that has been, uh . . . released into an area by humans?

P: Uh . . . sometimes . . . but not necessarily. The term "introduced species" is simply used to refer to any non-native species that, well . . . that enters an ecosystem. [Q7] OK, they can be brought in by people and by the forces of nature, like the wind. Introduced species are also known as exotic species, naturalized species, or . . . if they've become pests, they're called invasive species. [Q6] Today, we are going to examine the impact that an introduced plant species has had on an ecosystem.

Actually, it's very common for people in the United States to import plants from other continents. This is because the local plants are often not considered decorative enough. So plants from other regions are brought in . . . and sometimes they have problems adjusting. They may require more water than is available, for example. However, they often prosper too well, resulting in a negative effect on native species.

One such plant is the Russian olive, which was introduced to central and western United States in the 19th century as an ornamental. Let me describe this plant to you. It's a perennial shrub, meaning it has a life cycle of two or more years. It's a very attractive plant with thick silvery foliage. And people like the plant because it's dense, so it's ideal for use as a hedge. The plant was well suited to the climate, and it thrived and soon became a common addition to many people's lawns. [Q8] As with all exotic species, as long as the Russian olive was confined to areas of human habitation, it posed no threat to the surrounding ecosystem. The problem is, the fruit of this tree proved, well . . . popular with many birds, resulting in its seeds being deposited into the wild.

This proved to be a disaster because this plant is able to outcompete the native species. It consumes a high proportion of the available groundwater, which leaves little of this resource for other plants. [Q9] In addition, the dense shade produced by the Russian olive's foliage makes it almost impossible for the saplings of other trees to mature. As the Russian olive is able to grow in almost any type of soil, it spreads rapidly. [Q10] In fact, the only natural restriction on its potential habitat is a need for a lot of sunshine, which has led to its invading the southwestern portion of the country.

Q11 So . . . although introduced plants are often visually appealing, they usually negatively impact the ecosystem. That is why many environmental groups are now trying to discourage this practice by promoting native species as symbols of their respective regions. Whether this will succeed remains to be seen.

Now get ready to answer the questions. You may use your notes to help you answer.

6. What is the main topic of this lecture?
7. Why does the professor mention the wind?
8. What can be inferred about introduced plants?
9. According to the professor, what is one negative effect of the dense shade produced by the Russian olive?
10. According to the professor, what is a reason the Russian olive grows well in the southwestern United States?

Listen again to part of the lecture. Then answer the question.

P: So . . . although introduced plants are often visually appealing, they usually negatively impact the ecosystem. That is why many environmental groups are now trying to discourage this practice by promoting native species as symbols of their respective regions. Whether this will succeed remains to be seen.

11. What can be inferred about the professor?

P: 시간이 된 것 같군요. 시작해 봅시다. 우리는 도입종에 대해 잠시 이야기할 거예요. 그러니까, 이것은 사실 세계의 많은 지역에서 중요한 문제입니다. 음... 도입종이 무엇인지 누가 말해 볼 수 있나요?

S: 사람에 의해서 어떤 지역으로 풀어진, 어... 종들 아닌가요?

P: 어... 때때로는요... 하지만 꼭 그렇진 않아요. '도입종'이라는 용어는 단순히 그 지역 태생이 아닌, 음... 한 생태계로 유입된 종을 가리키는 데 쓰입니다. 자, 그것들은 사람에 의해 유입되기도 하고 바람과 같은, 자연의 힘에 의해 유입되기도 합니다. 도입종은 외래종, 귀화종이라고도 알려졌고, 또... 만약 그것들이 해충이 되면, 침입종이라고도 불려요. 오늘은, 식물 도입종들이 한 생태계에 미치는 영향에 대해 알아보도록 하겠습니다.

사실, 미국 사람들에게는 다른 대륙으로부터 식물을 수입하는 것이 매우 흔한 일입니다. 현지 식물들은 보통 충분히 장식적이라고 생각되지 않기 때문이죠. 그래서 다른 지역의 식물들을 들여오고... 때때로 그것들은 적응하는 데 어려움을 겪기도 해요. 예를 들면, 그것들은 구할 수 있는 것보다 더 많은 물을 필요로 할 수도 있죠. 하지만, 또한 종종 너무 잘 자라서, 토착종들에게 부정적인 영향을 끼치기도 합니다.

그러한 한 가지 식물은 러시안 올리브로, 19세기 미국 중서부에 장식용 식물로 소개되었습니다. 이 식물을 설명해 볼게요. 그것은 다년생 관목인데, 이는 그것이 2년 이상의 생명 주기를 가지고 있다는 뜻입니다. 그것은 두꺼운 은색의 잎을 가진 아주 매력적인 식물이죠. 그리고 사람들은 그것이 울창해서, 울타리로 사용하는 데 적합하기 때문에 좋아합니다. 이 식물은 기후에 잘 적응했고, 잘 자라서 곧 많은 사람들이 정원에 흔히 추가하는 것이 되었습니다. 모든 외래종과 마찬가지로, 러시안 올리브는 인간의 주거지역에 갇혀 있는 한, 주변 생태계에 위협을 가하지 않아요. 문제는, 이 나무의 열매가, 음... 많은 새들에게 인기가 있어서, 씨앗들이 야생에 놓이게 되었다는 점입니다.

이 식물이 토착종을 능가할 수 있기 때문에 재앙이 된다는 거예요. 그것이 이용 가능한 지하수의 많은 부분을 소비해버리자, 다른 식물들을 위한 이 자원이 거의 남아 있지 않게 되었거든요. 게다가, 러시안 올리브의 잎으로 만들어진 빽빽한 그늘은 다른 나무들의 묘목들이 성장하는 것을 거의 불가능하게 만들었죠. 러시안 올리브는 거의 모든 종류의 토양에서 자랄 수 있기 때문에, 급속하게 퍼져나가요. 사실, 그것의 잠재적 서식지에 대한 유일한 자연적 제한은 많은 햇빛이 필요하다는 것뿐이고, 이는 그것이 미국 남서부 지역에 침입하는 것으로 이어졌습니다.

그래서... 도입종들은 종종 보기에는 매력적이어도, 생태계에 보통 부정적으로 영향을 끼쳐요. 이게 바로 현재 많은 환경 단체들이 토착종을 각 지역의 상징으로 장려함으로써 이런 관행을 단념시키려고 하는 이유죠. 이게 성공할지 아닐지는 지켜봐야겠지만요.

어휘

introduced species 도입종   exotic[igzátik] 외래의   naturalize[nǽtʃərəlàiz] 귀화시키다   pest[pest] 해충
invasive[invéisiv] 침입하는   decorative[dékərətiv] 장식적인   prosper[práspər] 잘 자라다
ornamental[ɔ̀ːrnəméntl] 장식용 식물   perennial[pəréniəl] 다년생의   shrub[ʃrʌb] 관목   foliage[fóuliidʒ] 잎
dense[dens] 울창한, 빽빽한   hedge[hedʒ] 울타리   thrive[θraiv] 잘 자라다   habitation[hæ̀bitéiʃən] 주거지
deposit[dipázit] 놓다   disaster[dizǽstər] 재앙   outcompete[àutkəmpíːt] 능가하다   sapling[sǽpliŋ] 묘목
mature[mətʃúər] 성장하다   restriction[ristríkʃən] 제한   discourage[diskə́ːridʒ] 단념시키다   respective[rispéktiv] 각각의

[12-17]
Listen to part of a lecture in a music class.

P: It seems like all forms of modern music include sounds that are produced electronically.
Q12 However, it's important to note that electronic music is also a distinct art form. And one of
the most popular genres of this type of music is electronica . . .
So, what is electronica? Well, this term started being used in the 1990s to refer to the various
styles of electronic music that were becoming popular . . . such as, um, techno music and
house music. Uh, do you have a question?

S1: Um, I just wanted to clarify something. Are you saying that electronica is, uh . . . dance music?

P: That's part of it . . . Q13 but electronica also includes music that is, well . . . that's not really
suitable for dancing. For example, one subgenre is ambient music. Uh, this is electronic music
that is intended to, you know . . . to function almost as background music. It doesn't have
catchy rhythms or melodies . . .
Anyway, in the late 1980s and early 90s, electronica was, um . . . it was an underground art
form. It was rarely played on the radio or in major performance venues. Some critics even
claimed that it wasn't really music . . .

S1: Uh, that seems like kind of an extreme position . . . Why did they feel that way?

P: That's a good question . . . Q14 The main issue was that electronica breaks many of the rules
regarding song structure . . . um, basic elements such as verses and choruses are missing, for
example. In addition, it isn't created by musicians who play conventional instruments. And, of
course, electronica often involves sampling . . . Um, small sections of other songs are included
in a piece. These critics found electronica confusing and so . . . they didn't know how to react
to it. It didn't match their expectations about how music should sound.
Q15 But this is actually what appealed to the early fans of the genre. Electronica was an entirely
new form of music. It was all about creating unique sounds and audio effects. And these were
combined in unusual ways to, um . . . to arouse emotional and even physical responses in
listeners. To do this, artists took full advantage of new music technologies. One of the most
important was the synthesizer . . . Um, is everyone familiar with this instrument?

S2: It's sort of like an electronic piano, right?

P: Well, they're similar in appearance . . . Both have keyboards. Q16 But a synthesizer produces a
much wider range of sounds. It can convincingly imitate other instruments . . . or create totally
new sounds. This is why it was so vital to early electronica artists. Another important
technological development involved the editing of sounds. Um, there were computer
programs that allowed musicians to manipulate recorded sounds . . . this enabled them to
create very distinctive music.
Now, by the late 90s, electronica had entered the mainstream. And it had a significant impact

on other forms of music. Major pop stars began incorporating electronica into their songs, and, after a while . . . other musical combinations started appearing . . . and they were somewhat surprising. I mean, even punk music showed signs of being influenced by electronica. In fact, electronica became so popular that it was even used in commercials . . . a practice that continues today.

S2: That's true . . . It seems like every time I see a car commercial on TV, there's . . . um, there's some sort of upbeat electronic music playing in the background.

P: Right. And it makes sense when you think about it . . . ^{Q17} On the one hand, electronica is associated with youth and energy. On the other, there is nothing controversial about it . . . um, no chance of inappropriate lyrics or anything in a commercial. Why wouldn't an advertiser use it?

Now get ready to answer the questions. You may use your notes to help you answer.

12. What is the main topic of the lecture?
13. Why does the professor mention ambient music?
14. Why did some critics claim that electronica was not real music?
15. What does the professor imply about early fans of electronica?
16. Why was the synthesizer important to the development of electronic music?

Listen again to part of the lecture. Then answer the question.

P: On the one hand, electronica is associated with youth and energy. On the other, there is nothing controversial about it . . . um, no chance of inappropriate lyrics or anything in a commercial. Why wouldn't an advertiser use it?

17. What does the professor mean when he says this:
    P: Why wouldn't an advertiser use it?

P: 모든 형태의 현대 음악이 전자적으로 만들어지는 소리를 포함하는 것처럼 보여요. 하지만, 전자 음악 또한 별개의 예술 형태라는 것에 주목하는 것이 중요합니다. 그리고 이러한 종류의 음악에서 가장 인기 있는 장르 중 하나가 일렉트로니카죠...
    자, 일렉트로니카란 뭘까요? 음, 이 용어는 1990년대에 인기 있어진 다양한 양식의 전자 음악을 지칭하는 데 사용되기 시작했습니다... 예를 들어, 음, 테크노 음악과 하우스 음악 같은 것 말이에요. 어, 질문이 있나요?

S1: 음, 좀 분명하게 하고 싶은 게 있어요. 교수님께서는 일렉트로니카가, 어... 댄스 음악이라고 말씀하시는 건가요?

P: 그건 일렉트로니카의 일부죠... 하지만 일렉트로니카는 또한, 음... 사실 춤에는 어울리지 않는 음악을 포함하기도 해요. 예를 들어, 하나의 하위 장르는 환경 음악입니다. 어, 이것은, 그러니까... 대부분 배경 음악의 기능을 하도록 의도된 전자 음악이에요. 그것은 기억하기 쉬운 리듬이나 멜로디를 가지고 있지 않거든요...
    어쨌든, 1980년대 후반과 90년대 초반에, 일렉트로니카는, 음... 비전통적인 예술 형태였어요. 그것은 좀처럼 라디오나 주요 공연 장소에서 연주되지 않았죠. 심지어 일부 비평가들은 그건 진짜 음악이 아니라고 주장했어요...

S1: 어, 그건 좀 극단적인 태도처럼 보이는데요... 그들이 왜 그렇게 생각했죠?

P: 주된 문제는 일렉트로니카가 노래의 구조에 관한 많은 규칙을 어겼다는 거였어요... 음, 예를 들어, 절과 후렴 같은 기본적인 요소들이 빠져있죠. 게다가, 그건 전통적인 악기를 연주하는 음악가들에 의해 만들어지지 않아요. 그리고, 물론, 일렉트로니카는 보통 샘플링을 포함해요... 음, 다른 노래의 일부분이 작품에 포함되는 것 말이죠. 이 비평가들은 일렉트로니카가 혼잡하다고 생각해서... 그것에 어떻게 반응해야 할지 몰랐던 거예요. 그것은 음악이 어떻게 들려야 하는지에 대한 그들의 기대에 부응하지 않았으니까요.
    하지만 사실 이게 바로 이 장르의 초기 지지자들의 마음에 들었던 것이었습니다. 일렉트로니카는 완전히 새로운 형태의 음악이었죠. 독특한 소리와 음향 효과를 만들어내는 것에 관한 모든 것이었어요. 그리고 이것들은, 음... 듣는 사람들에게서 감정적이고 심지어 신체적인 반응을 불러일으키는 특이한 방식으로 결합됐어요. 이를 위해, 예술가들은 새로운 음악 기술을 충분히 이용했습니다. 가장 중요한 것 중 하나는 전자 음향 합성 장치였어요... 음, 모두들 이 악기에 익숙한가요?

S2: 그건 뭐랄까 전자 피아노 같은 거잖아요, 맞죠?

P: 음, 보기에는 비슷하죠... 둘 다 건반을 가지고 있으니까요. 하지만 전자 음향 합성 장치는 훨씬 폭넓은 범위의 소리를 만들어냅니다. 그것은 다른 악기들을 그럴듯하게 흉내 내고... 혹은 완전히 새로운 소리를 만들어낼 수 있죠. 이것이 바로 초기 일렉트로니카 예술가들에게 그게 정말 필수적이었던 이유예요. 또 다른 중요한 기술적 발달은 소리의 편집을 포함했어요. 음, 음악가들이 녹음된 소리를 조작할 수 있게 해준 컴퓨터 프로그램이 있었죠... 이는 그들이 매우 독특한 음악을 만들 수 있도록 해줬고요.

자, 90년대 후반 쯤, 일렉트로니카는 주류에 들어갔어요. 그리고 다른 형태의 음악에 커다란 영향을 끼쳤죠. 일류 팝 스타들은 일렉트로니카를 그들의 노래에 포함하기 시작했어요, 그리고, 얼마 후에... 다른 음악적 조합들이 등장하기 시작했죠... 그리고 그것들은 다소 놀라웠습니다. 제 말은, 펑크 음악마저도 일렉트로니카의 영향을 받고 있는 조짐을 보였거든요. 사실, 일렉트로니카는 정말로 인기 있어서 광고에도 사용됐어요... 오늘날에도 계속되고 있는 관행이죠.

S2: 맞아요... TV에서 자동차 광고를 볼 때마다... 음, 배경에 연주되는 어떤 활기찬 전자 음악이 있는 것처럼 보여요.

P: 그래요. 그리고 생각해 보면 이해가 갈 거예요... 한편으로, 일렉트로니카는 젊음과 활기에 관계가 있어요. 반면에, 그것에는 논란의 여지가 되는 게 아무것도 없죠... 음, 광고에 어울리지 않는 가사나 뭐 그런 것이 있을 리가 없어요. 광고주가 왜 그것을 사용하지 않으려고 하겠어요?

어휘

electronically[ilektránikəli] 전자적으로 subgenre[sʌ́bʒàːnrə] 하위 장르 ambient music 환경 음악
catchy[kǽtʃi] 기억하기 쉬운 underground[ʌ́ndərgràund] 비전통적인 venue[vénjuː] 장소 position[pəzíʃən] 태도
verse[vəːrs] 절 chorus[kɔ́ːrəs] 후렴 conventional[kənvénʃənl] 전통적인 piece[piːs] (음악 등의) 작품
synthesizer[sínθəsàizər] 전자 음향 합성 장치 convincingly[kənvínsiŋli] 그럴듯하게 manipulate[mənípjulèit] 조작하다
mainstream[méinstriːm] 주류 incorporate[inkɔ́ːrpərèit] 포함하다 commercial[kəmə́ːrʃəl] 광고
controversial[kàntrəvə́ːrʃəl] 논란의 여지가 있는

[18-22]

Listen to a conversation between a professor and a student.

S: Excuse me, professor? You wanted to see me?

P: Ah, Laurie! Yes, come in. I wanted to speak to you. You see, Q19 I think you give very detailed answers during class when I ask you specific questions, and . . . you've been doing fairly well on your assignments. Q18/Q19 But why aren't you participating more actively in my American literature seminar? You know, your participation affects your final grade.

S: Um, to be honest, Professor . . . it's my first time taking a seminar like this . . . so I'm not really used to this style of class . . . I'm more used to classes with, you know, hundreds of students listening to the teacher . . . And it's easy for me to answer questions when it's just facts, but giving my opinion is something different entirely.

P: Q18 Well, I'd rather hear you say something—anything—instead of just sitting back and letting everyone else talk. Anyway, I'm sure you have opinions on the topics we discuss. Don't you ever feel like contributing to the discussions?

S: I don't know, I—I guess other students have more background in this subject . . . they can give better answers than I can. And, uh . . . I'm actually majoring in mathematics. Math problems always have one correct answer, you know? It's comforting to me. Q20 But literature? It's not like that . . . I mean, it seems so subjective . . . you know, how every person has a different perspective and so there's no real agreement about anything . . . And like I said, it's hard when you don't have background in a subject.

P: Hmm . . . I understand where you're coming from, but you have to realize . . . well, just because other students have more background knowledge than you, it doesn't necessarily mean they will be correct or have a more valid point of view. Q21 The whole point of the seminar is the students learn and benefit from each other. So I'd like you to actively take part in my seminar from now on. You want to do well in my class, don't you?

S: Yes, I do.

P: And I think you find the subject itself interesting too, right? Otherwise you wouldn't have signed up in the first place . . . or you would have dropped the course a long time ago.

S: That's true . . . I do enjoy the stuff we're reading and discussing. I mean, I don't know that much about literature, but I want to learn to appreciate it.

P: Here, let me give you a quick example. You remember last week's seminar when I finished talking about different movements that emerged through American literature?

S: I think so . . . you mentioned Realism and Naturalism . . .

P: That's right. Well, I was going to continue discussing them next class . . . Q22 As I said, although the Realists and the Naturalists had the same goal . . . describing things objectively rather than idealizing them like the Romanticists did . . . they achieved it in slightly different ways. Did you notice any differences between the two readings I assigned?

S: Oh, sure. The Naturalist writer seemed to be less sympathetic towards human beings than the Realist one . . .

P: Yes, that's an excellent point! See? This is exactly what you should bring to the seminar!

S: I'll try, professor. Hopefully I—I won't freeze up.

Now get ready to answer the questions. You may use your notes to help you answer.

18. Why does the professor want to see the student?
19. What does the professor imply about the student's performance in his literature class?
20. What does the student imply about literature?
21. According to the professor, what is the objective of the seminar?
22. Why does the professor discuss Realism and Naturalism?

S: 실례합니다, 교수님? 저를 보자고 하셨나요?

P: 아, Laurie! 그래, 들어오렴. 너와 이야기하고 싶었단다. 그러니까, 수업 시간에 내가 너에게 구체적인 질문을 할 때 너는 상당히 상세한 답변을 한다고 생각해. 그리고... 과제도 꽤 잘하고 있어. 그런데 왜 내 미국 문학 세미나에 더 적극적으로 참여하지 않는 거니? 그러니까, 너의 참여도는 네 최종 성적에 영향을 준단다.

S: 음, 솔직히, 교수님... 저는 이런 세미나를 듣는 게 처음이에요... 그래서 사실 이런 형식의 수업에 익숙하지 않아요... 저는, 그러니까, 몇백 명의 학생들이 선생님의 수업을 듣는 것에 더 익숙하거든요... 그리고 저는 정확한 사실에 대한 질문에는 답하기 쉽지만, 제 의견을 제시하는 건 완전히 다른 것이에요.

P: 음, 나는 네가 무언가 말하는 것을 좀 듣고 싶단다, 어떤 것이든지 말이야, 그냥 뒤에 앉아서 다른 모든 학생이 말하도록 놔두는 대신 말이지. 어쨌든, 우리가 토론하는 주제에 대한 견해가 있으리라 생각하는데. 토론에서 의견을 말하고 싶은 기분이 들 때는 없니?

S: 모르겠어요, 저, 저는 다른 학생들이 이 과목에 대해 더 많은 배경 지식을 가지고 있다고 생각하거든요... 그들은 저보다 더 나은 답변을 할 수 있어요. 그리고, 어... 저는 사실 수학을 전공하고 있어요. 그러니까, 수학 문제는 항상 하나의 정확한 답을 가지고 있잖아요? 저에게는 그게 편해요. 하지만 문학이요? 그렇지 않아요... 제 말은, 그건 너무 주관적인 것 같아요... 그러니까, 정말 모든 사람이 각기 다른 관점을 가지고 있어서 무언가에 대한 진정한 합의는 없어요... 그리고 제가 말씀드린 것처럼, 과목에 대한 배경 지식이 없으면 어렵고요.

P: 흠... 어디서 기인한 건지는 알겠다, 하지만 깨달아야 해... 음, 단지 다른 학생들이 너보다 더 많은 배경 지식을 가지고 있다고 해서, 반드시 그들이 맞다거나 더 타당한 관점을 가지고 있다는 걸 의미하는 것은 아니란다. 세미나의 중요한 핵심은 학생들이 서로에게 배우고 이득을 얻는다는 점이니까. 그래서 난 네가 이제부터 세미나에 활발하게 참여했으면 해. 내 수업에서 좋은 성적을 얻고 싶잖아, 그렇지 않니?

S: 네, 그래요.

P: 그리고 내 생각에는 네가 이 과목 자체에 흥미를 느끼고 있는 것도 같은데, 맞지? 그게 아니라면 애초에 등록하지도 않았을 테니까... 아니면 오래 전에 이 수업을 취소했겠지.

S: 사실이에요... 우리가 읽고 토론하는 내용은 즐기고 있어요. 제 말은, 제가 문학에 대해 그리 많이 알지는 못하지만, 그것을 어떻게

감상하는지를 배우고 싶거든요.

P: 여기, 짧은 예를 들어 볼게. 지난주 세미나에서 미국 문학을 통해 나타난 다양한 운동들에 관한 이야기를 끝냈던 거 기억하니?

S: 그런 것 같아요... 교수님께서는 사실주의와 자연주의를 언급하셨죠...

P: 맞아. 음, 나는 다음 수업에서도 그것들을 계속 논의하려고 했는데... 내가 말했듯이, 비록 사실주의 작가들과 자연주의 작가들은... 낭만주의 작가들처럼 대상을 이상화하지 않고 객관적으로 묘사하려는 같은 목적을 가졌지만... 그들은 그것을 약간 다른 방식으로 이뤄냈다. 내가 과제로 내준 두 개의 읽기 자료에 어떤 차이점이 있다는 것을 알아챘니?

S: 오, 그럼요. 자연주의 작가는 사실주의 작가보다 인간에 대해 덜 동정적인 것처럼 보여요.

P: 그래, 정말 좋은 지적이야! 알겠지? 이게 정확히 네가 세미나로 가져와야 하는 거야!

S: 노력해 볼게요, 교수님. 제, 제가 얼어붙지 않길 바랄게요.

어휘

specific[spisífik] 구체적인   contribute[kəntríbjuːt] 의견을 말하다   major in ~을 전공하다   comforting[kʌ́mfərtiŋ] 편한
subjective[səbdʒéktiv] 주관적인   perspective[pərspéktiv] 관점   valid[vǽlid] 타당한   benefit[bénəfit] 이득을 얻다
appreciate[əpríːʃièit] 감상하다   objectively[əbdʒéktivli] 객관적으로   idealize[aidíːəlàiz] 이상화하다
sympathetic[sìmpəθétik] 동정적인   freeze up 얼어붙다

[23-28]
Listen to part of a lecture on biology.

If I asked you what sets humans apart from the rest of creation, what would you say? Um, probably something about complex communication, right? We know that primates, birds, and dolphins can also communicate on a basic level, but did you know that other life forms—like plants, and even bacteria—can communicate as well? Q23 So what I want to talk about today is bacteria communication.

You'll all be interested to know that it was actually a student who was the first to realize this. Back in the 60s, a microbiologist and one of his students were studying these bacteria called *Vibrio fischeri* . . . um . . . if you've ever been in a tropical ocean at night and seen luminescence in the water, then you've seen *Vibrio fischeri* . . . they're able to light themselves up. Q24 The student . . . Ken Nealson was his name . . . did his own research and determined that the bacteria only light up once their local population has reached a certain size.

Q24/Q25 What happens is something called quorum sensing. Um . . . a quorum is the number of people you need at a meeting to take a vote. So each of these little individual bacteria sends out a signal—a special molecule called an autoinducer—to sort of say, "Hello, I'm here!" If enough bacteria are gathered in one place saying, "I'm here!" and there are lots of these autoinducer molecules swimming around, eventually, by detecting these autoinducers, the bacteria can work together to trigger a certain phenomenon.

Q26 Now, *Vibrio fischeri*, the bioluminescent bacteria I mentioned earlier, don't make any light until they have detected a large enough number of other bacteria through quorum sensing. Why waste the energy? But suddenly, when enough bacteria are present, all of them will light up together.

As another example, let's talk about the bacteria that make us sick. If there were just a few of them releasing toxins, your immune system would wipe them out, just like that. But now, if there were thousands, or even millions, of these bacteria all ganging up together . . . waiting, quorum sensing, and spitting out their autoinducers . . . Q27 then, bam! They detect enough autoinducers and all decide to release their toxins at once. Your immune system is overwhelmed . . . it can't immediately fight back against so many toxins . . . so you get an infection that takes several days to go away. You can see why quorum sensing is effective, right?

Nealson's research didn't really have much credibility until about 10 years ago, so this is a very new field of study. Scientists still don't know how some bacteria are able to light up or how many bacteria, exactly, are needed to make a quorum that triggers an event. But now that we've found out how important this bacterial communication is in causing sicknesses and infections, it's being studied in much more detail. ^{Q28} If there's some way we can block this quorum sensing from happening . . . and you know, there are certain species of bacteria that can actually do this . . . kind of like microscopic computer hacking . . . if we can learn how to hack the bacteria communication system, then we can prevent lots of medical conditions. As you can imagine, medical research departments are starting to devote significant resources to this goal.

Now get ready to answer the questions. You may use your notes to help you answer.

23. What does the professor mainly discuss?
24. What does the professor say about Ken Nealson?

Listen again to part of the lecture. Then answer the question.

P: What happens is something called quorum sensing. Um . . . a quorum is the number of people you need at a meeting to take a vote. So each of these little individual bacteria sends out a signal—a special molecule called an autoinducer—to sort of say, "Hello, I'm here!"

25. Why does the professor say this:
    P: Um . . . a quorum is the number of people you need at a meeting to take a vote.

Listen again to part of the lecture. Then answer the question.

P: Now, *Vibrio fischeri*, the bioluminescent bacteria I mentioned earlier, don't make any light until they have detected a large enough number of other bacteria through quorum sensing. Why waste the energy? But suddenly, when enough bacteria are present, all of them will light up together.

26. What does the professor imply when he says this:
    P: Why waste the energy?

Listen again to part of the lecture. Then answer the question.

P: . . . then, bam! They detect enough autoinducers and all decide to release their toxins at once. Your immune system is overwhelmed . . . it can't immediately fight back against so many toxins . . . so you get an infection that takes several days to go away. You can see why quorum sensing is effective, right?

27. What does the professor mean when he says this:
    P: You can see why quorum sensing is effective, right?

28. Why does the professor mention computer hacking?

제가 인간을 나머지 생물들과 구별하는 것이 무엇이냐고 묻는다면, 여러분은 뭐라고 말할 건가요? 음, 아마도 복잡한 의사소통에 관한 무언가일 거예요, 그렇죠? 영장류, 조류, 그리고 돌고래 또한 기본적인 수준에서는 의사소통할 수 있지만, 다른 생명체들, 식물과 심지어 박테리아도 의사소통할 수 있다는 것을 알고 있었나요? 그래서 오늘 제가 이야기하고 싶은 것은 박테리아의 의사소통입니다. 이것을 처음 알아낸 사람이 사실 학생이었다는 것을 알면 여러분 모두 흥미로워하겠죠. 60년대로 돌아가서, 한 미생물학자와 그의 학생 중 한 명이 '비브리오 피셔리'라고 불리는 박테리아를 연구하고 있었어요... 음... 여러분이 열대 지방의 바다에 가서 밤에 물속에서의 발광을 본 적이 있다면, '비브리오 피셔리'를 본 거예요... 그들은 스스로 빛을 낼 수 있거든요. 그 학생은... 이름이 켄 닐슨인데... 스스로 연구해서 그 박테리아의 지역 개체 수가 특정 크기에 도달했을 때만 빛을 낸다는 것을 알아냈어요.

이는 정족수 인식이라고 불리는 것이 발생한 거예요. 음... 정족수란 한 모임에서 투표를 하는 데 필요한 사람 수를 말합니다. 그래서 각각의 작고 독립적인 박테리아는 신호를 보내서, 이는 자가 유도 물질이라고 불리는 특별한 분자인데, "안녕, 나 여기 있어!"라는 식으로 말하는 거예요. 만약 충분한 박테리아가 "나 여기 있어!"라고 말하며 한곳에 모여 있고 많은 자가 유도 물질 분자들이 주변에 떠다니고 있으면, 마침내, 이 자가 유도 물질들을 인지함으로써, 박테리아는 특정 현상을 함께 일으킬 수 있죠.

자, '비브리오 피셔리', 제가 앞서 언급한 생물 발광을 하는 이 박테리아는, 정족수 인식을 통해 다른 박테리아의 수가 충분히 많다는 것을 감지하기 전까지는 어떤 빛도 내지 않아요. 왜 에너지를 낭비하겠어요? 하지만 갑자기, 충분한 박테리아가 있으면, 모두 함께 빛을 낼 거예요.

또 다른 예로, 질병을 일으키는 박테리아에 관해 이야기해 봅시다. 만약 독소를 내보내는 박테리아가 소수뿐이라면, 여러분의 면역 체계는 순식간에, 그들을 없애버릴 거예요. 하지만 이제, 수천 개, 또는 심지어 수백만 개의 박테리아가 모두 함께 단결해서... 기다리다가, 정족수를 인지하고, 자가 유도 물질을 뿜어낸다면... 그러면, 빵! 그들은 충분한 자가 유도 물질을 감지하고 모두 동시에 독소를 뿜어내기로 하겠죠. 여러분의 면역 체계는 압도당하고요... 그렇게 많은 독소를 즉시 저지할 수가 없거든요... 그래서 없어지는 데 며칠 걸리는 감염이 되는 거예요. 정족수 인식이 효과적인 이유를 알겠죠, 그렇죠?

닐슨의 연구는 약 10년 전까지만 해도 사실 그다지 신빙성이 없었기 때문에, 이건 굉장히 새로운 연구 분야예요. 과학자들은 아직도 일부 박테리아가 빛을 낼 수 있는 방법이나 어떤 현상을 일으키는 정족수가 되기 위해서는, 정확히, 얼마나 많은 박테리아가 필요한지 알지 못해요. 하지만 이제 이 박테리아의 의사소통이 병이나 감염을 일으키는 데 얼마나 중요한지 알아냈으니, 훨씬 더 구체적으로 연구되고 있죠. 만약 정족수 인식이 일어나는 것을 막을 수 있는 방법이 좀 있다면... 그리고 그러니까, 실제로 이런 일을 할 수 있는 특정 박테리아 종이 있거든요... 미세한 컴퓨터 해킹 같죠... 만약 우리가 박테리아의 의사소통 체계를 해킹하는 방법을 알게 된다면, 그럼 많은 질병을 예방할 수 있어요. 여러분이 상상할 수 있다시피, 의학 연구부는 이 목표에 상당한 자원을 투입하기 시작했죠.

어휘

microbiologist[màikroubaiáɡædʒist] 미생물학자 **luminescence**[lù:mənésns] 발광 **determine**[ditə́ːrmin] 알아내다
quorum[kwɔ́ːrəm] 정족수 **autoinducer**[ɔ̀ːtouindjúːsər] 자가 유도 물질 **trigger**[trígər] 일으키다
bioluminescent[bàioulùminésnt] 생물 발광을 하는 **toxin**[táksin] 독소 **immune system** 면역 체계 **infection**[infékʃən] 감염
credibility[krèdəbíləti] 신빙성 **microscopic**[màikrəskápik] 미세한 **medical condition** 질병 **devote**[divóut] 투입하다

[29-34]
Listen to part of a lecture on geography. The professor is discussing lakes of the Rub' al-Khali.

To continue our ongoing discussion of desert geography, um, [Q29] I'd like to spend some time today talking about a giant patch of desert on the Arabian Peninsula . . . it covers a quarter of it, in fact. It's known as the Rub' al-Khali, which is usually translated as "the empty quarter" in English. It's an apt translation, because the place is almost completely barren. There are very few plants and animals, and certainly no people! But, uh, that wasn't always the case . . . seeing as [Q29] there's lots of geological evidence pointing to lakes and grasslands teeming with life from long ago. [Q30] Scientists figure . . . rather, they speculate . . . it's hard to say for sure . . . that monsoon rains— the ones we see in India nowadays—had shifted a couple of times to pour rain in the Arabian desert. The first monsoon happened around 37,000 years ago, and the second one more recently . . . like 10,000 years ago. These two monsoons caused desert lakes to form. It's clear that heavy rain was necessary, but another condition was needed for this to happen— [Q31] there had to be some clay or silt present. If there were only sand, the water would filter down and not remain standing, but the other materials would stop it from seeping away.

So the geological record points to there having been two distinct sets of lakes in the area. [Q32] The older lakes appear to have been formed in the valleys between the giant sand dunes running through the empty quarter. These lakes tended to be quite long . . . some of them were a kilometer in length . . . and they likely lasted for several years before they evaporated. The newer lakes were much smaller, so they probably didn't exist for very long. Like I mentioned before, the older lakes were long and thin . . . almost finger-like. This is because the sand dunes themselves were long and rounded, so the water would run down them, taking the clay with it, and sit in the long gaps between the dunes. In the period between the monsoons, scientists guess that some sort of climate change occurred. There must have been hotter, drier conditions which brought heavy winds along to reshape the sand dunes and to make them choppier and more abrupt . . . giving them a crested shape like they have today instead of a smooth, rounded one. Scientists assume that the rainwater started to pool and form lakebeds on these newly shaped dunes. Another point I want to discuss is the fossils found near each set of lakes. [Q33] With the lakes, conditions suddenly became livable and animals started to migrate over . . . which was a mistake because the lakes only lasted a short time. In the older lakes, fossils of large animals, such as water buffalo and hippopotamus, were found. In the newer lakes, however, only fossils of smaller animals were discovered—which gives you an idea of how shallow the newer ones probably were in comparison. Both types of lakes were apparently very salty as well, if mineral deposits are any indication. The fossil record backs this up. [Q34] We can find snail and clam shells in abundance there, but no fossilized remains of fish. Since the lakes were not fed by a freshwater source, they became saltier and saltier . . . and such conditions are uninhabitable to fish.

Now get ready to answer the questions. You may use your notes to help you answer.

29. What is the professor mainly discussing?

Listen again to part of the lecture. Then answer the question.

P: Scientists figure . . . rather, they speculate . . . it's hard to say for sure . . . that monsoon rains— the ones we see in India nowadays—had shifted a couple of times to pour rain in the Arabian desert.

30. What can be inferred about the monsoon rains?
31. According to the professor, why was clay or silt necessary to form the lakes?
32. According to the professor, what are two characteristics of the older lakes?
33. What is the professor's opinion on animal migration to the lakes?
34. According to the professor, what is the evidence that the lakes were very salty?

사막 지리에 관해 진행 중인 논의를 계속하자면, 음, 오늘은 아라비아 반도에 있는 거대한 지역의 사막에 대한 이야기를 하면서 시간을 좀 보내고 싶어요... 사실, 그것은 아라비아 반도의 4분의 1을 차지하죠. 그것은 룹알할리라고 알려져 있고, 영어로는 보통 "비어 있는 4분의 1"로 번역돼요. 그건 적절한 번역이에요, 왜냐하면 그곳은 거의 완전한 불모지라서, 식물과 동물이 거의 없고, 당연히 사람도 없죠! 하지만, 어, 항상 그랬던 것은 아니에요... 오래 전에 생명체로 넘치는 호수와 초원이 있었다고 말해주는 많은 지질학적 증거들이 존재하거든요.

과학자들은 생각해요... 그렇다기보다, 추측하죠... 확실하게 말하긴 어려우니까요... 우리가 요즘 인도에서 보는, 우기가 방향을 여러 번 바꾸어 아라비아 사막에도 비를 뿌렸을 것이라고요. 첫 우기는 37,000년 전쯤에 발생했고, 두 번째는 더 최근에... 10,000년 전쯤이었어요. 이 두 번의 우기는 사막호가 형성되게 했죠. 폭우가 필요했던 건 당연하지만, 이것이 발생하기 위해서는 또 다른 조건이 필요했어요, 약간의 찰흙이나 토사가 존재했어야 하죠. 만일 모래만 있었다면, 물은 고이지 않고 스며들었을 거예요, 하지만 다른 물질들은 그것이 스며들지 못하도록 하는 거죠.

그래서 지질학적인 기록들에 의하면 그 지역에는 별개의 두 호수 군락이 있었어요. 더 오래된 호수들은 비어 있는 4분의 1지역에 퍼져 있는 거대한 사구 사이의 계곡에 형성된 것으로 보여요. 이 호수들은 꽤 긴 편이었어요... 어떤 것들은 길이가 1km나 됐죠... 그리고 그것들은 증발되기 까지 수 년 동안 지속됐을 거예요. 새로운 호수들은 훨씬 작았어요, 그래서 그것들은 아마도 그리 오래 존재하지는 않았을 거예요. 제가 앞서 언급했듯이, 더 오래된 호수들은 길고 가늘었어요... 거의 손가락처럼요. 이는 사구 자체가 길고 둥글어서, 물이 사구를 흘러내려 가면서, 찰흙을 함께 내려 보내고, 사구들 사이의 긴 틈에 자리잡았기 때문이에요. 우기 사이의 기간에, 과학자들은 일종의 기후 변화가 일어났을 거라고 추측해요. 거센 바람을 일으키는 더 덥고, 건조한 상태가 사구를 더 거칠고 가파르게 변형시켰을 거라고요... 평평하고, 둥근 모양 대신 오늘날처럼 벗이 있는 것 같은 모양을 만들면서요. 과학자들은 빗물이 고이기 시작하면서 이 새롭게 형성된 사구에 호수 바닥을 만들었을 거라고 추정해요.

제가 다루고 싶은 또 다른 점은 각 호수 군락 근처에서 발견된 화석이에요. 호수가 생기니까, 갑자기 살기에 좋은 환경이 되어서 동물들이 이주해오기 시작한 거예요... 호수는 짧은 시간 동안만 지속되었기 때문에 이건 잘못된 선택이었죠. 오래된 호수들에서는, 물소와 하마같은, 커다란 동물의 화석들이 발견되었어요. 하지만, 새로운 호수들에서는, 오직 작은 동물의 화석만이 발견되었는데, 이는 아마도 새로운 호수들이 비교적 얼마나 얕았는지를 짐작하게 해주죠. 분명 두 종류의 호수 모두 소금기 또한 아주 많았을 겁니다, 만약 광물 퇴적물들이 어떤 증거가 된다면요. 화석 기록도 이를 뒷받침해주죠. 우리는 거기서 달팽이와 조개껍데기를 풍부하게 찾을 수 있지만, 화석화된 물고기의 자취는 남아있지 않아요. 호수에 민물을 제공하는 수원이 없었기 때문에, 그것들은 점점 더 소금기가 많아진 거예요... 그리고 이런 환경에서는 물고기가 살 수 없고요.

어휘

ongoing[ángòuiŋ] 진행 중인 peninsula[pənínsjulə] 반도 apt[æpt] 적절한 barren[bǽrən] 불모지인
geological[dʒìːəládʒikəl] 지질학적인 grassland[grǽslænd] 초원 teem with ~으로 넘치다 monsoon rain 우기
silt[silt] 토사 distinct[distíŋkt] 별개의 sand dune 사구 evaporate[ivǽpərèit] 증발하다 choppy[tʃápi] 거친
abrupt[əbrʌ́pt] 가파른 crested[kréstid] 벗이 있는 lakebed[léikbèd] 호수 바닥 fossil[fásəl] 화석 livable[lívəbl] 살기에 좋은
migrate[máigreit] 이주하다 water buffalo 물소 hippopotamus[hìpəpátəməs] 하마 in comparison 비교적
indication[ìndikéiʃən] 증거 in abundance 풍부하게 uninhabitable[ʌ̀ninhǽbitəbl] 살 수 없는

• 각 문제에 대한 정답단서는 지문에 보라색으로 표시되어 있습니다.

1. (B) Main Purpose/Topic	2. (D) Connecting Contents II	3. (B) Inference
4. (A) Detail	5. (A), (C) Detail	6. (A) Main Purpose/Topic
7. (D) Detail	8. (A) Connecting Contents II	9. (B) Connecting Contents II
10. (B), (D) Detail	11. (B) Detail	12. (D) Main Purpose/Topic
13. (C) Detail	14. (C) Function & Attitude	15. (B) Connecting Contents II
16. (B) Detail	17. (B), (C), (E) Detail	18. (D) Main Purpose/Topic
19. (B), (C) Detail	20. (B) Function & Attitude	21. (D) Detail
22. (B) Inference	23. (D) Main Purpose/Topic	

24. Connecting Contents I

Step 1	Combine seawater with chemicals
Step 2	Purify the solution and allow it to dry
Step 3	Use electricity to separate the elements
Step 4	Refine the metal and process it for use

25. (B) Detail	26. (C) Function & Attitude	27. (A) Inference
28. (B) Function & Attitude		

[1-5]
Listen to a conversation between a student and a professor.

S: Professor Watson, I'm glad I caught you. One of the other students mentioned you were leaving early today to attend a conference.

P: Hi Richard. Actually, I had to cancel my plans. It's a shame, too, because I was really looking forward to it. I've just got too many papers to mark this week. But, um . . . how are things going? Last time we talked, you, uh . . . you mentioned being uncertain about what to do for your sophomore year . . .

S: Q1 Actually, I've decided to do a semester abroad. Um, as you know, I'm a Spanish major. It'd be good to spend time in a country where I can . . . you know . . . use the language every day.

P: That's a good idea . . .

S: But, um, I'm having trouble deciding where to go. I was hoping you'd have some advice for me.

P: I see. Do you have a few places in mind?

S: Yep . . . Spain is the most obvious choice. Aside from the chance to improve my Spanish, Spain is appealing because it's got a lot of history and, um, culture.

P: That's true . . . You'd probably learn a lot in Spain. But you should think about practical matters . . . like cost. Spain can be expensive, so you should, um, have a budget in mind before making your decision.

S: Oh, good point. I hadn't even started thinking of money . . . Is Spain really that pricey, though?

P: Yes. Especially if you want to live in a major city like Barcelona. Q2 The smaller towns are, of course, cheaper . . . However, I wouldn't recommend living in these areas. They don't have the same cultural opportunities. They don't have many museums or performance venues . . . So many students get bored living in places like that.

S: I want to live somewhere I can try lots of different restaurants and festivals. Spain doesn't sound like a good option if it's too expensive to, well . . . to live in a big city. Um, let's see . . . Another place I was thinking of was Argentina.

P: I've heard great things about Argentina . . . It's a popular destination for Spanish language majors at this university. At least a dozen go there every semester.

S: As a matter of fact, that's why I'm hesitant about it. Q3 If I go somewhere with a lot of students from back home, it would be tempting to just spend time with them and not meet local people.

P: Right. Then you wouldn't be truly immersed in the culture.

S: That would be such a waste . . .

P: Well, have you considered another country in South America?

S: Q4 I've looked into Peru a bit. It's got several historical sites I'd love to visit . . . especially Machu Picchu. I've always been interested in ancient cities . . . Travel websites say it's a must-see place. However, there are only a few study-abroad programs that involve universities in Peru . . . so it's hard to find information about studying there.

P: I think Peru's an excellent destination. Q5 I happen to know a student who went there for a semester and loved it. I'd be happy to put you in touch with her.

S: Sure. I have a lot of things I'd like to ask her.

P: No problem. I'll email you her, um, information. Q5 Also, I can write a letter of recommendation for you . . . Uh, you usually need to include one or two in your application.

S: That's great, thanks! OK, I guess Peru is my new top choice! Now I just have to decide whether to go in the fall semester or the spring . . .

P: I say go during the spring. That way, you'll finish studying in June and, well . . . then you can take the summer to visit other countries in South America before the fall semester starts.

S: Good tip! I'm already excited for next year.

Now get ready to answer the questions. You may use your notes to help you answer.

1. What are the speakers mainly discussing?
2. Why does the professor mention museums and performance venues?

Listen again to part of the conversation. Then answer the question.

S: If I go somewhere with a lot of students from back home, it would be tempting to just spend time with them and not meet local people.

P: Right. Then you wouldn't be truly immersed in the culture.

S: That would be such a waste . . .

3. What does the student imply when he says this:
   S: That would be such a waste . . .

4. Why does the student want to visit Peru?
5. What does the professor offer to do for the student?

S: Watson 교수님, 때마침 뵙게 되어 다행이에요. 다른 학생들 중 한 명이 교수님께서 오늘 일찍 학회에 참석하러 가실 거라고 말했거든요.

P: 안녕 Richard. 사실, 내 계획을 취소해야 했단다. 아쉬운 일이기도 하지, 그 학회를 정말 기대하고 있었거든. 이번 주에 채점해야 할 보고서가 너무 많구나. 그, 음... 어떻게 지내고 있니? 지난번에 이야기할 때, 너는, 어... 2학년 때 무엇을 할지 잘 모르겠다고 말했었지...

S: 사실, 한 학기를 해외에서 지내기로 했어요. 음, 교수님도 아시다시피, 저는 스페인어 전공자잖아요. 제가... 그러니까... 그 언어를

매일 사용할 수 있는 나라에서 시간을 보내는 게 좋을 것 같아서요.

P: 좋은 생각이구나...

S: 그런데, 음, 어디로 가야 할지 결정하는 데 어려움을 겪고 있어요. 교수님께서 조언을 좀 주셨으면 했어요.

P: 그렇구나. 몇 군데 생각해둔 곳이 있니?

S: 네... 스페인이 가장 명백한 선택이에요. 제 스페인어를 향상할 기회 이외에도, 스페인은 많은 역사와, 음, 문화를 가지고 있어서 매력적이거든요.

P: 맞는 말이야... 아마 스페인에서 많이 배울 수 있겠지. 하지만 현실적인 문제들도 생각해 봐야 한단다... 비용 같은 것 말이야. 스페인은 돈이 많이 들 수 있으니, 네가, 음, 결정을 내리기 전에 예산을 생각해 보는 것이 좋겠구나.

S: 오, 좋은 지적이에요. 돈은 아직 생각해 보지도 않았거든요... 그런데, 스페인이 정말 그렇게 돈이 드나요?

P: 그렇지. 특히 네가 바르셀로나와 같은 주요 도시에 살고 싶다면 말이야. 더 작은 소도시들은, 물론, 더 저렴하겠지... 하지만, 이러한 지역에 사는 것은 추천하고 싶지 않구나. 그곳들이 동일한 문화적 기회를 가지고 있지는 않거든. 그곳에는 박물관이나 공연 장소가 없단다... 그래서 많은 학생이 그런 곳에 사는 것을 지루해하지.

S: 저는 많은 다양한 식당과 축제를 경험할 수 있는 곳에서 살고 싶어요. 만약 대도시에 사는 것이, 음... 돈이 너무 많이 든다면, 스페인은 좋은 선택지가 아닌 것 같네요. 음, 어디 보자... 제가 생각했던 또 다른 장소는 아르헨티나였어요.

P: 아르헨티나에 관한 훌륭한 점들을 들어본 적이 있어... 우리 대학 스페인어 전공자들에게 인기 있는 행선지란다. 학기마다 적어도 12명이 그곳에 가지.

S: 사실은, 그게 바로 제가 주저하는 이유예요. 만약 제가 모국에서 온 많은 학생이 있는 곳으로 간다면, 저는 그저 그들과 시간을 보내도록 유혹받고 현지 사람들을 만나지 않을 거니까요.

P: 맞아. 그러면 그 문화 속에 진정으로 몰두할 수가 없지.

S: 그건 정말 낭비일 거예요...

P: 음, 남미에 있는 다른 나라를 생각해 봤니?

S: 페루를 약간 조사해 봤어요. 제가 방문하고 싶은 역사 유적지가 몇 곳 있거든요... 특히 마추픽추요. 저는 고대 도시에 대해 항상 관심을 가져왔어요... 여행 관련 웹사이트들은 그곳이 꼭 봐야 하는 곳이라고 말하고요. 하지만, 페루에는 대학과 연계된 해외 유학 프로그램이 몇 개뿐이에요... 그래서 그곳에서 공부하는 것에 관한 정보를 찾기가 어려워요.

P: 페루는 아주 훌륭한 목적지가 될 것 같구나. 페루에서 한 학기를 보내고 그곳을 좋아했던 학생 한 명을 우연히 알게 되었는데. 기꺼이 너를 그녀에게 소개줄 수 있단다.

S: 물론이죠. 그녀에게 물어보고 싶은 것들이 많아요.

P: 그래. 내가, 음, 그녀의 정보를 네게, 음, 이메일로 보내주마. 또, 널 위해 추천서를 써줄 수도 있단다... 어, 보통 한두 개를 지원서에 포함해야 할 거야.

S: 잘됐군요, 감사합니다! 좋아요, 페루가 새로운 최상의 선택이 된 것 같네요. 이제 가을학기에 갈지 봄학기에 갈지만 결정하면 되겠어요...

P: 봄에 가라고 말해주고 싶구나. 그렇게 하면, 6월에 학업을 마치고 나서, 음... 가을 학기가 시작하기 전에 남미에 있는 다른 나라들을 방문하면서 여름을 보낼 수 있잖니.

S: 좋은 정보네요! 벌써부터 내년이 정말로 기대돼요.

어휘

catch[kætʃ] 때마침 만나다   sophomore[sáfəmɔ̀ːr] 2학년   appealing[əpíːlin] 매력적인   practical[præktikəl] 현실적인
budget[bʌ́dʒit] 비용   pricey[práisi] 돈이 드는   venue[vénjuː] (콘서트·경기 등의) 장소   immerse[imɔ́ːrs] 몰두하게 하다
must-see[məstsíː] 꼭 봐야 하는   happen to 우연히 ~하게 되다   letter of recommendation 추천서

[6-11]

Listen to part of a talk on art history.

P: All right, everyone. Q6 Today we're going to focus on Victorian art. And let me just say, to understand Victorian art, you've got to understand what occurred during this period of history. Before we get going though, I should probably ask . . . Does anyone know why it is called the Victorian era?

S: Well, it was during the reign of Queen Victoria . . . back in the 19th century, right?

P: That's right. She ruled from 1837 to 1901. OK, Q6 Victorian art was a response to the technological developments and social upheavals that occurred during this period. The Industrial Revolution was in full swing, the Reform Act was passed, which granted more people the right to vote, and a burgeoning middle class was developing. In the realm of art, major innovations were being made in the fields of fine art and design . . . in particular with fabrics, wallpaper, and ceramics. At the same time, Q7 with the invention of the steel-plate printing process, printing became an increasingly important element of design. Artwork suddenly became affordable to the common people, thanks to this new technology, which allowed printers to make thousands of copies at a time. Steel-plate printing also brought about an enormous growth in the production of newspapers, magazines, and books . . . so public access to art increased as well. Q8 People were fascinated with these images, subscriptions to publications increased, and pretty soon, people wanted to buy prints of these artworks . . . so you had a growing audience of art collectors. This was particularly evident at the World Expo in 1851 . . . It was held in London and over six million visitors came to the city for the event over the course of five and a half months. Commentators at the time remarked with some astonishment at how much more knowledgeable about art the visitors were compared to past audiences.

Let's think about this for a moment. In the past, who was it that patronized the arts?

S: Wouldn't it have been mostly the aristocrats? You know . . . those born into wealth?

P: That's true. Q9 But in Victorian times, there was a new class of wealthy individuals. These were the businesspeople that made their money during the Industrial Revolution, and they became interested in art . . . but not the art of the aristocracy. These guys wanted the work of living artists and not the work of masters from long ago. An example of this new breed of collectors was John Sheepshanks. Q10 He was a manufacturing baron during the mid-1800s who donated a very large collection of contemporary British art to the Victoria and Albert Museum in London just before his death. It was individuals like Sheepshanks who became the main collectors of Victorian art.

OK . . . so we've seen how the typical art collector changed, but what about the art itself? How did that change? Well, Victorian art was different in two major ways. First of all, it tended to be smaller because the patrons, well, they tended to live in villas, as opposed to the gigantic castles in which the aristocracy lived. This led to the development of the cabinet-sized painting. Q11 A second difference was in the subject matter. As art audiences expanded to include those people outside the nobility, there was a renewed focus on pieces that were inspired by the things found in day-to-day life. This helped make the art of the era more comprehensible and easy to appreciate because patrons didn't need any sort of specialized knowledge in order to enjoy it.

Now get ready to answer the questions. You may use your notes to help you answer.

6. What does the professor mainly discuss?
7. What was a benefit of the steel-plate printing process?
8. Why does the professor mention the 1851 World Expo?
9. Why does the professor discuss businesspeople?
10. What does the professor say about John Sheepshanks?
11. According to the professor, what was the influence the new class of wealthy individuals had on the art world?

P: 자, 여러분. 오늘 우리는 빅토리아 시대의 미술에 초점을 맞춰 볼 거예요. 그리고, 빅토리아 시대의 미술을 이해하기 위해서는, 역사상 이 시기에 무슨 일이 일어났는지 이해해야 한다고 말하고 싶네요. 살펴보기 전에, 질문을 하나 해야 할 것 같네요... 그게 왜 빅토리아 시대라고 불리는지 아는 사람 있나요?

S: 음, 빅토리아 여왕의 통치 시기였으니까요... 19세기요, 맞나요?

P: 맞아요, 그녀는 1837년부터 1901년까지 통치했어요. 빅토리아 시대 미술은 이 시기에 일어난 기술적인 발전과 사회 변화에 대한 반응이었지요. 산업 혁명이 한창이었고, 영국 선거법 개정법이 통과되어서, 더 많은 사람들이 투표할 권리를 받았으며, 급성장하는 중산층이 발달하고 있었어요. 예술계에서는, 미술과 디자인 분야에서 주요한 혁신이 이루어지고 있었죠... 특히 직물, 벽지, 그리고 도자기에서요. 동시에, 금속판 인쇄 공정의 발명으로, 인쇄술이 디자인에서 점점 더 중요한 요소가 되었어요. 갑자기 일반 사람들도 미술 작품을 구매할 수 있게 되었는데, 이는 인쇄기가 한 번에 수천 장의 복사본을 만들 수 있게 한, 이 새로운 기술 덕분이었죠. 또한 금속판 인쇄술은 신문, 잡지, 그리고 책 생산에 엄청난 성장을 가져왔어요... 그리하여 대중이 미술을 접할 기회도 증가했어요. 사람들은 이러한 그림들에 매혹되었고, 출판물의 구독이 증가했으며, 그리고 이내, 사람들은 이러한 미술 작품을 사고 싶어했어요... 그래서 미술품 수집가들이 늘어난 거죠. 이는 특히 1851년 세계 엑스포에서 분명하게 나타났어요... 엑스포는 런던에서 열렸고 6백만 명이 넘는 방문객들이 5개월 반의 기간 동안 이 행사를 위해 런던에 왔습니다. 당시의 논평가들은 방문객들이 과거의 관객들에 비해 미술에 대한 지식이 얼마나 많은지에 대한 놀라움을 표현했고요.

이것에 대해 잠시 생각해 보죠. 과거에는, 누가 미술을 후원했을까요?

S: 대부분 귀족이 아니었을까요? 그러니까... 부유하게 태어난 사람들이요?

P: 사실이에요... 하지만 빅토리아 시대에는, 부유한 개인들로 이루어진 새로운 계층이 있었어요. 이들은 산업 혁명 동안 돈을 번 사업가들이었고, 미술에 관심을 가지게 되었죠... 하지만 귀족의 미술에 대해서는 아니었습니다. 이 사람들은 살아 있는 미술가들의 작품을 원했고 오래전 대가들의 작품을 원하진 않았어요. 이 새로운 부류의 수집가의 한 예로는 존 시프생크스가 있어요. 그는 죽기 직전 런던의 빅토리아 앤드 알버트 미술관에 당대 영국 미술의 수많은 수집품들을 기부한 1800년대 중반의 제조업계 부호였어요. 빅토리아 시대 미술의 주요 수집가가 된 사람들은 바로 시프생크스와 같은 사람들이었죠.

좋아요... 그래서 우리는 전형적인 미술 수집가들이 어떻게 변했는지를 보았는데, 미술 그 자체는 어떨까요? 그건 어떻게 변했을까요? 자, 빅토리아 시대 미술은 두 가지 주요한 면에서 달랐어요. 첫째로, 후원자들은, 음, 귀족이 살았던 거대한 성과는 반대로, 주로 빌라에 살았기 때문에 빅토리아 시대 미술은 더 작은 경향이 있었어요. 이것은 진열장 크기의 그림이 발전하게 했죠. 두 번째 차이점은 작품의 주제예요. 미술 관람객들이 귀족 이외의 사람들까지 포함하도록 확장되었기 때문에, 일상 생활에서 발견되는 사물에 영감을 받은 작품들에 대한 새로운 관심이 생겼어요. 이는 후원자들이 작품을 즐기기 위해서 아무런 특별한 지식을 갖추지 않아도 되었기 때문에 그 시대의 미술이 더 이해하기 쉽고 감상하기 쉽도록 하는 것을 도왔어요.

어휘

reign[rein] 통치 burgeon[bə́ːrdʒən] 급성장하다 fine art 미술 fabric[fǽbrik] 직물 wallpaper[wɔ́ːlpèipər] 벽지 ceramic[sərǽmik] 도자기 subscription[səbskrípʃən] 구독 publication[pʌ̀bləkéiʃən] 출판물 commentator[káməntèitər] 논평가 remark[rimáːrk] 표현하다 astonishment[əstániʃmənt] 놀라움 knowledgeable[nálidʒəbl] 지식이 많은 patronize[péitrənàiz] 후원하다 aristocracy[æ̀rəstákrəsi] 귀족 master[mǽstər] 대가 breed[briːd] 부류 manufacturing[mæ̀njufǽktʃəriŋ] 제조업계 baron[bǽrən] 부호 contemporary[kəntémpərèri] 당대의 gigantic[dʒaigǽntik] 거대한 nobility[noubíləti] 귀족 comprehensible[kàmprihénsəbl] 이해하기 쉬운

[12-17]

Listen to part of a lecture in an astronomy class. The professor is discussing star catalogs.

P: As I mentioned earlier, astrometry is the, uh, branch of astronomy concerned with calculating the positions and movements of objects in space. Q12 The field is highly dependent on star catalogs . . . and this is what I want to go over in detail today.

A star catalog is essentially a list of stars that have been identified by astronomers. Normally, it will include a star's name or number and the coordinates for its location in the sky. Um . . . coordinates are sets of numbers that are used to indicate points on a map. Q13 Now, to get precise coordinates, astronomers have to measure two angles. The first angle is expressed in degrees, and the second one is expressed in hours . . . Essentially, it's like drawing an imaginary cross in the sky and finding where the two lines of the cross intersect. The more detailed star catalogs may also include other data, such as a star's brightness. Some indicate whether they're part of a larger cluster or group of stars.

S1: Q14 Um, I actually saw a star catalog recently at, uh, the Museum of Science . . . It was interesting . . . One has to wonder . . . how did the idea for these things even come about?

P: Let's see . . . Um, if you go back into ancient history, everyone from the Chinese to the Arabs produced star catalogs at one time or another. Q15 Each civilization had different motivations for producing star catalogs . . . Some tracked the stars for religious reasons . . . Um, the Babylonians, for example, assigned names to stars because they thought these were spirits living in the sky. Others had more practical concerns. The ancient Greeks, for instance, were the first to seriously study astronomy as a science. They were searching for a way to explain the world around them . . . Why the Sun, the Moon, and the stars seemed to move across the sky . . . Or why some stars appeared in the sky at different times of the year . . .

S2: Sorry, but, uh . . . what did they use to observe stars? I mean, the telescope wasn't invented until the 17th century, right?

P: Exactly . . . Um, 1608, to be precise . . . Before this, astronomers didn't really use any special device to study the stars . . . Just the naked eye. Anyway, it was the Greek astronomer Hipparchus who put together the first comprehensive star catalog in the . . . um, it was the second century B.C. This catalog listed 850 stars in total, more than any previous catalog. Actually, Hipparchus was inspired by an earlier Greek star catalog . . . There's a story that says he was looking up at the sky one evening . . . Q16 and he noticed one star that seemed out of place. It didn't match what the earlier catalog had predicted. Because of this apparent error, Hipparchus made it his goal to produce a new and more accurate star catalog . . .

But what is a star catalog used for? Well, at its most fundamental, a star catalog is simply used to create a map of outer space . . . Such maps or charts give us a clearer picture of the universe we inhabit. But they do have some other uses . . . For instance, in ancient times, Q17 star catalogs were used to track the seasons, um, like a calendar. By observing how the positions of certain groups of stars changed over time, one could tell what time of the year it was. Additionally, star catalogs may be used to judge the distances to stars from Earth . . . This is invaluable to researchers investigating the age of our universe. And lastly, they provide a means for navigation. Whether at sea, on land, or in the air, you can figure out your location on the planet by finding your position in relation to certain stars.

Now get ready to answer the questions. You may use your notes to help you answer.

12. What is the main purpose of the lecture?
13. How do astronomers determine a star's coordinates?

Listen again to part of the lecture. Then answer the question.

S: Um, I actually saw a star catalog recently at, uh, the Museum of Science . . . It was interesting . . . One has to wonder . . . how did the idea for these things even come about?

14. What does the student mean when she says this:
    S: One has to wonder . . .

15. Why does the professor mention the Babylonians?
16. What may have prompted Hipparchus to produce a star catalog?

17. According to the professor, what are some practical uses of star catalogs?

P: 제가 앞서 언급했던 것처럼, 측성학은, 어, 우주에 있는 물체의 위치와 움직임을 계산하는 것과 관련 있는 천문학 분야입니다. 이 분야는 성표에 상당히 의존적이죠... 그리고 바로 이게 오늘 상세하게 살펴보고 싶은 거예요.

성표는 기본적으로 천문학자들에 의해 발견되어온 별의 목록입니다. 보통, 그것은 별의 이름 또는 번호와 하늘에서 그것의 위치에 대한 좌표를 포함할 겁니다. 음... 좌표란 지도에서 특정한 지점을 나타내기 위해 사용되는 일련의 숫자고요. 자, 정확한 좌표를 얻기 위해서, 천문학자들은 두 개의 각을 측정해야 합니다. 첫 번째 각은 도로 표현되고, 두 번째 것은 시로 표현되죠... 기본적으로, 그것은 가상의 십자를 하늘에 그리고 그 십자의 두 선이 교차하는 곳을 찾는 것과 같습니다. 더 상세한 성표는 별의 밝기와 같은 다른 자료를 포함할 수도 있어요. 일부는 그것들이 별의 더 큰 무리 또는 집단의 일부인지를 나타내죠.

S1: 음, 사실 저는 최근에, 어, 과학박물관에서 성표를 봤는데요... 그건 흥미로웠어요... 누군가는 궁금해할 거예요... 이런 것들에 대한 생각이 도대체 어떻게 생겨났는지 말이죠?

P: 어디 봅시다... 음, 고대사로 돌아가 보면, 중국인에서 아랍인까지 모두 한 번쯤은 성표를 만들었어요. 각 문명은 성표를 만드는 데 서로 다른 동기를 가지고 있었고요... 어떤 사람들은 종교적인 이유로 별을 추적했어요... 음, 바빌로니아인들은, 예를 들어, 별에 이름을 부여했는데, 이것들이 하늘에 사는 영혼이라고 생각했기 때문이죠. 다른 사람들은 더 현실적인 관심사를 가지고 있었습니다. 고대 그리스인들은, 예를 들어, 처음으로 천문학을 과학으로서 진지하게 연구했어요. 그들은 그들 주위의 세계를 설명하기 위한 방법을 찾고 있었죠... 왜 태양이, 달이, 그리고 별들이 하늘을 가로질러 움직이는 것처럼 보이는지... 혹은 왜 어떤 별들은 연중 서로 다른 시기에 하늘에 나타나는지를요...

S2: 죄송해요, 그런데, 어... 그들은 별을 관측하기 위해 무엇을 사용했나요? 제 말은, 17세기까지는 망원경이 발명되지 않았잖아요, 그렇죠?

P: 맞아요... 음, 정확히 말해서, 1608년이죠... 이 전에는, 천문학자들은 사실 별을 연구하기 위한 어떤 특별한 장치도 사용하지 않았어요... 그저 맨눈을 사용했죠. 어쨌든, 첫 번째 포괄적인 성표를 만든 사람은 바로 그리스 천문학자 히파르쿠스였는데... 음, 기원전 2세기였죠. 이 목록은 총 850개의 별을 포함했는데, 이전의 그 어떤 목록보다도 많은 거였어요. 사실, 히파르쿠스는 앞선 그리스 성표에 영감을 받은 거예요... 다음과 같은 이야기가 있어요, 어느날 밤에 그가 하늘을 올려다보고 있었어요... 그리고 그는 제자리에서 벗어난 것처럼 보이는 별 하나를 발견했습니다. 그건 앞선 성표가 예측했던 것과 일치하지 않았죠. 이 분명한 오류 때문에, 히파르쿠스는 새롭고 더 정확한 성표를 만드는 것을 그의 목표로 삼은 거예요...

하지만 성표는 어디에 사용될까요? 음, 가장 기본적으로, 성표는 단순히 우주 공간의 지도를 만드는 데 사용됩니다... 그러한 지도나 도표는 우리에게 우리가 살고 있는 우주를 더 분명하게 묘사해줘요. 하지만 그들은 몇 가지 다른 용도를 가지고 있습니다... 예를 들어, 고대에는, 성표가 계절을 추적하기 위해 사용되었어요, 음, 달력처럼. 특정 별 집단의 위치가 시간이 지남에 따라 어떻게 변하는지 관찰함으로써, 그때가 연중 어떤 시기인지를 알 수 있었습니다. 게다가, 성표는 지구로부터 별들의 거리를 판단하는 데 사용될 수도 있죠... 이는 우리 우주의 나이를 조사하는 연구원들에게 매우 유용합니다. 그리고 마지막으로, 그것들은 항해를 위한 수단을 제공해요. 바다, 육지, 혹은 상공에 있더라도, 특정 별들과 비교해서 여러분의 위치를 찾음으로써 지구에서 여러분의 위치를 알아낼 수 있는 거죠.

어휘
astrometry[əstrámətri] 측성학 astronomy[əstránəmi] 천문학 star catalog 성표 coordinate[kouɔ́ːrdənət] 좌표
intersect[intərsékt] 교차하다 cluster[klʌ́stər] 무리 concern[kənsə́ːrn] 관심사 comprehensive[kàmprihénsiv] 포괄적인
out of place 제자리에서 벗어난 invaluable[invǽljuəbl] 매우 유용한

[18-22]
Listen to a conversation between a student and a university employee.

W: Q18 Hi, I need to talk to someone about my meal card.

M: Your meal card? Is there a problem with it?

W: Um . . . no . . . not exactly. It's just that I haven't really been using it, so I'm wondering what to do next semester, and . . .

M: OK, first can you give me your card, please? Hmm . . . Did you know you have 60 meals left on your account? And there are only two and a half weeks to go in the semester! So, why haven't you used them? Wait . . . let me guess—you live off-campus, right?

W: Well, no, actually. In fact, I live in Barnard Dormitory, just next door. Q19 The problem is that I'm so busy with classes and work that I don't have time to get to the cafeteria. I'm always on the east side of campus for classes and my job is on the opposite end of town near the Westgate Mall.

M: Ah, I see. Do you work at the mall?

W: No . . . at an Italian restaurant close by. Q19 That's another thing—since I work at a restaurant, I get free dinners every night at the end of my shift.

M: Um, it's probably none of my business, but why did you buy such a big meal plan if you're never around?

W: Q20 Well, you see, I—I didn't get the job until mid-semester, so I wasn't planning on being all over the place so much. On top of that, I picked up a couple of audit classes about a month after the term began. I really didn't expect my schedule to be so full. I literally don't have time to breathe.

M: I see . . . well, Q21 you might want to adjust your meal plan then.

W: Can I do that?

M: Sure you can! There are three options: the full meal plan that you are on now, and then there is the, uh, part-time plan, which is one meal per day, six days per week . . . and finally, well, of course there's the cash option. Q22 You're actually not required to participate in a plan per se. It's just that most students like to take advantage of the discounted rate . . . it's a little more expensive to pay with cash on a meal-by-meal basis.

W: What a relief! I thought students who lived in dorms had to participate in the meal plan. You know what, though? I'm guessing it's probably way too late in the semester to do anything about it for this term.

M: I don't think so . . . We're pretty lenient with students.

W: If I'm able to change my plan for this semester, could I possibly get a refund for the meals I haven't used?

M: Oh, no, I think a refund wouldn't be likely. But you could definitely get the unused credit transferred to the fall. You don't lose value just because the semester ends . . . so, well, theoretically you could keep using your card indefinitely—as long as you're enrolled as a student here, that is . . .

W: Basically, I can change my plan and keep the balance? I mean, it seems like I wouldn't be really losing or gaining anything either way.

M: Exactly, and if your schedule changes in the future, you can just switch again if you need to.

W: So can I make the switch now?

M: You're allowed to do that only between semesters when you enroll.

W: That's good to know. Thanks . . . You've been a big help!

Now get ready to answer the questions. You may use your notes to help you answer.

18. What is the woman's problem?
19. According to the conversation, what are two reasons the student does not eat at the cafeteria often?

Listen again to part of the conversation. Then answer the question.

W: Well, you see, I—I didn't get the job until mid-semester, so I wasn't planning on being all over the place so much. On top of that, I picked up a couple of audit classes about a month after the term began. I really didn't expect my schedule to be so full. I literally don't have time to breathe.

20. Why does the woman say this:

    W: I literally don't have time to breathe.

21. What does the service center worker suggest the student do?

22. What does the service center worker imply about the school's meal plan?

W: 안녕하세요, 제 식권에 대해서 누군가와 이야기해야 할 것 같아요.

M: 식권이요? 거기 무슨 문제라도 있어요?

W: 음... 아니요... 그렇진 않아요. 그냥 제가 사실 한동안 사용하지 않아서, 다음 학기에는 어떻게 해야 할지 고민이에요. 그리고...

M: 알겠어요, 먼저 학생의 식권을 줘 볼래요? 흠... 학생의 계좌에 60번의 식사가 남아있는 것을 알고 있었나요? 그리고 이번 학기는 2주 반밖에 남지 않았고요! 그래서, 왜 그것들을 쓰지 않았죠? 잠깐만요... 제가 추측하자면, 학교 밖에서 사는군요, 그렇죠?

W: 음, 사실, 아니에요. 실은, 저는 바로 옆, Barnard 기숙사에 살아요. 제가 수업과 일 때문에 너무 바빠서 구내식당에 갈 시간이 없다는 게 문제죠. 저는 늘 캠퍼스 동쪽에서 수업을 듣고 제 일은 시내 반대편 끝의 Westgate 쇼핑센터 근처거든요.

M: 아, 그렇군요. 쇼핑센터에서 일하나요?

W: 아니요... 근처 이탈리아 식당에서요. 그게 또 다른 이유예요, 식당에서 일하기 때문에, 근무 시간이 끝날 때마다 무료로 저녁을 먹거든요.

M: 음, 아마 제가 상관할 일은 아니지만, 구내식당에 가지 않을 거면 왜 그렇게 많은 식사 제도를 구매했나요?

W: 음, 그게, 저, 저는 학기 중반까지는 일을 하지 않아서, 그렇게 많이 여기저기 다닐 계획이 아니었어요. 게다가, 학기가 시작하고 한 달쯤 후에 청강 수업 두 개를 신청했거든요. 사실 제 스케줄이 이렇게 꽉 찰 줄은 예상 못했어요. 말 그대로 저는 숨쉴 틈도 없어요.

M: 그렇군요... 음, 그럼 학생의 식사 제도를 조정할 수 있겠네요.

W: 그렇게 할 수 있나요?

M: 당연히 할 수 있죠! 세 가지 선택사항이 있어요. 학생이 지금 하고 있는 완전한 식사 제도가 있고, 그 다음, 어, 일주일에 6일간, 하루에 한 끼를 먹을 수 있는, 시간제 제도가 있죠... 그리고 마지막으로, 음, 물론 현금 선택사항이 있어요. 사실 반드시 제도 자체에 참여해야 하는 것은 아니에요. 그저 대부분의 학생이 할인율의 이익을 받는 것을 좋아하죠... 끼니마다 현금을 내는 것이 조금 더 비싸니까요.

W: 다행이네요! 기숙사에 사는 학생들은 식사 제도에 참여해야만 하는 줄 알았거든요. 하지만, 그거 아세요? 아마 이번 학기에는 무언가를 하기에 너무 늦은 것 같아요.

M: 그렇지 않을 거예요... 우린 학생들에게 꽤 관대하거든요.

W: 만약 이번 학기 제도를 바꿀 수 있다면, 제가 사용하지 않은 식권을 환불받을 수 있나요?

M: 오, 아니요, 환불은 불가능할 거예요. 하지만 분명 사용하지 않은 잔고를 가을로 넘길 수는 있어요. 단지 학기가 끝났다고 해서 식권이 끝나버리지는 않아요... 그래서, 음, 이론적으로 학생은 식권을 제한 없이 계속 사용할 수 있는 거예요, 이곳 학생으로 등록되어 있는 한 말이죠, 즉...

W: 기본적으로, 저는 제 식사 제도를 바꿀 수 있고 남은 횟수를 유지할 수 있다는 거죠? 제 말은, 어떤 방법이든 제가 무언가를 잃거나 얻지도 않을 것 같은데요.

M: 정확해요, 그리고 만약 앞으로 학생의 일정이 바뀌면, 필요시에 다시 바꾸기만 하면 돼요.

W: 그럼 지금 바꿔도 되나요?

M: 학기 사이에 등록할 때에만 바꿀 수 있어요.

W: 알게 되어 다행이군요. 고맙습니다... 정말 큰 도움이 되었어요!

어휘

off-campus[ɔ:fkǽmpəs] 학교 밖에서 mall[mɔ:l] 쇼핑센터 shift[ʃift] 근무 시간 all over the place 여기저기 on top of 게다가
audit class 청강 수업 literally[lítərəli] 말 그대로 per se 자체 lenient[lí:niənt] 관대한 get a refund 환불받다
credit[krédit] 잔고

[23-28]
Listen to part of a lecture in a chemistry class.

Today, I'd like to continue our exploration of the alkaline earth metals by . . . talking about a certain type of metal that forms the common soda can. Soda cans are made of an aluminum-magnesium alloy. The magnesium is what gives the can its strength . . . and this use, as an alloying agent, is one of the most common applications of magnesium. It has a wide range of uses, though—from industrial to final consumption goods.

The amount of magnesium produced and consumed has increased considerably since the 1960s. Q23 Today, worldwide production of magnesium is close to . . . 600,000 tons. Now, the manufacturing processes that have made this level of production possible have also evolved. But, basically, there are two main processes. The first uses electrolysis. Essentially, this involves passing electricity through elements that are fused or bonded together into compounds in order to separate them. As you know, metals and other elements are almost never found in their pure form. When you pass electricity through these compounds, it causes the elements to separate. The second process uses thermal reduction. Please understand that "reduction" is a chemistry term. It means "to separate from impurities." Q26 This is achieved by using a reducing agent—you know, a chemical that reduces metal from mineral ore. Actually, let's not get ahead of ourselves here. It's more important that you grasp the overall production process rather than the technical details, which you can pick up through your reading.

Let's go into more detail about electrolysis. Can a metal such as magnesium be obtained from seawater? Yes, it can. The whole thing starts with seawater. Q24 We make a conducting solution by adding chemicals to the seawater. The solution is then purified, I mean, refined, and then allowed to dry to obtain a solid piece of magnesium chloride. The solid is then melted down and an electric current is passed through it to separate the two elements of the compound—the liquid magnesium and the chlorine gas. In the last stage, the liquid magnesium metal is further refined, and then it's processed for other uses. One pound of magnesium can be extracted for every 100 gallons of seawater. This may not sound like a good ratio, but seawater is plentiful, so you can imagine that there is almost a limitless supply of magnesium.

Q27/Q28 But there's a catch: the electrolytic process requires 35 to 40 megawatts of electricity for every ton of magnesium. Can anyone conceptualize this figure? Well, 1 megawatt represents enough electrical capacity to supply 1,000 US households with electricity for one month. So for every ton of magnesium produced, you could power 35,000 to 40,000 households for a month! Q27 So even when seawater is accessible, the electrical capacity of a country can be a barrier to magnesium production.

The other method, thermal reduction process . . . well, this process allows almost any country to become a major producer of magnesium. For one, even though the total energy requirements are about the same as the electrolytic process, thermal reduction needs mainly heat energy. So there are potential cost savings from using cheaper fuel sources such as coal. Q25 The other advantage is that it allows all countries, even landlocked nations . . . I mean, countries without coasts . . . to become major magnesium producers because the mineral ore containing magnesium is easily obtained from the earth's crust. Magnesium is the eighth most abundant mineral and can be found in over 60 types of rocks. So, with the thermal reduction process, about six tons of ore is required to produce a ton of magnesium.

Now get ready to answer the questions. You may use your notes to help you answer.

23. What is the lecture mainly about?

24. In the lecture, the professor describes the process for producing magnesium from seawater. Put the steps listed below in the correct order.

25. According to the professor, why does the thermal reduction process allow almost any country to produce magnesium?

Listen again to part of the lecture. Then answer the question.

P: This is achieved by using a reducing agent—you know, a chemical that reduces metal from mineral ore. Actually, let's not get ahead of ourselves here. It's more important that you grasp the overall production process rather than the technical details, which you can pick up through your reading.

26. What does the professor mean when she says this:
   P: It's more important that you grasp the overall production process rather than the technical details . . .

27. What can be inferred about a coastal country that does not produce magnesium?

Listen again to part of the lecture. Then answer the question.

P: But there's a catch: the electrolytic process requires 35 to 40 megawatts of electricity for every ton of magnesium. Can anyone conceptualize this figure?

28. Why does the professor say this:
   P: Can anyone conceptualize this figure?

오늘은, 알칼리성 토류 금속에 대한 조사를 계속하고 싶네요... 보통의 소다 캔을 만드는 특정 금속 종류에 대해 이야기하면서요. 소다 캔은 알루미늄-마그네슘 합금으로 만들어지죠. 마그네슘은 캔을 견고하게 만들거든요... 그리고 합금화제로 사용되는, 이 용도는, 마그네슘의 가장 흔한 적용 중 하나입니다. 하지만, 그것은 넓은 범위의 용도로 쓰여요, 공업용에서 최종 소비재에 이르기까지 말이죠. 1960년대 이래로 마그네슘의 생산량과 소비량은 상당히 증가했습니다. 오늘날, 전세계의 마그네슘 생산량은... 60만 톤에 가까워요. 자, 이 수준의 생산을 가능하게 한 제조 공정 또한 발달했습니다. 그러나 기본적으로는, 두 가지 주요 공정이 있어요. 첫 번째는 전기 분해를 이용해요. 기본적으로, 이는 혼합물로 녹거나 결합되어 있는 물질들을 분리하기 위해 전기를 통과시키는 과정을 수반합니다. 여러분도 알다시피, 금속 및 다른 물질들은 순수한 형태로 거의 찾아보기 힘들어요. 이러한 혼합물에 전기를 통과시키면, 그것은 물질들이 분리되도록 하죠. 두 번째 공정은 열 환원법을 사용합니다. '환원법'은 화학 용어라는 것을 이해해두세요. 그것은 '불순물로부터 분리되는 것'을 의미해요. 이건, 그러니까, 무기물 광석에서 금속을 환원하는 화학 물질인 환원제를 사용하여 가능해지는 것입니다. 사실, 여기까지 앞서나가지는 말아야겠네요. 여러분이 전반적인 생산 공정을 이해하는 것이 읽기 자료를 통해 알 수 있는, 기술적인 세부사항을 이해하는 것보다 중요하니까요.

전기 분해에 대해 더 자세히 알아봅시다. 마그네슘과 같은 금속을 바닷물로부터 얻을 수 있을까요? 네, 가능해요. 모든 것은 바닷물로부터 시작하거든요. 바닷물에 화학 물질을 넣음으로써 전도 용액을 만들 수 있어요. 그 다음 용액이 걸러지고, 제 말은, 정제되고, 그 다음 염화 마그네슘의 고체 조각을 얻기 위해 말려집니다. 그리고 나서 그 고체를 녹이고 그 혼합물의 두 물질인, 액체 마그네슘과 염화 가스를 분리하기 위해 전류를 통과시킵니다. 마지막 단계에서는, 액체 마그네슘 금속이 더욱 정제되고, 그런 다음 다른 용도를 위해 공정되죠. 바닷물 100갤런 당 1파운드의 마그네슘이 추출됩니다. 높은 비율처럼 들리지 않을지도 모르지만, 바닷물은 풍부하기 때문에, 마그네슘은 거의 무한히 공급될 수 있다는 것을 상상할 수 있을 거예요.

하지만 한 가지 단점이 있어요. 전기 분해 공정은 1톤의 마그네슘당 35~40메가와트의 전기가 필요해요. 이 수치를 개념화할 수 있는 사람 있나요? 음, 1메가와트는 미국의 1,000가구에 한 달 동안 충분한 전력량을 공급할 수 있다는 것을 나타내요. 그래서 1톤의 마그네슘 생산당, 35,000~40,000가구에 한 달 동안 전력을 공급할 수 있는 거죠! 그래서 바닷물이 얻기 쉽다고 하더라도, 한 국가의 전력량은 마그네슘 생산에 장벽이 될 수 있는 거예요.

다른 방법인, 열 환원법 공정은... 음, 거의 모든 국가들이 마그네슘 주요 생산국이 될 수 있도록 해줍니다. 우선, 총 에너지 필요량은 전기 분해 공정과 거의 같지만, 열 환원법은 주로 열 에너지만을 필요로 하거든요. 그래서 석탄과 같이 더 저렴한 연료 공급원을 사용하여 잠재적인 비용 절감이 가능하죠. 또 다른 이점은 이것이 모든, 심지어 육지로 둘러싸인 나라들도... 제 말은, 바다에 인접하지 않은 나라들도... 주요 마그네슘 생산국이 될 수 있도록 하는데 이는 마그네슘을 함유한 무기질 광석은 지구의 표면에서 쉽게 얻을 수 있기 때문이죠. 마그네슘은 8번째로 풍부한 광물이고 60종류가 넘는 암석에서 발견할 수 있어요. 그래서, 열 환원법 공정에서는, 1톤의 마그네슘을 생산하는 데 약 6톤의 광석이 필요합니다.

어휘

alkaline[ǽlkəlàin] 알칼리성의   earth metal 토류 금속   alloy[ǽlɔi] 합금   alloying agent 합금화제
consumption goods 소비재   electrolysis[ilèktrálǝsis] 전기 분해   element[éləmənt] 물질   thermal[θə́ːrməl] 열의
reduction[ridʌ́kʃən] 환원법   impurity[impjúərəti] 불순물   reducing agent 환원제   ore[ɔːr] 광석   grasp[græsp] 이해하다
solution[səlúːʃən] 용액   purify[pjúərəfài] 거르다   refine[riːfáin] 정제하다   magnesium chloride 염화 마그네슘
electric current 전류   plentiful[pléntifəl] 풍부한   catch[kætʃ] 단점   figure[fígjər] 수치   capacity[kəpǽsəti] 양
power[pauər] 전력을 공급하다   landlocked[lǽndlɑ̀kt] 육지로 둘러싸인

* 각 문제에 대한 정답단서는 지문에 보라색으로 표시되어 있습니다.

1. (A) Main Purpose/Topic
2. (B) Function & Attitude
3. (C) Inference
4. (B) Detail
5. (D) Function & Attitude
6. (B) Main Purpose/Topic
7. (D) Detail
8. (B) Function & Attitude
9. Connecting Contents I

Step 1	Electricity consumption increases.
Step 2	Backup power flows from an alternative generator.
Step 3	Power flows through an indirect route.
Step 4	Overloading causes a power outage.

10. (C) Detail
11. (B) Inference
12. (B), (C) Main Purpose/Topic
13. (D) Connecting Contents II
14. (D) Detail
15. (B), (D) Detail
16. (D) Inference
17. (A) Main Purpose/Topic
18. (B) Inference
19. (C) Detail
20. (B) Connecting Contents II
21. (A), (C), (D) Detail
22. (C) Function & Attitude
23. (A) Main Purpose/Topic
24. (C) Detail
25. (B) Connecting Contents II
26. (D) Detail
27. (C), (D) Detail
28. (B) Function & Attitude

[1-5]

Listen to a conversation between a student and a university employee.

M: How can I help you?

W: Yeah, um, ^{Q1} I have a problem with my financial aid report for this upcoming semester. You see, it says here that I'm only receiving $5,000, which will leave about half of my tuition unpaid.

M: Were you expecting more?

W: Well . . . yes. I just transferred here from Carthage—that's a small private university on the west coast—and I was receiving a full scholarship there. My financial aid covered everything—tuition, room and board, books . . . and the tuition there is even higher than it is here! I can't understand why the amount I've been awarded is so low.

M: OK, hold on a second while I get your records. Ms. . . . uh, Wood, is that right?

W: Yes. Katherine Wood.

M: All right, Ms. Wood. ^{Q2} It says here that you are to receive 50 percent of your semester tuition in federal grants, but it doesn't list anything about other forms of financial aid, including scholarships.

W: How can that be? I was getting full tuition reimbursement plus living expenses at Carthage. The only reason I can afford college is because of that assistance.

M: Hmm . . . Private universities run under a completely different system—a lot of the funding they receive is from alumni donations and other private sources. In public universities, loans are handled directly by the federal government or finance associations such as big banks. The federal government also offers grants, but there's a cap on the amount a student can get. ^{Q5} If the university has any scholarships to give, the funding for this comes from the state government. Again, the student can't expect to get a lot.

W: Q5 But my scholarship was merit-based. You see, I received perfect marks in high school and scored high on my college entrance exam! I was planning on not working so I could focus on my classes and do better in school. And I was under the impression that a merit-based scholarship applies no matter what college you go to.

M: Well, not always. See, some scholarships are provided by independent agencies or the colleges themselves. In some cases, they are specifically designed for a particular college . . . or even students of a single department.

W: That doesn't seem fair. I mean, I earned it, after all . . .

M: I'm sorry, but I don't make the rules. Here at our university, there are only a certain number of aid packages offered to students each year. Q3 Honestly, you're pretty fortunate to receive the amount you did, as it is definitely more than what most students get. Actually, most students take out loans to pay for their education.

W: Well, what other options do I have? I really don't have the money to cover the remainder of my fees.

M: Q4 Let's see . . . it says here on your records that you are eligible for work-study, which is a great option. And if you don't want to work, you can always take out student loans, although this late in the year, you will only be eligible for private loans, which carry higher interest rates.

W: Seems like work-study is the best alternative. Where do I need to go to apply for that?

M: No need to apply, as you've already been approved. You just need to take your work-study record to a potential employer when going for an interview. Do you know where to find the job listings?

W: Um, yeah, on the website, right?

M: Sure, or, um, at the student job center down at Randall Hall.

W: OK, thanks for your help.

M: Good luck!

Now get ready to answer the questions. You may use your notes to help you answer.

1. Why does the woman visit the financial aid office?

Listen again to part of the conversation. Then answer the question.

M: It says here that you are to receive 50 percent of your semester tuition in federal grants, but it doesn't list anything about other forms of financial aid, including scholarships.

W: How can that be? I was getting full tuition reimbursement plus living expenses at Carthage.

2. Why does the woman say this:
   W: How can that be?

3. What does the man imply about the amount the woman received?
4. What does the man suggest the woman do?

Listen again to part of the conversation. Then answer the question.

M: If the university has any scholarships to give, the funding for this comes from the state government. Again, the student can't expect to get a lot.

W: But my scholarship was merit-based. You see, I received perfect marks in high school and scored high on my college entrance exam!

5. What does the woman mean when she says this:

W: I received perfect marks in high school and scored high on my college entrance exam!

M: 어떻게 도와드릴까요?

W: 네, 음, 다음 학기 학비 지원 통지서에 문제가 있어요. 그러니까, 여기에는 제가 5천 달러만 받는다고 나와 있는데, 그러면 제 수업료의 반 정도가 미납으로 남게 돼요.

M: 더 많을 거라고 예상했나요?

W: 음... 네. 저는 Carthage에서 여기로 막 편입했어요, 서해안에 있는 작은 사립 대학교죠, 그리고 저는 그곳에서 전액 장학금을 받고 있었거든요. 제 학비 지원은 모든 걸 포함했어요, 수업료, 방 그리고 식사, 교재... 그리고 심지어는 그곳의 수업료가 여기보다 더 높았고요! 제가 받은 금액이 왜 이렇게 낮은지 이해할 수 없어요.

M: 네, 학생의 기록을 살펴볼테니 잠시 기다리세요. 어, Wood... 양, 맞죠?

W: 네. Katherine Wood입니다.

M: 좋아요, Wood양, 여기에는 학생이 연방 보조금에서 한 학기 수업료의 50퍼센트를 받도록 되어 있는데, 장학금을 포함한, 다른 형태의 학비 지원은 아무것도 명시되어 있지 않네요.

W: 어떻게 그럴 수 있죠? 저는 Carthage에서 수업료 전액 상환에 더해서 생활비까지 받았는데요. 제가 대학에 다닐 수 있었던 단 하나의 이유는 그 지원이었고요.

M: 흠... 사립 대학교들은 완전히 다른 체계 아래에서 운영돼요, 그들이 받는 많은 금전적 지원은 졸업생 기부금과 다른 사적 출처로부터 와요. 공립 대학교에서는, 대출이 연방 정부나 큰 은행과 같은 금융 기관에 의해 직접적으로 다루어지죠. 연방 정부는 보조금도 제공하지만, 한 명의 학생이 받을 수 있는 금액에는 한계가 있어요. 만약 대학교가 아무 장학금이나 줄 수 있는 게 있다면, 이에 대한 금전적 지원은 주 정부로부터 오죠. 다시 말하지만, 그 학생은 많은 것을 기대할 수 없어요.

W: 하지만 제 장학금은 성적에 근거를 두고 있어요. 그러니까, 저는 고등학교에서 완벽한 성적을 받았고 대학 입학 시험에서도 높은 점수를 받았어요! 저는 수업에 집중하고 학교생활을 더 잘하기 위해서 일하지 않을 계획이었어요. 그리고 성적에 근거를 둔 장학금은 가려고 하는 어떤 대학에든 적용된다는 인상을 받았거든요.

M: 음, 항상 그렇지는 않아요. 보면, 몇몇 장학금은 개별 기관이나 대학 자체에 의해 제공돼요. 어떤 경우에는, 특정 대학교를 위해 특별히 만들어지죠... 혹은 단과 대학 학생들만을 위해서요.

W: 공평한 것 같지 않아요. 제 말은, 저는, 어쨌든, 장학금을 얻어낸 건데요...

M: 미안해요, 하지만 제가 규칙을 정하는 게 아니에요. 우리 대학교에는, 매년 학생들에게 제공되는 보조 방법들이 몇 개밖에 없어요. 솔직히, 학생이 받은 만큼의 돈을 받게 된 건 운이 꽤 좋은 거예요, 그건 대부분의 학생들이 받는 것보다 확실히 더 많으니까요. 사실, 대부분의 학생들은 그들의 학비를 내려고 대출을 받잖아요.

W: 음, 다른 선택사항은 어떤 게 있나요? 저는 나머지 수업료를 충당할 수 있는 돈이 정말 없거든요.

M: 어디 봅시다... 여기 기록을 보니 학생은 아주 좋은 선택인, 근로 장학의 혜택을 받을 자격이 있군요. 그리고 만약 학생이 일하고 싶지 않다면, 언제라도 학생 대출을 받을 수 있어요, 비록 올해에는 늦어서, 이자율이 더 높은, 사적 대출 밖에 못 받겠지만요.

W: 근로 장학이 가장 좋은 대안인 것 같아요. 지원하려면 어디로 가야 하나요?

M: 학생은 이미 승인받았기 때문에, 지원할 필요가 없어요. 면접을 보러 갈 때 고용주가 될 사람에게 근로 장학 기록만 가져가면 됩니다. 일자리 목록은 어디서 찾는지 아세요?

W: 음, 네, 웹사이트에서요, 그렇죠?

M: 맞아요, 아니면, 음, Randall 홀에 있는 학생 취업 센터에 가 보세요.

W: 알겠습니다, 도와주셔서 감사해요.

M: 행운을 빌어요!

어휘

financial aid 학비 지원 **federal** [fédərəl] 연방의 **grant** [grænt] 보조금 **reimbursement** [rìːimbə́ːrsmənt] 상환
living expense 생활비 **assistance** [əsístəns] 지원 **funding** [fʌ́ndiŋ] (금전적) 지원 **alumni** [əlʌ́mnai] 졸업생
donation [dounéiʃən] 기부금 **cap** [kæp] 한계 **merit-based** [méritbèist] 성적에 근거를 둔 **remainder** [riméindər] 나머지
work-study [wə́ːrkstʌ̀di] 근로 장학 **take out** (대출을) 받다 **interest rates** 이자율 **alternative** [ɔːltə́ːrnətiv] 대안

[6-11]
Listen to part of a lecture in a physics class.

P: Right . . . ^{Q6} Today, I want to talk a little about the semiconductor switch and why it has become so important in supplying people with uninterrupted power. When we think of problems with electricity, tell me, what's the first thing that comes to your mind? Any "bright" ideas?

S: Would it be power blackouts?

P: Yep, you got it. Aside from the inconveniences that we experience in our homes from blackouts, there are more serious consequences to consider. Businesses can lose hundreds of thousands of dollars for every hour that they don't have power. So electricity suppliers need to make sure they have technology that reduces the likelihood of power outages.

There are several phenomena that can cause blackouts. Hurricanes, for one, can bring down power lines. Lightning can strike lines or substations and destroy equipment. Technical faults are another major contributor to blackouts. But actually, the most common cause of widespread power outages is something called loop flow.

OK, you know that electricity flowing between a generator and a customer's home or business moves through all of the cables and wires connecting the two. But it doesn't always move along the shortest distance between the two points. What happens is, electricity follows the path of least resistance within the grid, and this can fluctuate according to changing conditions. Just so you understand how it works, let's say that we have three towns . . . A, B, and C. And each town has its own generator and power lines. But all of the towns' systems are connected to each other in a network. This is so that there's backup power in case any one town's demand exceeds its generating capacity. OK . . . imagine that it's a hot day in town A. ^{Q9} Everyone has their air conditioner running, and the generators there can't keep up with the demand. But in town B, they're not using so much power. ^{Q15} Now, ideally, power from town B would flow directly to town A. ^{Q7} But as I mentioned, electricity doesn't always take the shortest route! Sometimes, for various reasons, there's resistance . . . it's also called impedance . . . along a power line. Impedance prevents the electricity from flowing directly from town B to town A. ^{Q8/Q9} Instead, it takes the path of least resistance, from town B to town C, and then to town A. This is loop flow.

So what's the problem? Town A still gets all the power it needs, right? Well, not necessarily. The extra burden of power flowing through town C causes its generator to shut down. ^{Q15} Then town B's generator is overburdened and shuts down. This causes town A's generator to do the same, and all of this results in total blackout for the entire region.

This is where the semiconductor switch comes in. The magic of the semiconductor is that it can act as a conductor or an insulator. The switches operate by either conducting or blocking the flow of electrons through silicone crystals. And this can be done hundreds or even thousands of times a second. Uh, the switches can instantly alternate currents within the grid to reroute electricity in case of a system failure. It can switch to "block mode" to cut off a faulty, damaged, or overloaded power line, and then switch to "conduct mode" to connect to a backup source instantaneously. And all of this takes place without interrupting the flow of electrical current. ^{Q10} Semiconductor switches can be strategically placed along network grid paths. Thus, the problem I just described could have been avoided. It would have kicked in automatically by instantly redirecting the electricity to flow along the shortest route to town A instead of flowing through town C and overloading their system. ^{Q11} The simple semiconductor switch can save the nation hundreds of millions of dollars in damage and lost productivity. Once they're completely integrated into the power network, loop flow will become a thing of the past.

Now get ready to answer the questions. You may use your notes to help you answer.

6. What is the main purpose of the lecture?
7. According to the lecture, why does electricity not always take the shortest route as it flows?

Listen again to part of the lecture. Then answer the question.

P: Instead, it takes the path of least resistance, from town B to town C, and then to town A. This is loop flow. So what's the problem? Town A still gets all the power it needs, right? Well, not necessarily. The extra burden of power flowing through town C causes its generator to shut down.

8. Why does the professor say this:
   P: So what's the problem?

9. The following are steps in the process of loop flow. Put the steps listed below in the correct order.
10. According to the professor, what is the main function of semiconductor switches in the power supply industry?
11. What does the professor imply about the status of the nation's power networks?

P: 자... 오늘은, 반도체 스위치와 사람들에게 끊임없는 전력을 공급하는 데 있어 이것이 왜 그렇게 중요해졌는지에 대해 좀 이야기하고 싶군요. 전기와 관련한 문제에 대해 생각할 때, 가장 먼저 떠오르는 것이 무엇인지, 말해 볼까요? 어떤 '기발한' 생각이 있나요?
S: 정전이 아닐까요?
P: 네, 바로 그거예요. 정전 때문에 가정에서 겪는 불편함 이외에도, 고려해야 할 더 심각한 결과들이 있어요. 기업들은 전력이 없는 매 시간마다 수백 수천 달러를 손해볼 수도 있습니다. 따라서 전기 공급업자들은 정전의 확률을 감소시키는 기술을 가지고 있는지 확인해야 하죠.
정전을 일으킬 수 있는 몇 가지 현상이 있어요. 우선, 허리케인은 전선을 손상시킬 수 있죠. 번개는 전선이나 변전소와 충돌하고 장비를 파괴할 수 있습니다. 기술적인 결함도 정전의 또 다른 주요 요인이에요. 그러나 사실, 넓은 지역에 걸친 정전의 가장 흔한 원인은 루프 순환이라고 불리는 것입니다.
자, 발전기와 고객의 가정 또는 기업 사이에서 흐르는 전기는 그 둘을 연결하는 모든 케이블과 선을 통해 이동한다는 것을 알고 있죠. 그러나 전기가 항상 두 지점 사이의 최단 경로를 따라 이동하는 건 아니에요. 실제로, 전기는 송전선 내에서 가장 저항이 적은 경로를 따라 흐르고, 이것은 변하는 상황에 따라 변동할 수 있습니다.
여러분이 이게 어떻게 작용하는지 이해할 수 있도록, A, B 그리고 C라는... 세 개의 도시가 있다고 가정해 봅시다. 그리고 각 도시는 발전기와 전선을 각각 가지고 있어요. 하지만 모든 도시의 시스템은 네트워크 내에서 서로 연결되어 있고요. 이는 한 도시의 수요가 발전 용량을 초과할 경우에 대체 전력을 공급해주기 위해서죠. 자... A 도시에 무더운 날이 찾아왔다고 상상해 보세요. 모든 사람들이 에어컨을 가동시켜, 그 도시의 발전기는 수요를 따라갈 수가 없어요. 하지만 B 도시에서는, 사람들이 그렇게 많은 전력을 사용하지 않고 있습니다. 이제 원칙적으로는, B 도시의 전력이 직접적으로 A 도시로 흘러가겠죠. 하지만 제가 말한 것처럼, 전기는 항상 최단 경로를 따르지는 않아요! 때때로, 여러 이유로 인해, 저항이 있어요... 임피던스라고도 불리죠... 전선을 따라서 말이에요. 임피던스는 전기가 B 도시에서 A 도시로 직접적으로 흐를 수 없게 해요. 대신, 전기는 저항이 가장 작은 길을 따라갑니다, 즉 B 도시에서 C 도시로, 그 다음 A 도시로 말이에요. 이게 루프 순환이죠.
그렇다면 무엇이 문제일까요? A 도시는 필요한 전력을 계속해서 모두 얻죠, 그렇죠? 음, 꼭 그렇지는 않아요. C 도시를 통해 흐르는 과도한 양의 전력은 발전기가 정지하게 만들거든요. 그러면 B 도시의 발전기도 과부하되어 정지하죠. A 도시의 발전기에서도 같은 현상이 일어나, 그 결과 전 지역에서 정전이 발생합니다.
이런 현상 때문에 반도체 스위치가 등장하게 되었어요. 반도체의 매력은 그것이 도체 또는 절연체의 기능을 한다는 것입니다. 스위치는 실리콘 유리를 통해 전자의 흐름을 전도하거나 막아서 작동해요. 그리고 이는 1초에 수백 번 또는 심지어 수천 번 행해지죠. 어, 이 스위치는 시스템 결함이 있을 경우 송전선 내에서 즉각적으로 전류의 흐름을 바꾸어 전기를 다른 길로 수송할 수 있습니다. 그것은 '차단 모드'로 변환하여 결함이 있고, 손상됐거나, 과부화된 전선을 차단할 수 있고, 그리고는 '전도 모드'로 변환하여 즉시 대체 전력으로 연결할 수 있습니다. 그리고 이 모든 과정은 전류의 흐름을 방해하지 않으면서 일어납니다.
반도체 스위치는 네트워크 배전선 길을 따라 전략적으로 설치될 수 있어요. 따라서, 제가 설명한 문제점은 막을 수 있다는 거죠. 그

스위치는 전류가 C도시를 거쳐 가며 시스템을 과열시키지 않도록, 전류의 흐름을 A 도시로 가는 최단 경로로 즉시 바꾸어 줌으로써 자동적으로 작동합니다. 간단한 반도체 스위치는 국가가 피해와 생산성 저하로 잃을 수 있는 수백만 달러를 절약하도록 해주는 거죠. 반도체 스위치가 전력 네트워크에 완전히 통합된다면, 루프 순환은 과거의 문제가 될 거예요.

어휘

semiconductor[sèmikəndʌ́ktər] 반도체 power blackout 정전(=power outage) power line 전선
substation[sʌ́bstèiʃən] 변전소 generator[dʒénərèitər] 발전기 grid[grid] 송전선 fluctuate[flʌ́ktʃuèit] 변동하다
backup power 대체 전력 generating capacity 발전 용량 shut down 정지하다 conductor[kəndʌ́ktər] 도체
insulator[ínsəlèitər] 절연체 current[kə́:rənt] 전류 reroute[rì:rú:t] 다른 길로 수송하다 instantaneously[ìnstəntéiniəsli] 즉시
strategically[strətí:dʒikəli] 전략적으로 integrate into ~을 통합하다

[12-16]
Listen to a conversation between a student and a professor.

S: Good afternoon, Professor Chow. Um, your office hours begin now, right?

P: Hi, Brittany. Yes, I can talk. What do you need?

S: ᵠ12 Um, I wanted to check if the midterms were marked yet. I'm a little nervous about how I did . . .

P: I'm really sorry . . . I just haven't gotten around to it yet. I was planning to do it this weekend.

S: No problem. I just thought I'd check. Um, while I'm here . . . the paper you assigned on the history of the American West . . .

P: Right. Do you need help with it?

S: Sort of. I've decided what area to focus on . . . silver mining in the 19th century. That industry had such a huge impact on the country's development. ᵠ12 The thing is, the topic is pretty . . . big. I need help narrowing it down.

P: Well, let me think . . . There are quite a few books and articles about the first silver mining boom, so I'd recommend looking at that . . . It happened after a large deposit of silver was found in, um . . . in a Nevada mountain. It was called the, uh, Comstock Lode . . . and one that huge had never been discovered before in the US. Its discovery started the silver rush.

S: I have done a little research on that . . . Um, the Comstock Lode was first discovered in 1857, wasn't it?

P: Right. ᵠ13 But at first, no one realized that there was silver in the area . . . You see, the early prospectors were . . . well, they were looking for gold. But they had trouble extracting the gold because there was all this, um, bluish clay in the way . . . When this material was analyzed, it was found to contain high concentrations of silver. As a result, miners soon started flooding into the area.

S: Everyone wanted to get rich, I guess.

P: Exactly. And a lot of people did get rich . . . But that newfound wealth had a price. There were dangers involved. For example, the mining tunnels often collapsed. Um, let me explain . . . The silver ore was unusually soft . . . so soft, in fact, that miners could dig it out themselves using shovels and didn't have to rely on machines. ᵠ14 But it also meant that the mine tunnels were weak and unstable . . . The walls frequently fell in and killed miners.

S: Uh-huh . . . Mining technology back then must not have been very sophisticated . . . It sounds like miners had, well . . . they had a very dangerous job.

P: ᵠ14 But actually, that's another thing you should know about the Comstock Lode . . . It prompted the development of new, safer mining technologies. The problem of weak tunnels, for instance, led to square set timbering . . . Um, it's a way of stabilizing tunnel walls using wooden blocks. The blocks are sort of stacked against the walls to prevent them from collapsing.

S: That's interesting . . . So what happened to the mines? I read that about 20 years after the discovery, their output dropped dramatically . . . Did the silver just dry up?

P: Pretty much. ^{Q15} Over a few decades, more than 700 million dollars in silver was taken out of the mountain . . . but that couldn't last forever. Around 1880, the mines started to decline, and people began leaving the area.

S: This definitely sounds like an interesting topic.

P: Wonderful, I'm glad it works.

S: ^{Q16} I'm heading straight to the library while this information is fresh in my mind . . . and I'm going to start writing well in advance of the deadline . . . I don't want to suffer like the last time a paper was due.

P: That's a good idea. Let me know if you have more questions.

Now get ready to answer the questions. You may use your notes to help you answer.

12. Why does the student go to see the professor?
13. Why does the professor mention the bluish clay found in the mines?
14. Why were new mining technologies developed for the Comstock Lode?
15. What does the professor say about the mines of the Comstock Lode?

Listen again to part of the conversation. Then answer the question.

S: I'm heading straight to the library while this information is fresh in my mind . . . and I'm going to start writing well in advance of the deadline . . . I don't want to suffer like the last time a paper was due.

16. What does the student imply when she says this:
    S: I don't want to suffer like the last time a paper was due.

S: 안녕하세요, Chow 교수님. 음, 교수님의 근무 시간이 이제 시작하죠, 맞나요?

P: 안녕, Brittany. 그래, 이야기를 나눌 수 있단다. 무엇이 필요하니?

S: 음, 혹시 중간고사 점수가 채점되었는지 확인하고 싶었어요. 제가 어떻게 했는지 좀 걱정돼서요.

P: 정말 미안하지만... 아직 처리하지 못했단다. 이번 주말에 하려고 했어.

S. 괜찮아요. 저는 그냥 확인하려고 한 거예요. 음, 여기 온 김에... 미국 서부의 역사에 관한 과제 말인데요...

P: 그래. 그것에 도움이 필요하니?

S: 조금요. 어떤 부분에 초점을 맞출지는 정했어요... 19세기의 은광이요. 그 산업은 나라의 발전에 거대한 영향을 끼쳤잖아요. 문제는, 그 주제가 너무... 커요. 그걸 좁히는 데 도움이 필요해요.

P: 음, 생각해 보자... 초기의 은광 호황에 관해 꽤 많은 책과 논문들이 있으니, 그걸 보는 것을 추천해주고 싶구나... 그건, 음... 네바다 산에서 거대한 은의 매장 층이 발견된 뒤에 발생했단다. 그건, 어, 캄스톡 광맥이라고 불렸고... 그렇게 거대한 광맥은 이전에 미국에서 발견된 적이 없어. 그것의 발견은 실버러시가 시작되게 했단다.

S: 그것에 관해 조사를 좀 했어요... 음, 캄스톡 광맥은 1857년에 처음으로 발견되었죠, 그렇지 않나요?

P: 맞아. 하지만 처음에는, 그 지역에 은이 있다는 것을 아무도 알아차리지 못했단다... 보렴, 초기의 탐사자들은... 음, 금을 찾고 있었어. 그런데 길을 막는 이, 음, 푸르스름한 진흙 때문에 금을 채굴하는 데 어려움을 겪었지... 이 물질이 분석됐을 때, 짙은 농도의 은을 포함하고 있다는 게 밝혀졌어. 결과적으로, 광부들은 곧 그 지역으로 몰려들기 시작했단다.

S: 제 생각에, 모두 부자가 되고 싶었나 봐요.

P: 그렇지. 그리고 많은 사람이 부자가 되었어... 하지만 그 새로 발견된 부에는 대가가 있었지. 위험이 포함되어 있었단다. 예를 들어, 광산 터널은 자주 무너졌어. 음, 설명을 좀 하자면... 은 광석은 대단히 부드러웠단다... 사실, 너무 부드러워서, 광부들은 그들 스스로 삽을 이용해 그걸 파낼 수 있었고 기계에 의존할 필요가 없었지. 하지만 그건 또한 광산 터널이 약하고 불안정하다는 것을 의미했단다... 벽들은 자주 무너져서 광부들을 죽게 했어.

S: 아... 그 당시 광산 기술이 그다지 정교하지는 않았겠죠... 광부들은, 음... 매우 위험한 직업을 가졌다는 것으로 들리네요.

P: 하지만 사실, 그게 캄스톡 광맥에 대해 네가 알아야 하는 또 다른 부분이란다... 그것이 새로운, 더 안전한 광산 기술의 발전을 유도했다는 거지. 예를 들어, 약한 터널의 문제는 스퀘어 세트 지주로 이어졌어... 음, 그건 나무벽돌을 사용해서 터널을 안정시키는 방법이야. 그 벽돌들은 벽이 무너지는 걸 막기 위해 벽에 맞대어 쌓여졌단다.

S: 그거 흥미롭네요... 그래서 광산에 무슨 일이 발생했죠? 발견 약 20년 후에, 광산의 생산량이 급격하게 떨어졌다고 읽었어요... 은이 다 고갈되었나요?

P: 거의 그랬지. 몇십 년 동안, 7억 달러 이상의 은이 산에서 채굴되었어... 하지만 그게 영원히 지속될 수는 없었지. 1880년 즈음에, 광산은 쇠퇴하기 시작했고, 사람들은 그 지역을 떠나기 시작했단다.

S: 이건 확실히 흥미로운 주제처럼 들리네요.

P: 잘됐구나, 그렇다니 기쁘다.

S: 이 정보가 제 머릿속에 생생할 때 바로 도서관으로 가야겠어요... 그리고 기한 훨씬 전에 작성하기 시작할 거예요... 지난번 보고서 마감 때처럼 시달리고 싶지 않거든요.

P: 좋은 생각이구나. 질문이 더 있다면 알려주렴.

어휘

office hours 근무 시간   boom[bu:m] 호황   deposit[dipázit] 매장 층   prospector[práspektər] 탐사자
extract[ikstrǽkt] 채굴하다   bluish[blú:iʃ] 푸르스름한   in the way 길을 막는   concentration[kὰnsəntréiʃən] 농도
flood into ~으로 몰려들다   collapse[kəlǽps] 무너지다   dig out ~을 파내다
square set timbering 스퀘어 세트 지주(12개의 갱목(坑木)을 입방체로 짜맞춘 형틀 지주(支柱))   stack[stæk] 쌓다
output[áutpùt] 생산량   dry up 고갈되다

[17-22]

Listen to part of a lecture in an anthropology class.

So, um, the Mayan civilization began in 2000 BC and lasted until the, um . . . the 16th century. Last class, we went over the three main periods that divide its long history. And there's one thing that remained consistent throughout this time . . . a strong economy. Q17 I bet you're wondering how the Mayans created such prosperity . . . Well, there were a number of factors involved . . .

The first was that they had access to abundant natural resources. The lands they occupied in Central America were fertile and diverse. Plus the climate was mild and tropical . . . there was lots of sun and rain. Q18 The combination of fertile soil and good weather meant that the Mayan food supply was . . . well, let's just say that the average Mayan rarely had to worry about where his or her next meal was coming from . . . This, of course, helped to ensure stability and security. There were, uh, other resources, too . . . besides food, I mean . . . The Mayans discovered useful minerals under the hills and mountains. With resources like these, they could create more wealth. Q19 Some of the minerals were used in luxury items . . . you know, jewelry, ornaments, stuff like that . . . uh, jade and turquoise were especially popular in this respect. Other minerals were used to produce tools and, um, weapons.

Now, another big part of the Mayans' economy was trade. Trade, as you know, is an important factor in all successful civilizations. I mean, the health of a civilization really depends on its ability to distribute its resources effectively. That's why these trade networks were so essential . . . they ensured people got what they needed to survive. The Mayans traded extensively among themselves . . . uh, between their cities and towns. Usually, towns offered surplus items and received other goods in return. For example, a coastal town could trade fish for corn with a farming community.

The Mayans also maintained trade networks with cultures outside of their lands . . . They traded basic necessities like salt and cotton, as well as high-value minerals like obsidian. This not only generated wealth, but also contributed to the overall development of Mayan society . . . Q20 Um, these economic interactions often resulted in cultural exchanges as well . . . For instance, it was the Zapotec civilization that developed the writing system that was used by the Mayans . . .

The third element I should mention is the system of tribute and, um, tax collection used by the Mayans. Um, let me explain. At times, cities fought each other over resources and trade routes. But, once a conflict was settled, the victorious cities collected tribute . . . um, some form of payment, from the conquered ones. In exchange, they guaranteed peace, stability, and continued trade. These powerful cities also, um, collected taxes from residents in the form of goods. Overall, this system produced a concentration of wealth in cities.

The Mayans benefited greatly from this wealth. Q21 For instance, it gave them the ability to support a large population . . . Um, it also allowed them to invest in new technologies . . . which, of course, led to improvements in farming, architecture, and other industries . . . And a third consequence was the growth of a Mayan middle class. Um, what I mean is, even Mayans who were not members of the nobility could experience lives of relative luxury. They had their basic needs met and enjoyed recreational activities in their free time. Q22 Um, if any of this sounds familiar, it should. The same indicators of a strong economy . . . deep resources, large markets, solid governance, and so on . . . These can all be found in the example of the United States, arguably the most prosperous nation in history to date.

Now get ready to answer the questions. You may use your notes to help you answer.

17. What is the main topic of the lecture?
18. What can be inferred about the Mayan food supply?
19. What does the professor say about the minerals discovered by the Mayans?
20. Why does the professor mention Zapotec civilization?
21. According to the professor, what were the benefits of Mayan wealth?

Listen again to part of the lecture. Then answer the question.

P: Um, if any of this sounds familiar, it should. The same indicators of a strong economy . . . deep resources, large markets, solid governance, and so on . . . These can all be found in the example of the United States, arguably the most prosperous nation in history to date.

22. What does the professor mean when she says this:
    P: Um, if any of this sounds familiar, it should.

자, 음, 마야 문명은 기원전 2000년에 시작해서, 음... 16세기까지 계속되었습니다. 지난 시간에, 우리는 마야 문명의 긴 역사를 나누는 세 개의 주요 시기를 살펴봤습니다. 그리고 이 시간에 걸쳐서 일관되게 유지되었던 한 가지가 있었는데요... 튼튼한 경제입니다. 여러분은 분명 마야인들이 어떻게 그러한 번성을 만들어냈는지 궁금해하고 있을 것 같은데... 음, 수반된 여러 가지 요소가 있었죠...

첫 번째는 그들이 풍부한 천연자원을 이용할 수 있었다는 것입니다. 그들이 중앙아메리카에서 차지했던 토지는 비옥했고 광범위했어요. 게다가 기후가 온화하고 열대성이었죠... 많은 햇빛과 강수량이 있었어요. 비옥한 땅과 좋은 날씨의 조합은 마야의 식량 공급이... 음, 보통 마야인들은 그들의 다음 식사가 어디에서 오는지에 대해 거의 걱정하지 않았다고만 말해두죠... 이건, 물론, 안정과 안보를 보장하는 데 도움이 되었고요.

어, 다른 자원들도 있었습니다... 제 말은, 식량 이외에도요... 마야인들은 언덕과 산 아래에서 유용한 광물들을 발견했습니다... 이러한 자원으로, 더 많은 부를 창출할 수 있었어요. 광물 일부는 사치품에 사용되었어요... 그러니까, 보석, 장신구, 그런 것들이요... 어, 이 점에서 옥과 터키석이 특히 인기 있었습니다. 다른 광물들은 도구와, 음, 무기를 생산하는 데 사용되었죠.

자, 마야 경제의 또 다른 커다란 부분은 무역이었습니다. 무역은, 알다시피, 성공한 모든 문명에서 중요한 요소예요. 제 말은, 한 문명의 번영은 정말이지 그것의 자원들을 효과적으로 분배하는 능력에 달려있거든요. 그게 바로 이러한 교역망들이 매우 중요했던 이유입니다... 그들은 사람들이 생존하는 데 필요한 걸 얻는 것을 보장해주었죠. 마야인들은 자신들 사이에서 광범위하게 무역했습니다... 어, 도시와 마을 사이에서요. 보통, 마을은 잔여 물품을 제공하고 보답으로 다른 물건을 받았습니다. 예를 들어, 해안 마을은 농업 공동체의 옥수수와 생선을 교환할 수 있었죠.

마야인들은 또한, 그들의 토지 밖 문화권들과의 교역망도 유지했습니다... 그들은 소금과 면직물 같은 생활필수품뿐 아니라, 흑요석과 같은 고가의 광물을 교환했어요. 이는 부를 산출했을 뿐만 아니라, 마야 사회의 전반적인 발전에 기여했습니다... 음, 이러한 경제적 상호작용은 종종 문화적 교류 또한 야기했어요... 예를 들어, 마야인들에 의해 사용된 문자 체계를 발전시킨 것은 바로 사포텍 문명이었죠...

제가 언급해야 할 세 번째 요소는 마야인들에 의해 사용되었던 공물과, 음, 세금 징수 체계입니다. 음, 설명하도록 하죠. 가끔, 도시들은 자원과 무역로를 두고 서로 싸웠습니다. 그러나, 갈등이 해결되고 나면, 승리한 도시들은 공물을 징수했어요... 음, 정복된 도시들로부터의 일종의 지불 방식이었죠. 답례로, 그들은 평화, 안정, 그리고 지속적인 무역을 보장했습니다. 이러한 강력한 도시들은 또한, 음, 주민들로부터 물건의 형태로 세금을 징수했습니다. 대체로, 이 체계는 도시의 부의 편중을 초래했고요.

마야인들은 이 부로부터 상당한 이익을 얻었습니다. 예를 들어, 그것은 그들에게 큰 인구를 부양할 능력을 주었죠... 음, 그것은 또한 그들이 새로운 기술에 투자할 수 있도록 해줬는데요... 이는, 물론, 농업, 건축업, 그리고 다른 산업들의 발전으로 이어졌습니다... 그리고 세 번째 결과는 마야 중산층의 성장입니다. 음, 제 말은, 심지어 귀족 구성원이 아니었던 마야인들도 상대적으로 호화로운 삶을 경험할 수 있었어요. 기본적인 수요가 충족되었고 자유시간에는 여가 활동을 즐겼거든요. 음, 만약 이 중 어떤 것이라도 익숙하게 들린다면, 그래야 할 거에요. 튼튼한 경제의 똑같은 지표들... 풍부한 자원, 거대한 시장, 견고한 통치 방식, 기타 등등... 이것들은 모두 아마 틀림없이 오늘날까지 역사상 가장 번성한 나라인 미국의 예시에서도 발견되니까요.

어휘

prosperity[prɑspérəti] 번성   abundant[əbʌ́ndənt] 풍부한   fertile[fə́rtl] 비옥한   diverse[divə́rs] 광범위한
mineral[mínərəl] 광물   jade[dʒeid] 옥   turquoise[tə́rkwɔiz] 터키석   health[helθ] (국가·사회 등의) 번영
basic necessities 생활필수품   cotton[kɑtn] 면직물   obsidian[əbsídiən] 흑요석   tribute[tríbjuːt] 공물
conquer[kɑ́ŋkər] 정복하다   guarantee[gæ̀rəntíː] 보장하다   recreational activities 여가 활동   solid[sɑ́lid] 견고한
governance[gʌ́vərnəns] 통치 방식   arguably[ɑ́ːrgjuəbli] 아마 틀림없이

[23-28]

Listen to part of a lecture in a biology class.

P: So, animals communicate in a variety of ways . . . But the most common is a technique called vocalization. This is what I'll be focusing on this morning. ^{Q23} Specifically, we'll look at a familiar sound that cats make . . .

Purring is the most common vocalization among cats . . . It's a soft, rumbling sound. ^{Q24} It happens when cats tighten their vocal passages as they're breathing. The air vibrates in the cat's vocal box as it goes in and out, and causes purring. Depending on its volume, quality, and length, a purr can signify a few different things . . . Um, I'm sure we have some cat owners here. Would any of you have an idea what cats are trying to say by purring?

S1: Um, yeah, I own a couple of cats . . . And I've noticed they purr when they're relaxed . . . like when they sit on my lap.

P: OK, good. Yes, purring is most often associated with a positive emotional state such as contentment. And it's common for cats to feel happy and purr during physical contact, either with other cats or with, um, humans. Cats often rest and groom together . . . they enjoy these activities, so they purr. ^{Q25} Also, cats do something called kneading. They grab onto something with their paws and sort of massage it. It looks like they're kneading bread dough. This is also a behavior that shows contentment, and cats often purr during it to show that they're feeling good . . .

Another function of purring is to express that a cat is, um, hungry. Now, there was a study done in . . . where was it . . . in Britain that found a noticeable difference in the sound of a purr that was from hunger. ^{Q26} When the cats in the study wanted food, they purred . . . but they combined it with another sound . . . kind of like a cry or a whine that is similar to a baby's

Actual Test 2 **333**

cry . . . Some people have even mistaken a cat's cry for a baby's. Why would cats make this sound? Well, to get a response from humans . . . in this case, food. They've learned that people are sensitive to this sound . . . We are more likely to tend to the cat to make it stop. Cats realize this and make the sound intentionally . . . Pretty amazing, isn't it?

S2: Professor? I also have a cat, and she's always purring at weird times. Like, when I'm taking her to the vet . . . and she hates the vet. Could purring also mean a cat is . . . I don't know . . . stressed out or something?

P: That's actually my final point . . . that cats purr when they're sick or distressed. There are some theories about this . . . It's likely that cats purr as a way to comfort themselves when they're upset or in pain. [Q27] Researchers have linked purring to the release of endorphins, which are natural pain-killers. What's more, the purring may actually have the ability to heal cats when they're sick! You see, purring causes vibrations in the cat's body that, um, can make swelling go down . . . [Q27] Also, the low frequency of the vibrations has actually been shown to encourage bone and tissue healing . . . obviously that relieves discomfort. So purring not only helps them feel better . . . it literally helps them get better . . .

S1: [Q28] So how can we tell the difference between a happy purr and, uh, a stressed-out purr?

P: I wish there were a simple answer. You just have to pay attention. When interpreting vocalizations, context is important. The cat's condition and body language will usually provide some clues. Cats that, um, lick their lips a lot could be suffering. So if your cat is purring and licking its lips, it's probably uncomfortable.

Now get ready to answer the questions. You may use your notes to help you answer.

23. What is the main topic of the lecture?
24. According to the professor, how do cats produce purring sounds?
25. Why does the professor mention bread dough?
26. How do cats motivate people to feed them?
27. How can purring reduce pain?

Listen again to part of the lecture. Then answer the question.

S1: So how can we tell the difference between a happy purr and, uh, a stressed-out purr?
P: I wish there were a simple answer. You just have to pay attention. When interpreting vocalizations, context is important.

28. What does the professor mean when she says this:
P: I wish there were a simple answer.

P: 자, 동물들은 여러 가지 방법으로 의사소통합니다... 그런데 가장 흔한 건 발성이라고 불리는 기법이죠. 이것이 바로 오늘 아침 제가 초점을 맞출 것이에요. 구체적으로, 고양이가 내는 익숙한 소리를 보도록 하겠습니다...
그르렁거리기는 고양이들 사이에서 가장 흔한 발성인데요... 그건 부드러운, 우르릉거리는 소리예요. 그것은 고양이들이 숨을 쉬면서 후두를 조일 때 발생합니다. 공기가 들어오고 나가면서 고양이의 성대를 떨리게 하고, 그르렁거리도록 하죠. 음량, 질, 그리고 길이에 따라, 그르렁거리는 소리는 몇 가지 다른 것들을 의미할 수 있어요... 음, 여기 고양이 주인들이 몇 있을 거라고 확신하는데요. 여러분 중 누구라도 고양이가 그르렁거림으로써 말하려는 것이 무엇인지 알고 있나요?

S1: 음, 네, 저는 고양이 두 마리를 소유하고 있어요... 그리고 그들이 편안할 때 그르렁거린다는 걸 알게 됐죠... 제 무릎에 앉을 때처럼요.

P: 그래요, 좋아요. 네, 그르렁거리기는 만족감과 같은 긍정적인 정서 상태와 가장 자주 연관되죠. 그리고 고양이들이 신체적인 접촉 중에 기분 좋게 느껴서 그르렁거리는 것은 흔한 일이에요, 다른 고양이와의 접촉이든, 음, 사람과의 접촉이든 말이죠. 고양이들은

보통 함께 휴식을 취하고 털을 깨끗이 합니다... 그들은 이러한 활동을 즐기고, 그래서 그르렁거리죠. 또한, 고양이들은 주무르기라고 불리는 것을 해요. 발로 무언가를 잡고 일종의 마사지를 합니다. 그건 빵 반죽을 주무르는 것처럼 보이죠. 이 또한 만족을 보여주는 행위이고, 고양이들은 보통 주무르기 동안 기분이 좋다는 걸 보여주기 위해 그르렁거립니다...

그르렁거리기의 또 다른 기능은 고양이가, 음, 배고프다는 걸 표현하는 거예요. 자, 연구가 하나 있었습니다... 어디더라... 영국에서 배고픔에서 오는 그르렁거리는 소리에서 주목할 만한 차이를 발견했죠. 연구에서 고양이들이 먹이를 원할 때, 그르렁거렸습니다... 하지만 그들은 그걸 또 다른 소리와 결합했죠... 아기의 울음소리와 비슷한 울음 혹은 칭얼거리는 소리 같은 것을요... 몇몇 사람들은 심지어 고양이의 울음소리를 아기의 것으로 착각했습니다. 고양이들은 왜 이 소리를 내는 걸까요? 음, 사람들로부터 반응을 얻기 위해서죠... 이 경우에는, 먹이를요. 그들은 사람들이 이 소리에 민감하다는 걸 알게 된 거예요... 우리가 고양이를 멈추게 하려고 보살펴줄 가능성이 크잖아요. 고양이들은 이걸 깨닫고 의도적으로 그 소리를 내는 거랍니다... 상당히 놀라워요, 그렇지 않나요?

S2: 교수님? 저도 고양이가 있는데, 그녀는 항상 이상한 때에 그르렁거려요. 말하자면, 제가 수의사에게 그녀를 데려갈 때요... 그리고 그녀는 수의사를 싫어하죠. 그르렁거리기는 고양이가... 글쎄요... 스트레스를 받았다거나 뭐 그런 걸 뜻할 수도 있나요?

P: 사실은 그게 저의 마지막 요점입니다... 고양이가 아프거나 괴로울 때 그르렁거린다는 것 말이에요. 이에 관한 몇 가지 이론이 있어요... 고양이들이 속상하거나 아플 때 스스로를 위로하려는 방법으로 그르렁거릴 가능성이 있습니다. 연구원들은 그르렁거리기를 천연 진통제인 엔도르핀의 분비와 연관 지었습니다. 게다가, 아플 때 그르렁거리는 것은 실제로 고양이를 치유하는 능력을 가졌어요! 보세요, 그르렁거리기는 고양이의 몸 안에 진동을 일으키는데, 음, 그건 부기가 빠지게 할 수 있죠... 또한, 저주파 진동은 실제로 뼈와 조직의 치유를 촉진한다고 증명되었습니다... 그건 명백하게 불편함을 완화해줘요. 그래서 그르렁거리기는 그들 기분이 나아지도록 도울 뿐만 아니라... 말 그대로 호전되게 돕는 거죠...

S1: 그러면 우리가 기분 좋은 그르렁거림과, 어, 스트레스 받은 그르렁거림 사이의 차이를 어떻게 구별할 수 있죠?

P: 간단한 정답이 있었으면 좋겠네요. 그저 주의를 기울여야만 해요. 발성을 이해할 때에는, 맥락이 중요합니다. 고양이의 상태와 몸짓이 보통 어떤 단서를 제공할 거예요. 음, 입술을 많이 핥는 고양이는 고통스러워하고 있을 수 있어요. 따라서 여러분의 고양이가 그르렁거리면서 입술을 핥고 있다면, 아마도 몸이 불편한 걸 거예요.

어휘

vocalization[vòukəlizéiʃən] 발성 purr[pəːr] (고양이 등이) 그르렁거리다; 그르렁거리는 소리 rumbling[rʌ́mbliŋ] 우르릉거리는
tighten[taitn] 조이다 vocal passage 후두 vocal box 성대 contentment[kənténtmənt] 만족감
groom[gruːm] 털을 깨끗이 하다 knead[niːd] 주무르다 dough[dou] 반죽 whine[hwain] 칭얼거리는 소리
mistake A for B A를 B로 착각하다 sensitive[sénsətiv] 민감한 tend to 보살피다 vet[vet] 수의사 distressed[distrést] 괴로운
swelling[swéliŋ] 부기 literally[lítərəli] 말 그대로 context[kántekst] 맥락

Hackers TOEFL Listening Intermediate

Actual Test 2 335

|H|A|C|K|E|R|S|

TOEFL
LISTENING
Intermediate

본 교재 강의 · 교재 MP3 · 받아쓰기 MP3 · iBT 리스닝 실전모의고사 · 해커스인강(Hackersingang.com)
토플 실전모의고사 · iBT 리스닝 · 무료 토플 스피킹/라이팅 첨삭 게시판 · 토플 공부전략 강의 · 토플 자료 및 유학 정보 고우해커스(goHackers.com)

해커스 어학연구소